Changing American Education

SUNY Series, Teacher Preparation and Development
Alan R. Tom, editor

Changing American Education

Recapturing the Past or Inventing the Future?

edited by
Kathryn M. Borman and Nancy P. Greenman*

*Placement of the editors' names is alphabetical. The editors worked collegially and editorship of this volume is equal: fully collective and collaborative.

State University of New York Press

Published by
State University of New York Press, Albany

For information, address State University of New York
Press, State University Plaza, Albany, NY 12246

Production by Dana Foote
Marketing by Bernadette LaManna

Library of Congress Cataloging-in-Publication Data

Changing American education : recapturing the past or inventing the
    future? / edited by Kathryn M. Borman and Nancy P. Greenman.
        p.   cm. — (SUNY series, teacher preparation and development)
    Includes bibliographical references and index.
        ISBN 0–7914–1659–3 (alk. paper). — ISBN 0–7914–1660–7 (pbk.
    alk. paper)
        1. Educational change—United States.   2. School improvement
    programs—United States.   3. Curriculum change—United States.
    4. School management and organization—United States.   I. Borman,
    Kathryn M.   II. Greenman, Nancy P.   III. Series: SUNY series in
    teacher preparation and development.
    LA210.C46   1994   1993
    371.2′00973—dc20   92–42842
                                                            CIP

10 9 8 7 6 5 4 3 2 1

Contents

II
Rhetoric versus Reform and Restructuring
in the District and Community

III
Rhetoric versus Reform and Restructuring
in the School and Classroom

Introduction

The title of this edited volume, *Changing American Education: Recapturing the Past or Inventing the Future?*, poses what might appear to be a simple question: In the enterprise of changing education and schooling, are we looking backward or forward? The choices are not dichotomous; however, the pursuit of an answer to the question reveals the web of issues associated with any discussion of educational change.

On one level, the question might conjure a debate between those educators who propose a Eurocentric common core curriculum and those who might envision multicultural curricula joined with the new learning technology. This volume, however, was not framed to address issues at this level of the debate; rather, it focuses on some of the more *fundamental* concerns that *might* give rise to such debates.

The chapters in this volume are organized into three major sections. Following this introductory chapter, the next six chapters explore broad themes drawn from historical and theoretical analyses of educational and school change. The second section includes four chapters that analyze recent and ongoing efforts at the school district level to reorder roles, relationships, and the social and economic structures that support them. Finally, the volume's concluding section is organized to examine reform and restructuring at the school and classroom levels.

This book has three central purposes. The first is to examine the nature of comprehensive, large scale historical and social changes that contextualize educational reform. A second and related purpose is to amplify the meaning of lessons learned by those who have assisted in particular change efforts. Many of the chapters draw upon rich case material that provides documentation of the possibilities and hazards awaiting those who undertake reform of educational practice and structures. Finally, several chapters examine how the rhetoric of educational change may fall short of the reality as translated to processes and practices at different levels of the enterprise.

The importance of the volume resides in the extent to which it provides an understanding of current efforts at educational and school change including the effective schools movement and former President Bush's America 2000 proposals to create a "new generation of American schools" for the twenty-first century. Authors whose work is included here approach the issue of changing schools from interpretive and critical perspectives in policy studies and the anthropology, history, sociology, and psychology of education. In the remainder of this introduction, we examine major arguments put forward in each of the chapters in this volume.

PART I: HISTORICAL AND THEORETICAL BACKGROUND TO SCHOOL CHANGE IN THE UNITED STATES

In the first chapter, "Not All Caterpillars Become Butterflies: Reform and Restructuring as Educational Change," Nancy P. Greenman provides a conceptual framework for thinking about change and also unpacks one of the volume's salient themes: the rhetoric as contrasted with the realities of educational and school change. The chapter is a useful foray into the politically (and conceptually) murky landscape of the change literature. As Greenman shows, terms such as "reform" and, more recently, "restructuring" do not always have the same meanings in the discourse of those who use them. By articulating a number of schemes for both categorizing and interpreting different levels of change, Greenman illustrates how what can be termed "first wave" reform focuses on rearranging commonly accepted elements of schooling, such as how the school day is organized, while leaving power relations intact. The status quo is thus maintained while "reformers" fret over whether or not community members and teachers should be invited to the table. In order to more closely align the realities and the rhetoric, Greenman emphasizes, all of the players need critical awareness of their relationships to the cultural context and the process of change.

A major failure of would-be educational change-makers has resided in their focus on constructing rational models for altering forms such as teacher education while obscuring political and economic inequities. Thus, again giving attention to context and presuppositions therein, Thomas S. Popkewitz and Marie Brennan in "Certification to Credentialing: Reconstituting Control Mechanisms in Teacher Education" illustrate how state-mandated credentialing requirements have equated reform with "professionalization." Legislative and governmental texts are analyzed by the authors who show how new forms of control have been produced that both structurally organize educational practice and obscure power relations. Teachers have been reduced to the objects of a Foucaultian "clinical language," their praxis conceived as a discrete set of tasks. In addition, government at the state and federal levels has extended its control to school practice, eroding the legitimacy and direction of traditional local and democratic control. As did Greenman, Popkewitz and Brennan underline the importance of critical awareness (and perhaps deconstruction) of context to allow for the process of change; "to locate discontinuities is to open new systems of possibility."

Continuing the volume's consideration of reforms touching teacher education, teaching, and teachers, in chapter 3 Michael W. Apple addresses the question "Is Change Always Good for Teachers? Gender, Class, and Teaching in History" and concludes that it is not. Like Popekewitz and Brennan and most others in this volume, Apple argues that school is thoroughly political in nature. According to Apple, political dimensions of schools and schooling can be detected in the (1) relationship of class, race, and gender with school processes and outcomes, (2) the kinds of knowledge that are (and are not) selected to imbed in the curriculum and, (3) the work teachers do in school. Apple's historical analysis also leads the reader through an account of the changing nature of the job of teaching. As a predominantly male occupation in the 1850s, teaching was a supplementary activity—a way to augment wages earned in farming or to enhance a career in local politics since some degree of prestige was associated with the position. As a form of mobility and a haven of respectability for women, however, teaching from the late nineteenth century forward has fallen increasingly under the control of patriarchal ideologies. As teaching became feminized, Apple argues, teaching itself became increasingly subject to state and local regulations while salaries relative to earlier pay scales fell off—women received only two-thirds of the pay earned by men. Historically, as Apple shows, women have resisted the patriarchal forms and structures that have been imposed on their jobs in an attempt to regulate their behavior. The scenario continues to play itself out as women continue to mobilize against further erosion of their autonomy and ability to define parameters of their position.

Networks of college of education deans are a potentially important source of educational change-making, particularly if these networks are connected with highly visible and influential universities. This argument is put forward by Barbara Schneider and Stafford Hood in their chapter, "Pathways to Institutional Change: From the Deans' Network to the

Holmes Group." Schneider and Hood demonstrate how initial concerns of Big 10 and Big 8 college of education deans who constituted the membership of an informal deans' network became the centerpiece of the later Holmes Group deans. Concerns of the deans included: (1) enhancing both teacher and administrator education, and (2) forming closer alliances with the field through a "multidirectional collaborative process involving scholars, practitioners, administrators, and linking agents." These two themes have continued to dominate the Holmes agenda. The authors show how both the Deans' Network and later the Holmes Group deans battled in their individual university contexts to overcome the "professional liability" in research universities associated with teacher education programs. The authors conclude that the Holmes Group continues to face major difficulties in its efforts to restructure teacher education and must address a remaining set of problems, not the least of which includes the needs and interests of both non-research oriented institutions and those with large minority enrollments.

The next chapter, "The 1989 Education Summit as a Defining Moment in the Politics of Education," by Susan R. Martin, moves the focus from teacher education reform to the broader federal agenda in the politics of education. Although the federal government's connections with business-related interests and state-level concerns are hardly recent phenomena, the summit meeting reemphasized and formalized the shift toward exclusion of other interests, particularly those of professional educators. The analysis in the chapter is organized to show how the media uncritically accepted President Bush's explanations of the U.S. educational "crisis." Bush and others, such as William Bennett linked the faltering U.S. economy with the failure of students to acquire skills making them "internationally competitive." The fact that the U.S. has undergone a structural reordering of its economy in the wake of failing productivity in manufacturing was not taken into account. The President's desire to improve the performance of U.S. schools, shaped by advisors representing the Carnegie Corporation, was symbolically shifted to the state level. This shift has continued to be played out in the emphasis on state certification policies as argued in chapter 3 by Popkewitz and Brennan and in the continuing involvement of business interests in such federal initiatives as the New American Schools Design Team Initiatives Corporation as mentioned here by Martin.

The final chapter in this section is by Erwin V. Johanningmeier. In "It Was More Than a Thirty Years' War, but Instruction Won: The Demise of Education in the Industrial Society," Johanningmeier argues that compulsory schooling, the dominance of educational psychology and a lack of progression from the requirements of a nineteenth century industrial state have served to create a public educational system out of touch with realities confronting U.S. post-industrial society. Johanningmeier emphasizes, as Popkewitz and Brennan also note, the strong and almost exclusive psychological orientation of education that has shaped and limited alternatives for schooling. Goals to change the school grounded in the rationales provided by these forces will not serve society well according to the author. Rather, educators at all levels must take up concerns about educating students that seriously engage the instructional goals of teaching. Training in basic skills and evaluation using standardized testing procedures are window dressing. This chapter speaks to a critical national concern to examine assumptions underlying our system of universal public education.

PART II: RHETORIC VS. REFORM AND RESTRUCTURING IN THE DISTRICT AND COMMUNITY

The four chapters included in Part II of this volume bring the analysis to the level of the school district and its surrounding community. The first chapter in this section, "Community Involvement and Staff Development in School Improvement," by William T. Pink and Kathryn M. Borman, uses two local case studies to argue that restructuring strategies must be articulated by teachers and community members, particularly parents, if change is to occur. Citizens in "North Riverside," an urbanized working class suburb in southwestern Ohio, perceived themselves to be responsive and civic-minded despite longstanding hostilities between the city's majority white and minority African-American communities. After an effort to evaluate and alter classroom and school-wide practices, the schools remained disengaged from a commitment to change. In the case of Chicago, an ambitious ongoing attempt to restructure district practices continues to be threatened both by political agendas and a lack of common purpose. The authors provide a set of operating principles that could be applied to other settings, particularly settings where participants are emotionally embroiled and conflicting agendas serve to immobilize key actors.

Continuing an analysis of the Chicago case, G. Alfred Hess, Jr. and John Q. Easton describe conditions giving rise to the radical changes in the system and present data from the first year's implementation of the reform agenda. In their chapter "Monitoring the Implementation of Radical Reform: Restructuring the Chicago Public Schools," these authors pay particularly close attention to the work accomplished during the first year by the Local School Advisory Council (LSAC), arguing that accountability provisions may prove to be the most important aspect of the state-mandated reforms in Chicago. The LSACs are important to the success of the enterprise because resources and important school governance decisions are in the hands of these groups. Hess and Easton present a number of useful and often surprising findings. These include the rather heartening news that LSACs actually *do* spend large portions of their meeting time discussing the school's curricular program, school safety and security, and the school budget, although a considerable amount of attention is also given at these meetings to council procedures. By continuing their longterm evaluation of the Chicago experiment, Hess, Easton, and their colleagues at the Chicago Panel will not only provide objective reports but will also inform LSACs of their findings which in turn may then modify their practices.

The Chicago case, of course, is simply one of many reform efforts being carried forward in urban school districts. In their chapter, "Educational Reform and the Urban School Superintendent: A Dilemma," Louis Castenell, Cornell Brooks, and Patricia Z. Timm examine the reform agendas currently put forward by urban school superintendents representing twenty-one large city school systems. The authors conclude that the rhetoric of school reform, embodied in such activities as "curriculum development" and "climate building" often masks another agenda, one concerned with improving students' "basic skills" and enhancing student performance on standardized tests. The authors conclude that many school superintendents are "abdicating their transformative opportunities."

While "parent involvement" in school reforms promises the opportunity to radically alter school decision-making, the term itself can be and frequently is manipulated to satisfy various interests. Marianne N. Bloch and B. Robert Tabachnick make this argument in their chapter "Improving Parent Involvement as School Reform: Rhetoric or Reality?" Parent involvement may encompass volunteer work, representation on parent councils, or school choice voucher privileges. It seldom, however, is aimed at working *with* teachers in defining, shaping, and effectively meeting professional responsibilities. Using a series of vignettes drawn from their field work at "Greendale," "Oakhill," and "Lakelawn" schools, the authors examine the extent to which the efforts of parents, teachers, and the authors were largely symbolic or, in fact, real transformations of existing school practices. Not only do Bloch and Tabachnick find that there are "real and important differences in belief, priority, definition and practice" in the area of parental involvement but they also discover the real time constraints that prevent participants from breaking down the substantial barriers to communication leading to "greater transformative involvement" of parents.

PART III: RHETORIC VS. REFORM AND RESTRUCTURING IN THE SCHOOL AND THE CLASSROOM

In the volume's concluding section, the authors of five chapters move directly into the school and classroom to address changes in curricular practices, structural arrangements and patterns of interaction leading to new ways of "doing school." Several authors have been key participants in the processes of change they set about analyzing in their texts.

Dorothy Angell, the author of "Can Multicultural Education Foster Transcultural Identities?" picks up the thread and more fully embroiders the notion of critical understanding of cultural context and the self as cultural construction noted by Greenman and others in this volume. Angell describes the concept of culturally mediated personal identity, and argues its importance as a focal point in education. Based on ethnographic work as well as her work with students in teacher education, Angell reflects on the response her students have to their culturally "different" students and makes a strong case for the value and practice of empathy in human affairs. Angell cautions, however, that a fully empathetic response, while essential in understanding "the bonds of feeling that hold people together or tear them apart," demands a response "consonant with the other's reality." In a nation so long divided in its sentiments along class and ethnic lines, empathy has never been easy to achieve. However, as Angell's analysis points out, in an increasingly "minority majority" society, we have paramount need to develop empathic orientations. Thus, in looking for alignment of "rhetoric and reality," one of the recurring themes in this volume, she identifies empathy as a possible "bridge between the rhetoric about valued cultural diversity and the reality of 'troublesome' cultural differences."

Julie Binko, in her chapter "Using the Future to Create Community and Curricular Change," suggests that one way to align rhetoric and reality is to direct curricular change through juxtaposition of observed current reality and desired projected reality. Binko focuses on the community as directing the changes, seeing the reformation of a K-12 curriculum and the direction of community change as interactive. According to Binko, the three dimensions of time (past, present, and future) "will direct the evolution of meaning for a reformed, procreative, pro-formative curriculum." The case study through which she demonstrates this process linked the current state of the community—obtained with ethnographic techniques—to citizens' desirable futures—obtained via ethnographic futures research—and produced ten recommendations based on the juxtapositions. Just as the notion of "shared vision" has been discussed elsewhere in this volume as an essential part of change, Binko notes that "common choice of a future" is the first step toward directing actual change in the community through educational change.

In order to generate shared visions in our heterogeneous society, obviously we need to allow those visions to be more inclusive than we individually may desire; we need some sense of common identity. In addition to Angell's development of empathy, and perhaps fostering development of that empathy, collaborating and working together in teams may help to create a sense of belonging and common identity. Joanne M. Arhar, in her chapter "Interdisciplinary Teaming: Can It Increase the Social Bonding of Middle-Level Students?," looks at interdisciplinary teaming as a key to middle level restructuring. According to Arhar, inherent in the "middle school philosophy and social structure" is a focus on the needs of students and the uniqueness of middle level students, and an evolution of responsive programs. These are usually interactive in nature; teaming is an integral part of the notion of middle schools. In Chapter 11, Angell noted that adolescents are especially receptive to the development of understanding difference through empathy. Arhar acknowledges the importance of personal relationships in the development of a sense of belonging and common identity—with peers, teachers, and school. She argues that social bonding, then, is both an intermediate step toward academic achievement and "an outcome worthy in and of itself." Teams have the potential to create conditions "conducive to formation of close, stable relationships between teachers and peers." Arhar's well designed study takes care to ensure that the rhetoric of teaming is a reality in the participating schools. A number of findings emerge from Arhar's study.

In the chapter entitled "Beliefs, Symbols, and Realities: A Case Study of a School in Transition," W. Wade Burley and Arthur S. Shapiro describe a case study of a southeastern school where externally facilitated change occurs in response to internally identified unmet needs. In this intervention, the authors, serving as change agents, helped elicit desired outcomes, identified barriers to change, and aligned the lived reality with rhetoric for desired change. As part of the process, this junior high school changed to a middle school with teaming as part of the social organization.

The final chapter of both this section and the volume has within it many of the recurring themes that have emerged throughout the book. Chester H. Laine, Lucille M. Schultz and M. Lynne Smith, in their chapter, "Interactions among School and College Teachers: Toward Recognizing and Remaking Old Patterns" offer a critical analysis of collaboration. The authors note the proliferation of failed university-school collaborations, and use a case study of six years of participation in a collaborative project involving a large urban school system and a comprehensive research university to explore the "danger inherent in the introduction of *innovations* within complex settings." This chapter provides a view of collaboration from the perspectives of various players and the agendas, usually unarticulated, motivating each. It is rich with dialogue and explication of the various cultural contexts, revealing many of the cultural constraints on collaboration. However, ultimately in collaboration, "personal agendas had to accommodate and serve the interests of the children and communities served by the urban schools." Development of understanding of the constraints and demands, of personal relationships, and of trust allowed for successful collaboration rather than individual attention to promoting individual agendas.

The volume, then, both begins and ends with an examination and possible dismantling of barriers to change that invents the future.

Kathryn M. Borman
Nancy P. Greenman

PART I

HISTORICAL AND THEORETICAL BACKGROUND TO EDUCATIONAL CHANGE IN THE UNITED STATES

Change is a fact of life. Technological, political, economic, cultural, educational—all types of change abound. As much as we may not like to alter what has become comfortable, we now acknowledge that we live in an age when change not only occurs, but does so rapidly and continually. For a nation whose credo is "If it ain't broke, don't fix it," this is difficult to admit and even more difficult to accept. Thus, with all the attention being directed toward American education, it is safe to assume we must be perceiving that it is "broke."

Articulation of a problem limits the alternatives available as solutions. If we see education as "broke," as not working anymore, then in what form must it be to be considered "fixed?" Does change constitute repair? Does a focus on repair limit our options to reconstruction of what was? Shrouded in a smokescreen of rhetoric about innovative change for the future, American education frantically holds on to normative change in efforts to "get education back to the way it was" in the mythical past. Even if this were possible, it would not be appropriate to present and future configurations.

Perhaps the question posed in the title of this edited volume is itself rhetorical; we have been trying to recapture the past rather than invent the future. While involved in the business of change, and its perceived urgency, we often are blinded to the patterns, assumptions, implications, and generally fundamental issues that obscure, at the very least, what we say we are about.

The purpose of Part I of this volume is to explore some of the issues fundamental to changing education in the United States. It offers a look at the very notion of change as well as consequences and efficacy of choices made and changes that have occurred. Through a sampling of issues, Part I provides a sketch of the broad context of changing American education.

NOT ALL CATERPILLARS BECOME BUTTERFLIES: REFORM AND RESTRUCTURING AS EDUCATIONAL CHANGE

Nancy P. Greenman

The time to release ourselves from simplistic and ineffective prescriptions has passed; the time to dream is upon us.
—Carl D. Glickman 1990, 69

For more than a decade, attention has been focused steadily on educational change. The rhetoric surrounding change has shifted from reform to restructuring, perhaps to indicate a difference in the approach to change, but there is a growing realization that "the more things change, the more they stay the same." As Albert Shanker observed, "Everyone may now be in favor of restructuring but very little restructuring is actually taking place" (Shanker 1990, 345). Assuming "everyone" *were* in favor of significant educational change, simply adopting the mantra "I think I can" may not be enough if we continue pushing on a door marked "pull." What must occur for the caterpillar that is American education to change into a butterfly?

The conceptualizing of change in the educational arena is extremely varied; as a result, discourse about change is somewhat confusing. Some scholars (e.g., Cuban 1990; Popkewitz 1988; Popkewitz, Tabachnik, and Wehlage 1982; Raywid 1990) suggest that this confusion constitutes a fog of rhetoric that gives the illusion of educational change, obfuscating the need to produce any actual significant change. Perhaps, as Popkewitz (1988) suggests, the notion of reform is in itself a part of the illusion:

> The activities of reform are framed in a manner that makes our institutions seem more responsive, progressive, and efficient in the face of their contradictions. The appeal of reform is related to the illusion of progress and the promise of our millennial dreams. Our language and cultural sensitivities continually create illusions about change and progress. (81)

Change also is sabotaged successfully by inadvertently imposing innovative concepts on archaic structures. The innovations often are misunderstood, resisted, and ultimately deemed ineffective, especially when evaluated by inappropriate criteria.

In this chapter I attempt to make sense of some recent patterns of educational change by examining reform and restructuring in their apparent theoretical contexts. First I discuss several frameworks for talking about change. Then I address the concepts of reform and restructuring in relation to the prevailing worldviews that shape these concepts and that often contribute to observable discrepancies between the rhetoric and the realities surrounding them. Some of these ideas may appear obvious, but they are *not* being addressed obviously—nor even subtly—by most facilitators in the effort to change education; although almost every case is analyzed as an instance of unique culture in order to explain the ramifications of the change process, the broader cultural context is overlooked. This contradiction fosters a cultural discontinuity and effectively sabotages the changes. In support of my premises, I draw examples from several case studies and give an overview of a restructuring effort that has not yet critically addressed the broad cultural context. Consequently, it is likely to be a transitory educational "quick fix." In contrast, I describe another effort that holds the promise of long-term success.

CHANGE, BY WHATEVER NAME...

How do we know what constitutes change? Golembiewski (1990) said, "[Y]ou have to define 'change' not only before you can estimate whether or not it occurs in a specific case but also before you can estimate how much of it occurs" (215). *Webster's Seventh New Collegiate Dictionary* (1972) defines change as a making, or becoming, distinctly different.

These definitions imply either radical transmutation of character or replacement of one thing with another. The terms *alteration* or *modification* are used to describe partial or moderate change. None of these definitions seems to address the situation in which "the more things change, the more they stay the same," or to apply to change that seems to perpetuate what exists. To say that general descriptions of change appear inadequate for understanding change phenomena is to grossly understate the problem.

As those persons who are involved in the process and discourse of change address refinements of meaning, new terms emerge to describe the precise change discussed; but the meanings of words also overlap. Constructive discourse is thwarted by the confusion: "Similar terms are used in debating dissimilar constructs and radically different positions. The resultant debates lead to a dialogue that is at best frustrating and at worst polarizing" (Bacharach 1990, 415). Often these terms become fashionable buzzwords that seem to embrace so many disparate meanings that they appear to lose any *significant* meaning. Lieberman and Miller (1990) spoke of the term *restructuring* in this way: "[It] has become the buzzword for the nineteen-nineties, but it has as many definitions as it has advocates" (761). Thus, the confusion is increased by (a) determining what constitutes significant change and (b) deciding how to speak about such change to distinguish it from other forms. The following review of several models of change provides some insight into these issues.

Most people have observed workers who always look busy but who actually get nothing done. These individuals have perfected the illusion of work. Watzlawick, Weakland, and Fisch (1974) identify a level of change called *first-order change*, which might be characterized by such workers. First-order change occurs within an invariant group or system. Problems identified at this level have predictable solutions mirroring the logic of the existing system; both problem and solution are perceived in the same frame of reference. The solutions become extensions of the problems and perpetuate them: The more things change, the more they stay the same. In contrast, *second-order change*, a virtual change *of* change, provides a way out of the existing group or system by generating a discontinuity or transformation. Problems at this level of change are reframed to produce solutions that would seem illogical from the perspective of the existing group or system; thus groups or systems are seen as dynamic rather than as self-perpetuating.

Bruckerhoff (1988) suggests that change occurs at two levels: In *surface change*, one simply might substitute one item or technique for another, whereas *change in principle* is a thorough reorganization of ideas according to a new principle. These levels approximate the model suggested by Watzlawick et al., but do not address the dynamics of the change.

Golembiewski's (1990) typology, couched in the organizational development model, addresses change based on intervention. *Alpha change*, like most designs for organizational development, recognizes only change occurring along relatively stable, invariant dimensions of reality or within a relatively fixed system, as in first-order change. *Beta change* still deals with a relatively stable environment, but measures variation. *Gamma change* is conceived as a radical shift in conceptualizing the salient dimensions of reality. It is a quantum shift in redefining the relevant psychological space as a consequence of intervention. Gamma change, like second-order change, is a change in state rather than the change in condition evident in alpha and beta change.

Another typology proposes four phases of change based on a biological model. Land (1973; Land and Ainsworth-Land 1982) suggests that *Phase I* change is accretive or formative in that the identity of an entity is established or developed and change is focused on survival. *Phase II* change is replicative or normative; most change of this type is an attempt at maintaining the status quo or the acknowledged normalcy. *Phase III* change is creative, collaborative, mutualistic, and integrative. *Phase IV* change is actually transformation—a destructuring and restructuring to create a new level and begin the cycle of phases again.

The transformation denoted by Land's Phase IV spans some of the current perceptions of educational restructuring, but it appears to represent the rhetoric more closely than the actualization or the reality. Raywid's (1990) typology specifically addresses efforts at educational change. What Raywid called "pseudo-reform" she suggests is "sheer rhetoric" and the most common type of change in education. As examples she cites actions such as lengthening the school day and denying driver's licenses to dropouts; she suggests that this level of change, actually an illusion or ritual of change (Cuban 1990; Popkewitz 1988; Popkewitz, Tabachnik, and Wehlage 1982), serves to deflect public attention from what matters in education.

Raywid's *incremental reform* aims to improve educational practice, but it functions within a limited sphere; it represents attempts at innovation within an invariant structure or system. In the third type of change, *restructuring,* Raywid suggests the language and emphasis are changed to express fundamental and pervasive alterations in organizational and institutional aspects of education, as exemplified by site-based management and "choice" of schools.

Elements of each of these models may surface in what I have described elsewhere (Greenman 1987) as the following three types of change: old or *intraparadigmatic change,* transitional or *interparadigmatic change,* and new change or *metamorphosis.* Here, and elsewhere in this chapter, the significant (though often overused and abused) term *paradigm* has the sense of a model of reality that gives rise to a philosophical or behavioral disposition (Pelletier 1985, 37), or a shared set of notions, ideas, assumptions, and/or expectations that society accepts as the consensual validation of reality. The term implies a megaparadigm in the sense of a worldview. This concept is to be distinguished from the concept underlying the term *scientific paradigm,* also used in this chapter, which refers to assumptions that inform scientific exploration and theory.

Intraparadigmatic change may be regarded as a whirlwind of energy in a nonporous box; this is surface, alpha, or first-order change—that which might occur in Land's Phases I and II—or pseudo-reform. Intraparadigmatic change does not challenge or permeate the assumptions that underlie the existing paradigm or worldview. In this type of change the same elements are simply rearranged; their validity is never questioned. The proposed change in this category might include tougher requirements, higher test scores, more tests, longer school days, and more homework.

Interparadigmatic change may be represented by the same whirlwind of energy as described above, but in this case it moves in and out of a porous box. The structure is the same, but there is some movement beyond it. This type of change would be transitional, as in Land's Phase III. Interparadigmatic change contains elements of a new structure, although at times only in rhetoric, because it is still anchored in the existing structure—the past. This type of change might envelop Raywid's incremental reform and Golembiewski's beta change. Perhaps—depending on the orientation and depth of the new conceptions of reality—it might also encompass Golembiewski's gamma change and Bruckerhoff's change in principle. Raywid's restructuring also might be classified here, depending on the perception of the concept and on the fidelity of treatment. This category includes new-sounding concepts that ultimately resemble what has gone before. I have described this transitional change elsewhere (Greenman 1987) as "parts of new and new parts."

Invoking the same imagery, metamorphosis is represented by the disintegration of the box or container, whether porous or nonporous, and by the creation of a new, differently shaped container from some of the pieces or the energy, infused with newly constructed pieces of different fabric, and with new energy and assumptions. This type of change, which might correspond partially to the destructuring and restructuring in Land's Phase IV, would be an example of second-order change or paradigm shift; the new fundamental assumptions necessitate invention and deep structural change, which will affect all aspects and even all conceptions of education.

For the purpose of this chapter, significant educational change entails fundamental restructuring of education—perhaps including but not limited to restructuring of schools, empowerment, site-based management, or any of the other features that may have become synonymous with restructuring in some arenas. Significant change is implied by metamorphosis, second-order change, Land's Phase IV, Raywid's restructuring, Golembiewski's gamma change, and Bruckerhoff's change of principle. In the remainder of this chapter I consider whether the reform of the early 1980s and the restructuring that is currently in vogue can be considered significant change.

REFORM

First-wave reform, as it is called in retrospect, was the response to a national diagnosis of a diseased educational system. It is generally recognized that we are in the midst of a series of waves of educational reform (Cuban 1990), though there may be some disagreement (e.g., Bacharach 1990; Kirst 1990; Murphy 1990) as to how many waves have rolled in or crashed upon the shores of American education. A plethora of commission reports initiated in the late 1970s and made public in the early 1980s (the best known of which is The National Commission on Excellence in Education's 1983 report, *A Nation at Risk*) looked to education as both the cause and the cure of American economic ills. The wave metaphor may have originated in observations by the United States Department of Education that the commission reports had initiated a "tidal wave of school reform which promises to renew American education" (quoted in Passow 1990, 10–11). First-wave reform did not question the basic structure of education nor the system of which it is a part. Instead, the players (limited here to teachers and students) and the way they played the game of education were considered to be at fault. "More is better" was the battle cry of first-wave reform: Legislators, on the advice of business leaders and administrators, mandated and legislated longer hours, more work, and stiffer requirements. Kirst (1990) reported, "The key variable in 1983 was thought to be a more rigorous curriculum. As one legislator told me, 'Let's make the little buggers work harder' " (21).

Because the commissions made up of business executives and government administrators had determined that teachers were essentially incapable of making correct decisions about the educational process, teachers were not included in decisions about the necessary reforms. Their already small areas of hard jurisdiction, or unquestioned decision making, virtually evaporated. Accountability was translated into mounds of paperwork for already overburdened teachers; teachers were "deskilled" as educators and "reskilled" as technicians and managers of technological and behavior management systems (Bennett and Le-Compte 1990, 140, 142).

In a study of the impact of first-wave reform on a group of outstanding teachers, McNeil demonstrated that teachers responded by leaving the teaching profession, by teaching only the bare bones (omitting controversial issues, engaging in "defensive simplification" of complex topics), by teaching "to the test" (providing outlines and lists of "important facts") at the expense of understanding and analysis, or by mystifying the curriculum (Bennett and LeCompte 1990, 141). First-wave reform essentially was imposed from outside the schools from the top down, so the resistance at the school level was understandable in light of what researchers know about change: The teachers were not invested in the process and were held accountable for results over which they had no control.

RESTRUCTURING

Second-wave reform, also known as restructuring, grew out of the realization that something was wrong with the first type of initiative for change: Nothing was really changing. Scholars identified problems in the culture of the school and the process of change, and the rhetoric changed from talk of reform to talk of restructuring. Theoretically, restructuring addresses the deep structure of education; it challenges long-held notions about what education is and how we carry it out.

Early rhetoric on restructuring stressed the grassroots creating of learning environments, curriculum, pedagogy, decision making, and virtually all other aspects of education. It also stressed the ongoing nature of such an enterprise; the schools, via the staff and the community, would be reflective and continually self-renewing, because that process would be part of the new structure. Actually, some of the restructuring rhetoric emerged in the early 1980s, built on the discourse of earlier reform efforts. State capitals provided scant support for proposals such as Sizer's 1984 model for secondary school reorganization (Kirst 1990), mainly because that model did not offer an easily measurable and demonstrable "quick fix."

Restructuring has been made more "manageable," however, by narrowing the focus to various segments. Some educators speak of restructuring *schools* or *schooling;* others envision restructuring *education.* For some educators, restructuring *is* empowerment of teachers *or* site-based management *or* shared decision making *or* middle schools *or* team teaching *or* effective schools *or* students' performance *or* involvement by parents *or.* . . . Although some of the elements identified as crucial to restructuring (see, e.g., Bacharach 1990; Barth 1988; Lieberman 1988a, 1988b; Maeroff 1988) are listed above, no one of those elements in itself constitutes restructuring. Reduction and segmentation may have made restructuring more accessible and more manageable, but also they have distorted the intended focus of restructuring on significant change, as defined earlier in this chapter.

RHETORIC VERSUS REALITY[1]

Restructuring begins theoretically at the school level—grassroots change, so to speak—but resistance from teachers, administrators, and parents is widespread (Timar 1989). Those who have an investment in the restructuring effort observe that *restructuring* is becoming just another buzzword (e.g., Lieberman and Miller 1990) and fear that it will be perceived as, and reduced to, another quick fix. Resistance to restructuring often emerges when the frame of reference from which the changes are generated and perceived is inconsistent with the fabric of the concepts embodied in restructuring, and the criteria against which the changes are evaluated are likewise inconsistent. As was observed to be the case in a Seattle suburb (Timar 1989, 269), opposition to reforms can emerge because restructuring may not reinforce the rituals associated with schooling.

This inconsistency between reform effort and philosophical orientation almost always exists in intraparadigmatic change, and often emerges in interparadigmatic change. The latter at times is creative, collaborative, mutualistic, integrative, and innovative, but the past is still used as a guide. First-order change is still being applied where second-order change is needed. In both intra- and interparadigmatic change, discourse about restructuring may be incongruent with the fidelity of treatment; the rhetoric does not match the reality. The following examples may illustrate this phenomenon.

The rhetoric of restructuring calls for an heterarchic organization (which entails an ever-changing locus of control, of power, and of leadership) rather than an hierarchic organization, but the reality usually is simply an extension of a bureaucratic, hierarchic organizational model in which the only possible alternative is perceived as horizontal. Such an alternative then is perceived as threatening to administrators, or as tokenism if teachers and others are given no real power. The superintendent of a Pennsylvania school district espoused a "strong bias in favor of restructuring" (Moloney 1989, 21), yet he said that it is harmful for teachers to spend time discussing changes in education over which they have no control:

> If empowering teachers simply means improving communication, enhancing collegiality, and meeting legitimate teacher needs, then such reform is useful, up to a point. If, on the other hand, empowering teachers means teachers are spending more time on committees debating other stakeholders about decisions they can't make anyway, then such change is less than useful. (Ibid)

In his article for *The Executive Educator* (Moloney 1989), directed toward an audience of administrators, Moloney never suggested that perhaps teachers *should* be able to make more decisions. A principal who shocked superintendents and other principals with his implementation of democratic decision making explained that even though he is the legal authority in his school, on the school's instructional council he, in equal status with all the other members of the council, has one vote with no veto power:

> Yes, I'm the legal authority, but decisions about schoolwide educational improvement are the prerogative [sic] of all professional educators. I'll sink or swim based on the decisions of a body of intelligent people. (quoted in Glickman 1990, 73)

The fact that this behavior is shocking to other administrators and the fact of widespread existence of tokenism in most schemata for shared decision making involving teachers rest on underlying assumptions about teachers and about the organizational structure of schools. If power is perceived as a fixed entity—if a zero-sum concept of power is held—then administrators theoretically would lose power if they gave some to teachers, and teachers would lose their power if they gave some to parents. Other concepts of power that perhaps are more consistent with the spirit of restructuring, such as facilitative, interactive power (Dunlap and Goldman 1991) or the notion of power as unlimited, would allow empowerment of others without threat to those currently making the decisions, because these concepts do not imply loss or removal of power. Unfortunately, the application of these concepts in the implementation of restructuring is rare. When it does occur (as in the example cited above), both the concepts and the application of them are discredited. The rhetoric of empowerment and shared decision making is inconsistent with the reality.

Though rhetoric about restructuring encourages teachers to invent education, or at least schooling, as they would have it, the reality contains district, state, and federal barriers that include rigid staffing policies, legal delegation of authority, regulations controlling accreditation and accountability, and mandated books and curricula. Apparently, examples of token authority are more common than meaningful decentralization (David 1991, 13). In Philadelphia, for example, although restructuring efforts focus on decentralized authority at the school level, the superintendent has been trying to enforce a standard curriculum and schedule (Gibboney 1991, 686). Likewise, some of the tenets of *America 2000* (U.S. Dept. of Education 1991) potentially undermine local restructuring processes. Supportive school districts have sought waivers to legal constraints, but these barriers generally are used as a rationale for aborting efforts at significant structural change. Gibboney notes that school-board members are not educated about education itself nor about educational reform. In a tally he conducted, 70 percent of the workshops available to school-board members were related to techniques (e.g., effective boardmanship) and to the routine maintenance of a school system (e.g., finance and budget procedures, personnel issues, and legal responsibilities; Gibboney 1991, 686–87).

School-board members need such information, but also they need to know about structure and other aspects of education beyond a layperson's knowledge; these individuals make decisions that directly affect teachers, children, and educational possibilities. If they are not critically aware of their own fundamental assumptions about education, teachers, power, and educational change, probably they will feel threatened by teacher-generated innovations and other initiatives for change. In addition, interpretation and implementation of some innovations may be distorted: The rhetoric may not reflect the practice in any way.

The concept of team teaching, for example, which has been discussed since the late 1950s (Anderson 1988, 17), is consistent with restructuring education. Anderson (1988) suggests that team teaching must include the following basic elements: (a) long-term and short-range planning by the total group of teachers and staff members working with a designated group of students; (b) co-teaching; (c) connection between the students in the group and all team members; (d) participation by all team members in evaluating the students, in which a final evaluation is often made in a conference; (e) team responsibility for assessing instructional progress; and (f) sharing of resources for the benefit of all. In many schools that claim to be involved in restructuring and that offer team teaching as evidence, the students actually move from one teacher and one self-contained classroom to another for instruction in different subjects, with independent evaluation by individual teachers. Departmentalization and "turn-teaching," whereby teachers take turns teaching the students, are the reality behind the team-teaching rhetoric.

Early rhetoric about restructuring produced concepts such as self-renewing schools, reflective practitioners, and lifelong learning. Rather than focusing on the best practice in education as an *end point,* on the final solution to arising problems, and on the "right" way to conduct a school, reflective practitioners (on an individual level) and self-renewing schools (on a collective level) recognize that creating effective education is a continual process. The process is analogous to the constant subtle and not-so-subtle adjustments necessary when one is sailing, windsurfing, or skiing, for example; one does not take a fixed position and stay there, because the environment and the conditions are constantly changing. Reflective practitioners are professionals who use their expertise to carefully assess the problem at hand, evaluate possible solutions, act, and assess the consequences of their actions in a continuous interaction with any problematic situation and with the process of teaching in general (Webb and Sherman 1989, 281–82). In self-renewing schools the faculty, staff, and administrators collectively would follow the same process of continually revisiting the visions and missions and reassessing the effectiveness of the school structure and procedures, and of creating change when needed.

In reality, however, educators search for nirvana, the *best practice,* in an effort to *fix* education once and for all. Perception of "wave after wave" of reform leaving education virtually unchanged can have a deleterious impact on those involved in the educational enterprise, as can attempts at improvement that create their own antitheses (Deal 1990). Deal suggests that constant change damages the culture of schools and the spirit of educators (6). Perhaps the harmful effect is due to perception: Does one focus on the destination, on the journey, or on both? Lifelong learning also necessitates a love of the journey, on which individuals continue to learn rather than load themselves with knowledge until they are full. The structure of schooling, however, does not encourage continual learning or the return of older students to school. Thus the rhetoric celebrates the notion of process, but the reality devalues the process and focuses on the product. There are those (e.g., Finn 1990) who insist that the recent "paradigm shift" in science supports an educational shift *from* process to product or outcome. The scientific evidence describing a universe in process rather than a fixed universe supports the opposite. We have, in fact, been focusing on product all along—we just defined differently the commodity. What Finn and others define as the process in the existing system is actually normative change in an attempt to maintain the same outcome. A celebration of process and change does not negate outcome, but rather acknowledges that outcomes are emergent and evolving—a series of markers rather than fixed end points.

Teachers' professionalism and collegiality are mentioned frequently in the rhetoric of second-wave reform or restructuring. Unfortunately, teachers are not necessarily the ones who define what professionalism is in relation to teachers; Weberian concepts of a profession, though not necessarily applicable to teachers, still are invoked as criteria. Collegiality generally has increased among those teachers who are involved in the efforts at restructuring, though usually they are not supported by existing structures of schools. Teachers often collaborate and plan after normal school hours, in the evenings, and on weekends. Teachers who must devote their own time and energy to creating new roles in the restructuring process also must maintain their old roles and responsibilities in order to function in an unchanged system (David 1991, 12). Also, because the usual procedure is to conduct a pilot restructuring program, not all teachers are involved in efforts at restructuring.

Because of existing politics, power structures, reward systems, and other aspects of organizational structure, jealousies, elitism, and divisive strategies often exist in the schools. In writing about the politics of restructuring, Timar (1989) cites examples of noncollegiality that accompanied restructuring in a Seattle suburb and in Jefferson County, Kentucky, schools: Competition rather than collaboration among teachers, a "we/they" mentality between teachers and administrators and between teachers involved in restructuring projects and those who were not so involved, widespread distrust, and a marked lack of "sense of common purpose."

The politics of restructuring comprise a specific example of the political nature of change, which must be recognized if change is to occur (Bruckerhoff 1988). Bruckerhoff states, "If teachers want to change education, they must understand change as a political act and collaborate to establish an ideological basis for teaching" (5). Perhaps because educators feel vulnerable, we fail to place on our agenda important questions that may represent necessary avenues of discourse because they are politically dangerous; but it is difficult to see where politics end and education begins (Hartoonian 1991, 22). One can recognize politics in schools and within school districts—sometimes so subtle as to be hardly detectable. The school and district politics may be elusive but they and their impact are strongly felt. Politics permeate the educational system on state and federal levels, the structure of the educational system as a whole, and the interface of education and society.

According to Cuban (1990), scholars propose the deflection of the political intensity of widespread social change to very slow change through the educational system as one of the reasons why Americans turn to schools in times of social turmoil. He states:

> Elite classes or dominant groups in the society that set directions for major social policies charge the public schools with the responsibility for solving national ills. . . . because the sources of those ills are deeply rooted in the structures of the society and . . . [if] the major problems of poverty, racism, drug addictions, and environmental destruction were addressed directly, grave upheavals in economic, social, and political institutions would occur. (8)

Education, then, is both permeated with politics and embedded in the politics of the larger cultural context. Politics is only one aspect of that context; all aspects of a culture both embody and are shaped by the philosophical orientation and the worldview of that culture.

THE CONTEXT OF CHANGE

To create significant change as defined in this chapter—to step out of the syndrome of "the more things change, the more they stay the same"—perhaps change initiators need to view reform and restructuring in the wider cultural context. As scholars and practitioners we may acknowledge and theoretically may address this context, but our own worldviews often obscure the fundamental issues. We give nod to the concept of the cultural construction of school and of educators, but critical consciousness in and of a cultural context can cause personal discomfort. Sizer (1991) admits that reexamining assumptions and simultaneously attending to all the consequential aspects of school restructuring can be painful, but that avoiding pain can mean avoiding change. He states, "To pretend that serious restructuring can be done without honest confrontation is a cruel illusion" (34).

Some scholars maintain that only direct challenge can alter the structure of education, but that most attempts in this area have been superficial. Emery (1980) notes:

> Most previous challenges . . . have failed to constitute a direct challenge because they have failed to see that the core of the educational paradigm lies outside of educational practices. That core does not lie in the character of the teacher-pupil relations; it does not lie in the freedom of the pupil to experiment with teaching materials; it does not lie in open classrooms, teacher teams, group project work and not even in the balance of rewards and punishments. . . . These things have been accommodated when and where they have been necessary and then expelled from the system when "real" education has been re-established as the goal. (2–3)

Thus Emery acknowledges some of the "rites" in the ritual of creating the illusion of educational change.

Emery's words echo the sentiments of educators who perceive no real change in education. Most explanations for the shifts of focus in education rely on either the pendulum or the cycle metaphor (Cuban 1990). The following words of a newly retired veteran teacher demonstrate the perception of education as a closed system with virtually no change beyond an established cyclic pattern:

> I just figured that I'd keep doing what I'd been doing all along. When you get to my age you can see that the whole thing runs in cycles—or in circles. . . . They put the wine in new bottles, but it's the same old wine. I knew that if I waited long enough what I was doing would come back into style.

So I decided not to go chasing after the fads but to sit still and let [the fads] come to me. (Quoted in Webb and Sherman 1989, 251)

This teacher identified any innovations as recurring fads because she or he views changes from the standpoint of firmly held philosophical assumptions.

Such a perspective encourages the application of new labels to old concepts on the part of educators strongly influenced by existing worldviews and philosophical assumptions. For example, instead of employing the dynamics of cooperative learning, educators simply may relabel traditional approaches to group work as "cooperative learning." In a similar vein, some educational scholars comment on the static nature of reform, as in McDaniel's statements that "all education reform movements ultimately fail—or at least fall short of expectations" and that the educational pendulum swings on a short stroke (McDaniel 1989, 16, 18). Cuban (1990) suggests that the metaphors for examining change—the pendulum and the cycle—in themselves imply motion but no change. Perhaps the criteria for determining the success of educational change and for defining "real" education need to be addressed.

According to Emery (1980), the core of the traditional educational paradigm lies in epistemology, or assumptions about how it is possible to gain knowledge. I believe that one must look critically several layers deeper, even beyond the axiological level that addresses values; we must address the ontological level, where the worldview prevails and permeates every molecule of one's being. Some of the restructuring literature acknowledges the need to include, or even begin with, a focus on ontology, but we still see it, including educational assumptions, as being "out there" rather than as an integral part of ourselves and the structures we create and reinforce. Sir Alfred North Whitehead observed that movement toward change invites action and reaction, both supported by subtle underlying assumptions that need articulation:

In each age of the world distinguished by high activity, there will be found at its culmination, some profound cosmological outlook, implicitly accepted, impressing its own type on the current springs of action. This ultimate cosmology is only partly expressed, and the details of such expression issue into derivative specialized questions of violent controversy. The intellectual strife of an age is mainly concerned with these latter questions of secondary generality that conceal an agreement upon first principles almost too obvious to need expression, and almost too general to be capable of expression. In each period there is a general form of the forms of thought; and, like the air we breathe, such a form is so translucent, and so pervading, and so seemingly necessary, that only by extreme effort can we become aware of it. (Quoted in Gregory 1980, 300)

My basic premise is that American efforts toward reform and restructuring, and even the notions of change employed in these efforts, are tied to the "form of the forms of thought" prevalent in the operational American worldview—that which informs the very structure of education and schooling. To create the kind of change demanded by a significant restructuring of education, we must make that "extreme effort" to examine education critically in relation to the cultural context and the prevailing paradigm, and to become aware of emerging paradigms that may provide more appropriate principles for the envisioned change.

Theoretically, education scholars are aware that unarticulated philosophical assumptions frame the perspective from which an individual and (by extension) a culture view the world. Human beings create cultures. These cultures generate knowledge about the universe and produce a worldview, a philosophical orientation, or what I defined earlier in this chapter as a megaparadigm, which forms the parameters of reality and limits the perception of reality *to* those parameters. The sociocultural institutions of a particular culture or society, such as education, are created within the boundaries of the created reality; in fact, they embody that reality. As many scholars (e.g., Harkins 1976; La Belle 1976; Ogbu 1974) remind us, education mirrors and transmits—both explicitly and implicitly, by inclusion and exclusion—the values, beliefs, attitudes, ideologies, and notions about the world, and notions about the self and about society.

The operational American worldview (those fundamental assumptions that guide all of our thought and action), or the current perception of the universe accepted by Western society, is based essentially on classical Newtonian physics, Aristotelian linearity, Cartesian duality and reductionism, and simple causality. It is static, inflexible, segmented, and monochronic, separating mind from body and body from environment. It purports that matter is the essence of the universe, that consensus knowledge prevails, and that reality must be validated scientifically (e.g., Greenman 1987; Korzybski 1958; Pelletier 1985). This prevailing American/Western perception has been identified as the Cartesian-Newtonian paradigm or worldview (e.g., Crowell 1989; Gibboney 1991). The impact of this view on American education can be observed in the following examples of how we choose to "do school": (a) the schools' focus on subject matter; (b) the segmentation of knowledge into subject areas, facts, and objectives; (c) how the school is divided; and (d) the emphasis on test scores.

Moreover, the very nature of first-wave reform derives its validity from this Cartesian-Newtonian worldview. Educational reforms in the wake of *A Nation at Risk* appeared to reflect a military metaphor: a hierarchical chain of command with top-down leadership, emphasis on regulation and standardization of practice, accountability, "basic training" for teachers and students, and focus on a fixed concept of the nature of excellence (McDaniel 1989, 17). The essence of the reform was mechanistic and quantitative, and it was governed by what Barth (1986) calls "list logic." If one believes that matter is the essence of a fixed universe, then the idea that "more is better," and the focus on content rather than on process, on a zero-sum concept of power, on standardized testing and measurement, and on methods and techniques, to name only a few elements of the first-wave effort at reform, make perfect sense.

The process of first-wave reform is intraparadigmatic. It focuses on maintaining the status quo; therefore modification, or rearranging the same elements, is the format. From the perspective of the prevailing American worldview, first-wave reform is successful. Some educational scholars (e.g., Murphy 1990, 35) are convinced that such reform is the key to successful educational change. First-wave reform is logical when viewed within its context and measured against the criteria: It is touchable, concrete, and thus defensible to school boards and state legislatures, and it enjoys face validity (Barth 1986). First-wave reform appears to supply a quick fix to educational ills without significantly altering a fixed universe. Schools as presently defined do what they are supposed to do: They express, define, maintain, and perpetuate rather than alter, transform, or invent ideologies (Cuban 1990; Greenman 1987).

Many scholars (e.g., Capra 1975, 1982; Ferguson 1980; Orenstein 1986; Pelletier 1985; Wolf 1981) believe that we are in a transitional phase, or in what Thomas Kuhn (1962) called a "paradigm shift." The emerging scientific paradigm supports a perception of the universe based on relatively new research in physics (such as quantum mechanics and chaos theory) and other scientific disciplines. The principles of this paradigm include process, integration, complexity, interconnection, and unbroken wholeness. The paradigm proposes such notions as the following: (a) Energy is the essence of the universe; (b) chaos is a natural state, and order might not be as we perceive and define order; and (c) the brain is a system that can be perceived as a hologram. Because science is the explainer and validator of reality in the Western (or, more specifically, American) worldview, this emerging scientific paradigm has initiated the emergence of a changing American worldview or megaparadigm.

Some of these principles support the rhetoric of restructuring. Concepts such as participatory school-based management, collegiality, empowerment of teachers, team teaching rather than turn teaching, an interdisciplinary curricular approach, cooperative learning, whole language, and equity receive validity in relation to the principles of interconnection, integration, complexity, and unbroken wholeness. Attention to variety in learning styles and to diversity in human beings is supported by the concept of complexity and by the idea of thriving on chaos rather than by a need for uniformity, linearity, and sameness. The concepts of reflective practitioners, self-renewing schools, and lifelong learning make sense in relation to a universe that is governed by process rather than being fixed.

There exists, then, theoretical support for redefining the criteria against which we measure successful educational change and for redefining the very essence of education itself. Yet, what Joel Barker (1984) calls "paradigm paralysis" prevails, resulting from visions framed by and within what are perceived as boundaries. The restructuring efforts are shaped by the same worldview that shapes the existing educational (and other sociocultural) structures. Some districts are attempting more successfully than others to address existing assumptions. The following review of several case studies of restructuring shows that those restructuring efforts that incorporate critical examination of broad cultural contexts appear less likely to result in ineffectual quick fixes and hold more promise of long-term success than those efforts that do not address assumptions implicit in prevailing politics, power relationships, and other aspects of the existing cultural contexts.

PERCEPTIONS FROM THE FIELD

Interviews from two pilot studies in progress, one in Hardrock County (pseudonym), a southwestern school district, and the other in Rivers County (pseudonym), a Florida district, corroborate reports from other documented studies (e.g., Casner-Lotto 1988; Conley and Bacharach

1990; Timar 1989) that indicate mistrust, misunderstanding, and an underlying feeling of being threatened in relation to restructuring efforts. These efforts have emphasized shared decision making as the avenue for change. In both districts, the restructuring effort was initiated at the top, and the teachers initially resisted vesting themselves in the process— many still do so. In another Florida district, Flatland County (pseudonym), a memorandum regarding site-based decision making was distributed to the teachers. The memo delineated areas in which decisions could be made, but excluded some areas essential for the freedom and power to restructure. The teachers would have nothing to say, for example, about the selection of textbooks, the structuring of the school day, the means of external evaluation (such as norm-referenced tests), or areas of content in the curriculum. The administrators apparently made no effort to suggest or support the seeking of waivers from, or changes of, federal, state, and county directives, mandates, and laws. Instead, the local administrators used these barriers in role-distancing tactics.

In the school district's rhetoric, the Rivers County middle school is identified as a model school, considered by some teachers and administrators, and by the school district, as engaged strongly in restructuring. After a pilot project was conducted at this school, all Rivers County schools adopted interdisciplinary teaming. The entire middle school is piloting a formalized school management project, which is oriented toward school-based decision making. In addition, various groups of teachers in the school are implementing other pilot projects.

The reality, then, is that this Rivers middle school does not have an integrated approach to restructuring so much as it serves as a testing ground for pilot projects initiated by the school board or at other levels of administration. Only 11 percent of the teachers felt that they had any real power over decisions that affected them directly as teachers. Forty-two percent felt they sometimes had that power as professional educators. Among the areas where teachers had decision-making power, very few allowed for any structural changes.

Almost all of the teachers perceived the restructuring efforts—or any changes—as initiated by the principal, the school board, and other administrators. Some teachers, however, believed that input by teachers was part of the process and that administrators actually considered their suggestions. Many teachers believed that their input was elicited, but that no action was taken on their ideas. Some of the faculty felt strongly that the process was elitist and that only "favored teachers" were involved. An alarming number of teachers said they either knew nothing about restructuring or were not aware that any restructuring was taking place at their school. Generally, the effort for educational change in the Rivers school appears to be fragmented, with no shared vision. Teachers' perceptions range from a feeling of total involvement in the process, through disenfranchisement, to resistance to any kind of educational change.

In the Hardrock district, the restructuring effort was initiated and supported by the superintendent, with strong support on many levels from a national foundation. This foundation was established by a prominent international corporation specifically to support American educational change by providing consultants, lobbyists, and some indirect funding. Initially, in this case the restructuring rhetoric at times was diametrically opposed to the reality. For example, empowerment of teachers was theoretically a prime objective. Yet although teachers were told they were being empowered, what little power they had was often drastically diminished. Factors influencing this incongruity included (a) state and federal mandates that took precedence over local decisions; (b) principals who felt threatened by the process; (c) politically powerful parents who held a conservative, classical (à la Allan Bloom), Cartesian-Newtonian view of what "real" education was supposed to be; (d) decisions by the school board, including the barring of any form of collective bargaining; and (e) implicit political manipulations that had been the traditional means of dealing with teachers, especially those who deviated from the norm or challenged traditionally structured education. Mistrust was prevalent, often to the greatest degree among those teachers who had been most innovative in the past. These teachers had believed in their ability to change education and "the system's" response to their efforts, only to be disappointed repeatedly. Resistance to the restructuring project prevailed at all levels. Most of the "restructuring" plans generated by the schools proposed first-order, intraparadigmatic changes, sometimes couched in restructuring rhetoric.

One school, however, was particularly successful in the Hardrock restructuring effort and emerged as a model for the district. Second-order change occurred at this school; some of the conditions that allowed for such change included the following: (a) Excellent reflective practitioners were scattered throughout the district, but in this school a majority of teachers already had accepted the principles of the emerging paradigm and viewed the restructuring effort as a vehicle for formalizing what they had been implementing individually in their classrooms. (b) Many of the teachers were part of a strong support network that had evolved over the years and were accustomed to looking at themselves, and at education in general, critically and in a cultural context. (c) The principal was extremely supportive, and he respected and trusted the teachers. The faculty and the staff of this Hardrock school were able to develop a shared vision, to involve the community, to develop a comprehensive plan, and to obtain a grant for implementation of the plan. They were encouraged to seek waivers from state mandates and to press to change state laws that were limiting the restructuring effort. The superintendent, who was committed to restructuring, helped to keep a nervous school board from reacting to the teachers' initiative.

Because of this success, some other groups of teachers received permission to create second-order change. Several teachers at one school had long challenged traditional and standard means of evaluation, including state-mandated norm-referenced tests. For years, they were viewed as "troublemakers." In the context of the restructuring initiative, they became heroes—models for other teachers. They were encouraged to develop and expand an alternative means of evaluation and to obtain waivers from state mandates. Another group of teachers helped design a new Hardrock County district school; they participated in shaping the architectural design, in selecting furniture and other hardware, in developing procedure and curricula, and in hiring the principal with whom they would work. Yet another group of teachers was involved in creating the ideal school for later development.

Other schools, unfortunately often motivated by the jealousy and competition long fostered in the district, nonetheless began to ask questions and to engage in critical self-examination in a cultural context. Through this process they began to understand the restructuring process. They were taking steps to initiate comprehensive plans in their schools and to develop shared visions beyond those dictated by presentism and by "paradigm paralysis."

Thus, after four years of efforts at restructuring in Hardrock, the resistance was beginning to dissipate. When the superintendent had to retire because of ill health, however, the entire process was threatened. The school board decided to hire a superintendent who was more conservative than the departing superintendent. Teachers' hiring of a new principal for one of the schools was interrupted, and the hiring decision was made by the new superintendent. Those teachers and administrators who are committed to restructuring are cautiously watching the Hardrock County district politics; they have not given up hope for significant change, and they believe that their new sense of empowerment will help to sustain the process of change, even though the momentum has slowed. The fact that restructuring may revolve around the power of one individual indicates the entrenchment of the traditional educational structure. "Empowerment" without authority, either given or negotiated, results in responsibility and blame, but not freedom or real power to initiate change and transform education.

CONCLUSION

If we are serious about creating significant educational change, we must work toward lessening the gap between the rhetoric of restructuring and the reality, as observed in the fidelity of treatment in implementation. This effort can be facilitated by helping the participants in the restructuring effort—from top to bottom and from bottom to top of the old organizational structure—to develop a critical awareness of how they relate to the cultural context and the process of change. Existing assumptions must be articulated, new assumptions must be imagined, and bridges between the two must be built. Deal (1990) suggests, "In order to transform schools successfully, educators need to navigate the difficult space between letting go of old patterns and grabbing on to new ones" (12). For meaningful educational change to occur, according to Shive (1980), the starting point is the vision; there needs to be something we can grab on to: "Until we develop a conceptualization of the future as we would have it, and use this conceptualization to guide education in the present, no educational reform of any significance is really possible" (11).

The concept of structural tension (Fritz 1984) suggests that one must first envision, then choose to have what one envisions. At the same time, we must know where we are in relation to the chosen vision, and continually reevaluate and readjust in relation to our choices and to the vision itself. The structural tension must be maintained; we can let go of neither the vision (though it can be refined with new information) nor the reality of the moment. This tension might help us to negotiate the anxiety associated with liminality. People may need to grieve the loss of old mind-sets:

> People must successfully negotiate the space between clinging to tradition and embracing a new worldview. This requires grief work, a historical connection between past, present, and future—and celebration. (Deal 1990, 12)

We cannot "get there from here" if we do not know where "here" is, but also we will not go very far if we define "there" only by what is already within our sights. To an uninformed observer, the caterpillar bears no resemblance to the butterfly. Perhaps metamorphosis—creating significant educational change—also requires a leap of faith in possibilities—even if they do not appear to be possible from where we are standing.

Notes

1. Increasingly, there are various uses of the word *rhetoric,* each with different implications. For the purpose of this discussion of the phrase *rhetoric versus reality, rhetoric* refers to the realities implied in the rhetoric and *reality* refers to the realities observable in practice.

References

Anderson, R. H. 1988. "Team Teaching: Quo Vadis?" *Florida ASCD Journal* (Fall): 17–22.

Atkin, J. M. 1989. "Can Educational Research Keep Pace with Educational Reform?" *Phi Delta Kappan* 71(3): 200–205.

Bacharach, S. B. 1990. "Education Reform: Making Sense of It All." In *Education Reform: Making Sense of It All,* edited by S. B. Bacharach, 415–30. Boston: Allyn & Bacon.

Ballinger, C. 1988. "Rethinking the School Calendar." *Educational Leadership* 45(5): 57–61.

Barker, J. 1984. *Discovering the Future: The Business of Paradigms.* Minneapolis: Filmedia.

Barth, R. S. 1986. "On Sheep and Goats and School Reform." *Phi Delta Kappan* 68(4): 293–96.

Barth, R. S. 1988. "Principals, Teachers, and School Leadership." *Phi Delta Kappan* 69(9): 639–42.

Bennett, K. P., and M. D. LeCompte. 1990. *How Schools Work: A Sociological Analysis of Education.* White Plains, N.Y.: Longman.

Brandt, R. 1988. "On Changing Secondary Schools: A Conversation with Ted Sizer." *Educational Leadership* 45(5): 30–36.

Bruckerhoff, C. 1988. "Education for the 1990's: What Will It Be, Change or More of the Same?" *Educational Foundations* 2(3): 5–9.

Bull, B. L. 1987. "Confronting Reform in Teacher Preparation: One State's Experience." *Educational Evaluation and Policy Analysis* 9(1): 25–40.

Capra, F. 1975. *The Tao of Physics.* New York: New Age Books.

Capra, F. 1982. *The Turning Point: Science, Society, and the Rising Culture.* New York: Simon & Schuster.

Carey, L. 1989. "On Alienation and the ESL Student." *Phi Delta Kappan* 71(1): 74–75.

Carroll, J. M. 1990. "The Copernican Plan: Restructuring the American High School." *Phi Delta Kappan* 71(5): 358–65.

Casner-Lotto, J. 1988. "Expanding the Teacher's Role: Hammond's School Improvement Process." *Phi Delta Kappan* 69(5): 349–56, 375–76.

Chion-Kenney, L. 1987. "A Report from the Field: The Coalition of Essential Schools." *American Educator* 11(4): 18–27.

Combs, A. W. 1988. "New Assumptions for Educational Reform." *Educational Leadership* 45(5): 38–43.

Conley, S. C., and S. B. Bacharach. 1990. "From School-Site Management to Participatory School-Site Management." *Phi Delta Kappan* 71(7): 539–44.

Cornbleth, C. 1986. "Ritual and Rationality in Teacher Education Reform." *Educational Researcher* 15(4): 5–14.

Crowell, S. 1989. "A New Way of Thinking: The Challenge of the Future." *Educational Leadership* 46(9): 60–63.

Cuban, L. 1988. "A Fundamental Puzzle of School Reform." *Phi Delta Kappan* 69(5): 341–44.

Cuban, L. 1990. "Reforming Again, Again, and Again." *Educational Researcher* 19(1): 3–13.

David, J. L. 1988. "The Use of Indicators by School Districts: Aid or Threat to Improvement?" *Phi Delta Kappan* 69(7): 499–502.

David, J. L. 1991. "What it Takes to Restructure Education." *Educational Leadership* 48(8): 11–15.

David, J. L., and B. C. MacPhee. 1988. "Changing School Structure in the Summer." *Educational Leadership* 45(5): 78–81.

Deal, T. E. 1990. "Reforming Reform." *Educational Leadership* 48(8): 6–12.

Dunlap, D. M., and P. Goldman. 1991. "Rethinking Power in Schools." *Educational Administration Quarterly* 27(1): 5–29.

Eisner, E. W. 1988. "The Ecology of School Improvement." *Educational Leadership* 45(5): 24–29.

Elam, S. M., and A. M. Gallup. 1989. "The Twenty-First Annual Gallup Poll of the Public's Attitude toward the Public Schools." *Phi Delta Kappan* 71(1): 41–54.

Elmore, R. F. 1987. "Reform and the Culture of Authority in Schools." *Educational Administration Quarterly* 23(4): 60–78.

Emery, F. 1980. Educational Paradigms: An Epistemological Revolution. Unpublished ms. London, Tavistock Institute.

Ferguson, M. 1980. *The Aquarian Conspiracy: Personal and Social Transformation in the 1980's.* Los Angeles: Tarcher.

Finn, C. E. 1990. "The Biggest Reform of All." *Phi Delta Kappan* 71(8): 584–92.

Fritz, R. 1984. *The Path of Least Resistance.* Salem, Mass.: DMA.

Georgeoff, J. 1989. "Let's Again Talk Sense about Our Schools." *Phi Delta Kappan* 71(1): 19–28.

Gibboney, R. A. 1991. "The Killing Field of Reform." *Phi Delta Kappan* 72(9): 682–88.

Ginsberg, R., and B. Berry. 1990. "Experiencing School Reform: The View from South Carolina." *Phi Delta Kappan* 71(7): 549–52.

Glickman, C. D. 1990. "Pushing School Reform to a New Edge: Seven Ironies of School Empowerment." *Phi Delta Kappan* 72(1): 68–75.

Gold, G. G. 1987. "A Reform Strategy for Education: Employer-Sponsored Teacher Internships." *Phi Delta Kappan* 68(5): 384–87.

Golembiewski, R. T. 1990. *Ironies in Organizational Development.* New Brunswick, Conn.: Transaction.

Greenman, N. P. 1987. "American Education: Emerging Contexts for a Model of the Future." Ph.D. Dissertation, University of New Mexico, Albuquerque. DAI 49/03A p. 476.

Gregory, M. S. 1980. "The Science-Humanities Program (NEXA) at San Francisco State University: The 'Two Cultures' Reconsidered." *Leonardo* 13:295–302.

Harkins, A. M. 1976. "Controls, Paradigms and Designs: Critical Elements in the Understanding of Cultural Dynamics." In *Educational Patterns and Cultural Configurations,* pp. 212–221. Edited by Joan I. Roberts and Sherrie R. Akinsanya. New York: David McKay Company, Inc.

Harkins, A. M. 1980. "Postscript: Systems Thinking for the Educational Futurist." In *Education: A Time for Decisions,* K. M. Redd and A. M. Harkins, 271–76. Washington, D.C.: World Future Society.

Hart, L. A. 1989. "The Horse is Dead." *Phi Delta Kappan* 71(3): 237–42.

Hartoonian, M. 1991. "Good Education is Bad Politics: Practices and Principles of School Reform." *Social Education* (January): 22–23, 65.

Henley, M. 1987. "Something is Missing from the Education Reform Movement." *Phi Delta Kappan* 69(4): 284–85.

Honetschlager, D., and M. Cohen. 1988. "The Governors Restructure Schools." *Educational Leadership* 45(5): 42–43.

Ken, S. T. 1989. "Reform in Soviet and American Education: Parallels and Contrasts." *Phi Delta Kappan* 71(1): 19–28.

Kirst, M. W. 1990. "The Crash of the First Wave." In *Education Reform: Making Sense of It All,* edited by S. B. Bacharach, 20–29. Boston: Allyn & Bacon.

Koepke, M. 1989. "Learning by the Block." *Teacher Magazine* (December): 52–60.

Korzybski, A. 1958. *Science and Sanity: An Introduction to Non-Aristotelian Systems and General Semantics.* 4th ed. Lakeville, Conn.: International Non-Aristotelian Library.

Kuhn, T. 1962. *The Structure of Scientific Revolutions.* Chicago: University of Chicago Press.

La Belle, T. J. 1976. "An Anthropological Framework for Studying Education." In *Educational Patterns and Cultural Configurations,* edited by J. I. Roberts and S. K. Akainsanya, 67–82. New York: David McKay.

Lambert, L. 1988. "Staff Development Redesigned." *Phi Delta Kappan* 69(9): 665–68.

Land, G. L. 1973. *Grow or Die.* New York: Dell.

Land, G. A., and V. Ainsworth-Land. 1982. *Forward to Basics.* Buffalo, N.Y.: DOK.

Lieberman, A. 1988a. "Expanding the Leadership Team." *Educational Leadership* 45(5): 4–8.

Lieberman, A. 1988b. "Teachers and Principals: Turf, Tension, and New Tasks." *Phi Delta Kappan* 69(9): 648–53.

Lieberman, A., and L. Miller. 1990. "Restructuring Schools: What Matters and What Works." *Phi Delta Kappan* 71(10): 759–64.

Maeroff, G. I. 1988. *The Empowerment of Teachers: Overcoming the Crisis of Confidence.* New York: Teachers College Press.

McDaniel, T. R. 1989. "Demilitarizing Public Education: School Reform in the Era of George Bush." *Phi Delta Kappan* 71(1): 15–18.

McDonald, J. 1989. "When Outsiders Try to Change Schools from the Inside." *Phi Delta Kappan* 71(3): 206–11.

Meadows, B. J. 1990. "The Rewards and Risks of Shared Leadership." *Phi Delta Kappan* 71(7): 545–48.

Michaels, K. 1988. Caution: Second-Wave Reform Taking Place. *Educational Leadership* 45(5):3.

Moloney, W. J. 1989. "Restructuring's Fatal Flaw." *The Executive Educator* 11(10): 21–23.

Murphy, J., ed. 1990. *The Educational Reform Movement of the 1980s.* Berkeley, Calif.: McCutchan.

National Commission on Excellence in Education. *A Nation at Risk: The Imperative for Educational Reform.* Washington, D.C.: Government Printing Office, 1983.

Ogbu, J. U. 1974. *The Next Generation: An Ethnography of Education in an Urban Neighborhood.* New York: Academic Press.

Orenstein, R. E. 1986. *The Psychology of Consciousness: The Classic Study, Completely Revised and Updated.* New York: Penguin Books.

Passow, A. H. 1990. "How it Happened, Wave by Wave: Whither (or Wither?) School Reform?" In *Education Reform: Making Sense Of It All,* edited by S. B. Bacharach, 10–19. Boston: Allyn & Bacon.

Pelletier, K. R. 1985. *Toward a Science of Consciousness.* 2d ed. Berkeley, Calif.: Celestial Arts.

Popkewitz, T. S. 1988. "Educational Reform: Rhetoric, Ritual, and Social Interest." *Educational Theory* 38(1): 77–93.

Popkewitz, T. S., R. Tabachnick, and G. Wehlage. 1982. *The Myth of Educational Reform*. Madison: University of Wisconsin.

Rallis, S. F. 1988. "Room at the Top: Conditions for Effective School Leadership." *Phi Delta Kappan* 69(9): 643–47.

Rallis, S. F., and M. C. Highsmith. 1986. "The Myth of the 'Great Principal': Questions of School Management and Instructional Leadership." *Phi Delta Kappan* 68(4): 301–3.

Raywid, M. A. 1990. "The Evolving Effort to Improve Schools: Pseudo-Reform, Incremental Reform, and Restructuring." *Phi Delta Kappan* 72(2): 139–43.

Richmond, G. 1989. "The Future School: Is Lowell Pointing Us toward a Revolution in Education?" *Phi Delta Kappan* 71(3): 232–36.

Seldon, R. W. 1988. "Missing Data: A Progress Report from the States." *Phi Delta Kappan* 69(7): 492–94.

Shanker, A. 1990. "The End of the Traditional Model of Schooling—and a Proposal for Using Incentives to Restructure Our Public Schools." *Phi Delta Kappan* 71(5) 345–57.

Shive, R. J. 1980. *The Future: Implications for the Learner.* (ERIC Document Reproduction Service No. ED 240117).

Sizer, T. R. 1991. "No Pain, No Gain." *Educational Leadership* 48(8): 32–34.

Timar, T. 1989. "The Politics of School Restructuring." *Phi Beta Kappan* 71(4): 265–75.

Timar, T. B., and D. L. Kirp. 1988. "State Efforts to Reform Schools: Treading between a Regulatory Swamp and an English Garden." *Educational Evaluation and Policy Analysis* 10(2): 75–88.

Tucker, M. S. 1988. "Peter Drucker, Knowledge Work, and the Structure of Schools." *Educational Leadership* 45(5): 44–46.

Tye, B. B. 1987. "The Deep Structure of Schooling." *Phi Delta Kappan* 68(4): 281–83.

Tyler, R. W. 1987. "Education Reforms." *Phi Delta Kappan* 68(4): 277–80.

U. S. Department of Education. 1991. *America 2000: An Education Strategy.* Washington, D.C.: GPO.

Watzlawick, P., J. Weakland, and R. Fish. 1974. *Change: Principles of Problem Formation and Problem Resolution.* New York: Norton.

Webb, R. B., and R. R. Sherman. 1989. *Schooling and Society.* New York: Macmillan.

Webster's Seventh New Collegiate Dictionary. 1972. Springfield, Mass.: Merriam.

Weiler, H. N. 1988. "The Politics of Reform and Nonreform in French Education." *Comparative Education Review* 32(3): 251–65.

Wise, A. E. 1988. "The Two Conflicting Trends in School Reform: Legislated Learning Revisited." *Phi Delta Kappan* 69(5): 328–32.

Wolf, F. A. 1981. *Taking the Quantum Leap.* San Francisco: Harper & Row.

2

CERTIFICATION TO CREDENTIALING: RECONSTITUTING CONTROL MECHANISMS IN TEACHER EDUCATION

Thomas S. Popkewitz and Marie Brennan

During the last decade, nationwide concern about the quality of schools has prompted hundreds of reform proposals that would change the work of teaching, the organization of teacher education, and the emphasis on public school education. One aspect of these reforms concerns the changing mechanism for certifying teachers through university professional programs. From the early 1970s to the late 1980s, legislative and administrative rules have shifted from a focus on certifying approved programs to credential procedures that specify individual traits, experiences, and information. This shift in focus has been based upon an assumption that the quality of schooling can be altered through judicious changes in the procedures and determinations of outputs in teacher education. These practices are often viewed as a problem of rational choice, in which assessments of the national economy, international competition, and cultural and social tensions produce a need to reform school practices so that schooling becomes more responsive to national priorities and the public interest.

In our research, we consider the problematic of rationality of change by examining the last two decades of legislative and governmental administrative texts covering university teacher education in Wisconsin and California. For the purposes of this research, the texts can be considered to be both a dynamic of social relations and a product of them.[1] The texts are understood not "just" as part of a formal mechanism to achieve prescribed outcomes, but also as part of the events in which new forms of control are produced. California and Wisconsin teacher education regulations stand within a field of power relations and institutional configurations. The regulations owe their plausibility to the networks of relations that are presupposed by the texts and the dynamics of culture, politics, and economics that make possible their production. Consequently, in this context, the term *text* takes on both a concrete and a theoretical meaning.

The administrative texts are significant mechanisms of control not only through the use of overt sanctions, but through the epistemology established for structuring intent and purpose to the events of schooling. The rules and standards establish categorical relations and distinctions that define the boundaries between the permissible and the impermissible, the unspoken and the omitted. These relations have the potential to discipline the individual who acts upon and internalizes the values, dispositions, and sensitivities that have been framed by administrative discourse. In this manner, the texts signify a direction, sense of will, and purpose that structurally organize educational practice, and that are independent of the specific author's intended effects.

When texts are viewed as practices of social regulation in this manner, a notion of the state enters into the analysis. The school is a cultural creation that has been consistently tied to the formation of the state in the United States. We use "state" as a theoretical concept to consider how macro- and microelements of social regulation occur to produce the governing of the "self" in daily practices, disposition, and cognition (see, e.g., Foucault 1980). The regulation appears as one of a neutral institution of society that operates through the formation of governmental and nongovernmental actors in the arena of schooling. Thus, our concern with the state embraces more than governmental agencies. We use the administrative texts to focus upon the formal actors (legislative and government agencies) who enter into coalitions with actors in other institutions, thereby steering the governance of schooling. We also consider the problem of social regulation in relation to the structures of dispositions produced within and among different institutions, and the power relations that have been invested with authority as a result of specific discourse strategies. These coalitions make up the "state" in teacher education. Thus from our perspective, the state is neither a neutral site in which interest groups play out their struggles, nor a tool used by one particular group or class to dominate others.

In the course of evaluating discourse about the regulation of schools and teacher education, we will first consider theoretical issues of texts, power relations, and education. We then proceed to look at the general pattern of change in California and Wisconsin with regard to the regulation of teacher education, and at the larger social and economic issues that are brought to bear on current reform practices. At this point, "state" is also used as a geographical concept to refer to practices such as those of the State of Wisconsin. As with most social life, publicly stated agendas have particular nuances, tensions, and social implications that may not be evident at first glance. By deconstructing the logic of regulatory texts, we can make possible alternative reconstructions that are based on a quite different logic. It is through critique that sciences of human affairs play an important role in a democracy: To locate discontinuities is to open new systems of possibility.

STRUCTURES OF POWER RELATIONS AND TEXTS

One way to understand the changing power relations in the current reforms is to consider historically the emergence of texts as steering mechanisms for social policy. Until recently, formal texts have not been an important dynamic in the construction of American society. At a very general layer, one could point to documents that are significant as symbols of the history of the country and its folklore. Texts such as the Constitution provide only a general mantle by which the tensions of change, and the demands and struggles within society, are considered, thereby serving as a symbol to legitimate the outcomes of struggles that have been decided in other arenas.

Most of our social institutions have been structured without the invention of formal steering texts; their functions or purposes have been defined in a manner that seems similar to the development of common law. The formation of school subjects, for example, had little to do with written policies, but were microdevelopments as issues of socialization and labor were struggled with within schooling (see, e.g., Popkewitz 1987). The ideological emphasis on "negotiated" rather than state-promulgated regulation is further legitimized through modern political theory of interest group pluralism. Modern political science, for example, considered behavioralism to be a methodological revolution. Its focus shifted from consideration of legislative texts to studies of the conditions, interests, and processes that influence the production and implementation of policy (Dahl 1963).

We can compare this to European contexts in which the merging of religion and government into a highly centralized and strong state made the formulation of official texts an important element in the processes of policy formulation and realization (Luke 1989). Yet the focus of American political science hides important and fundamental dynamics of political conduct. The concern with processes of government and pluralism has neglected the study of the state as a merging of society and government in the process of regulation as social identities are constructed. As state power became at once more localized and centralized in transportation, commerce, and sectors of social welfare at the turn of the century, the formalization of social patterns became more regularized and disciplined.[2] Legislation, administrative agencies (such as those in federal banking), and the development of an epistemology about social policy that was pragmatic and utilitarian helped to provide direction about the ways that social problems and individuality were to be interpreted and social improvement gained.

The development of schooling had, until recently, given rise to no significant national documents about purpose or direction. There has been no ministry of education, and it is only occasionally that legislation serves as a landmark. Prominent texts in schooling were, to a large extent, nonexistent, with historians turning to Horace Mann's reports to the Massachusetts state legislature in the 1840s, the Committee of Ten or Eight recommendations, and post hoc explanations of the emergence of school curricula. Government- and philanthropy-sponsored reports did appear sporadically, but did not have a sustained public presentation. School practice was given legitimacy and direction not through explicit governmental or administrative statements, but through a generalized faith in the educated citizen and local control. Negotiations in communities served to interpret and direct school practices within general parameters that in fact did relate to national discourses about schooling (Tlusty 1986).

The importance of other than textual means to establish social solidarity is expressed in the pedagogy of schooling. Emphasis has been upon "upbringing" throughout schooling, making socialization patterns in the classroom a central concern throughout high school and in sports, extracurricular activities, and "child-centered" pedagogy. For the most part, the focus upon interactional processes is legitimated by nineteenth-century lore about face-to-face interactions and communicative qualities that establish the requisites of social solidarity and national identity

(Bledstein 1976). This lore is recaptured in the emergence of interactional (qualitative) research studies in the past two decades. The "quantitative" research maintains assumptions that reassert the relation of individualism and community as a way to respond to changing social conditions (see Popkewitz 1981).

The informal mechanisms of social control and production served well in education until the post–World War II period (Spring 1976). The seemingly decentralized mechanisms did create solidarity. Local government provided flexibility in the school system when the economy was dominated locally, and allowed for the resolution of social and cultural conflict in both urban and rural settings. It also enabled coalitions of interest at a local level to organize reforms that rationalized existing dispositions and interests while, in the process, maintaining an appearance of a stateless state in the educational sector.

In the current situation, however, the older mechanisms of control have lost the ability to mobilize and give direction, requiring new institutional formations to steer schooling (Popkewitz 1987). Formal texts about school policy, regulation, and administration have emerged as central to the definition of social agendas. Within a relatively short period of time (1981–89), a number of books and reports have been issued about a national crisis of culture, economy, and schooling. The sheer number is impressive (for example, there are more than eighty commissioned reports related to mathematics education that are listed in the references of the National Research Council 1989).

Public rhetoric and reform practices make the problem seem as though there has been a sudden discovery of the limitations of progress produced through inadequate schooling. The language of reform is cast as a universal one, full of mythic imagery and religious calling. There is a moral and passionate language about culture, global economic competition, and social cohesion to unite a nation.

To view the reports, legislative practices, and standards as responses of social awareness is to obscure the dynamics of the current reform movement. The issues and dilemmas raised about teacher selection, the bureaucratic quality of schools, standards of achievement, and the forms of teacher education are not new problems but part of a long-term debate that began with the creation of mass schooling in the nineteenth century (Kaestle 1983). Further, the reconstitution of a state bureaucracy to make the schools more responsive to economic and cultural priorities has been in process since at least the end of World War II and is part of a long-term structural development in the dynamic of U.S. state building. The accountability movement of the late 1960s and early

1970s stressed the need to create nationwide competencies for teachers and students, to meet standards through more testing, and to rationalize teaching processes so that they provide a more efficient system for determining merit and outcomes. The increased regulation and administration of teacher education occurred in the late 1950s, through the National Defense Act and, in California, through the Fisher Act (1961) and the Ryan Act (1970). The current debate, rather than initiating a reform, can be viewed as part of changes that have already taken place.

We can now speak of a national public discourse for education at all levels. The U.S. Department of Education has assumed an active public role setting a national agenda for schooling and in creating systems for monitoring "outputs." In certain ways, a U.S. secretary of education sounds like a European minister who issues green papers and white papers to build a consensus for government policies, and who makes pronouncements about moral and social good. The discussions and texts make the problems of cultural "laxity," social resolve, and economic revival seem solvable through the schools. At the federal level, there is a new statistical and testing capacity to monitor children's achievement and teacher work. Data are also being collected to give state-by-state comparisons of school achievement. In addition, targeted research is mobilized to further the agenda through the establishment of a national network of more than thirty research laboratories and technical assistance centers. Thus, even though the national administration in education has little direct fiscal capacity to intervene in schooling and teacher education, it occupies an extremely important position, from which it can mobilize a discourse by which groups aligned with that focus can gain legitimacy.

Specific and localized mechanisms of control interrelate governmental agencies, universities, professional groups, and foundations in creating new monitoring systems. The massive production of legislative and administrative rules and standards during the 1980s steers current practice, ranging from the time spent in classes to the manner in which student and teacher credentialing is to be achieved. An administrative capacity to guide and monitor the reforms has been achieved through a mobilization of the educational sciences: Academic theories about effective schools and competency express the sentiments about reform that appear within the larger context of reform, defining the responsibility of economic recovery and cultural redefinition as a science of management.

Here we can distinguish between multiple types of texts produced during the past decade, as a discourse about reform is mobilized. There are government and foundation reports that are exhortatory, asserting that a nation is at risk, or that a nation needs to be prepared for a new economy, society, or culture (see, e.g., Popkewitz, Pitman, and Barry 1986). These reports are similar to green or white papers produced in the United Kingdom or Australia. They outline a problem and provide a set of categories and distinctions to organize potential solutions about the "crisis" of schooling. At a different layer of the reform discourse are legislative and administrative texts that have legal sanctions and prescriptive qualities backed by the administrative apparatus of government. While it is the latter, governmental texts that are the main focus of this chapter, the relations of various texts to institutional patterns needs to be recognized. The reform reports, administrative texts, and research projects organize particular practices of teachers through the language practices adopted (see Popkewitz 1991, chap. 4).

As developed during the past decade, the public texts of California and Wisconsin can be viewed as a part of these institutional practices and specific reform trends. The style of presentation and the categories need to be considered intertextually: They give preference to specific strategies in the reconstitution of power and control.

TEXTS AS DISCOURSES OF POWER AND TECHNOLOGIES OF CONTROL

We can view the rules and regulations of state government certification as "more" than an administrative language that conveys intent, purpose, and direction. Detailed procedures, rules, and obligations serve to differentiate behavior; and they separate, rank, and organize individuals. Certification rules govern the sort of talk about education that is possible and the parties who are to be taken as serious talkers.[3] The sanctioned, consecrated knowledge of certification selects, suppresses, shapes, and presents particular social interpretations in the guise of universal, absolute values. The categories of government embody political power in its most subtle and compelling form, as "to impose and inculcate a vision of divisions. . . . to make visible and explicit" (Bourdieu 1989, 23).

The power relations that are articulated in administrative rules, however, not only identify the actors involved in the production and maintenance of teacher certification. The rules and form of discourse provide ways through which individuals monitor not only institutional relations but also their conception of "self" within these relations. The certification rules are practices by which the self is to be produced: The distinctions and categories of the rules are to be internal as prescriptions for action. What is talked about and how that talk is carried on are parts of the mechanism whereby the world is produced and reproduced through the subjective elements of everyday life.

In this manner, we can consider the language of reform as having a normalizing function. The discourse of reform links prescribed changes with the public knowledge of the world in a manner that enables people to feel satisfied that the process will effectively attain personal as well as social ends. Thus, we can study the discourses of reform as part of power relations by which individual identities are constructed and produced; the categories, distinctions, and differentiations "carried" in the institutional patterns provide not only cognitive schema but dispositions toward what is possible, and not possible, as one is to act in the world. The construction of social identities occurs for teachers as well as students (Meyer 1987).

Part of understanding the relation of language, social practices, and social identity lies in the consideration of school practices neither as static sets of rules nor as universally defined standards. The commonplaces of curriculum that address conceptions of child development, categories of achievement, and practices for determining student competence consist of ordering procedures and selection mechanisms that are less than one hundred years old. They emerged as part of a complicated set of relations that, among others, combined multiple interests of power, achievement, and salvation into a discourse about schooling. That discourse was once contained in a moral and religious rhetoric that related schooling to various notions of salvation; today that rhetoric is secular and administrative, but the promise of salvation is maintained through a language that makes social relations seem universal, progressive, and beyond human reproach.

To pursue, for the moment, the ways in which similar words embody changes in concepts in different social practices, we can focus upon the making of "reform" and "professionalism" as an object of school practices (Popkewitz 1991). Both words were used in the formation of nineteenth-century mass schooling. By tracing the changing sets of relations that are presupposed in the use of these words to their present context, one comes to understand that the words are located in social arrangements and that they embody power relations. Reform in the early nineteenth century was intended to eliminate the evil of the unfortunate; professionalism in teaching was the task of "professing" Christian sincerity. By the twentieth century, reform focused on issues of labor socialization and upbringing in a society where older patterns of social, cultural, economic, and political authority were being redefined. The redefinitions of concepts occurred in multiple institutions, as micro-

and macrolayers of regulation were related. Reform and professionalism merged to respond to new patterns as expert knowledge and secular control through science gave reference to issues of power, achievement, and salvation.

The words about schooling, teaching, learning, and so on in texts carry assumptions, values, and social relations. All who read the school reform documents believe they understand them because of the commonsense familiarity associated with words like *teaching, learning,* and *professionalism.* Yet it is our contention that the concepts that underlie the words of reform change over time as they give reference to different sets of conditions and power relations.

We draw attention to the words of educational practice because of the importance of considering administrative texts about teacher education as socially produced in power relations. The reform discourse is part of a set of relations about self-regulation and monitoring. It is intertwined with institutional worlds and issues of power. As we will argue later, the educational administrative rules exist at a point where state government, schooling, universities, and educational sciences interrelate in the production of social regulation.

The problem of studying the reforms in teacher education, then, is to draw attention to the field in which the objects of study emerge and are assigned an identity, and to the authorities who code and interpret practice, and, finally, to the institutional grid that gives specification and classification to categories. Further study is required to understand how the objects that are constituted by the discourse of reform, in turn, discipline the motivating and cognitive patterns that arise in the construction of the self. What superficially seems to be rational and reasonable, consists of choices that are presupposed by particular power relations that exist within the social field of practice.

The current "truths" of teacher education may be examined in the substance of what is said about governmental certification, the identity of those who have authority over those pronouncements, and the power relations that are embodied in both form and content. From this viewpoint, the construction of national reports, such as *A Nation at Risk,* or the certification/credentialing of teacher education, should not be understood as singular events that have their own explanation. Instead, these practices should be recognized to be part of a composite that transcends the lines of particular people and events. Changes in teacher education entail an intersection of social fields that produces choice through a merging and production of a logic of classificatory thought. That is, the categories, distinctions, and differentiations in the administrative rules embody a logic about social practice, social relations, and the actions that are plausible for the constructions of the self within social patterns. The logic embodied in administrative rules intersect with other institutions to form patterns of social regulation. To understand power is to understand the multiplicity of centers, and the complex interaction of institutions, in which classificatory thought is produced. The new codes for regulating teacher education, the redefinitions of certification, and the program requirements of state departments of teacher education combine to offer systems of control and technologies as power is exercised.

If we view governmental administrative practices concerning teacher education as particular distinctions and categories that give form to reasoning about educational problems, we can inquire into the goals and motivations that they subsume. While seeming to serve as a vehicle to solve our current problems, the establishment of standards for teacher education and certification sets in motion an organization of affairs that draws on important power relations. As we will argue, state strategies contain their own relations of power.

WISCONSIN AND CALIFORNIA: FROM CERTIFICATION TO CREDENTIALING

A crisis of governing has been experienced differently by different U.S. states, yet the tendency to focus on teacher education is common to most. Wisconsin, for example, has a stable population and one of the most rigorous teacher standards according to national comparisons; entry into schools of education in the Wisconsin system is comparable to that in other fields, including engineering and liberal arts. Yet Wisconsin is no less impatient to introduce more certification control in line with public rhetoric than is a state like California—where a severe shortage of qualified teachers, important challenges from people of color, and enormous press coverage of poor service and inappropriate standards abound.

While states like Florida directly attempt to incorporate research on teaching effectiveness into their legislation, the California and Wisconsin legislatures have delegated responsibility for teacher certification standards and eligibility requirements to administrative bodies. Thus, the California Commission on Teacher Credentialing is a semiautonomous agency responsible to the legislature; Wisconsin's credentialing occurs through its Department of Public Instruction.

Across many states in the nation in the early 1970s, there was a tendency toward more-uniform certification for teachers (Di Sibrio 1973). Although the change in teacher certification has been dramatic in the last ten years, the extent of change is not obvious when we examine the publicly released statements of certification requirements from each state authority.[4] From the administrative descriptions of state certification statements, very little appears to have changed over this period: Even the length of the published formalities for each state remains at only a page or two in total.

Yet in this small period of time, significant changes in the focus and substance of control are contained in the parentheses and asterisks of documents and subsequent legislative and administrative rules. Life certification is no longer granted in Wisconsin or California, as of 1983 and 1985, respectively. Tests of competency and English are now mandatory in California, where none was necessary before. Furthermore, there are a number of teaching categories that previously did not require separate regulation or credentials.

The important changes in regulation have focused on the content, amount, and kind of directives that bear on institutional accreditation of teacher education programs. The changes are presented as a wealth of instructions about program requirements. The language makes the control become almost invisible, through the use of administrative discourse that is offered to prospective or second-degree (transferring) teachers and to the public at large. The existence and content of the new regulations may even pass largely ignored within institutions, except by those who are directly involved in administration or who are accountable to the agency bureaucracy. For many involved in teacher education, these changes have called upon huge amounts of time, energy, and financial resources, as elements within the university come to terms with the details of regulations within the decision-making processes of their own institution.[5]

The shift in the governing of university teacher education can be viewed as one that moved from certification to credentialing. Previously state education agencies set broad guidelines by which universities proceeded to form teacher education programs. For instance, the Ryan Act of 1970 established a commission to "develop rules and requirements of uniform and general applicability and not engage in prescription of courses and prescriptive unit counting" (California Legislature, Statutes of the 1970 Regular Session, chap. 557, sec. 13115). Previously, the emphasis was on approval of the university, which granted certificates; in contrast, the new governing strategy details the specific tasks, time elements, and relations that are to constitute teaching. In this sense, the movement has been away from certifying teachers' competence through participation in programs, and toward credentialing teachers by measures of outcomes that are placed into university programs through administrative and governmental regulations. In certain ways, the move to credentials can be viewed as altering the university's part in the setting of agendas vis-à-vis schooling; yet the actual changes may be in the manner by which control is articulated and in the coalitions that steer policy.

We want to argue that the shift from certification to credentialing extends control through the very processes used for generating text as well as in requiring compliance to the form and content of the texts themselves. The governmental administrative texts are pervasive not merely through the alliances established with sanctionary powers of legislation or through more subtle coercion associated with accrediting procedures, but because of the focus they provide for action and disagreement. An effect of administrative codes or legislation is to make the text rather than the particular contestants or actors the focus of scrutiny.

THE LANGUAGE OF REGULATION AS A MEANS OF CONTROL

To see the pervasiveness of these regulations, let us examine closely the content of a single section of a 209-page set of standards that the Wisconsin Department of Public Instruction (DPI) issued in 1986 and revised in 1988, pertaining to the Teacher Education Program, subcharter 4, "General and Professional Education Rules for Elementary, Secondary, and Early Childhood Education." Within this subcharter, section PI 4.08 covers fourteen items. These items are presented as a list, whose order and details are instructive. The section requires all professional education programs leading to certification to meet the following standards:

1. Study of the historical, philosophical, and social foundations underlying the development and purpose of education and current trends, issues, and various approaches in the specific education program in the United States and in Wisconsin;
2. study of the legal, political and economic aspects and the governance of education and the organization, operation, policy making and administration of schools and educational programs in the United States and in Wisconsin;

3. study to develop an understanding of the diverse family, cultural, and socioeconomic background of pupils;
4. study and experience specifically designed to develop the competencies needed to teach critical thinking;
5. study of issues related to children at risk including the pertinent law concerning child abuse and neglect; suicide, alcohol and other drug abuse; school age parents; delinquency and truancy; developmental disabilities; and the child welfare system including the children's code, juvenile justice, public health, and social services;
6. study of the pupil services programs and their relationship to other aspects of the total school program;
7. study of educational psychology including principles and theories of learning;
8. study of methods of identifying and evaluating the social, emotional psychological and physical behaviors of pupils as these behaviors may affect learning;
9. study to develop knowledge and skills in methods of creating a positive physical, psychological and social teaching and learning environment;
10. study of educational research and practice related to classroom management and classroom organization;
11. study of methods and materials needed to evaluate and to report pupil progress including the development, administration, scoring, interpretation and validation of teacher developed and standardized tests;
12. study of the use of the library and other instructional resources;
13. study of school instructional media programs, experience in evaluating and using instructional materials and equipment including computers, and experience in creating graphic and audio visual materials designed to meet specific learning objectives; and
14. study of the profession including the roles and responsibilities of the school board, the school superintendent, principals and teachers, and professional associations, organizations and learned societies.

In this small part of the current text of regulation, we find four elements that redefine control of teacher education.

First is a proliferation of regulation. There are thirteen requirements that focus on provisions for every teacher education program.

Those requirements focus on programs having students study, develop, and understand "the historical, philosophical, and social foundations" that underlie "the development and purpose of" schools; "the diverse family, cultural and socioeconomic backgrounds of pupils"; competencies "to teach critical thinking"; "issues related to children at risk" and laws "about child abuse and neglect"; pupil services available in schooling; psychological "principles and theories of learning"; "methods of creating a positive physical, psychological and social teaching and learning environment"; "development, administration, scoring, interpretation and validation of teacher developed and standardized tests"; "educational research and practice related to classroom management and classroom organization"; and use of the library (Wisconsin DPI, 1988, 70.8–70.9).

The range by which an executive rationalization of teacher education has occurred is evident in subsequent State Department of Public Instruction–proposed administrative licensure, which adds another thirty-one pages of rules. The particular rules and standards cross a range of activities that previously were not the direct concern of the agency. It defines credentials for school administrators, distance education, and curriculum coordinators, as well as defining a university course—"at least 2 semester credits related to the topic of study" (Wisconsin DPI 1990, 4).

A second element in the rules is language that homogenizes social distinctions and conflict. Policy is articulated as administrative problems that have universal application. For example, one standard is that a program should "study methods of identifying and evaluating the social, emotional, psychological, and physical behaviors of pupils as these behaviors may affect learning" (Wisconsin DPI 1988, P.I. 4.08, pp. 70–78). Standardized and routinized procedures are stressed, as consensus and stability are made central to discussions. There is no discussion of the moral, ethical, and political debate that surrounds the categories of psychology that focus solely on behaviors. The administrative rules pay no attention to new goals but take for granted the goals of the existing institutional relations. Human ends are no longer conceived as ends in themselves or as subjects of philosophic discourse.

The assumption is that there is a common school for all and that equity is only a matter of equalizing the effectiveness of "delivery systems." Teachers are to learn how to use multimedia centers, to apply research, to make tests valid, and to learn the proper procedures for scoring, administering, and interpreting tests. Eliminated from scrutiny are the social differentiations that occur between urban, suburban, and rural school; black, Hispanic, Asian, and white (as well as within different ethnic groups within the label *white*); male and female; poor and wealthy; and so on. These distinctions are obscured by the universal quality of teacher education program rules: "Creating a positive . . . learning environment" seems to have no temporal and spatial dimensions.

The universality of the requirements makes it more difficult to identify the particular values or assumptions about society that are to give purpose and direction to schooling. The movement of discourse to "a program requires" distances the individuals from loci of power, as it appears that no groups or institutions have responsibility and obligation for the ensuring practices.

Third, the set of standards mingles a variety of hopes and desires through its rhetorical form. There are social reforming elements in which the school is to reconstruct society—expressed as protecting the child from abuse and establishing a curriculum for a multicultural society. The development of standardized tests that are valid and the call for effective teaching strategies that provide equal opportunities resonate with conservative and liberal interests. The standard captures a long-standing and cherished desire for a utopian institution, where success is built on merit; at the same time, it gives expression to schooling as an objective, rational, and modern enterprise devoted to the "basics." The standard of critical thinking can be read as part of a debate concerning teaching performance. Critical thinking can be seen as a humanist project to develop a broadly educated teacher and to promote classroom flexibility, innovation, and imagination. Some groups support critical thinking as a functional skill in work situations where parameters are defined but flexibility is needed, such as in the service or computer industries, where adaptability is important. Others see critical thinking as existing where social issues are ill-defined and constantly shifting. The discourse of the administrative code makes the varied foci devoid of any tension, contradictions, or intellectual content.

When placed in relation to the other elements of the administrative code and other reform practices, a restricted interpretation of critical thinking occurs. An examination of the text reveals that psychology is given a privileged position through reference to learning theory, measurement, and testing, as well as categories such as "at risk." The psychology of education is not neutral. It is historically functional in purpose. Critical thinking concerns a problem solving in which the parameters are already established—with the mind as separate from social context and history (see, e.g., O'Donnell 1985; Napoli 1981). Thinking occurs in a world of harmony, stability, and rationally ordered change. It is a notion that is appropriate for middle-level bureaucracy and business; critical thinking does not mean creating questions that are systemic or historical.

Here, through references to psychology, research, testing, and measurement, the administrative categories of teacher education reforms interface with other institutional practices and discourses. The distinctions and categories relate governmental standards with particular forms of educational research and university discourse about reform (see, e.g., Holmes Group 1986, 1990). We can begin to understand at this point that the governmental discourse is related to specific university discourses about schooling, research, and progress, a point we return to later.

ORGANIZING THE CONTROL OF THE SOCIALLY DISADVANTAGED

The governmental text provides strategies to bring "deviant" interest claims and sociopolitical orientations under control. Debates in the wider community or within the educational arena are translated into technical and semiotic disputes, removed from their structural relations and activist purposes. Officially set categories make it possible to assist groups by channeling demands into language and practices that recontextualize and reformulate the issues. The exercise of power becomes invisible through a discourse that obscures the politics of the pronouncements. In this process, the power relations of those engaged in the debate are diffused and the issues are transmogrified into a naturalized language of administration. Sociologically significant, the fight by African Americans, Latinos, and other people of color for proper acknowledgment of their children's educational plight is produced within processes that normalize their struggle into systems of remediation.

The neutralizing of social conflict is evident in the language and tone of the teacher education standards. The directives represent the program rules as necessary for certification of all teachers. The standards imply that the pupil makeup of all schools is such that all schools are in need of teachers who know the specified topics. Remediation, "at-risk" children, juvenile justice, and delinquency are topics placed beside learning about child development and school services. As everything is given the same surface priority, then all must appear equal. However, the specific language, ordering, and content focus of these standards allows a different message to emerge. The control exerted is clearly intended for those individuals and groups who diverge from the norm.

One example of the logic of ordering in the 1988 Wisconsin regulations (items 4.08-3 to 4.08-10) will suffice. Student teachers are required to study the diverse backgrounds of pupils (item 3), then—in the order of the regulation text—children "at risk" (4), the welfare system (5), and special pupil services (6). Following this, they are asked to study educational psychology and learning theories (7), and immediately afterward to study methods of identifying and evaluating behaviors as they affect learning (8).

The sequence incorporates its own messages about how these groups (which, by inference, are expected to pose the most problems for schools) are to be dealt with. It may be that the particular sequence is accidental. If so, it could not have been calculated to demonstrate more clearly the groups that are deemed to be in need of a "positive physical, psychological and social teaching and learning environment" (item 9), and teachers with good classroom management and organizational skills (item 10), not to mention those for whom testing will be seen to be most necessary. What appears to be a set of minimum prescriptions for all merely disguises a particular form of regulation for those who are socially and economically at a disadvantage.

Promoting equality in schools has a paradoxical effect in these regulations. It makes it possible to consider narrow, social-engineering technologies without much public outcry. This production of social categories and technologies is part of longer-term processes of social regulation in which the Wisconsin standards are defined. Years of federal funding for small-scale projects have redefined marginal groups by introducing classification systems that make them subject to greater supervision, under the label *at risk.* The mobilization of a discourse about "at-risk" children is assisted by professional literature and research, which use the category to describe school failures and remediation (Franklin 1987). The teacher education regulations in Wisconsin draw on this "common sense" of school planning and assessment.

While the language of new governmental requirements is meant to defuse tensions, that is not always its result. During the last ten years in California, the arguments over the growth of non-English-speaking ethnic groups produced regulations governing the credentialing of teachers that include an English-language competence test as a prerequisite for teaching certification. At the same time, efforts to include specific social agendas to mute criticism have, in some instances, increased debate, as in the California bilingual requirements. The new subject-matter inclusions in Wisconsin's teacher education certification point to the contradictory location of academics. While language study, reading, and mathematics are categories of the new credentialing, these inclusions are debated as professors of history, for example, seek greater emphasis for their field. The credential requirements undermine the social positions of other academics.

SOCIAL TRANSFORMATIONS AND ISSUES OF CONTROL

We can explore the ways in which power is both hidden and exercised by focusing upon education as an intersection of three dynamics: economic changes in society, cultural conflict, and shifts in the loci of state government power. These dynamics of change enter into the credentialing processes as administrative rules, thus recasting political discourse about social purpose and direction into statements about implementation and evaluation.

What appears on the surface is a major public concern with strategies to make all levels of education respond to the seemingly precarious situation of the United States in world markets. What is not as clear in the debate is the way in which the new educational agenda responds to a global realignment of international corporate finance. Industrial countries are seeking to redefine the relation of economic centers to the periphery, as well as to redefine the "upbringing" requisites necessary to keep the center as a center. In Sweden, Germany, Japan, and the United States, among others, the centers of finance and management are located in the host country, while much of the productive labor is found in third-world nations. With the combining of economic markets, such as the European Community of ten nations, there have been new international corporate mergers and production in diverse national settings. The changing relation of capital, production, and labor has introduced new dynamics into markets and new demands upon the skills that are viewed as necessary for the economies of the center.

In the United States, the current call for reform in this global context has been explicitly incorporated into the agendas of state government elected officials and bureaucracies. Schools are treated as though they were directly related to commodity production that will attract both foreign and domestic capital to a region. State governors have sought to link schools to economic development, including attracting new investments.[6] Statistical data that compare achievement scores among states are used by politicians to "sell" the economic viability of their environs.

The executive state government focus upon the arena of power follows closely a national shift. Prior to the depression in the 1930s and

World War II, the focus of national governmental policy lay with the legislative rather than the executive branch. This has changed drastically in the intervening years, to the extent that some commentators refer to "an imperial presidency." Similar changes have occurred in local and state governments. Where once power was distributed among independent agencies and the legislature, with the governorship being a place to mark time until politicians could move to more prestigious positions in the U.S. Senate, there has been a centralization of authority in the executive branch. This has produced active policy formulation, long-range planning, and problem anticipation by governors and state administrative agencies, including departments of education.

The concern with economy and education has symbolic importance; yet the substantive elements of the current reforms may lie within the social and cultural spheres.[7] Education provides a universal symbol that functions in multiple ways. It contains images of a common and meritorious society, so that all segments of society can identify with an element of progress. It is a cultural commodity, which many believe can make the United States internationally competitive. Schooling is also a site of international competition that produces a nationalist fervor by calling forth an earlier ideology of a "manifest destiny." At the same time, the focus upon education in correspondence to labor markets focuses attention away from political and cultural crises involved in the current reconstitution of state and economy.

Economic agendas are linked to social agendas of the New Right and liberals. Under the label *pro-family policy,* the concern of the Right is with upbringing to counteract a whole range of values that give focus to "secular humanism"—teaching about sex, abortion, value relativism (Hunter 1988). The New Right agenda has focused upon strategies that provide more central control of teachers' work, and on the curriculum as a corrective for what is viewed as the moral corruption of schools. The historical interest of liberals in individual autonomy in service of collective goals produces a convergence in strategies with the Right to improve the schools. As issues of inequality persist, the school is considered the agency to provide civic competence, economic meritocracy, and social and culture harmony through strategies of instrumental reasoning. In its own irony, the correcting of inequality is to be accomplished through standardization of new credentialing that obscures the substantive conditions of social differentiation.

We can identify the different interests by focusing upon two types of administrative regulations that appear in the Wisconsin codes. One kind of rule gives focus to all professional programs as containing "study and experiences specifically designed to develop the competencies needed to teach critical thinking." A second element in the codes consists of requirements that programs contain study in school history, philosophy, law, and society, as well as in general history and political science courses about the development of the nation. These courses are viewed as foundations or background knowledge necessary for actual teaching and curriculum development.

These regulations can be read in multiple ways. They are a humanist project that would develop a broadly educated teacher and promote greater flexibility, innovation, and imagination in classrooms (e.g., the concern with "critical thinking"). The texts can also be read as part of a larger struggle and debate about getting "back to basics" in teaching performance. Some groups support "critical thinking" as a functional skill for people working in situations where parameters are defined but flexibility is needed. Others "see" problem solving as existing within social as well as economic contexts where issues and data are ill-defined and constantly shifting. The placement of the general courses that are called "foundations" and "critical thinking" in the administrative text, however, is one of many procedural concerns in which all regulations are made to seem equal. The structure and form of the codes make the varied foci seem devoid of any tension, contradictions, or intellectual content. It is plausible to assume that the ambiguity of the language of the regulations produces conditions in which, for example, a "whig history" is celebrated that emphasizes institutional evolution and current institutional arrangements.

"Critical thinking," when placed in its larger educational and social pattern of thought, obtains different readings from the more general rhetoric about broad education and enlightened citizenry. While not a necessary condition of critical thought, the language of the text is one that is oriented toward psychology, a discipline that in education has historically been functional in purpose. When one examines the meaning of critical thinking in educational practice, it is not concerned with understanding the relations of self and society, nor is it concerned with unmasking the facades of daily life to understand the pretensions, deceptions, and self-deceptions that organize our lives. Rather, critical thinking in schooling concerns problem solving in which the parameters of relations are already established and the learning task is to create flexibility and solutions in settings that have limited degrees of ambiguity. It is a notion that is appropriate for middle-level bureaucracy and business, but not for individual autonomy and civic responsibility.

A merging of both Right and liberal agendas in these seemingly different credentialing units occurs through the strategies that are adopted.

The strategies of reform homogenize and universalize social phenomena by considering the problem as though it consisted of administrative intervention in, and control over, the school world. Further, though on the surface the strategies seem to serve different purposes, they introduce technologies of control. There is a movement toward the production of regimented, isolated, and self-policing subjects. It is to this element of the discourse that we now turn.

REWORKING DEMOCRACY AND THE STATE

The change to increased specification of the credentialing process in university-government relations redesigns the notion of democracy. The shift toward defining teacher education as largely an administrative province for governmental agencies is part of a larger change in power relations that is occurring under the rhetoric of democratic control. Outwardly, it seems that the thrust of the current reform movement is to make universities more accountable. The process described above could be seen as "democracy through the public definition of tasks," where *public* is a loose term covering the responsibilities delegated to an agency by an elected legislature. The regulations can largely be read as an administrative interpretation of "community need" and concern. Teacher education is to demonstrate its responsiveness to wider community issues by being subject to accountability measures in the form of (and interpreted through) administrative regulation. Through the passage of legislation and the production of administrative codes and regulations for credentialing in the universities, we see the outward symbols of and vehicles for much more fundamental shifts in what passes for the "state" in the United States.

We now turn to how the reform discourse centralizes and ritualizes the discussion about social, cultural, and economic issues. Further, our interest is with the enfranchisement of certain types of expertise that result in a particular form and content of participation.

ENGINEERING OF CONSENT

The rhetoric of participation and professional accountability provides a way to mediate particular administrative values with larger social belief systems. It has been argued that changing teacher certification from a life award to a renewable license is a way to make teachers responsible for maintaining their professional competence. The frequent public scrutiny through renewal processes is expected to reflect changing priorities of the "community," with the changes open to public debate through the legislative and administrative hearings that precede the passage of a new code.

The more-frequent timing of renewal for teaching licenses has a symbolic potency. It allows for public demonstration by the government agency that the task of responding to "community" is being undertaken responsibly and publicly on behalf of the community. The increased number of hearings and debates has the concomitant effect of deflecting attention away from the voluminous administrative approaches used by the state. Concern is expressed with a specific regulation or detail rather than with the logic of the system itself. The regulations can then act as a facade, without any real accountability about the effects of the increased level of administrative involvement. The process of participation through testimony replaces sustained debate about political and social goals.

Accountability translates into increased "citizen" intervention into the certification process of the universities. In California, the 1961 Fisher Act and the 1970 Ryan Act seemed to disenfranchise higher education from the control of teacher education, in favor of increased teacher and lay participation in teacher licensing. Amendments during the 1970s gave a majority of seats to lay members, mostly at the expense of higher education (1978) and teachers (1979), but the issue of who is represented on the credentialing commission is still hotly debated. Through participation as "role groups," the "community" is to play a more direct role in the control of teacher education.

What occurs in the participatory arrangements is a distancing of the perceived and contested problems in schooling through reference to another body: either through referral to legislative processes, which are necessarily time-consuming, or through the membership of some "lay" persons on the credentialing body. The form of participation in policy-making agencies is emphasized and lauded as a form of democratic control, while the form of control through the generation of administrative work undercuts the democratic impulse.

A notion of community emerges as one of negotiation and equal power among the various groups. Ignored is the role of staff in framing the agenda of participatory settings, such as the California Commission on Teacher Credentialing, or the manner in which the mass of procedural detail required for action reduces the space for discussion of substantive issues in the framing of legislation. The ceremonies of democracy also obscure the unequal power relations as policy decisions respond to established interests. In studies of the power relations in reforms, the notion of community tends to tighten control of teachers' work and to make invisible the normative structures that organize the poor and the disenfranchised.[8] Thus, the appeal to popular sovereignty removes from scrutiny the dynamics and particular interests that underlie institutional relations.

The government, through the delegation of major portions of responsibility to a state agency (such as the California Commission on Teacher Credentialing or the Wisconsin Department of Public Instruction), can also distance itself from the specifics of regulations, and can still retain the capacity to act through the passage of more legislation. California's technique of changing the name and the charter of the group for credentialing does little to alter the basic approach, and masks a continuity across participating groups and the tendency to grow more specific with the years. The focus of power and decisions is diffused. No person or agency seems in control. The legislators can reproach the agency, the agency can say it is only carrying out the tasks of the legislature, the university can claim it is restricted by all the new regulation. Responsibility for the quality of teacher education becomes diffused through the symbolic rituals of democracy, while various patterns of control proliferate, ostensibly to ensure accountability.

COALESCING OF FACTIONS ACROSS INSTITUTIONS: THE UNIVERSITIES AND STATE DEPARTMENTS OF EDUCATION

The distancing of policy from its sources of contention does not mean, however, that legislative and administrative agencies in state government are sovereign in the current university reforms. There is relative autonomy among universities and government agencies, although there are changes in the factions that have authority to speak in each institution as technical compliance is secured.

The form of the debate makes it seem that the long and venerable traditions that govern the relationship of university to state government are being challenged. Yet when we examine the internal responses to the state regulations, we get a different reading. The coincidence of events across institutions produces a synchronization of crises in different social fields. The changes that occur are not "merely" in meeting new regulations, but in altering the relative strength of the coalitions within the institutions, and in the self-checking patterns. There is a realignment within the university as new coalitions assume dominant positions in the negotiations undertaken with state government. This occurs through at least two dynamics.

The university's own "self-management" is well integrated into government at the state level and into the national infrastructure of the organization and control of the educational sector.[9] There is a related occurrence within the university—a long-term change that has brought administrative and budgeting controls into its internal organization, including the gradual replacement of "older" cultural orientations of university leaders who assert humanist traditions as means to solve social problems with the newer, more "modern," managerial conceptions. The administrative qualities of higher education are brought into the social organization of universities through the budget-planning processes and data collection problems and procedures. The procedures shape and fashion the defining of staff and programatic issues, even though the major actors have changed. The rationalization through finance occurs as college of education deans have shifted from educational administration to other educational disciplines. This element of factions within the university "working" with the Wisconsin Department of Public Instruction against the dean of the school of education is ignored in an otherwise detailed description of the politics of the development of the certification rules (see Prestine 1991).

Institutional relations establish conditions in which calls among state governors and economic and social interests for more flexibility in higher education are given plausibility and structure for action. The new regulations, and administration from outside, give legitimacy to the university administration. A receptive climate is also produced for certain factions within the university. Faculty concerned with rationalization use the rhetoric of service to increase the managerial functions as ways to monitor faculty productivity. Thus a current executive order in California established teacher education as a concern of all faculty and sought assessment measures for liberal arts courses (McLibbing and Wright 1988; Boxer and Richmond 1988). Thus, university programs of assessment and governmental priorities are synchronized. Specific faculty in liberal arts and education have emerged in California to create performance criteria and assessment procedures.

The changing of internal power relations tends to enfranchise certain kinds of expertise. The need arises for people who can understand and also who can negotiate with state agencies and the state legislature, with a premium being placed on skills in administration, political negotiation, and the monitoring of regulation compliance. Existing competition within the university (for instance, in competing definitions of child growth or the relative merits of psychology and other foundational courses) is short-circuited through the operation of these regulatory mechanisms. The legitimacy of certain ways of framing issues and problems of teacher education is undermined, and the huge increase in work load that is related to evaluation and monitoring, and certifying program regulations, and course design, itself, redefines the "work" of a significant number of university personnel. Further, both new faculty hiring and discourse within teacher education tend to strengthen the instrumental concerns expressed in the regulations.

There is also a corresponding growth of bureaucracy in state agencies, as they endeavor to monitor and evaluate the growing "business" of regulation. New actors appear at the state level to monitor the degree to which an individual agency's regulation is supported and even possible to achieve. In California, some of the regulations had to be redrawn because their specificity produced demands greater than the bureaucracies could meet. New categories of state workers are emerging, to provide an infrastructure necessary to meet increased monitoring demands. (For example, four "auditor" positions were created in the Wisconsin Department of Public Instruction, to travel four days each week, to check school-district compliance through examination of documentation records. Similar personnel exist for the universities.)

At the same time, older work structures are reformed to meet the new tasks related to monitoring. Wisconsin curriculum consultants, who used to have important influence upon the standards and evaluation of university curriculum, have been replaced by personnel in agencies of teacher credentialing. The consultants now have increased responsibilities in the preparation of statewide tests and program evaluations that are dictated by the new credentialing requirements. In the process, the state agency consultants become less important in the development of local programs and university teacher education. The changing priority in organization can be examined through staffing in the Wisconsin Department of Public Instruction. In the mid 1970s, there were two to four people, each, working in teacher credentialing and auditing. The 1987 staff directory, in contrast, lists over twenty people in each section.

The current university response to regulation can be understood within these organizational conditions. The form of university autonomy is becoming more and more narrow as the regulations not only *add* topics to be covered, but also define more tightly the constitutive aspects of knowledge in the courses. However, the debate within the universities is not over the processes of regulation, but over which items are to be accepted. The university tries to keep its discretionary powers over allocation of resources and differentiation among departments, and this limited definition of autonomy makes it possible for there to be little outcry from the very groups within the university that might have been expected to provide leadership against the encroachment of regulations.

One can consider the deans of schools of education who formed the Holmes Group within this context of control. The Holmes Group (1986, 1990) plans for improving teacher education are initiated to prevent the interests of others (outsiders to teacher education) from intervening in the university's business. The writers of the Holmes report argue that the university research community provides the expertise necessary for instituting new controls for schools. The report calls for management guided by research, and increased professionalization through changes in teacher licensing that introduce greater stratification and differentiation in teaching. The universities' actions, wrapped in the rhetoric of freedom of academic rights, incorporate the issues being debated in the wider society, aiming to neutralize them under the rubric of the academy. At the same time, the report used the discourse of centralized standards to assert the role of university teacher education.

The Holmes reports can be read as responding to a changing social space within the academy. There have been shifts in the practical orientations of deans of education. Previously, university schools of education have been academically organized by departments of educational administration, and intellectually defined by departments of educational psychology (Labaree 1990; Schneider 1987). The experience of the past two decades has introduced a faculty that is trained in philosophy, curriculum, or educational psychology into administrative positions. When these changes in administrative actors are positioned in relation to the processes of rationalization in higher education, greater micromanagement is evident. One dean of education in a large land-grant college of education, for example, mandated that all faculty in the curriculum department "study" teacher education. While this is a single case, it needs to be placed in a context of the formation of the Holmes Group and other institutional practices emerging to regulate teaching and teacher education.

These changes also coincide with new actors within teacher education. Many people trained in psychological studies of teachers have shifted their attention to the study of teacher education, creating fields of study such as teacher thinking and pedagogical reasoning. Teacher educational research is redefined and extended through government-funded research centers, typically located in universities around the country (see, e.g., Popkewitz 1991, chap 7).

Changing resource allocations within the university also give emphasis to program-related concerns of teacher education. The new coalitions within schools of education occur as teacher education becomes a priority in research *and* program development. Academic capital is obtained for governance of schools of education by faculty in previously marginalized departments of curriculum, special education, and teacher education.

The California state university system has made an assessment of liberal arts courses for prospective elementary school teachers mandatory in order to forestall legislative mandates. In the process, assessment procedures developed in a collaborative effort that involved faculty, university administrations, the credentialing commission, and the state department of education. The language of the assessment maintains an instrumental focus and extends it to all elements of university life, through participatory mechanisms and training workshops (Boxer and Richmond 1988).

PROFESSIONALISM AND EDUCATIONAL RESEARCH AS REGULATORY STRATEGIES

Much of the reform rhetoric claims that teaching should be made professional. The Holmes Group uses law and medicine as exemplars of professionalism that should be brought into teacher education. There is a need for standards, paralleling that in medicine, the Holmes Group (1990) asserts, although "educators have not worked out ways and means to articulate principles that represent professional consensus on best practice" (77). Accepting the general state mandate, the creation of teaching standards, the Holmes Group asserts, must be linked with the "mission of educating teachers" (77), which is to begin in the university. The reports emphasize that "the claim to professional status rests on" development of a "body of specialized knowledge, codified and transmitted through professional education and clinical practice" (Holmes Group 1986, 63).

The knowledge base discussed, however, emphasizes consensus of goals, functionality of knowledge, and stability of institutions under a rhetoric of change. There is talk of "mastery of discourse" (Holmes Group 1990, 11), knowledge bases (40), and distributing knowledge (59); each imply consensus and stability of knowledge, in direct contrast to other claims of disciplines as multiple conversations and voices in constructing stories. Examples of the collaborative arrangement in professional development schools emphasize a functional character of teaching. University faculty are to work with teachers in varying teaching content and methods, to identify "how technology can enable them to invent" a better understanding of concepts (58). Central to this work is the university, providing research that can help teachers to develop a more professional career.

The university-generated rules for teacher education practices need to be viewed in relation to the administrative rules, which value problem-management and purposeful, rational planning. When the research that underlies the promise of professionalization is scrutinized, the concern is to rationalize teachers' thoughts (Popkewitz 1991, chap. 6). Social interactions are broken into more-detailed, discrete tasks. Teachers' thoughts are decontextualized and then reformulated into logical and psychological categories that deny the social, historical, and political complexities of schooling. Monitoring is to occur through a clinical perspective in which external research distinctions are applied to determine teachers' personal competence. In this professionalized context, the discourse practices of collaboration that are based on research can become a technique of social administration (Popkewitz 1989, 1991). The "clinical language," as Foucault (1975) has argued in a study of the medical clinic, makes the individual as the object of discourse, a subject whose intentions are revealed and ordered by empiricism (also see St. Maurice 1987).

The new forms of control seem merely to be a continuation and consolidation of older interests and older techniques of gaining consensus across groups. However, the cumulative impact of these incremental changes has an affect of creating what becomes, in effect, new forms of control that alter power relations within the university.

CONVENIENT FICTIONS AND MYTHS OF REFORMING STATE GOVERNANCE

One way of interpreting current power arrangements is to see them as a rational outgrowth of government intervention. This interpretation is assisted by such factors as the Jarvis Amendment in California, which limited the local property-tax percentage of funding for schools, and the nationwide growth of state government funding for local schools. Current New Right rhetoric on "small government" and the removal of government intervention, especially with regard to welfare provisions, tends to keep the focus firmly on the role of government.

We would argue, however, that this explanation merely replaces the myth of local control with another myth of government control, thereby masking the complex interrelationships that allow power to be exercised through choices that are made in a variety of locations within what are otherwise semiautonomous institutions. Certainly there is centralization. The focus for debate is firmly centralized: Rituals of negotiation have developed around hearings as new items come up for consideration in legislatures and state agencies. All the organizations involved must also have developed centralized structures, in order to organize responses to the hearings and to one another. This alters the way in which power structures work within institutions and enfranchises different coalitions who support the new forms of control.

Government or state agency hearings provide a convenient fiction of democracy: They look like the sites where decisions are made. However, the process merely acts to legitimate a new form of control through regulation. Those who participate accept the new technical form of discourse; and in the process they are included in a redefinition of the governing patterns, while others are excluded. The coalitions of actors across institutions are just as responsible as the government agencies for the content and existence of regulations. *For our purposes of analysis, the coalition of power groups across institutions can be viewed as part of the governing mechanisms of teacher education at this time, and defines the meaning of the state in the current reform situation.*

To assert that a redefinition of the state is occurring through realignments and coalitions is not to assume that the terrain is uncontested. There are different notions, even among the business community, about the forms of schooling that provide the best education. For some, a classical liberal education would best serve the purposes of business. Others focus upon a narrower conception of the practical, focusing upon the needs of scientific and technological production as the core of education. Within government and foundations, there is concern that control should remain with the local setting—stemming from a fear that greater flexibility at the center toward national priorities can also set into motion forms of tyranny and authoritarianism. Within university and state departments, the new power relations are continually being contested by alternative discourses that include older traditions of curriculum. While tensions occur, subtle processes of administrative control serve to structure the contests and to homogenize the conflict in a manner that makes individual self-discipline socially and psychologically tighter.

MAKING POWER INVISIBLE

In the preceding analysis, we have focused upon the changing formal texts of state government regulation of teacher education. The formal government documents enable us to focus upon the sites of contestation and the actors involved in a relational manner: That is, the texts are not merely "windows" onto the world of action; the texts themselves are dynamics in those power relations. The transformation of power in teacher education is not accessible immediately to those who operate daily in universities, because of the way in which the various governmental, philanthropic, and professional texts about education interrelate at different layers of the system and with agendas set in other social and cultural arenas. Further, there is a difficulty in locating the meanings of power relations, as policy is articulated through an instrumental language that makes the problems seem administrative in focus and universal in application.

The creation of formal governmental texts about reform signifies, we believe, important changes in the dynamics of power and control in the arena of education. The text production occurs at multiple layers of society, to embody new coalitions that form to govern schooling. The current emphasis upon formal texts not only articulates a way to plan and steer school processes. The texts give reference to a reconstitution of state regulation that has cultural, political, and economic significance. These changes, however, are hidden by the strategies implicit in the public discourse.

Older notions of the state, as the governmental agencies that issue rules and regulations in civil society, are no longer a viable way to understand how power is exercised, or how values are allocated and choices are made. An adequate notion of the state entails more than the issuance of regulations, the role of governmental agencies, or the traditional problem of who makes decisions about programs and course content. The current situation involves multiple sites, including universities and research communities, and a continually shifting set of dynamics that guide and manage the governing that takes place in schooling. There is a redefinition of coalitions and a corresponding shift in the forms of contestation and in the actors who are involved in the process of control.

The reformations of the relations of power make it difficult to interpret the meaning of the state and teacher education. The emerging relations are not "merely" corporatist, in that existing dominant interests assign the implementation of policy to other nonstate coalition groups within society. Rather, elements within government, university, and professional groups interrelate in the forming and implementing of control mechanisms. *The changes pose a redefinition of the meaning of democracy. Not only have the interests of those who participate been narrowed, but the discourse of participation also produces a restricted range of problems and possibilities.*

Further, one can look at the current situation as being, simultaneously, a breakdown in older forms of socialization and a reforming of new ones, in which the production of a new steering mechanism through formal texts becomes more important. The texts are strategies and representational practices that bring into play the current reconstitution of state power.

But the textual power is not only representative: The process makes the new mechanisms of control seem extensions, albeit better than those previous mythic structures of local control. The discourse practices that are expressed in the administrative texts act as a medium of social practice and the outcome of such practices. The potential exists not only to shape permissible practice but to become a part of the mechanisms whereby identity is itself constructed in various layers of institutional life. Fixed in the rules of the discourse are finer differentiations of everyday behavior that objectively separate and rank individuals. The categories of social life and the psychologies of school practice establish a combination of hierarchial observations and normalizing judgments that make all individuals a potential category for observation and administration.

What the analysis does not address is the structure of inequality that interrelates university, schooling, and government agencies with their wider social contexts. At one level, there is evidence that different coalitions have assumed dominance in governmental bureaucracies, school practices, and university programs. Further, because the changes are proposed as administrative strategies, opposition to the texts tends also to be formulated within these boundaries, rather than to oppose the context that made them possible. Yet the structural implications of the design of social institutions and the relations of factions are difficult to identify within any particular historical moment.

In this chapter, we do not consider the development of alternative teacher certification routes, which are typically tied to apprentice models within school districts. Nor do we consider privatization of teacher certification, such as Teach For America. The latter prepares teachers for urban and rural areas through funds received from businesses, foundations, and individuals. These alternative certification practices seem, at first glance, to be in opposition to established institutional relations.

When considered through their discursive practices, there is a relation in assumptions about instrumental knowledge, individuality, and power. The alternative programs "carry" the same "theories," folklore, distinctions, and categories that organize teacher education programs and the practices of teachers and pupils in school (see Popkewitz, Myrdal, and Cho 1991).

The long-term question is whether the reforms legitimate existing relations or whether they are a reconstitution of power arrangements within the education sector. The form of our analysis cannot fully address this issue and the inequalities of power embedded in the relations. We can only develop the necessary analysis through which more detailed studies related to enduring (?) historical structural issues can be pursued.

Notes

Part of this chapter appears in Popkewitz 1991. The authors wish to acknowledge the support provided by a grant from the University of Wisconsin-Madison, Graduate School Research Committee. The study also benefited from comments and critiques offered by Anna Richert, and by participants in the Wednesday seminar group at the University of Wisconsin.

1. For a discussion of texts as power relations in education, see Cherryholmes 1988. The general issue is found in Foucault 1980 and Martin, Gutman, and Hutton 1988.

2. For a discussion of state formation and the construction of identity in Sweden, see Boli 1989; theoretically, see Thomas et al. 1987 and Berger, Berger, and Kellner, 1973.

3. Here, again, we draw on Foucault 1980 and Martin, Gutman, and Hutton 1988; also Dreyfus and Rabinow 1983. Our use of Foucault, however, is modified by our interest in questions of how texts become privileged and how inequalities in power relations can be explained.

4. The University of Chicago Press has an annual publication of all U.S. state requirements for teacher certification that is now in its fifty-second edition.

5. This emerges from our observations in Wisconsin and from discussions with people in California.

6. This has involved a redesigning of governmental control, as the executive branches begin to replace the legislative branches in key policy formulation at the state government level (Stevens 1988).

7. There is an element of the reform movement that commodifies issues of curriculum. This reification occurs, however, as both an economic and a cultural issue. (See Berger, Berger, and Kellner 1973).

8. For a discussion of the cultural dynamics of discourse in legitimating and establishing power relations, see Popkewitz 1976 and Popkewitz and Lind 1987.

9. For a treatment of the role of the university in modern societies, see Wittrock and Elzinga 1985.

References

Advisory Panel Report to Commission on Teacher Credentialing 1986. *Subject Matter Preparation of Elementary Teachers.* Sacramento, CA:

State of California Amended in California Senate 17th June 1986. Repealing Teacher Preparation and Licensing Law of 1970 and creating the California Teaching Standards Board, Sacramento, CA. 1986.

Berger, P., B. Berger, and H. Kellner. 1973. *The Homeless Mind: Modernization and Consciousness.* New York: Vintage.

Bledstein, B. 1976. *The Culture of Professionalism, the Middle Class, and the Development of Higher Education in America.* New York: Norton.

Boli, J. 1989. *New Citizens for a New Society: The Institutional Origins of Mass Schooling in Sweden.* New York: Pergamon.

Bourdieu, P. 1989. "Social Space and Symbolic Power." *Sociological Theory* 7:14–25.

Boxer, M., and J. Richmond. 1988. *Resource Guide: Subject Matter Assessment of Prospective Elementary School Teachers. Report of the California State University Workgroup on Assessment of Prospec-*

tive Elementary School Teachers. Long Beach, Calif.: Office of the Chancellor, California State University.

Burks, M., ed. 1986. *Requirements for Certification.* 51st ed. Chicago: University of Chicago Press.

Calif. Senate Bill No. 1605. Introduced by Senator Bergeson, January 27, 1986.

California Education Code. 1984 (Including amendments through 1983). Sacramento, CA.

Commission on Teacher Credentialing (CTC). 1987a. *California Credentialing Information 1987.* Sacramento, CA.

Commission on Teacher Credentialing. 1987b. *Commission on Teacher Credentialing Credential Handbook.* Sacramento, CA.

California Professional Growth Manual. 1985. Sacramento, CA.

CTC *Manual for Developing, Evaluating, and Approving Professional Preparation Programs for Multiple and Single Subject Credentials.* 1985. Sacramento, CA.

CTC *Manual for Developing, Evaluating, and Approving Professional Preparation Programs for the Early Childhood Specialist Credential.* 1985. Sacramento, CA.

Cherryholmes, C. 1988. *Power and Criticism: Post-Structural Investigations in Education.* New York: Teachers College Press.

Dahl, R. 1963. "The Behavioral Approach in Political Science: Epitaph for a Monument to a Successful Protest." In *Politics and Social Life: An Introduction to Political Behavior,* edited by N. Polsby, R. Dentler, and P. Smith. Boston: Houghton Mifflin.

Dean's Study Group, University of Wisconsin–Madison. 1986. *Dean's Study Group on the Improvement of Teacher Preparation: Reflections and Recommendations.* Madison, WI:

Di Sibrio, R. A. 1973. "An Analysis and Comparison of Certification Requirements for Elementary Teachers in the United States." Ph.D. diss. Indiana University of Pennsylvania, Indiana, PA.

Dreyfus, H., and P. Rabinow. 1983. *Michel Foucault: Beyond Structuralism and Hermeneutics.* Chicago: University of Chicago Press.

Foucault, M. 1975. *The Birth of the Clinic; An Archeology of Medical Perception.* Translated by A. Smith. New York: Vintage.

Foucault, M. 1980. *Power/Knowledge: Selected Interviews and Other Writings by Michel Foucault, 1972–1977.* Edited by Colin Gordon. New York: Panetheon.

Franklin, B., ed. 1987. *Learning Disabilities: Dissenting Essays.* New York: Falmer.

Holmes Group. 1986. *Tomorrow's Teachers.* East Lansing, Mich.: Holmes Group.

Holmes Group. 1990. *Tomorrow's Schools.* East Lansing, Mich.: Holmes Group.

Hunter, A. 1988. "Children in the Service of Conservativism: Parent/ Child Relations in the New Right Pro-Family Rhetoric." (Legal history working paper.) Madison: University of Wisconsin, Institute of Legal Studies.

Kaestle, C. 1983. *Pillars of the Republic: Common Schools and American Society, 1780–1860.* New York: Hill & Wang.

Labaree, D. 1990. "Power, Knowledge, and the Science of Teaching: A Genealogy of Teacher Professionalization." School of Education, Michigan State University, East Lansing.

Luke, C. 1989. *Pedagogy, Printing, and Protestanism. The Discourse on Childhood.* Albany: State University of New York Press.

Martin, L., H., Gutman, and P. Hutton. 1988. *Technologies of the Self, a Seminar with Michael Foucault.* Amherst, Mass: University of Massachusetts.

McLibbing, M., and D. Wright. 1988. "State of California Commission on Teacher Credentialing." In *Multiple Subjects Waiver Program, Standards of Program Quality.* Sacramento, CA.

Meyer, J. 1987. "Self and Life Course: Institutionalization and its Effects." In *Institutional Structure: Constituting State, Society, and the Individual,* edited by G. Thomas, J. Meyer, F. Ramirez, and J. Boli. 242–60. Newbury Park, Calif.: Sage.

Napoli, D. 1981. *Architects of Adjustment: The History of the Psychological Profession in the United States.* Port Washington, N.Y.: Kennikat Press.

National Research Council's Board on Mathematics *Sciences and Mathematics* Education Board (1989) *Everyone Counts: A Report to the Nation on the Future of Mathematics Education.* Washington, D.C.: National Academy of Sciences.

O'Donnell, J. 1985. *The Origins of Behaviorism: American Psychology, 1876–1920.* New York: University Press.

Popkewitz, T. 1976. "Reform as Political Discourse: A Case Study." *School Review* 84:43–69.

Popkewitz, T. 1981. "Qualitative Research: Some Thoughts about the Relation of Methodology and Social History." In *The Study of Schooling: Field Based Methodologies in Educational Research and Evaluation,* edited by T. Popkewitz and B. R. Tabachnick, 155–80. New York: Praeger.

Popkewitz, T. ed. 1987. *The Formation of School Subjects: The Struggle for Creating an American Institution.* New York: Falmer.

Popkewitz, T. 1989. "Culture, Pedagogy, and Power: Issues in the Production of Values and Colonialization." *Journal of Education* 170:77–90.

Popkewitz, T. 1991. *A Political Sociology of Educational Reform: Power/Knowledge in Teaching, Teacher Education, and Research.* New York: Teachers College Press.

Popkewitz, T., and K. Lind. 1987. *Teacher Incentives as Reform: Implications for Teachers' Work and the Changing Control Mechanism in Education.* Madison: Wisconsin Department of Public Instruction.

Popkewitz, T., Myrdal, S., and Cho, S. 1991. *Teach for America Summer Institute 1990 Evaluation Report.* Madison: University of Wisconsin, Center for Education Research.

Popkewitz, T., A. Pitman, and A. Barry. 1986. "Educational Reform and Its Millennial Quality: The 1980s." *Journal of Curriculum Studies* 18:267–84.

Prestine, N. 1991. "Political System Theory as an Explanatory Paradigm for Teacher Education Reform." *American Educational Research Journal* 28 237–74.

Schneider, B. 1987. "Tracing the Provenance of Teacher Education." In *Critical Studies in Teacher Education: Its Folklore, Theory, and Practice,* edited by T. Popkewitz, 211–42. New York: Falmer.

Spring, J. 1976. *The Sorting Machine: National Educational Policy since 1945.* New York: David McKay.

St. Maurice, H. 1987. "Clinical Supervision and Power: Regimes of Instructional Management." In *Critical Studies in Teacher Education: Its Folklore, Theory and Practice,* edited by T. Popkewitz, 242–64. New York: Falmer.

Stevens, W. 1988. "Governors Are Emerging as a New Political Elite." *New York Times,* 22 March, 8.

Task Force on Teacher Education, University of Wisconsin System. 1984. *Benchmarks of Excellence 1984.* Madison, WI: Department of Public Instruction.

Teacher Education Program Faculty, University of Wisconsin–Madison. 1986. Proposed Plan to Meet DPI 4.08 Professional Education Common Rules. Madison, W.

Thomas, G., J., Meyer, F., Ramirez and J. Boli eds. 1987 *Institutional Structure: Constituting State, Society, and the Individual.* Newbury Park, Calif. Sage.

Tlusty, R. 1986. *Curriculum Transformation as Social History: Eau Claire High School, 1890–1920.* Ph.D. diss., University of Wisconsin, Madison.

Wisconsin Bureau of Teacher Education, Certification, and Placement. 1986. *The Equivalency Clock-Hour Program 1986.*

Wisconsin Department of Public Instruction (DPI). 1977. *Wisconsin Certification Standards 1977.*

Wisconsin DPI. Division for Instructional Services. 1979. *Repeal and Recreation of Rules Relative to Teacher Certification, 1979.* Madison, WI: Department of Public Instruction.

Wisconsin DPI. 1984. *Certification Rules,* PI 3. Madison, WI: Wisconsin Department of Public Instruction.

Wisconsin DPI. Department of Public Instruction 1987. "Proposed Order of the State Superintendent of Public Instruction, Amending Rules." Madison, WI

Wisconsin DPI. 1988. *Teacher Education Program Approval Rules and Appeal Procedures PI 4.* Madison, Wisc.: Wisconsin DPI.

Wisconsin DPI. 1990. *Proposal Order of the State Superintendent of Public Instruction Creating/Amending Rules* (15 March, draft) Madison, Wisc.: Wisconsin DPI.

Wisconsin Legislative Council. (1975). *1975 Assembly Bill 740, Relating to Creation of School Personnel Certification Standards Council.* Madison, WI.

Wisconsin State Budget 1987–89. Wisconsin Legislative Fiscal Bureau. 1987. Madison, WI.

Wittrock, B., and A. Elzinga. eds. 1985. *The University Research System, the Public Policies of the Home of Scientists.* Stockholm: Almquist and Wiksell International.

Woellner, Elizabeth H., ed. 1976. *Requirements for Certification 1976–77.* 41st ed. Chicago: University of Chicago Press.

3

IS CHANGE ALWAYS GOOD FOR TEACHERS? GENDER, CLASS, AND TEACHING IN HISTORY

Michael W. Apple

THE POLITICAL CONTEXT OF CURRICULUM AND TEACHING

With the current emphasis on "reforming" education, it is important to realize that the language of reform has a history of multiple uses. It can be used to help create a movement toward more democratic institutions that are more responsive to students, teachers, and communities than what we have now. Or reform talk can be employed as part of a larger rhetorical strategy supportive of the tightening of control, of bringing the internal workings of schools more closely into line with the needs of groups in dominance. Only a political history of educational practice can make this clear. This is what I shall do here in my discussion of the history of the politics of the control of teaching. However, taking this political perspective requires that we see our educational institutions in a manner different from what many of us may be accustomed to.

THE POLITICS OF CURRICULUM AND TEACHING

What happens inside schools is not the result of some anonymous, neutral process. It does not arise from plans that match inputs and outputs, means and ends, in a smooth and rational way. Even though the dominant models of planning and evaluation, with their process/product inclinations, constantly ask us to treat schooling in this manner, they live in a world divorced from reality. For rather than being a neutral enterprise, schooling is through and through political.

This can be seen in its connections to the class, race, and gender divisions in the larger society, a society in which the gaps between rich and poor widen every day. It can be seen in the knowledge that is selected to become part of the official curriculum, knowledge that makes invisible the culture, histories, and lived experiences of so many people from formal study. We witness it repeatedly in the constant public and private battles over goals, over funding, over whose knowledge is or is not included in the curriculum, over who should decide all of this.[1] Not to recognize the inherently political nature of curriculum and teaching is to cut ourselves off from an understanding of how *and why* schools work the way they do and may prevent us from seeing what is required to alter them in progressive ways.

Perhaps the best way of seeing the ways politics forms the daily life of schools and of the curriculum and teaching that go on within them is to focus on one of the social movements that is currently having such a widespread impact in education. This is what has been called the "conservative restoration."[2]

A powerful conservative alliance has been more than a little successful in altering our public discourse, not only about what should go on in schools—about our teaching and curricula—but what schools are *for.* The impact of this alliance can be seen in a number of educational policies and proposals: (1) calls for voucher plans, tax credits, or programs of "choice" to make schools more like a thoroughly idealized free-market economy; (2) the movement in state legislatures and state departments of education to "raise standards" and mandate both teacher and student "competencies" and basic curricular goals and knowledge, thereby centralizing even more at a state level the control of teaching and curricula; (3) the increasingly effective assaults on the school curriculum for its supposedly antifamily and anti-free-enterprise bias, its lack of patriotism, its secular humanism, its neglect of the qualities of character and values that "made this country great," its lack of focus on work skills and dispositions, and its neglect of the "Western tradition"; and (4) the growing pressure to make the needs of business and industry into the primary goals of the educational system.[3]

Much of this can be seen in the words of a former secretary of education, William Bennett:

> The national debate on education is now focused on truly important matters: mastering the basics, . . . insisting on high

standards and expectations; ensuring discipline in the classroom; conveying a grasp of our moral and political principles;
and nurturing the character of our young.[4]

This focus on "truly important matters" is coupled with greater
emphasis on closer business/education linkages. In the words of the Business Roundtable, education "is not keeping up with the pace of change in
business, technology and commerce.... Too few of our young people
are equipped with the skills, versatility and values needed in our growing
and changing economy. When our young people cannot compete as individuals, we cannot compete as a nation."[5]

In essence, this new alliance has integrated education into a wider
set of ideological commitments. The objectives in education are the
same as those that guide its economic and social welfare goals. These
include the expansion of the "free market," the drastic reduction of government responsibility for social needs, the reinforcement of an intensely competitive structure of limited mobility, the lowering of
people's expectations for economic security, and the popularization of
what is clearly a form of social Darwinist thinking.[6]

As I have argued at length elsewhere, the political Right in the
United States has been very successful in mobilizing support not for but
against the educational system, often exporting the crisis in the economy to the schools. Thus, one of its major victories has been to shift the
blame for unemployment, underemployment, the supposed breakdown
of "traditional" values, standards, and sense of sacred knowledge and traditions in the family, education, and the paid workplace *from* the economic, cultural, and social policies of business and industry *to* the school
and other public agencies.[7]

This process is heightened by the federal and state governments,
which literally bombard the public with a particular *selection* of statistical data about the well-being, or lack of it, of our society. I say "selection" here because the United States government sets up "great
manufactories of 'facts and figures' " that are distributed to the public.
These are usually economic and serve to construct a view of reality as
fundamentally centered around the economics of profit and loss, usually
in terms of the agenda set by business's concern for national and international competition in which the benefits increasingly go to a minority
of people in the United States.[8]

In the process, the value of education is increasingly being reduced
to only its economic utility. Other curricular goals such as critical understanding, political literacy, personal development, self-esteem, and
shared respect are beside the point or "too expensive."[9] The issues of

care and connectedness—issues that, as feminists have so crucially re-
minded us, count so critically in building a society based on the common good—are disenfranchised as well.[10] Instead, schools are to
perform one primary function for society: to supply the "human capital"
to underwrite "the promise of individual success in competitive labor
markets and national success in competitive global markets."[11]

Simultaneously, as education's purpose is being drastically reduced
to its role in reaching the ideological and economic goals of the new alliance, its inner world has continuously tended to adopt the procedures
of standardization and rationalization that accompany these goals. Increasingly, teaching methods, texts, tests, and outcomes are being taken
out of the hands of the people who must put them into practice. Instead,
they are being legislated by state departments of education, state legislatures, and central office staff, who in their attempts to increase "the
quality of educational outcomes" are often markedly unreflective about
the latent effects of their efforts.

Some of these negative effects have been widespread, especially in
our urban areas. The tendency for the curriculum to be rationalized and
"industrialized" at a central level focuses largely on competencies measured by standardized tests and encourages the use of more and more
predesigned commercial material written specifically for those states
that have the tightest centralized control and the largest guaranteed
market.[12] The most obvious result here is what I have called the "deskilling" of teachers. When individuals cease to plan and control a large portion of their work, the skills essential to doing these tasks well and self-
reflectively atrophy and are forgotten. The skills that teachers have built
up over decades of hard work—setting relevant curriculum goals, establishing content, designing lessons and instructional strategies, individu-
alizing curricula and teaching based on an intimate knowledge of
students' desires, needs, and culture, working closely with the community on all of this, and so on—are lost. In many ways, given the centralization of authority and control and given the reduction of the primary
mission of the school into, mainly, its economic utility, they are simply
no longer "needed."[13]

In the larger economy, this process of separating conception from
execution and deskilling has been appropriately called the "degradation
of labor." Importing these procedures into the school under the banner
of improving educational quality, as many segments of the conservative
coalition advocate, can have exactly the same effects as when they have
been employed in all too many industries: a loss of commitment and respect, bitter battles over working conditions, a lowering of quality, and a

loss of skill and imagination.[14] In the economic workplace, this process has also ultimately reduced the power of employees to have any significant say in the goals and procedures of the institutions in which they work. All these characteristics run directly counter to what we are beginning to know about what will lead to effective curricula and teaching in schools.[15] And while the press may report instances where there are less hierarchical, less authoritarian, and more democratic attempts at educational reform, as many of you know, in so many of our states and in many of our urban school systems in particular the language may be about teacher and community empowerment but the reality may be something else again.[16]

All of this is not new by any means, of course. It is quite similar to the situation lamented by Margaret Haley—one of the leaders of the first teachers' union in the United States—at the beginning of this century. In her campaign to have teachers continue their struggles for a more democratic educational system, Haley was quite clear about one of the most important ingredients of her platform. Deskilling—or as she so cleverly called it, "factoryizing"—had to be overcome. For Haley, teachers had to constantly organize toward altering conditions in which they were expected "to carry out mechanically and unquestioningly the ideas and orders of those clothed with the authority of position and who may or may not know the needs of the children or how to minister them."[17]

Supporting the growing call for teachers' councils in actually running urban schools, Haley quoted John Dewey approvingly: "If there is a single public school system in the United States where there is official and constitutional provision made for submitting questions of methods of discipline and teaching, and the questions of curriculum, text-books, etc. to the discussion of those actually engaged in the work of teaching, that fact has escaped my notice."[18]

My reason for raising this historical example is not to suggest that we are at the stage we were at eighty years ago. Of course we aren't. Teachers and schools have made immense gains in making the curriculum less totally subject to administrative control. Teachers and local communities have gained considerably more autonomy in many urban areas in deciding what to teach and what counts as good teaching. However, we are in danger of losing the collective memory of how many years it took, and how many sacrifices were made, to make these gains. In the process, we may allow a slow but steady return to prior conditions, if the conservative restoration continues undebated.

Yet the story of Margaret Haley points out something else of considerable importance, given the topic of this chapter. Haley recognized the political fact that, as women, teachers constantly had to work even harder to gain respect and legitimacy for their skills and power. This is a crucial issue. As I have argued in *Teachers and Texts,*[19] it is nearly impossible to understand why curricula and teaching look the way they do, and the ways power is used in building and controlling them, unless we also ask *who* is doing the teaching. The ways teaching and curricula have historically been controlled have been connected to the fact that by and large teaching has been conceived as *women's labor.* Thus, the growing attempts by central authorities and by legislatures to rationalize teaching and to gain greater control over pedagogy, curriculum, and evaluation can also be seen as an attack, though not necessarily a conscious one, on the self-control of women's labor. Unfortunately, our society, like so many others, seems to care less about work that is done largely by women. In general, when a job has been defined as mainly women's paid work, it is subject to greater external control, less respect, and lower salaries, and its autonomy is reduced. In times of serious crisis, as we are experiencing in education and the larger society currently, it has been all too usual to attempt to reduce such autonomy even more.

In essence, I want to argue here that the issues of deskilling and the degradation of teachers' labor—issues so central to the possibilities of democratizing curricula and teaching—must be seen as not only a general problem, but one that speaks directly to the politics of gender relations in the larger society. For we must remember that nearly 90 percent of elementary school teachers and over 65 percent of teachers overall are, in fact, women. Understanding the political dynamics behind educational "reform" movements, hence, may require that we pay considerably more attention to the underlying relations of power in schools and the larger society.

These power relations have a history. How is it that teaching became women's paid work? How is it that women's paid work in education became the target for both rationalization and attempts by powerful groups to gain control over its means and ends? In this chapter, I will inquire into how women came to be in a position to be so targeted. Not only here in the United States, but in other countries as well, the control of teaching and curricula had a strong relationship to sex, class, and race divisions. I shall focus historically on the United States and England, though the arguments I shall present are not necessarily limited to these countries. While most of my analysis will deal with gender and class relations, in no way do I wish to diminish the utter centrality of race in any complete discussion of the politics of control of teaching.[20]

THE STRUCTURE OF WOMEN'S WORK

As one of the very best historians of women's labor has recently argued, most historical analyses of the rationalization and control of labor have been "preoccupied with artisans or skilled workers" such as weavers, shoemakers, or machinists or with those people who worked in heavy industry, such as miners and steelworkers. Almost by definition this is the history of men's work. Only a relatively few individuals—though luckily this number is growing rapidly—"have considered the implications of rationalization for women workers, despite the steadily growing number of women in the work force."[21]

Let me begin by going into even more detail about what the shape of women's paid work currently looks like. Such work is constructed around not one but two kinds of divisions. First, women's work is related to a *vertical* division of labor in which women as a group are disadvantaged relative to men in pay and in the conditions under which they labor. Second, such work is involved in the *horizontal* division of labor where women are concentrated in particular kinds of work.[22] Thus, 78 percent of all clerical workers, 67 percent of service workers, 67 percent of teachers (but a much higher percentage in the elementary school), and so on, are women, in the United States. Less than 20 percent of all administrative, executive, or managerial workers in the United States are women, and up to a decade ago less than 10 percent in England, were women.[23]

The connections between these two divisions, however, are quite striking. Low-wage, competitive-sector employment contains a large share of women in both countries. In England, 41 percent of jobs women hold are part-time, thereby guaranteeing lower wages and benefits and less control, but also documenting the linkages between patriarchal relations in the home (it is the woman's place to only work part-time and take care of children) and the kinds of work made available in the wage-labor market.[24]

We can get an even better idea of the concentration of women in certain occupations in the following data. As of 1979, in England, two-thirds of all women engaged in paid work were found in three occupational groups. Over 31 percent were working in clerical and related jobs; 22 percent worked in personal service occupations; and approximately 12 percent were employed in "professional" and related occupations in health and welfare. Within nearly all occupations, however, "women were over-represented in the less-skilled, lower status or lower-paid jobs, while men were over-represented in the highly-skilled and mana-gerial jobs."[25]

Though showing some differences, the figures are similar in the United States. Clerical work constitutes 35 percent of women's paid la-bor, followed by service work at 21 percent, educators, librarians, and social workers at 8 percent, retail sales at 6 percent, nurses and health technicians at 5 percent, and clothing and textile work at 4 percent.[26] Michele Barrett and others have pointed to the close correspondence between the kinds of paid work women tend to do and the division of labor in the family. Service work, the "caring professions," domestic service, clothing, human needs, and so forth, all remain part of this relationship between work inside and outside the home.[27] As I shall document in my next section, this relationship has a long history in education.

While these statistics are important in and of themselves, what they do not reveal is working conditions and class dynamics. Historically, women's jobs have been much more apt to be "proletarianized" than men's. There have been constant pressures to rationalize them. This is brought home by the fact that in our economy there has been a major expansion of jobs with little autonomy and control, while the number of jobs with high levels of autonomy has declined. These proletarianized positions were largely filled by women.[28] Evidence of this is given by the fact that the majority of working-class positions (54 percent) in the United States are held by women, a figure that is increasing.[29] These fig-ures actually speak to a complicated and dialectical process. As the labor market changes over time, the decrease in jobs with autonomy is related closely to changes in the sexual division of labor. Women will tend to fill these jobs. Just as importantly, as jobs—either autonomous or not—are filled by women, there are greater attempts to control from the outside both the content of those jobs and how they are done. Thus, the sepa-ration of conception from execution and what has been called the "deskilling" and "depowering" of jobs have been a particularly powerful set of forces on women's labor. (The current transformation of cleri-cal work by word processing technologies, with its attendant loss of of-fice jobs and mechanization of those jobs that remain offers a good ex-ample here.)[30]

These points have important implications for the analysis I am pre-senting. The sex-typing of a job is not likely to change unless the job it-self undergoes substantial alteration in some respects. The surrounding labor market needs to change and/or the tasks of the job itself need to be restructured.[31] But sex-typing, when it has occurred, has had a distinct impact on conflicts in the workplace and on negotiations over such things as the definitions of jobs, pay level, and determining whether or not a job is considered skilled.[32]

In general, there seems to be a relatively strong relationship between the entry of large numbers of women into an occupation and the slow transformation of the job. Pay is often lowered, and the job is regarded as low-skilled so that control is "needed" from the outside. Added to this is the fact that "those occupations which became defined as female were expanded at a time when the skills needed to do them were [seen as being] commonly held or easily learned and when there was a particularly high demand for labour, or an especially large pool of women seeking work."[33]

Of course, sometimes the very tasks associated with a job reinforce such sex-typing. Since teaching, for instance, does have a service and nurturing component to it, this reconstitutes in action the definition of it as women's work. And given "our" association of service and nurturing activity as less skilled and less valued than other labor, we thereby revivify patriarchal hierarchies and the horizontal and vertical divisions of labor in the process.[34] In many ways, the very perception of an activity is often saturated with sexual bias. Women's work is considered somehow inferior or of less status simply due to the fact that it is women who do it.[35] Because of these conditions, it has been exceptionally difficult for women to establish recognition of the skills required in their paid and unpaid work.[36] They must fight not only the ideological construction of women's work, but against both the tendencies for the job to become something different and for its patterns of autonomy and control to change as well.

In my presentation of data to show the progression of teaching from being largely men's work to being women's work, in many ways we shall want to pay close attention to how teaching may have changed and to the economic and gender conditions surrounding this. In essence, we may not be describing quite the same occupation after elementary school teaching becomes women's work. For jobs *are* transformed, often in significant ways, over time. A good example here is again clerical work. Like teaching, this too changed from being a masculine occupation in the nineteenth century to being a largely female one in the twentieth. Yet the labor process of clerical work was radically altered during this period. It was deskilled, came under tighter conditions of control, lost many of its paths of upward mobility to managerial positions, and lost wages during the end of the nineteenth century, both in the United States and England, as it became "feminized."[37] Given this, it is impera-

Table 3.1. Teachers in Public Elementary Schools in England and Wales, 1870–1930

Year	Total Number	Number of Women Teachers per 100 Men Teachers
1870	13,729	99
1880	41,428	156
1890	73,533	207
1900	113,986	287
1910	161,804	306
1920	151,879	315
1930	157,061	366

Source: Reconstructed from Barry Bergen, "Only a Schoolmaster: Gender, Class, and the Effort to Professionalize Elementary Teaching in England, 1870–1910," *History of Education Quarterly* 22 (Spring 1982): 4.

tive that we ask whether what has been unfortunately called the "feminization" of teaching actually concerns the same job. I will claim in fact that in some rather substantive economic and ideological aspects it was not. This transformation is linked in complex ways to alterations in patriarchal and economic relations that were restructuring the larger society.

GENDER AND TEACHING OVER TIME

Where does teaching fit in here? Some facts may be helpful. What has been called the "feminization" of teaching is clearly seen in data from England. Before the rapid growth of mass elementary education, in 1870, men in teaching actually slightly outnumbered women. For every 100 men there were only 99 women employed as teachers. This, however, is the last time men have a numerical superiority. Just ten years later, in 1880, for every 100 males there were now 156 women. This ratio rose to 100 to 207 in 1890, and 100 to 287 in 1900. By 1910, women outnumbered men by over 3 to 1. By 1930, the figure had grown to closer to 4 to 1.[38]

Yet these figures would be deceptive if they were not linked to changes in the actual numbers of teachers being employed. Teaching became a symbol of upward mobility for many women, and as elementary schooling increased, so did the numbers of women employed in it, points I shall go into further later on. Thus, in 1870 there were only 14,000

Table 3.2. Teachers in Public Elementary Schools in the United States, 1870–1930

Year	Number of Men	Number of Women	Total Number of Teachers	Percentage of Women
1870	—	—	—	59.0 (estimate)
1880	—	—	—	60.0 (estimate)
1890	121,877	232,925	354,802	65.6
1900	116,416	286,274	402,690	71.1
1910	91,591	389,952	481,543	81.0
1920	63,024	513,222	576,246	89.1
1930	67,239	573,718	640,957	89.5

Source: Adapted from Willard S. Elsbree, *The American Teacher* (New York: American Book Co., 1939), 554, and Emery M. Foster, "Statistical Summary of Education, 1929–30," *Biennial Survey of Education 1928–1930,* vol. 2 (Washington: U.S. Government Printing Office, 1932), 8.

teachers in England, of which more were men than women. By the year 1930, 157,601 teachers worked in state-supported schools in England and Wales. Close to 120,000 of these were women.[39] The definition of teaching as a female enclave is given further substantiation by the fact that these numbers signify something quite graphic. While the 40,000 men employed as teachers around 1930 constitute less than 3 percent of the occupied male workers, the 120,000 women teachers account for nearly 20 percent of all women working for pay outside the home.[40]

If we compare percentages of male to female teachers in the United States to those of England for approximately the same time period, similar patterns emerge. While there was clear regional variation, in typical areas in, say, 1840, only 39 percent of teachers were women. By 1850, it had risen to 46 percent.[41] The increase later on is somewhat more rapid than the English experience. The year 1870 finds women holding approximately 60 percent of the public elementary school teaching positions. This figure moves up to 71 percent by 1900. It reaches a peak of fully 89 percent in 1920 and then stabilizes within a few percentage points over the following years.

Given the historical connection between elementary school teaching and the ideologies surrounding domesticity and the definition of "women's proper place," in which teaching was defined as an extension of the productive and reproductive labor women engaged in at home,[42] we should not be surprised by the fact that such changes occurred in the gendered composition of the teaching force. Although there are clear connections between patriarchal ideologies and the shift of teaching into being seen as "women's work," the issue is not totally explained in this way. Local political economies played a large part here. The shift to non-agricultural employment in male patterns of work is part of the story as well. Just as important was the relationship between the growth of compulsory schooling and women's labor. As we shall see, the costs associated with compulsory schooling to local school districts were often quite high. One way to control such rising costs was in changing accepted hiring practices.[43] One simply hired cheaper teachers—women. Let us examine both of these dynamics in somewhat more detail. In the process, we shall see how class and gender interacted within the limits set by the economic needs of our social formation.

Some simple and well-known economic facts need to be called to mind at the outset. In the United Kingdom, although women teachers outnumbered their male colleagues, the salaries they were paid were significantly less. In fact, from 1855 to 1935, there was a remarkably consistent pattern. Women were paid approximately two-thirds what their male counterparts received.[44] Bergen claims, in fact, that one of the major contributing factors behind the fact that schools increased their hiring of women was that women would be paid less.[45]

In the United States, the salary differential was often even more striking. With the rapid growth of schooling stimulated by large rates of immigration as well as by struggles by a number of groups to win free compulsory education, school committees increased their rate of hiring women, but at salaries that were originally a half to a third as much as those given to men.[46] But how did it come about that there were positions to be filled in the first place? What happened to the people who had been there?

Elementary school teaching became a woman's occupation in part because men *left* it. For many men, the "opportunity cost" was too great to stay in teaching. Many male teachers taught part-time (e.g., between harvests) or as a stepping-stone to more lucrative or prestigious jobs. Yet with the growth of the middle class in the United States, with the formalization of schools and curricula in the latter half of the nineteenth century, and with the enlarged credentialing and certification requirements for teaching that emerged at this time, men began to, and were often able to, look elsewhere.

Strober summarizes these points nicely.

> All of these changes tended to make teaching less attractive to men. When teaching was a relatively causal occupa-

tion that could be engaged in for fairly short periods of time, it was attractive to men in a variety of circumstances. A farmer could easily combine teaching in the winter with caring for his farm during the rest of the year. A potential minister, politician, shopkeeper or lawyer could teach for a short period of time in order to gain visibility within a community. However, once standards rose for teacher certification and school terms were lengthened and combined into a continuous year, men began to drop out of teaching. In urban areas, where teaching was first formalized, and then, later, in rural areas, most men found the opportunity cost of teaching was simply too great, especially since although annual salaries were higher once standards were raised and the school term lengthened, the average teaching salary remained inadequate to support a family. Men also disliked losing their former classroom autonomy. And at the same time attractive job opportunities were developing for men in business and in other professions.[47]

Thus, patriarchal familial forms in concert with changes in the social division of labor of capitalism combine here to create some of the conditions out of which a market for a particular kind of teacher emerges. (Regarding England, we should add the fact that a considerable number of men sought employment both there and abroad in the civil service. Many of the men who attended "training colleges," in fact, did so as a point of entry into the civil service, not into teaching.[48] The "Empire," then, had a rather interesting effect on the political economy of gendered labor.)

Faced with these "market conditions," school boards turned increasingly to women. Partly this was a result of successful struggle by women. More and more women were winning the battles over access to both education and employment outside the home. Yet partly it is the result of capitalism as well. Women were continuing to be recruited to the factories and mills (often, by the way, originally because they would be sometimes accompanied by children, who could also work for incredibly low wages in the mills.)[49] Given the exploitation that existed in the factories and given the drudgery of paid and unpaid domestic labor, teaching must have seemed a considerably more pleasant occupation to many single women. Finally, contradictory tendencies occurred at an ideological level. While women struggled to open up the labor market and alter patriarchal relations in the home and the paid workplace, some of the arguments used for opening up teaching to women were at the expense of reproducing ideological elements that had been part of the root causes of patriarchal control in the first place. The relationship between teaching and domesticity was highlighted. "Advocates of women as teachers, such as Catherine Beecher, Mary Lyon, Zilpah Grant, Horace Mann and Henry Barnard, argued that not only were women the ideal teachers of young children (because of their patience and nurturant qualities) but that teaching was ideal preparation for motherhood."[50] These same people were not loath to argue something else. Women were "willing to" teach at lower wages than those needed by men.[51] When this is coupled with the existing social interests, economic structures, and patriarchal relations that supported the dominance of an ideology of domesticity in the larger society, we can begin to get a glimpse at the conditions that led to such a situation.

Many men, however, did stay in education. But as Tyack, Strober, and others have demonstrated, those men who stayed tended to be found in higher-status and higher-paying jobs. In fact, as school systems became more highly bureaucratized, and with the expansion of management positions that accompanied this in the United States, many more men were found in positions of authority than before. Some men stayed in education; but they left the classroom. This lends support to Lanford's claim that from 1870 to 1970, the greater the formalization of the educational system, the greater the proportion of women teachers.[52] It also tends to support my earlier argument that once a set of positions becomes "women's work," it is subject to greater pressure for rationalization. Administrative control of teaching, curricula, and so on increases. The job *itself* becomes different.

Thus, it is not that women had not been found in the teaching ranks before; of course they had. What is more significant is the increasing numbers of women at particular levels "in unified, bureaucratic, and public schools" with their graded curricula, larger and more formally organized districts, growing administrative hierarchies,[53] and, just as crucially, restructuring of the tasks of teachers themselves.

Such sex segregation was not an unusual occurrence in the urban graded school, for instance. At its very outset, proponents of these school plans had a specific labor force and labor process in mind. "Hiring, promotion and salary schedules were routinized." Rather than being left up to teachers, the curriculum was quite standardized along grade-level lines, with both teachers and students divided into these grades. New managerial positions were created—the superintendent and non-teaching principal, for instance—thereby removing responsibility for managerial concerns out of the classroom. Again, women's supposed

nurturing capabilities and "natural" empathic qualities and their relatively low salaries made them ideally suited for teaching in such schools.
Even where there were concerns about women teachers' ability to discipline older students, this too could be solved. It was the principal and/
or superintendent who handled such issues.[54]

This sexual division of labor within the school had other impacts. It
enhanced the ability of urban school boards to maintain bureaucratic
control of their employees and over curriculum and teaching practices.
The authors of a recent historical analysis of the relationship between
gender division and control demonstrate this rather well. They argue:

> By structuring jobs to take advantage of sex role stereo-
> types about women's responsiveness to rules and male au-
> thority, and men's presumed ability to manage women, urban
> school boards were able to enhance their ability to control
> curricula, students and personnel. Male managers in
> nineteenth-century urban schools regulated the core activi-
> ties of instruction through standardized promotional exami-
> nations on the content of the prescribed curriculum and
> strict supervision to ensure that teachers were following
> mandated techniques. Rules were highly prescriptive. Nor-
> mal classes in the high schools of the cities prepared young
> women to teach in a specified manner; pictures of the normal
> students in Washington, D.C., for example, show women stu-
> dents performing precisely the same activities prescribed for
> their future pupils, even to the mid-morning "yawning
> and stretching" session. Given this purpose of tight control,
> women were ideal employees. With few alternative occupa-
> tions and accustomed to patriarchal authority they mostly did
> what their male superiors ordered. [This, by the way, is partly
> questionable.] Difference of gender provided an important
> form of social control.[55]

Given these ideological conditions and these unequal relations of
control, why would women ever enter such labor? Was it the stereotypical response that teaching was a temporary way station on the road to
marriage for women who loved children? While this may have been
partly accurate, it is certainly overstated, since in many instances this
was not even remotely the case.

In her collection of teachers' writings from the nineteenth and
twentieth centuries, Nancy Hoffman makes the point that most women
did not enter teaching with a preoccupation with a love of children or

with marital plans as the main things in mind. Rather, uppermost in their minds was one major concern. They entered teaching in large part because they needed work. The teachers' comments often document the following:

> Women had only a few choices of occupation; and compared with most—laundering, sewing, cleaning, or working in a factory—teaching offered numerous attractions. It was genteel, paid reasonably well, and required little special skill or equipment. In the second half of the century and beyond, it also allowed a woman to travel, to live independently or in the company of other women, and to attain economic security and a modest social status. The issue of marriage, so charged with significance among male educators, emerges in stories of schoolmarms pressured reluctantly into marriage by a family fearful of having an "old maid" on their hands, rather than in teachers' accounts of their own eagerness or anxiety over marriage. There are also explicit statements, in these accounts, of teachers *choosing* work and independence over a married life that appeared, to them, to signify domestic servitude or social uselessness. Finally, the accounts of some women tell us that they chose teaching not because they wanted to teach children conventional right from wrong, but in order to foster social, political, or spiritual change: they wanted to persuade the young, move them to collective action for temperance, for racial equality, for conversion to Christianity. What these writings tell us, then, is that from the woman teacher's perspective, the continuity between mothering and teaching was far less significant than a paycheck and the challenge and satisfaction of work.[56]

We should be careful in overstating this case, however. Not a few women could and did train to be teachers and then worked for a relatively short period. As Angela John puts it, "Because the dominant ideology argued that woman's place was in the home, it conveniently enabled elementary teaching to be viewed in theory (if not in practice) as a profession for which women could train and work for a limited time."[57] Obviously, by constructing the image of teaching as a transient occupation, this "permitted the perpetuation of low wages," since such waged labor was merely a way of "tiding women over until they were married."[58] Many women teachers in England, the United States, and elsewhere, however, never married, and hence the situation is considerably more complicated than conventional stereotypes would have it.[59]

Yet while many teachers in the United States and undoubtedly in the United Kingdom approached their jobs with a sense that did not necessarily mirror the stereotypes of nurturance and preparation for marriage, this did not stop such stereotypes from creating problems. The increase in women teachers did not occur without challenge. Conservative critics expressed concern over the negative effects women teachers might have on their male pupils. Such concerns increased as the proportion of students going on to secondary schools rose. "While recognizing the beneficial effects on primary-level pupils, the continuation of the female teacher-male student relation into higher grades was viewed as potentially harmful."[60] (The longer tradition of single-sex schools in England partially mediated these pressures). That this is not simply an historical dynamic is evident by the fact that even today the proportion of male teachers is considerably higher in the high schools than in the elementary schools.

CLASS DYNAMICS AND TEACHING

The general picture I have painted so far has treated the constitution of teaching as primarily a part of the sexual division of labor over time. While this is crucially important, we need to remember that gender was not the only dynamic at work here. Class played a major part, especially in England, but most certainly in the United States as well.[61] Class dynamics operated at the level of who became teachers and what their experiences were.

It was not until the end of the nineteenth century and the outset of the twentieth that middle-class young women began to be recruited into teaching in England. In fact, only after 1914 do we see any large influx of middle-class young women entering state-supported elementary school teaching.[62]

Class distinctions were very visible. While the concept of femininity *idealized* for middle-class women centered around an image of the "perfect wife and mother," the middle-class view of working-class women often entailed a different sense of femininity. The waged labor of working-class women "tarnished" them (though there is evidence of between-class feminist solidarity).[63] Such waged labor was a departure form bourgeois ideals of domesticity and economic dependence. With the emergence of changes in such bourgeois ideals toward the end of the nineteenth century middle-class women themselves began to "widen their sphere of action and participate in some of the various economic and social changes that accompanied industrialization" and both the restructuring of capitalism and the division of labor. Struggles over legal and political rights, over employment and education, became of considerable import. Yet because of a tension between the ideals of domesticity and femininity, on the one hand, and the struggle to enlarge the middle-class woman's economic sphere, on the other, particular jobs were seen as appropriate for women. Teaching, and often particular kinds of stenographic and secretarial work, were among the more predominant ones.[64] In fact, of the white women who worked outside the home in the United States in the mid to late nineteenth century, fully 20 percent of them were employed at one time or another as teachers.[65]

This entrance of women, and especially of middle-class women, into paid teaching created important pressures for improvements in the education of women, both in the United States and England.[66] Equalization of curricular offerings, the right to enter into traditional male enclaves within universities, and so on were in no small part related to this phenomenon. Yet we need to remember an important social fact here. Even though women were making gains in education and employment, most middle-class women still found themselves *excluded* from the professions and other areas of employment.[67] Thus, a dynamic operated that cut both ways. In both being limited to and carving out this area of employment, women "held on to it as one of the few arenas in which they could exert any power, even at the expense of further reinforcing stereotypes about women's sphere."[68]

Having said this, we again should not assume that teachers were recruited only from middle-class homes in the United States or England. Often quite the opposite was the case. A number of studies demonstrate that working-class backgrounds were not unusual. In fact, one American study completed in 1911 presents data on the average woman teacher's economic background. She came from a family in which the father's income was approximately $800 a year, a figure that places the family among skilled workers or farmers rather than the middle class.[69]

These class differences had an impact not only on an ideological level, but in terms of education and employment within education as well. Girls of different class backgrounds often attended different schools, even when they both might wish to be teachers.[70] Furthermore, by the end of the nineteenth century in England, class differences created clear distinctions in patterns of where one might teach. While middle-class women teachers were largely found in private secondary and single-sex schools "which catered especially to middle class girls" or as governesses, women teachers from working-class backgrounds were found elsewhere. They dominated positions within state-supported elementary schools, schools that were largely working-class and mixed-sex.[71] In many ways these were simply different jobs.

These class distinctions can hide something of considerable import, however. Both groups still had low status.[72] To be a woman was still to be involved in a social formation that was defined in large part by the structure of patriarchal relations. But again patriarchal forms were often colonized and mediated by class relations.

For example, *what* was taught to these aspiring teachers had interesting relationships to the social and sexual divisions of labor. Many aspiring working-class "pupil teachers" in England were recruited to work in working-class schools. Much of what they were expected to teach centered around domestic skills, such as sewing and needlework, in addition to reading, spelling, and arithmetic. For those working-class pupil teachers who might ultimately sit for an examination to enter one of the teacher training colleges, gender divisions were most pronounced. In Purvis's comparison of these entrance tests, the different expectations of what men and women were to know and, hence, teach are more than a little visible. Both men and women were examined in dictation, penmanship, grammar, composition, school management, history, geography, French, German, Latin, and Welsh. Yet only men were tested in algebra, geometry, Euclid, and Greek. Only women took domestic economy and needlework.

The focus on needlework is a key here in another way, for not only does it signify clear gender dynamics at work, but it also points again to class barriers. Unlike the "ornamental sewing" that was more common in middle-class households, these working-class girls were examined on "useful sewing." Questions included how to make the knee part of "knickerbocker drawers" and the sewing together of women's petticoats of a gored variety. (This was one of the most efficient uses of material, since less material is needed if the fabric is cut and sewn correctly.)[73] The dominance of utility, efficiency, and cost saving is once more part of the vision of what working-class girls would need.[74] Purvis notes, "It would appear then that female elementary teachers were expected to teach those skills which were linked to that form of femininity deemed appropriate for the working classes."[75]

But teaching, especially elementary school teaching, was not all that well paid, to say the least; a teacher earned somewhat more than a factory operative but still only the equivalent of a stenographer's wages in the United States or England.[76] What would its appeal then have been for a working-class girl? In England, with its very visible set of class relations and articulate class culture, we find answers similar to, but—given these more visible class relations—still different from, those for the United States. First, the very *method* by which girls were first trained in the 1870s to become teachers was a system of apprenticeship, a system that was "indigenous to working class culture." This was especially important since it was evident at the time that female pupil teachers were usually the daughters of laborers, artisans, or "small tradesmen." Second, and here very much like the American experience, compared to occupations such as domestic service, working in factories, dressmaking, and so on—among the only jobs realistically open to working-class women—teaching had a number of benefits. It did increase status, especially among working-class girls who showed a degree of academic ability. Working conditions, though still nothing to write home about, were clearly better in many ways. They were relatively clean and, though often extremely difficult, given overcrowded conditions in schools, had that same potential for job satisfaction that was evident in my earlier quotation from Hoffman and that was frequently missing in other employment. And, just as significantly, since teaching was considered to be on the mental side of the mental/manual division of labor, it gave an opportunity—though granted a limited one—for a certain amount of social mobility.[77] (This question of social mobility and "respectability" may have been particularly important to those women and families newly within a "lower middle class" location, as well, given the increasing proportion of such people in teaching in England by the beginning of the second decade of this century).

There was a price to pay for this "mobility" and the promise of improved working conditions that accompanied it. Women elementary school teachers became less connected to their class origins, and at the same time class differences in ideals of femininity still kept her from being totally acceptable to those classes above her. This contradictory situation is not an abstraction. The fact that it was lived out is made clear in the frequent references by these teachers about their social isolation.[78] Such isolation was of course heightened considerably by other lived conditions of teachers. The formal and contractual conditions under which teachers were hired were not the most attractive. As many of you already know, women teachers in the United States, for example, could be fired for getting married, or if married, for getting pregnant. There were prohibitions about being seen with men, about clothes, about makeup, about politics, about money, about nearly all of one's public (and private) life.

It would be wrong to trace all of this back to economic motives and class dynamics. For decades married women were prohibited from teaching, on both sides of the Atlantic. While single women were often young, and hence were paid less, the notion of morality and purity as powerful symbols of a womanly teaching act undoubtedly played a large part. The very fact that the above-mentioned array of controls of women's physicality, dress, living arrangements, and morals speaks to the import of these concerns. Ideologies of patriarchy, with the teacher being shrouded in a domestic and maternal cloak—possibly combined with a more deep-seated male suspicion of female sexuality—are reproduced here.[79] It is the very combination of patriarchal relations and economic pressures that continue to work their way through teaching even to this day.

These controls are strikingly evident in a relatively standard teacher's contract from the United States for the year 1923. I reproduce it in its entirety since it condenses within itself so many of the ideological conditions under which women teachers worked.

TEACHERS CONTRACT 1923

This is an agreement between Miss _____, teacher, and the Board of Education of the _____ School, whereby Miss _____ agrees to teach for a period of eight months, beginning Sept. 1, 1923. The Board of Education agrees to pay Miss _____ the sum of ($75) per month.

Miss _____ agrees:

1. Not to get married. This contract becomes null and void immediately if the teacher marries.
2. Not to keep company with men.
3. To be home between the hours of 8:00 p.m. and 6:00 a.m. unless in attendance at a school function.
4. Not to loiter downtown in ice cream stores.
5. Not to leave town at any time without the permission of the chairman of the Board of Trustees.
6. Not to smoke cigarettes. This contract becomes null and void immediately if the teacher is found smoking.
7. Not to drink beer, wine, or whiskey. This contract becomes null and void immediately if the teacher is found drinking beer, wine, or whiskey.
8. Not to ride in a carriage or automobile with any man except her brother or father.

9. Not to dress in bright colors.
10. Not to dye her hair.
11. To wear at least two petticoats.
12. Not to wear dresses more than two inches above the ankles.
13. To keep the schoolroom clean
    a. to sweep the classroom floor at least once daily.
    b. to scrub the classroom floor at least once weekly with hot water and soap.
    c. to clean the blackboard at least once daily.
    d. to start the fire at 7:00 so the room will be warm at 8:00 a.m. when the children arrive.
14. Not to use face powder, mascara, or paint the lips.

In many ways, the contract speaks for itself. It is important to note, though, that this did not end in 1923. Many of these conditions continued on for decades to be ultimately transformed into the more technical and bureaucratic forms of control now being instituted in many areas of the United States.

Let me give one further concrete example. The larger political economy, in combination with patriarchal ideological forms, shows its power once again whenever the question of married women who engage in waged work appears historically. By the turn of the century hundreds of thousands of married women had begun to work outside the home. Yet during the depression, it was very common for married women to be fired or to be denied jobs if they had working husbands. The state played a large role here. In England, governmental policies and reports gave considerable attention to women's domestic role.[80] In the United States, in 1930–31 the National Association of Education reported that of the fifteen hundred school systems in the country, 77 percent refused to hire married women teachers. Another 63 percent dismissed any woman teacher who got married during the time of her employment. This did not occur only at the elementary and secondary levels. Some universities as well asked their married women faculty to resign. Lest we see this as something that affected only women teachers, the federal government itself required in 1932 that if a married couple worked for the government, one must be let go. This law was applied almost invariably to women only.[81]

The very fact that these figures seem so shocking to us now speaks eloquently to the sacrifices made and the struggles that women engaged in for decades to alter these oppressive relations. These struggles have been over one's control of one's labor and over the control of one's very life. Given the past conditions I have just pointed to, these historically significant struggles have actually brought no small measure of success. It is to these activities that I shall briefly turn in the concluding section of my analysis.

BEYOND THE MYTH OF THE PASSIVE TEACHER

Women teachers were not passive in the face of the class and gender conditions I described in the previous sections of this chapter. In fact, one of the major but lesser-known stories is the relationship between socialist and feminist activity and the growth of local teachers' organizations and unions in England and the United States.

Even while they worked internally to alter the frequently awful conditions they faced in urban schools on both sides of the Atlantic—such as crowded, unsanitary buildings, a teacher/student ratio that was often incredibly high, and an impersonal bureaucracy that, especially in the United States, was daily attempting to transform, rationalize, and control their work—a good deal of the unified action teachers took was concerned with their economic well-being. For example, grade school teachers in Chicago worked long and hard for adequate pensions. Out of this experience, the Chicago Federation of Teachers (CFT), headed by Catherine Goggin and Margaret Haley, was born in 1897. It soon led a successful fight for salary increases and succeeded in organizing more than half of the city's teachers in less than three years. Still an organization made up primarily of elementary school teachers, it was quite militant on economic matters. And while the women leaders and rank-and-file teachers were not necessarily as radical as some other leftist unions in cities such as Chicago, they still actively supported women's issues, municipal ownership of all utilities, popular elections and recalls, and labor solidarity. They did this in the face of middle- and upper-class resentment of unions. There was a constant struggle between the school board and the CFT, with the school board voting in 1905 to condemn the teachers for affiliating with the Chicago Federation of Labor (CFL). Such an affiliation was, according to the board, "absolutely unjustifiable and intolerable in a school system of a democracy."[82]

While these teachers were never totally successful in either their economic demands or their organizing plans,[83] they did succeed in forcing school boards to take elementary teachers—women—seriously as a force to be reckoned with. In the process, they also partially challenged the economic and ideological relations surrounding women's work.

For many others in England and the United States, the conditions under which they labored had a radicalizing effect. Thus, many of the leaders of feminist groups were originally teachers who traced their growing awareness of the importance of the conflict over patriarchal domination to the experience they had as teachers. Their resentment over salary differentials, over interference in their decisions, over the very ways they were so tightly controlled, often led in large part to their growing interest in feminist ideas.[84]

These examples offer us a glimpse at politicized activities. But for a large portion of the teachers in London or New York, Birmingham or Chicago, Liverpool or Boston, they struggled in "cultural" ways. They developed practices that gave them greater control of the curriculum; they fought to have a much greater say in *what* they taught, *how* they were to teach it, and how and by *whom* their work was to be evaluated. These everyday efforts still go on, as teachers continue to defend themselves against external encroachments from the state or from capital.

The history of elementary school teaching (and curriculum in part, as well) *is* the history of these political/economic and cultural struggles. It is the history of a gendered work force who, in the face of attempts to restructure their jobs, fought back consciously and unconsciously. Sometimes these very battles reinforced the existing definitions of women's work. Sometimes, perhaps more so in England, they lead to a cutting off of ties to one's class background. And sometimes, they supported class-specific ideals of work and professionalism. Just as often, however, these efforts empowered women, either by radicalizing some of them, by giving them much more say in the actual control of what they taught and how they taught it, or by demonstrating that patriarchal forms could be partially fractured in equalizing both salaries and hiring-and-firing conditions.

What ultimately shapes how curricula and teaching are controlled at the level of classroom practice is, hence, an *ongoing* process. It involves a complex interplay among the ideological and material structures of control of gendered labor that arise from bureaucratic management, the forms of resistance, and self-organization of teachers, and then employer counterpressures,[85] which once again produce a response by teachers themselves. I have shown one moment in this process. As teaching changes from a predominantly male to a predominantly female occupation, the constitution of the job itself changes as well. It entails significantly greater controls over teaching and curriculum at the level of teacher education and in the classroom. It is structured around a different set of class and gender dynamics. Finally, women are active, not passive, figures in attempting to create positions for women as teachers based on their own positions in the social and sexual divisions of labor. These efforts may have had contradictory results, but they were part of a much larger movement—one that is still so necessary today—to challenge aspects of patriarchal relations within both the home and the workplace.

Yet, as I have also argued, the transformation of teaching also led to the job itself becoming a breeding ground for further struggles. Many women were politicized. Some created unions. And others fought "silently" every day on their jobs to expand or retain control of their own teaching and curriculum. In a time when the state and capital are once more searching for ways to rationalize and control—to "reform"—the day-to-day work of teachers, these overt and covert efforts from the past are of more than historical interest. For elementary school teaching *is* still gendered labor. It is not too odd to end this chapter by saying that the past is still ahead of us.

Notes

This chapter is based on a longer analysis in Michael W. Apple, *Teachers and Texts: A Political Economy of Class and Gender Relations in Education* (New York and London: Routledge & Kegan Paul, 1988). A briefer version appears in *Teachers College Record* (Spring 1985).

1. I have discussed this in much greater detail in Michael W. Apple, *Ideology and Curriculum,* 2d. ed. (New York: Routledge & Kegan Paul, 1990); Michael W. Apple, *Education and Power* (New York: Routledge & Kegan Paul, ARK Edition, 1985); and Apple, *Teachers and Texts.* and Michael W. Apple, *Official Knowledge* (New York: Routledge, 1993).

2. Ira Shor, *Culture Wars* (New York: Routledge & Kegan Paul, 1986).

3. Michael W. Apple, "Redefining Equality," *Teachers College Record* 90 (Winter 1988): 167–84.

4. William Bennett, *Our Children and Our Country* (New York: Simon & Schuster, 1988), 10.

5. Business Roundtable, *Business Means Business about Education* (New York: Business Roundtable, 1989), 1.

6. Ann Bastian, Marilyn Gittell, Colin Greer, and Kenneth Haskins, *Choosing Equality* (Philadelphia: Temple University Press, 1986), 14.

7. See Apple, *Education and Power* and *Teachers and Texts.*

8. See Donald Horne, *The Public Culture* (Dover, N.H.: Pluto Press, 1986), 189–90, and Joshua Cohen and Joel Rogers, *On Democracy* (New York: Penquin Books, 1983).

9. Bastian et al., *Choosing Equality,* 157.

10. Carol Gilligan, *In a Different Voice* (Cambridge: Harvard University Press, 1982).

11. Bastian et al., *Choosing Equality,* 21.

12. For further discussion of the political economy of textbooks, see Apple, *Teachers and Texts.*

13. Apple, *Education and Power,* especially chapter 5.

14. Ibid.

15. Bastian et al., *Choosing Equality.*

16. See Michael W. Apple and Susan Jungck, "You Don't Need to Be a Teacher to Teach This Unit," *American Educational Research Journal* 27 (Summer 1990): 227–51.

17. Margaret Haley, quoted in James W. Fraser, "Agents of Democracy: Urban Elementary School Teachers and the Conditions of Teaching," in *American Teachers,* ed. Donald Warren (New York: Macmillan, 1989), 138.

18. Ibid.

19. Apple, *Teachers and Texts.*

20. Some of the history of African-American teachers can be found in Linda M. Perkins, "The History of Blacks in Teaching: Growth and Decline within the Profession." in *American Teachers,* ed. Warren, 344–69. For a more detailed theoretical and political argument for the centrality of race in education, see Cameron McCarthy and Michael W. Apple, "Race, Gender, and Class in American Educational Research," in *Class, Gender, and Race in American Education,* ed. Lois Weis (Albany: State University of New York Press, 1988).

21. Barbara Melosh, *The Physician's Hand: Work Culture and Conflict in American Nursing* (Philadelphia: Temple University Press, 1982), 8.

22. Michele Barrett, *Women's Oppression Today* (London: New Left Books, 1980), 154–55.

23. Alice H. Cook, *The Working Mother: A Survey of Problems and Programs in Nine Countries* (Ithaca: New York State School of Industrial and Labor Relations, Cornell University, 1978), 11.

24. Barrett, *Women's Oppression Today,* 155. This is, of course, reproduced in education, where substitute teachers in the elementary school are largely women.

25. Linda Murgatroyd, "Gender and Occupational Stratification," *Sociological Review* 30 (November 1982): 582.

26. Nancy S. Barrett, "Women in the Job Market: Occupations, Earnings, and Career Opportunities," in *The Subtle Revolution: Women at Work,* ed. Ralph E. Smith (Washington, D.C.: Urban Institute, 1979), 49. Similar but slightly different figures can be found in Cook, *The Working Mother,* 12.

27. Barrett, *Women's Oppression Today,* 156–57.

28. This is quite a complicated process, one including changes not only in the division of labor in capitalism, but in the family/household system as well. See Johanna Brenner and Maria Ramas, "Rethinking Women's oppression," *New Left Review* 144 (March/April 1984), 33–71.

29. Erik Olin Wright, et al. "The American Class Structure," *American Sociological Review* 47 (December 1982): 723.

30. See, for example, Jane Barker and Hazel Downing, "Word Processing and the Transformation of the Patriarchal Relations of Control in the Office," in *Education and the State*. Volume 2: *Politics, Patriarchy, and Practice,* ed. Roger Dale, Geoff Esland, Ross Furgusson, and Madeleine MacDonald. (Barcombe, England: Falmer Press, 1981), 229–56, and Rosemary Crompton and Stuart Reid, "The Deskilling of Clerical Work," in *The Degradation of Work?* ed. Stephen Wood, (London: Hutchinson, 1982), 163–78.

31. Murgatroyd, "Gender and Occupational Stratification," 591.

32. Ibid, 575.

33. Ibid, 588.

34. Ibid, 595.

35. Ibid, 581.

36. Barrett, *Women's Oppression Today,* 166–68. Barrett goes on to say here that the extent to which any job is seen as requiring a high level of skill is often dependent on the ability of the people who do it to have the power to establish that definition over competing ones.

37. Veronica Beechey, "The Sexual Division of Labour and the Labour Process: A Critical Assessment of Braverman," in *The Degradation of Work?* ed. Wood, 67. See also Margery Davies, *Women's Place Is at the Typewriter* (Philadelphia: Temple University Press, 1982).

38. Barry Bergen, "Only a Schoolmaster: Gender, Class, and the Effort to Professionalize Elementary Teaching in England, 1870–1910," *History of Education Quarterly* 22 (Spring 1982): 12.

39. Ibid.

40. Ibid, 5.

41. Myra Strober, "Segregation by Gender in Public School Teaching: Toward a General Theory of Occupational Segregation in the Labor Market," (Stanford University, 1982, manuscript), 16. Figures for the eastern cities of Canada are similar (though individual cities—such as Tor-

onto and Montreal—do differ, often for ethnic and religious reasons). See Marta Danylewycz and Alison Prentice, "Teachers, Gender, and Bureaucratizing School Systems in Nineteenth Century Montreal and Toronto," *History of Education Quarterly* 24 (Spring 1984): 75–100.

42. See, for example, Sheila Rothman, *Women's Proper Place* (New York: Basic Books, 1978), and Barrett, *Women's Oppression Today.* The role women were meant to play in upholding the religious and moral "fiber" of the nation should not go unnoticed here, as well. Native-born Protestant women were often recruited by the National Board of Popular Education to teach on, say, the American frontier to "redeem" the West. Many women themselves combined this vision with a clear sense both of economic necessity and of the possibilities of independence and adventure. These women were as a rule somewhat older than beginning teachers and were looking for both personal and professional autonomy in conjunction with their "moral mission." Attempts at controlling the religious and other content of the curriculum were also visible in these western schools. However, many of these woman teachers were successful in resisting such pressures on their teaching practices. See Polly Welts Kaufman, *Women Teachers on the Frontier* (New Haven: Yale University Press, 1984), especially Part 1.

43. John Richardson and Brenda Wooden Hatcher, "The Feminization of Public School Teaching, 1870–1920," *Work and Occupations* 10 (February 1983): 84. Following Douglas and others, Richardson and Hatcher also associate this with the relationship between middle-class women and religion.

44. Bergen, "Only a Schoolmaster," 13.

45. Ibid, 14.

46. Nancy Hoffman, *Women's "True" Profession: Voices from the History of Teaching* (Old Westbury, N.Y.: Feminist Press, 1981), xix. Conditions in Canada were very similar. See Danylewycz and Prentice," Teachers, Gender, and Bureaucratizing School Systems," 88.

47. Strober, "Segregation by Gender in Public School Teaching," 18. On the difficulties schools had in keeping male teachers, even in earlier periods, see Joan M. Jensen, "Not Only Ours but Others: Teaching Daughters of the Mid-Atlantic, 1790–1850," *History of Education Quarterly* 24 (Spring 1984): 3–19.

48. See the discussion in Frances Widdowson, *Going Up into the Next Class: Women and Elementary Teacher Training 1840–1914* (London: Hutchinson, 1983).

49. David Gordon, Richard Edwards, and Michael Reich, *Segmented Work, Divided Workers: The Historical Transformation of Labor in the United States* (New York: Cambridge University Press, 1982), 68. Many "native-born" women, however, fled the factories for other reasons. Not only had working conditions deteriorated, but a significant portion of these women preferred not to work alongside the immigrant women who were being hired to work in the mills. For further analysis of the changing conditions of women's labor and the tension between immigrant and native-born women workers, see Alice Kessler-Harris, *Out to Work: A History of Wage-Earning Women in the United States* (New York: Oxford University Press, 1982), 108–41.

50. Strober, "Segregation by Gender in Public School Teaching," 19. See also Keith E. Melder, "Mask of Oppression: The Female Seminary Movement in the United States," *New York History* 55 (July 1974): 261–79.

51. Strober, "Segregation by Gender in Public School Teaching," 19. This "willingness" often had *religious* roots. Thus, evangelical religious imperatives, and the history of protestant denominationalism, may have led to "moral" reasons for women to teach. See Joan Jacobs Brumberg, "The Feminization of Teaching: 'Romantic Sexism' and American Protestant Denominationalism," *History of Education Quarterly* 23 (Fall 1983): 383.

52. Lanford, quoted in Strober, "Segregation by Gender in Public School Teaching," 21.

53. Richardson and Hatcher, "The Feminization of Public School Teaching," 82.

54. Myra Strober and David Tyack, "Why Do Women Teach and Men Manage? A Report on Research on Schools," *Signs* 5 (Spring 1980): 499.

55. Ibid., 500. The authors also note that men made it to the top in school systems in part because of the advantages they had over women

in linking schools to the surrounding community. Maleness was an asset in meeting with the mostly male power structures of organizations such as Kiwanis and Lions clubs. This point was also made much earlier by Willard Elsbree in *The American Teacher* (New York: American Book Co., 1939), 555.

56. Hoffman, *Woman's "True" Profession,* xvii–xviii. For a general discussion of related points, see Keith E. Melder "Women's High Calling: The Teaching Profession in America, 1830–1860," *American Studies* 13 (Fall 1972): 19–32.

57. Angela V. John, Forward to Widdowson, *Going Up into the Next Class,* 9.

58. Ibid.

59. See, for example, Danylewycz and Prentice, "Teachers, Gender, and Bureaucratizing School Systems."

60. Richardson and Hatcher, "The Feminization of Public School Teaching," 87–88.

61. On the importance of thinking about the United States in class terms, see David Hogan, "Education and Class Formation: The Peculiarities of the Americans," in *Cultural and Economic Reproduction in Education: Essays on Class, Ideology, and the State,* ed. Michael W. Apple (Boston: Routledge & Kegan Paul, 1982), 32–78, and Erik Olin Wright, *Class, Crisis, and the State* (London: New Left Books, 1978). The most complete historical analysis to date of the class position of teachers is John Rury, "Who Became Teachers? The Social Characteristics of Teachers in American History," in *American Teachers,* ed. Warren, 9–48.

62. June Purvis, "Women and Teaching in the Nineteenth Century," in *Education and the State,* vol. 2, ed. Dale et al., 372. See also Widdowson, *Going Up into the Next Class.*

63. See the interesting and historical analysis of the place of socialist women here in Mari Jo Buhle, *Women and American Socialism, 1870–1920* (Urbana: University of Illinois Press, 1981).

64. Purvis, "Women and Teaching in the Nineteenth Century," 361–63. See also Rothman, *Women's Proper Place.* We should not assume that such educational and political struggles by middle-class

women meant that these gains simply reproduced a "safe liberalism" and bourgeois hegemony. For an argument that liberal discourse can be progressive at times, see Apple, *Education and Power* 123–125, and Herbert Gintis, "Communication and Politics," *Socialist Review* 10 (March–June 1980): 189–232.

65. Carl Degler, *At Odds: Women and the Family in America from the Revolution to the Present* (New York: Oxford University Press, 1980), 381.

66. Purvis, "Women and Teaching in the Nineteenth Century," 372. I stress *paid* teaching here, since Purvis also argues that middle- and upper-class women often worked as voluntary teachers in working-class literacy programs. Philanthropy and voluntary teaching could solve the problem brought about by the dominance of bourgeois ideals of femininity. A women *could* work, but only for the highest ideals and without remuneration.

67. Strober and Tyack, "Why Do Women Teach and Men Manage?" 496. See also Mary Roth Walsh, *Doctors Wanted, No Women Need Apply: Sexual Barriers in the Medical Profession, 1835–1975* (New Haven: Yale University Press, 1977). For England, see Jane Lewis, *The Politics of Motherhood* (London: Croom-Helm, 1980), and Sheila Rowbotham, *Hidden from History* (New York: Random House, 1974).

68. Sandra Acker, "Women and Teaching: A Semi-Detached Sociology of a Semi-Detached Profession," in *Gender, Class, and Education,* ed. Stephen Walker and Len Barton (Barcombe, England: Falmer Press, 1983), 134.

69. Degler, *At Odds,* 380. Paul Mattingly, as well, argues that by the 1890s even many normal schools had become almost exclusively female and had directed their attention to a "lower-class" student body. See Paul Mattingly, *The Classless Profession* (New York; New York University Press, 1975), 149. The significant portion of teachers who came from working-class families in Canada, as well, is documented in Danylewycz and Prentice, "Teachers, Gender, and Bureaucratizing School Systems," 91–93.

70. Interestingly enough, some believed that upper-middle-class young women were at an academic disadvantage to working-class young

women in teacher training institutions in England. See Widdowson, *Going Up into the Next Class.*

71. Purvis, "Women and Teaching in the Nineteenth Century," 364. Widdowson claims, however, that in general by the first decade of the twentieth century "the early education of the nation's children was predominantly in the hands of aspiring ladies recruited mainly from the lower-middle classes" (*Going Up into the Next Class,* 79). She also makes the interesting point that the ultimate entry of significant numbers of lower-middle-class young women into such positions contributed a good deal to the "professionalization" and increase in status of teaching.

72. Purvis, "Women and Teaching in the Nineteenth Century," 364.

73. Ibid, 366. For further discussion of the effect of such needlework on the women teachers of working-class girls, see the interesting treatment in Dina Copelman, "We Do Not Want to Turn Men and Women into Mere Toiling Machines: Teachers, Teaching, and the Taught" (Department of History, University of Missouri, Columbia, 1985, manuscript).

74. I wish to thank Rima D. Apple for this point.

75. Purvis, "Women and Teaching in the Nineteenth Century," 366.

76. Rothman, *Woman's Proper Place,* 58. For a discussion of how secondary schools grew as "training grounds" for preparing women for clerical work, see John L. Rury, "Vocationalism for Home and Work. Women's Education in the United States, 1880–1930," *History of Education Quarterly* 24 (Spring 1984): 21–44.

77. Purvis, "Women and Teaching in the Nineteenth Century," 367.

78. Ibid. See also William Edward Eaton, *The American Federation of Teachers, 1916–1961* (Carbondale: Southern Illinois University Press, 1975). The problem of a lack of connection between working-class parents and teachers in England is still a serious one. See, e.g., C.C.C.S. Ed-

ucation Group, *Unpopular Education: Schooling and Social Democracy in England Since 1944* (London: Hutchinson, 1981).

79. See Barrett, *Women's Oppression Today,* 187–226. See also her discussion of class differences in this section.

80. See Ann Marie Wolpe, "The Official Ideology of Education for Girls," in *Educability, Schools, and Ideology,* ed. Michael Flude and John Ahier (London: Halsted Press, 1974), 138–159.

81. Degler, *At Odds,* 413–14. Degler does point out, however, that the depression did not ultimately drive women out of the paid work force. Their rates of participation continued to increase. See p. 415. Similar policies were put into effect elsewhere as well. In New South Wales in Australia, married women were dismissed from their teaching jobs during the depression to protect men's positions. See R. W. Connell, *Teachers' Work* (Boston: George Allen & Unwin, 1985), 154.

82. Eaton, *The American Federation of Teachers,* 5–8. In his nicely written study of the history of teachers' organizations in the United States, Wayne Urban argues, however, that most of the members of these early teachers' organizations were significantly less radical than many of their leaders. Economic, not political, demands were more important for the bulk of the teachers. This, though, needs to be situated within the history of women's struggles over disparities in income, since in terms of this history economic issues may be less conservative than they seem at first glance. See Wayne J. Urban, *Why Teachers Organized* (Detroit: Wayne State University Press, 1982).

83. The leadership of the CFT believed that teachers might be lost in an amalgam of other unions and, to be taken seriously nationally, had to form their own national union. The attempt was first made in 1899 and again in 1902 by Haley and Goggin. The National Teachers Federation, an early precursor of the AFT, limited membership to grade school teachers, and while it did attract some national membership, it ultimately failed. See Eaton, *The American Federation of Teachers,* 10.

84. See Geraldine Clifford, "The Female Teacher and the Feminist Movement," University of California, Berkeley, 1981. Manuscript. Similar struggles occurred in Canada, as well. See, e.g., Danylewycz and Prentice, "Teachers, Gender, and Bureaucratizing School Systems," 93–94.

For England, see Copelman, "Mere Toiling Machines." Copelman has also analyzed the relationship between women teachers, feminism, and professional struggles in England in her interesting paper "The Politics of Professionalism: Women Teachers, 1904–1914," (University of Missouri, Department of History, Columbia, 1985, manuscript).

85. Craig Littler, "Deskilling and Changing Structures of Control," in *The Degradation of Work?* ed. Wood, 141. The importance of class as well as gender dynamics is made visible in Gerald Grace's argument that external control of teaching and curriculum by the state in England was lessened in the 1920s because of fears that a Labor government would use its power over teachers and curriculum to instill socialist ideas. Though Grace could have made more of gender issues, his points are provocative. See Gerald Grace, "Judging Teachers: The Social and Political Contexts of Teacher Evaluation," *British Journal of Sociology of Education* 6 (no. 1, 1985): 3–16.

4

PATHWAYS TO INSTITUTIONAL CHANGE: FROM THE DEANS' NETWORK TO THE HOLMES GROUP

Barbara Schneider and Stafford Hood

INTRODUCTION

Organizations have their own ideologies that become part of a collective historical tradition even when missions and operations shift from their initial purposes. Sometimes such organizations exist for relatively short periods of time but their cultural identities linger in the oral histories of their one-time members and in written documents. Such cultural histories are often obscured as the rhetoric of new organizations replaces the rhetoric of former ones. Yet these histories are important to understand, for they constitute a social resource that can profoundly shape the direction and activities of other groups that these one-time members may join. This chapter traces the organizational evolution of the Deans' Network, an association of school of education deans in research universities, and links its development with the formation of the Holmes Group, a consortium of education deans from major research universities in each of the fifty states dedicated to the improvement of teacher education (Holmes Group, 1986).

For over twenty-five years, twenty-one deans of schools of education in research universities participated in an initially informal, and later formal, organization referred to as the "Deans' Network." Formally constituted in 1974, this group was specifically designed to help schools and colleges of education make sustained and effective efforts to improve the quality of their undergraduate and graduate programs and faculties (Deans' Network 1974). Reviewing the formation and dissolution of the network is especially useful in understanding the challenges facing newer, comparable organizations such as the Holmes Group. Linking the network with the Holmes Group has special relevance, as some have perceived the Holmes Group to be an extension of the Deans' Network (Meade 1984).

Concern with the quality of education in the United States has a deep and lengthy history among education leaders in universities. From the early beginnings of schools of education in research universities, deans have sought to improve the quality of their teacher education programs (Powell 1976). While their views and enthusiasm sometimes have not been shared by their faculties or embraced by policymakers (Clifford and Guthrie 1988; Powell 1976; Schneider 1987), many deans have formed or joined organizations that have as their aim the reform and improvement of teacher education (AACTE 1948; Hemsing 1970; Deans' Network 1974; Holmes Group 1986).

Explanations for the successes or failures of the deans' efforts have received little attention. One reason for this may be that in many research universities, in comparison to other types of institutions such as doctorate-granting or comprehensive universities, the control over program and student requirements for admission, advancement, and graduation rests with the faculty (Bowen and Schuster 1986; Kenen and Kenen 1978). Deans are frequently seen as the administrative leaders of their schools or colleges, primarily responsible for finances rather than programs. Furthermore, the capacity of deans of schools and colleges of education to articulate and implement a reform agenda is considerably limited, in stark contrast to the power of the social structure both within and outside universities to mobilize resources toward defining what educational issues are of importance and require immediate action (Popkewitz 1991).

The Deans' Network was an attempt by a group of deans to move forward an agenda to improve the quality of graduate programs in schools of education. Some of the deans' efforts were achieved within the organization, while others were not. The mark of the network's success can perhaps best be seen through the work of other organizations that have championed some of the network's initial ideas and reforms. But just as some of the deans' recommendations continue to be carried on, so have some of the same organizational problems that contributed to the end of the network. Our inquiry examines the social interactions among these leaders and their relationships with groups outside and within their institutions in order to gain an understanding of the obstacles deans face in bringing about educational change through similar organizations. This analysis has particular relevance in light of recent controversies surrounding how to reform teacher education (Goodlad 1990; Holmes Group 1986).

The data for this analysis originate from a series of interviews, letters, memos, and reports written by deans and faculty in schools of education in research universities during the 1970s and early 1980s. Several of the memos and position papers had limited circulation, although many of the concepts and strategies for current reforms in teacher education can be traced to these original documents. Consequently, we have deliberately included many of these materials as examples.

TRANSFORMING AN INFORMAL GROUP INTO
A FORMAL ORGANIZATION

Deans of schools of education in research universities prior to 1974 had no formal networking organization other than the American Association of Colleges for Teacher Education (AACTE), which had as its major activity the creation of standards for teacher education (AACTE 1948). The AACTE, concerned with issues of educational quality, had at this time a membership of nearly nine hundred institutions, many of which were small undergraduate colleges with limited interest in pursuing a research agenda in education (Hemsing 1970). In addition to the AACTE, some schools of education in research universities also belonged to the National Association of State Universities and Land Grant Colleges, whose membership principally consisted of the leading public universities in the fifty states. But as with the AACTE, the membership included institutions with varying degrees of commitment to research (Bailey 1975).

Beginning in the early 1960s, the deans from the Big Ten universities (i.e., Indiana University, Michigan State University, Northwestern University, Ohio State University, Purdue University, the University of Illinois, the University of Iowa, the University of Michigan, the University of Minnesota, and the University of Wisconsin, Madison) would informally meet at the annual meeting of the AACTE to share both professional and personal information. Neither incandescent nor revolutionary, these informal sessions were used to exchange information on potential faculty hires, the state of the deanship at each institution, and the degree to which the interests of their respective institutions were being protected in the AACTE and other major organizations (Chandler 1978).

There are several important characteristics of this informal network that need to be underscored. First, these males, nearly all about the same age, race, and ethnicity, shared for the most part a common professional history; they had received their doctorate degrees in schools of education in the Midwest, and many had experience as public school administrators (1984). Second, many of the deans were personal friends who frequently telephoned each other and saw each other socially. These friendship ties solidified the group and helped to reinforce a common view and understanding of the purposes of education. Third, institutional rivalry was focused on athletics rather than questions of educational quality. Nearly all of the deans could point to various reputational quality surveys (Cartter 1966; Roose and Andersen 1970) to demonstrate that their schools or colleges of education were among the best in the country.

At the same time that the Big Ten institutions were meeting, their geographical sisters, the Big Eight (Iowa State University, Kansas State University, Oklahoma State University, the University of Colorado, the University of Kansas, the University of Missouri, the University of Nebraska, and the University of Oklahoma) were also holding independent informal gatherings. The Big Eight meetings were similar in content to the big ten meetings, and their deans exhibited many of the same demographic characteristics as their Big Ten counterparts. Friendships existed among the deans from both the Big Ten and the Big Eight institutions, and although there was some posturing over which was the more "prestigious" group, relationships were fairly amicable (Chandler 1978).

In 1973, the United States Office of Education sponsored a national effort, Project Open, to bring together people of similar role positions to identify common problems in education. Led by the reputedly vitriolic, ardent civil-rightist, B. J. Chandler, who at that time was dean of the School of Education at Northwestern University, a team of several of the Big Eight and Big Ten deans was assembled to respond to this initiative. Their efforts were successful, and with the support of Project Open, a coordinator was employed to convene the deans and associate deans of education from both the Big Eight and the Big Ten institutions for a series of formal meetings. The goals of these meetings were to identify concerns, share information, establish a communication network, and provide opportunities for follow-up activities on specific topics (Deans' Network 1974).

Conceivably there are several explanations as to why these two groups of deans were willing to interact on a more sustained, formal basis. First, the demographic characteristics of schools of education had begun to change significantly. The steady decline in undergraduate preservice enrollments in the early 1970s placed new constraints on faculty hires. Rising tuition at research universities made many schools of education less financially attractive to students than other types of institutions where undergraduate and graduate degrees could be obtained for a third of the cost of the more prestigious ones. Second, opportunities to compete for external grants and contracts were also restricted as foundations and state and federal governments began "tightening their belts" as the recession of the early 1970s cut deeply into their revenues. The loss of external research and training support placed new pressures on many school of education budgets, which already were compressed as a result of declining enrollments. For some schools of education, institutional collaboration was a key to stability and, in some more extreme cases, survival (Schneider et. al 1984).

FORMULATING THE NETWORK AGENDA: EMPHASIS ON CONTINUING EDUCATION

During the initial funding year, the deans identified two major objectives: (1) to institute mechanisms for the continuous renewal and development of school of education faculty; and (2) to improve the university role in programs for the continuing education of teachers and administrators in elementary and secondary schools (Deans' Network 1974). These topics grew from mutual concerns of nearly all the deans. A majority of the schools of education had sizable proportions of tenured, middle-aged faculty whose areas of research expertise were regarded as outmoded and nonproductive. "Retooling" such faculty by encouraging them to either enter new fields or take early retirement was a priority of many of the deans. On the practitioner side, continued expansion of comprehensive universities into the training and in-service market was severely curtailing the pool of new undergraduate and graduate students as well as opportunities to provide consultative services. It would be simplistic, however, to characterize the interest of the deans as purely monetary for there was a strong conviction among them that increasing fragmentation and irrelevance of much educational research especially in teacher education was gradually eroding its policy relevance. This perspective was articulated at this time in the Deans' network mission statement:

> ... the continued linkage between the theoretical/concep-
> tual base in education and the practice of education: i.e.,
> application of theory in educational institutions. The key
> elements in this theme are the production, dissemination,
> and use of knowledge in the areas of preparation and con-
> tinued development of professional educators. (Deans'
> Network 1974).

The aim of the network to form a closer alliance with the field
dominated the conversations of the informal deans' group and remained
a familiar topic throughout the network's brief existence. This initial focus on the need to form tighter relationships between the university and
the field invoked similar language that currently characterizes much of
the discussion in the Holmes Group (1986, 1990) documents.

From the deans' perspective, many faculty who published extensively in scholarly journals, viewed their role in relation to the field of
education as that of knowledge producers and expected others to translate their abstract ideas and concepts into practice. Professors who were
directly engaged with schools were seen as nonscholarly, second-rate
colleagues. In the university social structure, education as a field had traditionally been, and continued to be, regarded as having low intellectual
status compared to other social science disciplines. The nature of work
conducted in education was oftentimes seen as "not real science," and
faculty who openly worked with the schools were often regarded as further degrading the "intellectual" core of the field. Such values, according
to the deans, were seriously undermining the potential for improving the
quality of education.

> Universities operate from a tradition and social structure that
> provides reward and sanction largely on an individual basis.
> The traditional concept of linear, one-way knowledge produc-
> tion and use through research, development, dissemination,
> and application is proving inadequate in education. The no-
> tion that knowledge production flows naturally from re-
> search institutions through development systems to practical
> users is simply unreal and detrimental in the field of educa-
> tion. (Deans' Network 1974).

Thus the challenge to the deans was to construct a "multidirectional collaborative process involving scholars, practitioners, administrators, and linking agents" (Deans' Network 1974). The deans recognized

that to orchestrate such changes would require not only more communication and interaction with the field, but also socializing faculty and other university administrators in the value of such exchanges (Deans' Network 1974).

An analogous argument is made by the Holmes Group:

> First, as an institutional change effort, Holmes universities must work out new agreements and arrangements among a large cast that includes faculty and administrators in the arts and sciences and in the schools of education, K–12 school faculties, administrators, and their organizations, and public representatives at state and district levels. (Holmes Group 1989)

As with the Deans' Network, the Holmes Group deans claimed that such changes can be brought about not only by forming "new agreements and arrangements" but by "challenging deeply held beliefs and traditions . . . that violate conceptions of self-interest" (Holmes Group 1989).

The second objective of the Deans' Network, that is, the improvement of the university role in the continuing professional development of teachers and administrators in elementary and secondary schools, was operationally conceived as developing a collaborative relationship with teachers and administrators in school systems. Some of the activities planned to achieve this objective were a case study to develop knowledge and information on successful and failed attempts to collaborate with field professionals, on-site visits to model programs, discussions of techniques and instruments, and descriptions of effective delivery systems. Furthermore, the deans envisioned regional meetings that would bring together deans and faculty of schools of education, university administrators, school superintendents, state education personnel, teacher leaders, and state and local policymakers, for the explicit purpose of forging cooperative relationships between themselves and other groups and identifying potential barriers.

After a year of operation under Project Open, the deans decided to continue their relationship. To this end, the Deans' Network submitted a proposal to the W. K. Kellogg Foundation. The proposal outlined a series of activities that were directed at supporting programs for continuing education of university and school personnel, creating staff development projects for university faculty, sharing resources, disseminating information, and increasing knowledge productivity among faculties of colleges of education (Deans' Network 1978).

FORMALIZING THE DEANS' NETWORK

In 1975, the W. K. Kellogg Foundation approved a thirty-six-month grant of $148,980 to the Deans' Network. The members of this group included deans from the Big Eight and Big Ten universities and the University of Chicago, the University of Illinois, Chicago, and the University of Wisconsin, Milwaukee. Each member institution was expected to contribute $450 per year for membership dues and provide in-kind contributions of faculty time and travel for various network activities. A permanent full-time director and support staff were appointed. Thus, the informal "social clubs" of the Big Eight and Big Ten schools and colleges of education of the 1960s and early 1970s formally became the Deans' Network.

Increasing external support and in-kind contributions from participating institutions provided the resources for the network to greatly expand its activities from the Project Open year. Briefly, the network decided to embark on three efforts: (1) to stimulate collaborative research activities among faculty in network institutions; (2) to improve the university role in the continuing professional development of teachers and administrators in elementary and secondary schools; and (3) to engage in cooperative staff development activities. In addition to these initiatives, the network also distributed an issues-paper series, provided a national education legislation information service, developed alternative models for university program reviews, and organized four regional conferences on continuing and bilingual and multicultural education, resource management in times of fiscal constraint, and the impact of handicapped legislation on teacher preparation programs. (These activities are described in detail in Deans' Network 1978.)

Examining the accomplishments of the Deans' Network under the W. K. Kellogg grant, one is immediately struck by the limited number of activities directed at improving relations between the university and elementary and secondary schools. Promoting collaborative research projects, organizing and holding research conferences, workshops, and seminars, and creating a research presence among national policymakers were the types of projects that attracted the participation of the deans and faculty. Regardless of the rhetoric, issues related to teacher education and professional development of school personnel remained a low priority.

At the close of the grant period, the Deans' Network voted unanimously to continue the organization. One major change was to broaden the membership to include additional schools and colleges of education in public and private universities with research missions outside the Midwest. The purpose of the expansion was to develop a small, select, national organization that would assume a leadership position for research and development from an academic institutional base. To meet this objective, the deans decided to use as a criterion for membership that the school or college of education be housed in a university that belonged to the Association of American Universities (AAU), a small, elitist organization that represents universities with strong programs of graduate and professional education and research.

Even with an expanded membership, many of the deans believed that the network would still be small enough to continue with its original goals. Invitations were sent to the twenty or so institutions.[1] The first meeting of the expanded network was held in October 1979 in Boston.

At the time the network decided to increase its membership, another organization was being formed. A small group of deans representing universities from around the country met a dozen or so times over the course of several years to address how deans could increase the capacity of schools of education to further inquiry and scholarship associated with the process of education (Tucker 1981; Gideonse and Koff 1982). Called the "Salishan Deans" (after the lodge in Oregon where they first met), this group of twelve or more deans, half of which were Deans' Network members, sought to examine the intellectual underpinnings of teacher education (Gideonse and Koff 1982).[2] The formation of the Salishan Deans is noteworthy in relation to the Deans' Network history, for it tried to pull together an even smaller group of quite different types of institutions to pursue a theoretical issue. Although organized for an even shorter time than the Deans' Network, the Salishan Deans group was significant because it symbolized to some extent the interest and seriousness with which educational leaders were addressing the role of universities in improving professional training in education.

PROGRAMMATIC INTERESTS OF THE BROADENED NETWORK

The expanded Deans' Network strove to separate itself both organizationally and ideologically from other associations such as the AACTE. The deans deliberately planned a relatively modest governance arrangement unencumbered by a complex administrative structure. An elected dean was to act as the chair of a five-member executive committee that developed the agenda for the year's activities, approved in turn by the full membership at biannual meetings.

The underlying purpose of this governance structure was to create an organization that could be marshaled effectively to advocate on behalf of schools of education in research universities. This is perhaps best exemplified by the network's revised agenda, which limited the operation of the group to two major initiatives: (1) an empirical study of the quality of the doctorate in education, and (2) an examination of the role of teacher education in research institutions. Here again, we find that only activities with a strong research focus were considered legitimate. Both of these efforts were designed to form a wedge between the network and other schools of education located in universities and colleges without a research mission. The study of the doctorate, for example, stemmed from the suspicion among the deans that the quality of graduate training throughout the United States was of varying quality. The deans assumed that if among their institutions there was considerable variation, then in institutions where research was less of a priority, standards were certainly being compromised.

Funded by the Ford Foundation, the study "The Quality of the Doctorate" (see Schneider et al. 1985) was designed to provide a comprehensive knowledge base that would assist university administrators, faculty, students, and educational policymakers in determining standards for assessing the quality of graduate programs in education. The study attempted to identify valid descriptors of program quality, exemplary quality programs, and characteristics these programs shared. The design of the study included interviews with forty-two deans of schools of education, thirty-two on-site visits to schools of education, and surveys of 1,410 faculty and 1,438 students and alumni.

Results indicated that the strong culture of the research tradition among these institutions was clearly evident in degree structures, faculty reward systems, program requirements, and student employment aspirations. However, the opportunities to conduct research were found to be unevenly distributed among faculty in various specializations. Scholarship in the field of education, which was closely aligned to traditional social science disciplines, such as psychology and history, was more highly regarded than other specializations, particularly teacher education. Even though research was highly valued, few graduate students actually engaged in such activities as data collection or analysis, other than through the dissertation experience. (The rationale, conduct, and results of this study can be found in Schneider et. al. 1985.)

ROLE AND FUNCTION OF UNDERGRADUATE
TEACHER EDUCATION

The second initiative was charged with inquiring into the relationships that exist between undergraduate teacher education programs and other research efforts, such as establishing research centers, that customarily take place in universities that place a high value on research and scholarship. The serious economic conditions facing many universities had raised several questions regarding the place, role, and function of teacher education programs in major research institutions. It was suspected that as universities continued to face more stringent resource problems, inevitably, support for and the place of undergraduate teacher education programs would be brought into question. The ultimate aim of this effort was to specify the reasons for continuing teacher training programs in major universities and to resolve some of the conflicts, problems, and issues surrounding and affecting such programs (Gardner et al. 1980).

The sentiment among many of the deans was that in the types of institutions they represented, teacher education programs should be of the highest quality, attracting the very best students and faculty. Most of the deans suspected that this was not the case, although no empirical evidence existed to support or disconfirm these suspicions. To gain a more complete understanding of the state of teacher education in research universities, the deans agreed to begin a series of studies related to teacher education programs.

In the spring of 1980, a committee of deans from Ohio State University, the University of Texas, Michigan State University, the University of Wisconsin, the University of Illinois, Northwestern University, and the University of Michigan began working on these issues. Their first task was to ferret out some of the inherent problems of teacher education in research universities. After considerable discussion, five conflictual areas of "discontinuity" were identified:

> 1) The claim is frequently made that faculty who teach in the undergraduate programs become (or are to begin with) second class citizens doing important (meat and potatoes) work of the institution but standing behind the "graduate" faculty when rewards are distributed.

> 2) Virtually all of the research and development capacity in education exists in major universities, yet very little is used to address the problems related to the process of teacher ed-

ucation.... If this is ... true, it would seem that there is no
need for a college of education to have undergraduate programs for research purposes.

3) Increasing control by state governments and increasing
influence of teachers' organizations on teacher education
programs have narrowed the latitude available to institutions
to create different kinds of programs and have served to make
all programs very much the same in the last analysis. If so,
there can be no valid claim for uniqueness of product.

4) Nearly all land grant institutions have a mission statement which includes or accepts the training of teachers as important. However, most states have developed a set of
regional institutions which have teacher education missions
at their core. This development raises substantial questions as
to whether the mission statement of the land grant institution
is still as powerful and potent as it once was.

5) Lacking a knowledge base to inform and to define practice in the field, teaching is not a profession in the usual sense
of the word. Nor is there any apparent movement toward the
development of teaching as a profession. If universities are
places which include liberal arts programs and professional
programs, teacher education appears misplaced. (Gardner et
al. 1980)

To address these concerns, the deans organized four study groups
around the following themes: (1) the characteristics of teacher education departments in research and development universities; (2) the
goals, career patterns, relationships, and interactions among these faculty members; (3) the problems of elementary and secondary teaching
and how they relate to teacher education programs; and (4) the association between research and development centers in universities and
teacher education departments (Gardner et al. 1980).

STATUS OF TEACHER EDUCATION
IN NETWORK INSTITUTIONS

One of the study groups attempted to describe salient variables that portrayed the status of teacher education in Deans' Network institutions.
Among the network institutions, thirty-eight had teacher education
programs; five of these had teacher training programs that did not include elementary education. The committee designed and undertook a

mail survey to the thirty-three deans in those institutions with elementary and secondary teacher education programs, thirty-one of whom responded. The content of this instrument focused on student admissions standards, characteristics of the faculty, and advantages and disadvantages of teacher education programs in universities with research missions.

With respect to student admissions, the study group found that "intellective measures such as SAT scores of students admitted to elementary education programs remained the same as in prior years or increased" (Raths 1981, 1). This result seemed inconsistent with research at the time that clearly indicated a decline in the SAT scores of students who intended to pursue education as a major in college. The committee suspected that some of the deans had misinterpreted the question and had not taken into account these traditional indicators of student quality.

In evaluating the characteristics of the faculty, the deans overwhelmingly responded that the research productivity of their faculty was about the same or slightly lower than faculty in other programs. Deans in twenty-nine out of thirty-one institutions reported that graduate assistants taught undergraduate courses in the professional education sequence and, in all but one institution, also assisted in the supervision of student teachers; faculty members retained primary responsibility for supervising student teachers.

As for the impact of research and development on teacher education, the answers from the survey were not reassuring with respect to exposure to research opportunities. The most frequent experience students had with research during their teacher preparation period was limited to "methods of instruction," and for 80 percent of the students this practice occurred only several times in a single course. Slightly fewer responses indicated that students had been involved in research projects that examined the evaluation of curricular materials in teacher education. Overall, in fewer than half the institutions were students given opportunities to participate in research activities other than those directed at the process of becoming a teacher (Raths 1981).

When asked what recently adopted innovations in the elementary teacher education program might be attributed to the influence of researchers located in the college or school, the majority of deans pointed to the work of several key individuals in their institutions as being particularly influential in restructuring teacher education programs. According to the deans, faculty research activities had changed the curriculum of five special education programs, four science education courses, four professional seminars, four learning courses, and one new computerized testing program. Citing the work of several researchers outside their institutions, seven deans reported that they were redesigning their teacher education programs to make them longer, more intensive, and more directly linked to research. Five deans commented that the presence of researchers had no effect on their programs. However, these individuals were in the minority.

Two-thirds of the deans saw clear advantages to their elementary teacher education programs as a result of their affiliation with universities heavily committed research and development activities. Benefits were predominantly perceived as making the faculty more up-to-date in their fields of interest and in giving students an enriched educational experience. This is perhaps most illustrative in the comments of one dean who states: "The research and development environment primarily creates a better climate for change and staying at the forefront of knowledge production. It is not just research and development in education that makes this so, but the ethos of the entire university which encourages a strong content orientation for students" (Raths 1981, 15).

The disadvantages were also interesting, yet not unexpected. One dean reported, "The disadvantages are the typical ones reported in institutions like this one. They have to do with institutional priority setting in which undergraduate teaching is not invested with the same value as graduate teaching and research (Raths 1981, 15). This issue of "rewards" for working in teacher education elicited a number of comments. One dean stated that the "reward system emphasizes research/scholarship at the expense of intensive teaching" (Raths 1981, 15). Another commented, "Due in part to faculty reward structure at most research and development institutions, the faculty engaged in research tend to be disinterested in undergraduate students and courses, hence much instructional responsibility falls to graduate students who are pre-occupied with their own work. Instructors tend to over-emphasize theory and research and under-emphasize its relation to practice (Raths 1981, 15). And from another dean, "University promotion and tenure committees have high research expectations while our teacher education faculty have heavy teaching and service loads" (Raths 1981, 15).

Another problem identified by a dean but not related to the reward structure concerned the intrusion of research in "the education of the students." The dean maintained that the major difficulty with education as a field is that "the students themselves become objects of research" (Raths 1981, 15).

In summary, this work group came back to the organization with a clear message that there are major advantages for faculty in universities with strong commitments to research. However, the findings continued to demonstrate, as in the "Quality of the Doctorate" study (Schneider 1987), that faculty attached to teacher education departments suffer major professional liabilities. While a mission to engage in professional education may be present, the reward structure and attitudes of other faculty make teacher education an undesirable field.

RELATIONSHIP OF RESEARCH TO TEACHER EDUCATION PROGRAMS

The other study group to produce written work sought to examine (1) how research activities and teacher education programs within the same institution affect the scholarship of faculty within and outside teacher education departments; and (2) how faculty in other fields work cooperatively with teacher education staff and programs. This group also surveyed the members, but responses were considerably fewer than those received by the other group (Palmer 1980). Only six institutions (15.8 percent) responded, two of which had organized research and development centers funded by the National Institute of Education. Responses appeared thoughtful and detailed (Palmer 1980) and in some ways directly related to efforts later initiated by the Holmes Group.

A healthy relationship between teaching and research was purported to exist among faculty who work in this area. Use of research results appeared to be pervasive in the development of curriculum for preservice and graduate education courses, whereas the service mission seemed neglected and devalued. There seemed to be little indication that in-service teacher education was being initiated by the university.

These results may have prompted the authors to conclude that faculty in teacher education should be more deeply involved in elementary and secondary schools first-hand, so that they can keep abreast of the needs of such schools (Palmer 1980). Futhermore, the group suggested that commercial publication of research results and development of teacher guides, instructional materials, and in-service material may not be the "most rapid and efficacious means of bringing new knowledge to the schools." Teacher education departments should identify more appropriate mechanisms for keeping schools informed of developments on the leading edge of new knowledge, and of means for dissemination of knowledge (Palmer 1980).

Focusing on the substance of publications commonly produced by teacher education faculty, the study group supported the position that teacher educators were deeply concerned to make the results of their research useful in improving their teaching. This desire, in fact, seemed to be the driving force for their scholarly productivity. The study group concluded that while much of the research and development output apparently never appears in refereed journals, it does find its way into technical reports, books, and classrooms. The long-term benefits of these products formed the basis for "changed collegiate curricula, courses, and the environment for instruction" (Palmer 1980).

On a totally different topic, but not unrelated to the Holmes Group proposal for a "professional school," several deans responding to the survey expressed dissatisfaction with the fit between current teacher training programs and the pedagogical demands of the "typical American classroom." Many of the Deans' Network universities at one time had laboratory schools that served as exemplars of teaching practices. While several were now closed for reasons of fiscal exigency, a small number still remained operational. However, the school context in which such exemplary teacher training models exist often bears little resemblance to disadvantaged urban schools where many new teachers are given their first regular positions. If model training schools were to be kept operational, they should expose student teachers to a wider range of classroom situations.

In evaluating the reports of the study groups, a growing sense of uneasiness began to surface among the deans concerning the nature of their teacher education programs. It was clear that teacher education among the network institutions needed a distinctive mission, purposeful activities, and enforceable quality standards. The question was whether the network, which had never functioned like the regulatory body of the AACTE, could act as a standards and accrediting organization. The answer turned out to be no.

DISSOLUTION OF THE DEANS' NETWORK

One can examine the end of an organization and point to several reasons for its termination. In the case of the Deans' Network, a set of interlinking circumstances contributed to its discontinuation. The first, was lack of leadership. In the network's beginning stages it had the benefit of charismatic leaders who had a vision of education and who were willing to take risks, challenge the positions of educational leaders, and create a platform from which deans from schools of education in research universities could command the attention of federal and state policymakers. By the early 1980s, there were no individuals willing to take such a leadership position.

A second issue was research legitimacy. What brought the organization together was a collective institutional focus on research, as well as the prestige of the universities in which the schools and colleges of education were housed. This institutional elitism provoked some nonmember deans to question whether the research being conducted in their schools and colleges was any less valuable than that occurring in the network institutions. Moreover, some deans within the organization, as well as those outside, questioned if indeed network members represented the "premiere" institutions in their states or the country.

Nationwide, strong interest was emerging in building the research capability of all major schools and colleges of education. Presidential blue-ribbon committees and commissions were bringing educational research and its policy implications into the limelight. Scholarly and development activities were increasingly seen as central to nearly all universities, regardless of their overall commitment to research. Furthermore, some institutions were making considerable resource allocations to their schools of education for the explicit purposes of expanding their research capabilities in the area of education. Identifying schools of education as potential network members using the AAU list seemed inconsistent with the actual research commitments and productivity occurring in many colleges and schools of education whose institutions were not AAU members.

Thus, an organization constructed on the basis of a hierarchical institutional ranking that clearly separated institutions on the basis of their research productivity (often measured in dollars and publications) could not derive legitimacy in the context of the general field of education. The initial criteria for restricted membership based on a defined research eligibility requirement was proving itself to be politically divisive and unpalatable to both members and nonmembers.

Third, external economic support for research was becoming more difficult to obtain. Institutional competition, spurred in part by increasingly intensive federal research center competitions and scarcity of research and development funds from public and private sources, signaled that collaborative efforts among two or three institutions might be more economically efficient than larger ones. With smaller collaborative projects, more dollars could be generated through indirect overhead rates, which would then flow directly back to the schools and colleges. In contrast, wide-scale collaborative initiatives were likely to produce fewer dollars for each institution. In addition to the lack of economic resources, the social and political benefits derived from such large collaborative efforts also seemed unclear. Thus, small collaborative efforts

targeted at mutual interests among a relatively limited number of institutions seemed especially attractive. Sustaining a large collaborative organization like the Deans' Network seemed fiscally and politically
incompatible with these smaller efforts.

Fourth, the agenda that initially drew the institutions together was
completed. The deans had an empirical data base demonstrating that the
quality of doctoral training was similar across institutions. The larger
problem—how to improve the quality of teacher education in research
universities—proved to be an agenda item far more complex than other
efforts undertaken by the network. The configuration of the network
lacked the institutional support and social resources required to carry
out such an endeavor. A different type of organization was needed to undertake such a mission, one with an ideological agenda that could serve
not only elitist institutions but the field of education more generally. And
to that end, Judith Lanier, who at the time was dean of the College of
Education at Michigan State University, and several other network deans
helped to establish a new organization.

CREATION OF HOLMES GROUP

In many respects, the Deans' Network laid a foundation for continued
efforts under the rubric of the Holmes Group to address reforms in
teacher education. First, the network made substantial progress in spec-
ifying many of the problems in current teacher education programs in
universities with research and development missions. Second, the structure of the network could be viewed as an organizational prototype for
creating a consortium built on an ideological vision. Third, the network
brought together a group of strong deans to work constructively on issues underlying teacher education. Many of the deans in the network
formed the initial core members of the Holmes Group. Thus, the Holmes
Group began with considerable intellectual and social resources.

The issues of developing teaching as a profession and the redesign
of teacher education programs are both addressed in the reform agenda
of the Holmes Group (1986, 1990). The first major report produced by
the Holmes Group, *Tomorrow's Teachers* (1986), calls for more rigorous
standards in entry to and exit from teacher preparation programs and an
examination of the relevance and quality of the curriculum and clinical
experiences in these programs. The main features of the initial Holmes
Group proposal include an increased period of teacher training, differentiated staffing, and more preparation in subject matter content and
pedagogy (Sedlack 1987; Gordon 1988). The first report was severely

criticized by African-American teacher educators and researchers, as insensitive to the problems of preparing teachers for schools with a substantial number of educationally disadvantaged students. The second report, *Tomorrow's Schools* (1990), responded to the critics by advocating the concept of a professional development school model. The model includes both intensive clinical experiences and collaboration between teacher education programs and public schools.

If we refer back to the Deans' Network task force reports, we can see some of the underpinnings of these recommendations. For example, the study group reports indicated that in-service and research activities in network institutions had a minimal impact on practices in elementary and secondary schools. Therefore, it was suggested that the interactions between teacher education faculty and the practitioners be increased so that university faculty could become more deeply involved with the field. The professional development school model proposed by the Holmes Group is an attempt to address this concern. In this manner, the Deans' Network study of teacher education programs may have provided initial prototypes for addressing the concerns of schools and colleges of education at research institutions.

However, the larger contribution of the Deans' Network to the creation of the Holmes Group may have come from the intellectual capital that was present in the network and moved on to the Holmes Group. The first discussion for the creation of the Holmes Group was reported to have been held in the fall of 1983 at the Johnson Foundation's Wingspread Conference Center (Sedlack 1987). Seventeen deans from research schools and colleges of education met to discuss "alternative ways of involving the major research universities in an effort to enhance the quality of teacher education" (Holmes Group 1986, 71). A review of the Holmes Group's executive board membership list in 1986 reveals that eight of the fourteen institutions that were represented on this board had been members of the Deans' Network. Additionally, of the thirty-five deans reported as "participants in the development of the reform agenda" for the Holmes Group, twenty-five represented institutions that had been members of the Deans' Network. Indeed, most of the twenty-five deans had been members of the network. Thus, the Holmes Group collectively was formed by a majority of Deans' Network members. Equally important was the fact that those Deans' Network members (Judith Lanier, John Palmer, and William Gardner) who had been at the forefront of the network's studies on teacher education were ready to get the Holmes Group "off and running." Furthermore, the selection of Judith Lanier as president of the Holmes Group proved to have special significance.

From their beginnings, the Deans' Network and the Holmes Group were criticized for both their elitism and their minimal production of teacher education graduates. Teacher education programs at major research institutions produced such a small percentage of teacher education graduates that the question of the seriousness of their commitment to train teachers naturally arose. Neither the Deans' Network nor the Holmes Group provided any indication that they were in any way responsible for preparing more minorities to enter the teaching profession. The Deans' Network never addressed this issue, while the Holmes Group limited its discussion of this issue to two paragraphs in *Tomorrow's Teachers* and virtually excluded historically black colleges from the Holmes Group guest list. Both the Deans' Network and the Holmes Group made it clear that only major research universities would be invited to be members. Only subsequently were a few historically black colleges and universities invited to join the Holmes Group.

The charges of elitism and lack of credibility in the training and production of teachers made the acceptance of the Holmes Group objectives, like those of the network, problematic. Michigan State University had a commendable reputation in teacher training and was also considered to have a more applied, and hence less elitist, stance when contrasted with many of the Deans' Network and other Holmes Group members. Thus Michigan State University was in a position to elicit support from institutions not in the club. It was also important for the Holmes Group institutional base to be connected with a university with an established history of support for its teacher education programs. Combining Michigan State's institutional support and ability to draw a diverse membership, the Holmes Group became a more credible and marketable entity for government and foundation support, which were essential for its survival.

LINKAGES BETWEEN THE HOLMES GROUP
AND THE DEANS' NETWORK

The Holmes Group continues to face major challenges that will determine its ability to carry out its reform agenda and ultimately survive. These challenges include (1) holding the consortium together around the Holmes Group's articulated ideology; (2) addressing the multiplicity of needs and concerns of non-research-oriented institutions (particularly historically black colleges and universities); (3) raising the status of teacher education programs; and (4) establishing grassroots support among public schools. Some of these issues were also addressed by the Deans' Network, with limited success.

One of the major differences between the Deans' Network and the Holmes Group is the foundations upon which they were created. The initial members of the network were all white males who had been friends and colleagues and shared common histories as graduates of midwestern research universities (Denny and Hood 1984). These friendships created close social ties among the members that greatly facilitated communication and consensual decision making on various topics.

On the other hand, the members of the Holmes Group do not share a common history and were brought together to refine and implement an ideological agenda. Therefore, it is not surprising that consensus on many issues has not been easy to achieve. Goodlad (1990) reported that "after a most auspicious beginning and then substantial expansion in membership [the Holmes Group] began to have difficulty agreeing on the specifics of an agenda for their internal restructuring of teacher education" (146). Similarly, one of the Holmes Group deans reported that he and seven other deans opposed the elimination of undergraduate teacher education programs, and speculated that issues of content and strategies in the teacher education curriculum were not addressed in *Tomorrow's Teachers* because achieving consensus was "extremely difficult" (Tom 1987). In view of the large membership of the Holmes Group and its creation around an ideology not fully shared by its members, it is quite possible that some of the tougher issues facing the restructuring of teacher education programs will remain unattended to.

The necessity for the Holmes Group to be more responsive to the needs and interests of non-research-oriented institutions and institutions with large minority enrollments remains a critical issue. The Holmes Group was severely criticized for being elitist in limiting its membership to large research universities and ignoring the implications its reform agenda would have on the preparation of minority teachers (Dilworth 1988; Gordon 1988; Wilson 1988). Consequently, concern has been expressed by outside critics over the recommendations made by the Holmes Group for the recruitment and production of minority teachers and the quality of teacher preparation programs at historically black colleges and universities (Gordon 1988; Smith 1988).

By 1988, ninety-six institutions had agreed to work toward the implementation of the Holmes principles. Of this number, only one historically black institution (Howard University) was invited to join the Holmes Group. The exclusion of teacher preparation programs housed at institutions viewed as less prestigious supported the notion of elitism.

At the same time this action implied that those teacher education programs preparing a disproportionate share of minority teachers (historically black institutions) were not welcome. Recently the Holmes Group has been making considerable efforts to minimize some of these criticisms. It has increased the number of members from historically black colleges and universities to a total of six, and articulated its intention to "infuse the pursuit of equity and cultural diversity into all aspects of the Holmes Group Agenda" (*Holmes Group Forum* 1991, 1).

After five years there is little indication that the Holmes Group has been successful in its efforts to increase the status of teacher education programs in research-oriented schools and colleges of education. Furthermore, there is little evidence that institutions have responded to the Holmes Group by establishing a reward system that would encourage faculty to take up teacher training rather than research (Goodlad 1990). Finally, many faculty in schools and colleges of education directly or indirectly involved with teacher education continue to have little knowledge of the Holmes Group's reform agenda. These matters remain formidable obstacles to the Holmes Group reform agenda.

While the professional development school model has gained acceptance within the Holmes Group, there is little evidence that the grassroots support from the public schools for the establishment of professional schools has materialized. Few of the Holmes Group member institutions have substantial experiences or strong ties with inner-city schools. The complexities of these schools and the diversity of the educational needs of the students is new territory for most Holmes Group member institutions. If the Holmes Group's reform agenda is to be judged in the future, its success in working with urban schools and preparing teachers for these schools will be perhaps its most difficult test.

In conclusion, the long-term success of the Holmes Group is dependent not only on the forcefulness of its leadership but on the organizational structure and status of teacher education in schools of education in the broader university context. Bringing about sustained change in teacher education programs, especially within research universities, is extremely difficult (Schneider 1987). The problems with teacher education are really symptomatic of a field not highly valued within the university or external community. Regardless of how effective an organization of deans is, the deans must still contend with their own institutions. Even the most powerful ideas for reform are likely to go unheard without faculty and institutional commitment undergirded by strong cooperation with the field.

The Deans' Network had an agenda that was partially completed by that organization and partially transmitted to the Holmes Group. In contrast to the Deans' Network, the Holmes Group has an internal organization that is somewhat troublesome, for it has to achieve ideological consensus among institutions that share very different histories. However, all the Holmes Group institutions do share a common purpose, that is, the reform of teacher education.

The work of the Deans' Network was not dependent on the faculty at any of the institutional members or upon any external groups, for its agenda was in some ways self-serving to the deans themselves. Here perhaps lies the greatest challenge for the survival of the Holmes Group. To fulfill its purpose, the Holmes Group will need to build an extensive constituency of supporters beyond the deans, including the commitment of university faculty outside of education as well as administrators and teachers at all levels of the educational system.

Notes

1. The following institutions agreed to participate: Florida State University; Harvard University; New York University; Stanford University; Syracuse University; Teachers College, Columbia University; Temple University; University of California, Berkeley; University of California, Los Angeles; University of Georgia; University of Florida; University of Maryland; University of Massachusetts; University of North Carolina; University of Oregon; University of Rochester; University of South Carolina; University of Southern California; University of Texas; University of Washington.

2. The following were the Salishan Deans: Tomas Arciniega, California State University-Fresno; J. Myron Atkin, Stanford University; Arthur P. Caladarci, Stanford University; Robert L. Egbert, University of Nebraska; William Gardner, University of Minnesota; Hendrik D. Gideonse, University of Cincinnati; Robert D. Gilberts, University of Oregon; Robert H. Koff, State University of New York, Albany; Joan S. Stark, University of Michigan; Robert Stout, Arizona State University; Sylvia B. Tucker, Oregon State University; Richard Wisniewski, University of Oklahoma.

References

American Association of Colleges for Teacher Education (AACTE), National Education Association. 1948.

Bailey, S. 1975. *Interest Groups in the Nation's Capital.* Washington, D.C.: American Council on Education.

Bowen, H., and J. Schuster. 1986. *American Professors: A National Resource Imperiled.* Oxford: Oxford University.

Cartter, A. 1966. *An Assessment of Quality in Graduate Education.* Washington, D.C.: American Council on Education.

Chandler, B. J. 1978. Personal conversation with Barbara Schneider. May, 1978.

Clifford, G., and J. Guthrie. 1988. *Ed School: A Brief for Professional Education.* Chicago: University of Chicago Press.

Deans' Network. 1974. *A Consortium of Deans of Education in Major Midwestern Universities. A Proposal to the W. K. Kellogg Foundation.* Evanston, Ill.: Northwestern University.

Deans' Network. 1978. *A Final Report to the W. K. Kellogg Foundation.* Evanston, Ill.: Northwestern University.

Denny, T., and S. Hood. 1984. "Selected Characteristics of Study Participants." Paper presented at the Wingspread Conference Center, Racine, Wisconsin: Johnson Foundation.

Dilworth, M. 1988. "A Continuing Critique of the Holmes Group." *Journal of Negro Education* 57 (2): 199–201.

Gardner, W., G. Piché, K. Howey, J. Raths, J. Lanier, and H. Carter. 1980. "Outline Discussion Deans' Network Study on Undergraduate Teacher Education in R&D Institutions." University of Minnesota. Unpublished memo.

Gideonse, H., and R. Koff. 1982. "Inquiry, Scholarship, and Teacher Education: Issues and Implications." Paper prepared for the annual meeting of the American Educational Research Association, New York.

Goodlad, J. 1990. *Teachers for Our Nation's Schools.* San Francisco: Jossey-Bass.

Gordon, B. 1988. "Implicit Assumptions of the Holmes and Carnegie Reports: A View from an African American Perspective." *The Journal of Negro Education* 57 (2): 195–98.

Hemsing, E. 1970. *Realignments for Teacher Education, AACTE Yearbook.* Washington, D.C.: AACTE.

Holmes Group. 1986. *Tomorrow's Teachers.* East Lansing: Michigan State University.

Holmes Group. 1989. *Work in Progress: The Holmes Group One Year One.* East Lansing: Michigan State University.

Holmes Group. 1990. *Tomorrow's Schools.* East Lansing: Michigan State University.

Holmes Group Forum. 1991. 5:1–2.

Kenen, P., and R. Kenen. 1978. "Who Thinks Who's in Charge Here: Faculty Perceptions of Influence and Power in the University." *Sociology of Education* 51:113–23.

Meade, E. 1984. Personal conversation with Barbara Schneider March, 1984.

Palmer, J. 1980. *The Relationship of R&D Activity to Teacher Education Programs: Report of Study Group 4, Teacher Education Committee, The Deans' Network.* Madison: University of Wisconsin.

Popkewitz, T. 1991. *A Political Sociology of Educational Reform: Power/Knowledge in Teaching, Teacher Education, and Research.* New York: Teachers College, Columbia University.

Powell, A. 1976. "University Schools of Education in the Twentieth Century." *Peabody Journal of Education* 12: 3–20.

Raths, J. 1981. "Unpublished report of the Task Force, Status of Teacher Education in R & D Institutions." Champaign: University of Illinois.

Roose, K., and C. Andersen. 1970. *A Rating of Graduate Programs.* Washington, D.C.: American Council on Education.

Schneider, B. 1987. Tracing the Provenance of Teacher Education. In *Critical Studies in Teacher Education: Its Folklore, Theory, and Practice,* edited by T. Popkewitz, 211–41. London: Falmer Press.

Schneider, B., L. Brown, T. Denny, C. Mathis, and W. Schmidt. 1984. "The Deans' Perspective: Challenges to Perceptions of Status of Schools of Education." *Phi Delta Kappan* 65: 617–30.

Schneider, B., L. Brown, T. Denny, C. Mathis, and W. Schmidt. 1985. *The Quality of the Doctorate in Schools of Education: Final Report to the Ford Foundation.* Evanston, Ill.: Northwestern University.

Sedlack, M. 1987. "Tomorrow's Teachers: The Essential Arguments of the Holmes Group Report." *Teachers College Record* 88: 314–26.

Smith, C. P. 1988. "Tomorrow's White Teachers: A Response to the Holmes Group." *Journal of Negro Education* 57(2): 178–94.

Tom, A. 1987. "The Holmes Group Report: Its Latent Political Agenda." *Teachers College Record* 88: 430–35.

Tucker, S. 1981. "Increasing the Research Capacity of Schools of Education: A Policy Inquiry." A report prepared for the National Institute of Education. Oregon State University.

Wilson, R. 1988. "Recruiting and Retaining Minority Teachers." *Journal of Negro Education* 57(2): 195–98.

5

THE 1989 EDUCATION SUMMIT AS A DEFINING MOMENT IN THE POLITICS OF EDUCATION

Susan R. Martin

In September 1989, President George Bush hosted a two-day "summit meeting" attended by fifty state governors, who gathered at the University of Virginia to formulate a national education plan. Wearing the university's blue-and-orange-striped tie, Bush announced that the meeting was "a major step forward in education," a "historic" moment.[1] Later Bush declared, "The most notable product of the two-day meeting was an agreement between the President and the state leaders to work together to improve the schools."[2]

The historic significance of the 1989 summit meeting resides in its symbolic significance as a public ceremony to announce a new national leadership in education. The self-proclaimed "education president" vested governors and their states with policy-making responsibilities while excluding professional educators from involvement in framing the issues. Although not directly in the summit spotlight, business leaders, individually, as well as collectively through the Carnegie Corporation, provided inspiration for the Bush administration's leadership in education, and are therefore an integral part of the analysis put forward in this chapter. The 1989 education summit provides a focal point for analyzing this emergent leadership in education.

This chapter puts forward an historical framework for understanding the influence on education exerted by politicians and the business community during the 1980s and offers an interpretation of print media related to the 1989 education summit. The next section examines the historical patterns of leadership in education during the twentieth century to show the increasing federal presence in education, the diminution of the role of professional educators, and the deterioration of educators' relationship with the business community.

Throughout the chapter I analyze news articles related to the summit meeting, most of which appeared in *Education Week* (published since 1981, with 50,878 subscribers and an estimated national readership of approximately 228,000).[3] Using news articles, I examine the language, the images, and the events to show how the education summit announced a new policy-making thrust in education, led by politicians assisted by business leaders.

PATTERNS OF EDUCATIONAL LEADERSHIP

Since 1830, when Horace Mann first proposed the common school concept to create a universal public system in the United States, leaders in politics, business, education, and community affairs periodically have initiated education reform. The strength and duration of each group's influence has varied during the past 160 years. I next examine patterns of leadership in twentieth-century education reform.

At the beginning of the twentieth century, during the Progressive Era (1900–1917), reorganization of schools occurred under the leadership of civic elites, typically business or professional leaders who were eager to remove politics from the schools and who declared school governance to be corrupt and controlled by political ward bosses, particularly in large cities. Reformers called for at-large school board elections, an increase in school system bureaucracy, and increased administrative power for superintendents. Schools were to be organized and operated efficiently like corporations, with a school board—essentially a corporate board of directors—made up of civic elites.[4] This reform movement in public education was led at the local level by civic reformers and supported by school administrators because the proposed changes in school governance enhanced their administrative authority.

At the national level professional educators, according to historian David Tyack, included Commissioner of Education William Harris; the "university men," who were presidents of universities and professors in colleges of education; and the "school men," who were school administrators at the state and local level. Many belonged to the National Education Association (NEA), a major influence on the development and dissemination of education policy during the last quarter of the nineteenth century and early decades of the twentieth century.

In the Progressive Era, professional educators, especially university presidents, allied themselves with business and professional leaders to create an "interlocking directorate" of administrative progressives, as described by Tyack.[5] According to Upton Sinclair's critique of higher education in 1922, business leaders created a network of influence, founded universities, and established fellow members of their elites as presidents of these institutions.[6] Business leaders continued to be heavily involved in education reform during the early decades of this century.

Enduring private financial support for education reform was created during the Progressive Era by Andrew Carnegie, one of the most prominent financial figures in the industrializing United States, according to historian Ellen Condliffe Lagemann.[7] In 1911 the Carnegie Corporation, the last of the Carnegie trusts,[8] was endowed with $125 million and chartered "to promote the advancement and diffusion of knowledge and understanding among the people of the United States." Lagemann also states that

> a foundation so chartered could exercise power beyond that inherent in its extraordinary wealth. The Corporation's self-imposed mandate to define, develop and distribute knowledge was, in a sense, a franchise to govern, in important indirect ways.[9]

Thus, the Carnegie Corporation employed "private power for the public good" and created educational policies and structures in its role as an element of the interlocking directorate of corporate and professional educators. During an NEA meeting in 1901, professional educators expressed the hope that "some Rockefeller or Carnegie would one day see the wisdom of extending his donations for educational purposes in the public school."[10] However, not all of those professional educators gathered in Chicago agreed that private money should be used in education. Margaret Haley,[11] the militant business manager of the Chicago Teachers' Federation (CTF), demanded to speak from the floor. Breaking the tradition of silence for female NEA members, Haley urged that

> no Rockefeller or Carnegie would ever contribute from their ill-gotten millions to the public schools. Such a gift would close the eyes and seal the mouths of the teachers, who of all people should have their eyes open and their mouths free to

state the facts. The public schools should get their revenue
and their support from public taxation and never from private gifts.[12]

Although voices such as Haley's and Sinclair's were heard in opposition to "private power" in education, the alliance between the NEA and
the business community was strong in the early decades of the century.

The depression, however, altered this alliance when school districts were forced to retrench as a result of economic hardship. Conflict
erupted at the local level as business leaders advocated major cuts in
property taxes and school spending; professional educators responded
by defending their budgets against what they saw as attacks from the
business community.

Professional educators at first supported the New Deal, but when
the economic woes deeply affected the previously affluent and powerful
urban school districts, they turned against their former allies—business
leaders, state legislators, and the governors—considering them "selfish
and un-American . . . budget slashers."[13] By 1935, the professional educators' mood was even angrier. The NEA advocated financial support
from the federal government with no strings attached. President
Roosevelt chose to bypass the educational bureaucracy in order to chan-
nel the money directly to poor school districts; consequently, the alliance between the NEA and the New Deal administration also became
strained.[14] Professional educators became more isolated without the
support of business leaders, state politicians, or the federal government,
and their leadership role in educational change became severely limited.

In the Cold War period of the 1950s, virtually all previous governmental alliances with education were severed. Schools were attacked by
government critics, by military and business leaders, and by the general
public for offering courses that were generally anti-intellectual and particularly inadequate in the areas of mathematics and science.[15] The NEA
was no longer influential in determining education policy. By the late
1950s the federal government assumed a stronger leadership role in education through the funding and development of programs in mathematics and science. In establishing vehicles for supporting and advancing
school-based instructional materials, a strong national presence was created for determining the direction of education policy. Not surprisingly,
federal funding to education during this period occurred in the form of
categorical grants for specifically mandated purposes.

In the political and social turbulence of the 1960s, the forces influencing education changed dramatically. Major educational reform resulted from initiatives led at the grassroots level by civil rights activists,

teachers, and parents. As evidence of vast cultural and economic disparities among schools and school districts, the issues of equity and quality
of education were at the forefront of these groups. In response to these
grassroots initiatives, the federal government gave education a major
role in the War on Poverty, developing programs to enrich the school
experiences of the poor. To assist the implementation of desegregation, the federal government created the Civil Rights Act of 1964, mandating schools to comply with desegregation regulations in order to receive federal funds. In this period, the federal government assumed an
unprecedented and forceful role in educational leadership in the name
of equity.

Teachers previously had been almost invisible in the arena of educational policy, but in 1960 the first major teachers' strike, held in New
York City, changed forever their position. At the local level teachers'
militancy in the 1960s altered their relationships with school administrators, school boards, and the general public. Several highly successful strikes were organized by the American Federation of Teachers
(AFT), affiliated with organized labor.[16] In the 1960s, as a result of the
competition with the AFT, the NEA became more teacher-oriented;
within a decade, school administrators left the NEA to form their
own organizations.[17]

Teachers became a major national force in education in the 1960s
and 1970s, in part through their activities at the local level but primarily
as a result of their lobbying efforts at the state and national levels. In
1976, for the first time, the NEA supported a presidential candidate,
Democrat Jimmy Carter. In return for the NEA's support during his campaign, Carter established the U.S. Department of Education with cabinet-
level status in 1979; thus fulfilling a longtime goal of that organization.[18]
During the Carter administration a favorable relationship was forged between the White House and professional educators as a culmination of
less than two decades of teachers' political activism.

This unique teacher-initiated alliance between professional educators and the federal government came to an abrupt end in 1980 with the
election of Ronald Reagan during a period that Ira Shor calls "the conservative restoration."[19] Reagan had received the support of neither the
NEA nor the AFT, both of which have steadfastly supported Democrats
since 1976. During the Reagan years, the alliance between teachers and
federal-level policymakers deteriorated. Instead, governors and business
leaders became involved in educational reform, an effort squarely focused on academic excellence and the "professionalization" of teaching.

Supported by many who favored educational "choice," Reagan proposed tax credits as an alternative to public education, advocated school

prayer, vowed to dismantle the Department of Education, and announced that he would cut federal spending on education.[20] Both the NEA and the AFT focused their lobbying efforts on defeating Reagan's support of choice in education, an option that would have eroded the economic base supporting public schools.[21]

In sum, Reagan dramatically altered the federal role in education. In addition to cutting federal spending in this area by one-third, his administration supported policy-making at the state level through a systematic effort aimed at deregulation. During the early 1980s the Reagan administration simplified or revoked many existing federal regulations regarding education, reduced enforcement of the remaining structures, and shifted the responsibility for implementation of federal programs to the states. In addition, many categorical federal grants were changed to block grants, resulting in greater state control of federal funds.[22]

The year 1983 was pivotal in the politics of education. Recession gripped the nation in the early 1980s—plant closings and widespread unemployment created an atmosphere of anxiety. In April, Secretary of Education Terrel H. Bell's National Commission on Excellence in Education released *A Nation at Risk: The Imperative for Educational Reform,* sounding a clarion call for reform. With powerful and alarmist language, the report leveled harsh criticism at the schools, stating that

> the educational foundations of our society are presently being eroded by a rising tide of mediocrity that threatens the very future as a Nation and a people. If an unfriendly foreign power had attempted to impose on America the mediocre educational performance that exists today, we might well have viewed it as an act of war.

The report continued,

> As it stands, we have allowed this to happen to ourselves. . . . We have, in effect, been committing an act of unthinking unilateral, educational disarmament.[23]

The image of U.S. vulnerability expressed in military terms was intended to shock the nation and did. A week later *Action for Excellence: A Comprehensive Plan to Improve Our Nation's Schools* was released by the Education Commission of the States, a body established in 1982 with forty-one members, including eleven governors and thirteen chief executive officers of leading corporations.[24]

A number of other reports and scholarly studies on the state of education followed in quick succession, and by 1984 educational reform had become a national political issue. Excellence in education was touted as the means to gain competitiveness in the international marketplace.[25]

Prior to 1982, governors had not been involved in framing educational policy; however, the possibility of linking school reform with hopes for economic recovery now made education a "hot political topic," according to Thomas Toch, and governors joined the "front ranks of the reform movement." Governors, over half of whom had adopted austerity budgets in 1982, latched on to the call for educational reform as a way to bolster their states' failing economies. In an effort to attract new investors, some governors used improved education as a selling point. Some governors, such as Lamar Alexander of Tennessee, created their own education reform programs.[26]

Business leaders, like the governors, had not been significantly involved in matters of national educational policy prior to the 1980s. The education reform movement gained boosters in the business community at the local, state, and national levels who saw a poorly prepared work force as the root cause of the slumping U.S. economy. According to Toch, "Business backing of the national educational agenda was especially important in winning the support of fiscal conservatives among national elected politicians."[27] Thus, business leaders exerted influence in the political arena, supporting increased appropriations and tax hikes for education.

Members of the business community played yet another significant role in the educational reform movement of the 1980s—forming partnerships with school districts in an effort to have a more direct influence. The Reagan administration, having cut back federal funding for education by one-third, encouraged such "entrepreneurial spirit" and "welcomed with open arms" the offer of the business community to give financial support directly to the schools.[28] The number of such partnerships increased from 17 percent of all school districts in 1983 to 40 percent by 1989.

Because public response to the educational reform movement was overwhelming, Reagan altered his position on education as the 1984 election year approached. In an attempt to retain conservative supporters who opposed a centralized educational reform agenda and also to appear as "a friend of public education," Reagan chose to support the professionalization of teaching as an issue.[29] During his campaign the President emphasized education, making it a factor in national presidential politics. In Reagan's second term, William Bennett, his highly visible and outspoken second secretary of education, led a campaign for excellence that stressed competition, curricular content, and school choice. To promote this program, Bennett freely used the media to augment his "bully pulpit."[30]

Teachers' organizations responded to the education reform movement in an unpredictable fashion. Albert Shanker, staunch militant and president of the labor-affiliated AFT with a membership of 750,000, completely reversed his union orientation in 1983 and became an equally committed advocate of the reform movement to professionalize teaching through such means as career ladders, performance-based pay, peer appraisal, a national teacher exam, and alternative routes into teaching. In an equally unexpected role-reversal, the NEA, traditionally the professional organization, with a membership of approximately 1.5 million, vehemently opposed the movement to reform teaching, arguing that education only needed more money.[31]

The combined efforts of the governors, the business community, the president, and the AFT produced a positive public response. In a 1983 *New York Times* poll, 81 percent of the respondents said that they would be willing to pay higher taxes for education; in a 1984 *Boston Globe* poll, 86 percent indicated that it was more important to improve education than to lower taxes—a significant change from the Massachusetts taxpayer revolt in 1980.[32]

Educational reform remained an important national political issue throughout the Reagan administration. To capture the impetus of this important issue, George Bush in his 1988 presidential campaign declared his intention to be the first "education president," although his candidacy was supported by neither the NEA nor the AFT. One of his first actions as president was to move William Bennett from the Department of Education to a newly created position as the first "drug czar" in the war against illicit drugs. In this way he cleared the bully pulpit for himself. "Prominent men" advised Bush to adopt this strategy, according to Marc Tucker, director of the National Center on Education and the Economy,[33] an agency initially funded by the Carnegie Corporation.

In addition to clearing the bully pulpit, President Bush moved Bennett to a new program. Schools were considered an essential part of the war on drugs, and Bennett's new department was responsible for the allocation of funds to schools for their antidrug programs. In this way the president created a new office while maintaining Bennett's influence over programs and funding in education,[34] and diminished the role and power of the Department of Education.

The term *education president* misrepresents the reality of President Bush's leadership. In fact, most educational policy-making has been routed to the states and the business community. The 1989 summit meeting was a carefully orchestrated media event designed to enhance the president's image as an educational leader determined to solve the "crisis" in education despite his focused effort to propel the federal government away from financial commitments to educational reform.

THE EDUCATION SUMMIT OF 1989

As a crystallizing event in the politics of education, the education summit meeting of 1989 provided a focal point for turning the nation's attention to the crisis in American education as defined by the Bush administration. According to Martin Linsky, attracting media attention to a public event such as the education summit involves the aspect of journalism that "dictates that whatever important people say is news whether or not it is well founded or true." Linsky argues that "the ability of elected officials, especially governors and the president, to set an agenda by their utterances"[35] cannot be overemphasized.

Through his statements about the education summit, President Bush set the agenda and elicited support for changes in educational leadership and priorities. He also contributed to the rhetoric linking the weakened economy to the "crisis" in education. His words became news, although a logical link between "the educational mess" and the national economic situation was virtually nonexistent.

Bush's education summit was regarded as newsworthy because his political prominence, coupled with that of the governors who were key participants, made it so. Through statements to the press, the president and the governors were able to use the news media as a forum for promoting their ideas about education.[36] The coverage of the education summit offered no analysis or debate. Instead, the media consistently presented rhetorical images that enhanced the credibility of the president and the governors as skilled political craftsmen (no women were present in these roles).

In the following analysis, it is my goal to put the images, events, and participants of the 1989 education summit into a broader context and to draw reasoned conclusions that I hope will encourage further deliberation and debate. Through the activities of the summit meeting, President Bush confirmed that a "crisis" in education was contributing to the national economic problems, declared himself the national leader to solve this crisis, and chose a political team to function as professional educators. In addition he devalued traditional professional educators, such as those constituting NEA and AFT memberships. I will examine each of these points in turn.

The "Crisis" in Education

Reporting the White House message, the media uncritically declared that the crisis in American education was evident in the poor test scores of American students as compared with those of students from other in-dustrialized nations. According to a joint statement from President Bush and the governors issued after the summit meeting, "the caliber of the educational system and the nation's economy are *inextricably inter-twined*" (emphasis added).[37] A one-year study was declared essential to identify the "skills students need to be *internationally competitive*" (emphasis added).[38] According to the popular wisdom of the time, the failure of our international trade was linked to the failure of our students. In other words, the U.S. economy depended upon the state of our edu-cational system. This faulty logic was generally accepted by the public in 1989, as it was in 1983 when *Nation at Risk* was released.

The nation's real economic problems had begun to develop during the Reagan years with a decline in international competitiveness on the part of U.S. businesses. Many U.S. goods and services, in comparison with foreign-made products, were in fact shoddy and shunned by consumers. In addition, U.S. top executives earned salaries and bonuses crippling to the profit margin of many firms. As the U.S. position in global trade di-minished, a decline in student test performance became the scapegoat. Actually, the 1970s and early 1980s had been a time of high unemploy-ment largely in response to the increase in the youthful population, declining productivity, and declining American capital investment.[39] Be-tween 1960 and 1978, the average annual rate of increase in productivity in the United States was 1.7 percent, compared to 7.5 percent in Japan.[40] By the late 1980s, 20 percent of the output of American companies was produced by foreigners. Five hundred of America's largest corporations added no new jobs from 1975 to 1990, and their share of the labor force dropped from 17 percent in 1975 to less than 10 percent in 1990.[41]

Political economist and secretary of labor under President Clinton, Robert B. Reich argues that the spread of American corporations to a more "global web" of foreign locations resulted from the profit-based motive to obtain the cheapest possible labor worldwide. American cor-porations are stirred more by profit than by philanthropy in their deal-ings with the American educational system.[42] Business leaders in the late

1980s became interested in helping "at-risk" students from the inner cities. They were motivated, however, not by sudden altruism but by a reduced labor pool and by their changing employment needs. Throughout the 1980s, there was a 14 percent decline in the number of persons aged fourteen to twenty-four and a 20 percent decline in high school enrollees and graduates.[43] Although industrial corporations had moved 20 percent of their production to foreign centers during the 1980s, three million *new* jobs were created in the fast-food, bar, and restaurant businesses in the United States, more than the *total* number of "routine production jobs" in the auto, steel, and textile industries. To illustrate the further decline in the traditionally large corporations and the emergence of service businesses, Beverly Enterprises, the largest nursing home chain in the United States, employs almost as many workers as Chrysler.[44]

In the late 1980s, American business leaders stated that they needed workers who could think independently as well as perform highly technical tasks; consequently they supported increased training in mathematics and sciences. Some businesses created partnerships with local school districts for training local youths,[45] yet an estimated 50 percent of the work force in the 1990s will be employed in routine production or service jobs. Only 20 percent will perform tasks that require skills necessary to analyze and solve problems.[46] Increased mathematics and science instruction will not be necessary for the majority of the workers, despite business leaders' statements.

Even though states and local communities traditionally have been responsible for public education, there was no public debate of the issues before the meeting was held. The causal link between the economic and the education crises, the role of the president as the leader in implementing radical education reform, and the need to create national goals and standards—all were cast as beyond critical debate. The media simply presented the issues as a presidential mandate, and the public accepted them. It is not within the scope of this chapter to analyze the subsidiaries of the national corporate conglomerates in order to establish such links to the major media.[47] Nonetheless, the following analysis of media coverage of the summit illustrates that rhetoric and images created to shape public opinion were decidedly uncritical of presidential politics.

George Bush as the "Education President"

In calling the 1989 summit meeting, President Bush declared himself the creator of an historic event by virtue of both his chosen site for the meeting and his commentary during the course of the event. The news media linked President Bush with a wide variety of notable American leaders, including Thomas Jefferson and Franklin D. Roosevelt. These references carried heavy symbolic weight, dramatizing the historic importance of the summit.

The image of President Bush as philosopher and educational innovator was tied to the choice of the University of Virginia as the site. At the close of the meeting he declared, "Education is our most enduring legacy, vital to everything we are and can become . . . will we become children of the Enlightenment or its orphans?"[48] This allusion was to Thomas Jefferson, a student of the Enlightenment, the founder of the University of Virginia, and the first American to make the radical proposal for a limited system of public education available to all free children, including girls. Both through the selection of the site and through his reference to the Enlightenment, President Bush aligned himself with a founding father who was a consummate politician, philosopher, and radical educational leader.

In choosing to hold a "summit meeting" and to make broad use of media to generate interest and support, President Bush also created a historic link between himself and the charismatic Franklin Roosevelt. An article written before the meeting stated,

> Not since Franklin D. Roosevelt convened the governors for economic-recovery talks in the midst of the Great Depression have the White House and the state houses joined forces for a summit examining one issue.[49]

Thus President Bush was aligned with Roosevelt, a great reformer, and patrician like himself, who released the nation from the crippling economic crisis of the depression. The hidden message in much of the media was that if a solution to the current crisis in education were not found, an economic crisis similar to the depression might result.

"The American people are ready for radical reforms. We must not disappoint them," declared President Bush.[50] This statement is consistent with both Jefferson's and Roosevelt's images, and emphasizes the link between the presidency and the state governors as the "we" who would provide the solutions. The leader of this joint effort was not only a philosopher and a reformer, but also a military leader with a "battle plan," who declared that "the time for study is over . . . [we need] to set measurable national goals that all students must meet."[51]

President Bush also paid tribute to Andrew Carnegie, the business community, and others by stating that students, in addition to acquiring measurable skills, must also understand "the generosity of Andrew Carnegie, the genius of Alexander Graham Bell, and the heroism of Rosa Parks."[52] By first citing the largesse of the steel magnate, whose philanthropic legacy is directed toward education through the Carnegie Corporation, President Bush pointed to the historic alignment between education and business. Through their generosity, business leaders and private philanthropists had supported educational programs of their choice since the early decades of this century. The reference to Bell suggests the importance of technological developments and reinforces the link between education and industry. Finally, the reference to Parks would appeal to African Americans in their struggle for equal opportunity, which coalesced around the activity of this one private citizen.

Through all these allusions, President Bush appears to be a student of the Enlightenment, an advocate of education, a great reformer, and a military leader. In reality, he is a politician from an economically and socially privileged background and a friend of business. Like his predecessor Ronald Reagan, President Bush has encouraged corporate Americans to donate their financial resources to solve the problems of urban education, giving them some indirect power over schools. At the summit meeting, his choice of governors as participants provided business leaders with additional means for influencing education through their campaign contributions and political lobbying.

The New Educational Leaders

In calling together the "nation's chief state executives,"[53] President Bush identified the governors as the professional educators who would assist him in creating a national vision for education. "It is the first time that we've thought enough of education and understood its significance to commit ourselves to national performance goals," declared Bill Clinton, then the Democratic governor from Arkansas, before the summit meeting. [54] This statement illustrates how governors who were making the commitment renewed their leadership role.

In calling the meeting, President Bush also provided an occasion to publicly announce a federal-state partnership regarding funding, in which the governors would "examine Federal regulations under current law to move in the direction of greater flexibility." The president, following the pattern set in the Reagan administration, refused to increase federal funding to education, and the postsummit meeting agreement specified that the states and local districts "should bear the lion's share of the load. The Federal financial role is limited and has even declined."

With no promise of new money from the federal government, deregulation was a crucial issue, since it would provide governors the ability to determine which programs to support. The governors received this concession at the summit meeting. President Bush and the governors promised greater accountability for students' achievement in return for deregulation to meet the "urgent need for flexibility."[55]

As elected officials, the governors are directly responsible to their constituents for the economic well-being of their states. In 1989, governors' concerns included the goal of improving education to enhance students' future employment opportunities and to create more favorable business climates. As the new leaders in education, the governors shared the national spotlight with the president. Assisting the governors in their newly expanded and glorified roles as educational leaders of the nation are members of state legislatures who implement statewide educational policies. Consequently President Bush has placed the nation's educational leadership in the hands of elected officials, who in most cases have an unspoken allegiance to members of the business community for their financial campaign support. With governors as educational leaders, the states' educational programs are likely to change with each new administration and to remain linked to political campaign support from business. Governors are politicians, not professional educators; consequently, educational leadership becomes an aspect of their political aspirations. As a result, state educational programs are subject to shifting political tides and financial influence from vested interest groups.

Devaluation of Professional Educators

Professional educators, particularly those considered to be leaders in their fields, were excluded from the spotlight at the 1989 summit. By symbolically moving them from the center of the sphere of influence, President Bush devalued their opinions and demoted them to positions as advisors and functionaries in the hierarchy of the politics of education. Thus he encouraged a trend that had begun during the Reagan administration. During the meeting, Republican Governor Guy Hunt of Alabama voiced his animosity toward professional educators, saying that he wanted "a national policy that will help us overcome the educational professionals who have their heads in the sand."[56] Professional educators not only were viewed as inappropriate professional educators; they also had become the adversary.

In fact, many professional educators did not agree with the economic argument to explain the "crisis" in education. Rather than linking education with national economics, as had the politicians and business leaders, the professional educators who were consulted in presummit conferences voiced concerns about the basic questions of equity and economics in America. One of their major recommendations was "to attack the vexing social problems of poverty and poor health care that result in damaged children.[57] Many professional educators proposed looking beyond the schools to the larger problem of poverty in society. Except for proposing additional funds to Head Start, the postsummit report by the president and the governors did not address issues of poverty but focused instead upon national standards, an increase in state authority, and support for site-based school management.

Indeed, these themes persist in all aspects of Bush's America 2000 Plan, particularly in the creation of the New American Schools Development Corporation (NASDC). NASDC's board of directors, with the exception of ex-Congressman Thomas Kean, former governor of New Jersey, are uniformly chairs, presidents, and/or CEOs of their respective national firms. The express purpose of NASDC is to "underwrite the design of new high performance educational environments to jumpstart learning in America.[58] The 1989 summit, then, was a signal event whose occurrence provided a first rallying point for a new national educational agenda.

The summit did not materialize in a landscape entirely empty of some earlier business involvement, however. Since the mid 1980s, corporations have been encouraged by government and the public to provide financial support for educational programs in urban school districts struggling under severe economic limitations. Many corporations proposed programs in collaboration with school districts that they wished to fund. Under the prevailing economic conditions, it was understandable that professional educators did not become vocal in opposing either corporate America or the government during or after the summit—at stake was crucial financial support of many local school district initiatives.

To establish the summit spotlight for himself and the governors as the new leaders of educational reform, President Bush first had to displace or devalue the influence of the current professional educators at the national level. He began by diminishing the influence of the Department of Education. During the summit meeting, the president's prominent role eclipsed that of Secretary of Education Lauro F. Cavazos, whose low profile bordered on invisibility and mirrored his diminished influence on White House education policy.

Cavazos, a "low-key academic"[59] with "ideological pallor"[60] in contrast to Bennett, provided President Bush with no competition for the bully pulpit. Cavazos had a style and method that involved listening to others, identifying a problem, bringing people together to discuss it, and building consensus for a solution. Cavazos received initial criticism for being "all talk and no action,"[61] but he was supported by members of the higher education community, who considered him "light years ahead" of Bennett in his understanding of education issues."[62]

Not a politician, Cavazos was described by a Washington insider as "a sweet, naive college president . . . thrown into this den of political animals." An education lobbyist accurately stated that Cavazos "is not a part of the Bush team, and never will be."[63] Cavazos was, in fact, expressly excluded from the "Bush team." President Bush independently established an advisory panel on education that included business leaders, appointed John Chubb to a White House position that entailed the unofficial function of "education specialist,"[64] and delayed action on recommendations from Cavazos regarding key appointments to positions in the Department of Education.[65] Cavazos considered it his role "to espouse the viewpoints of the President,"[66] but he also maintained his personal convictions. For example, he opposed the Senate committee that voted $25 million for the National Board for Professional Teaching Standards (NBPTS), because he was unable to assure taxpayers that their money was being spent appropriately. He stated that "non-competitive grants are bad policy" and argued that without supervision by the Department of Education, which was constrained by NBPTS regulations, expensive and unwarranted duplication of research would occur.[67] This action placed the secretary of education in opposition to the president,[68] the Senate, and the leaders of the Carnegie Corporation who recommended and financially supported the NBPTS.[69]

Considering his weakened position in relation to the White House, it was not surprising that Cavazos was almost invisible at the summit meeting. He and President Bush attended two of three presummit meetings with representatives from school-related and research organizations; otherwise, he had no part of the summit process.[70] Cavazos's involvement was eclipsed by that of Roger Porter, the White House domestic policy advisor. Porter, with a background in government and business, attended all three of the presummit meetings. It was he, and not Cavazos, who prepared the document stating the executive position on education reform, which was presented to the news media as the "Porter Draft."[71]

The devaluation of Cavazos through exclusion from the education summit was complete within a year, at which time he was no longer secretary of education. Lamar Alexander, former governor of Tennessee who instituted one of the first statewide programs of education reform, was appointed the next secretary of education, and David T. Kearns, chief executive officer of Xerox Corporation, was later named undersecretary. These new leaders of the Department of Education, one from politics and the other from business, reflected the influential groups associated with the education summit in 1989.

The Role of the Business Community and the Carnegie Corporation

During the Bush administration, members of the business community were as interested in influencing education policy as a solution to the economic crisis as they had been during the Reagan administration. President Bush sought their involvement, according to Reagan Walker, a writer for *Education Week,* who noted that "the Bush administration has actively courted the business community's support in promoting its education agenda.[72] Leaders from national business organizations, including the Business Roundtable, an organization of the chief executive officers from two hundred of the largest corporations, met with Porter.[73] Of the thirty-eight participants in the presummit meetings with White House staff, twelve represented large corporations, two were from conservative research institutes, and two were from Carnegie Corporation–affiliated organizations.

In addition, the Carnegie Corporation heavily influenced the creation of an agenda for the summit and beyond; other business leaders were consulted because the "crisis" in education had been linked explicitly to the national economy (i.e., the state of business in America). Indeed, the Carnegie Corporation supported President Bush's role as the "education president" from the first month of his presidency.

The relationship between the Carnegie Corporation and the Bush administration recapitulated the "resonance" between the educational goals of the Carnegie Corporation and those of government leaders, whereby mutual agreement tended to prevail, according to Lagemann.[74] This "strategic philanthropy"[75] had the effect of establishing the normative deployment of private resources for the public good under governmental auspices. The Carnegie Corporation provided President Bush with a blueprint for educational reform through its agency, the National Center on Education and the Economy, under the direction of Marc Tucker and board chairman John Sculley, chief executive officer of Apple Computers.

The role of the National Center on Education and the Economy was defined as "policy development in education and human resources."

Their 1989 report, *To Secure Our Future: The Federal Role in Education,* "provided the new Bush administration with an agenda of actions the President could take to improve performance of American schools,"[76] urging the newly elected president to provide the national leadership and vision for education reform without increasing federal funding. Money, the report argued, was not the solution.[77] The report's recommendations regarding the goals of education reform and the role of the federal government heavily influenced the direction of the education summit. The following recommendations included in *To Secure Our Future* also appeared as goals emanating from the education summit:

1. National leadership with a federal-state partnership.
2. Federal financial responsibility in helping preschool children to prepare for school and in providing funds for research. Overall federal funding of 10 percent should not be increased.
3. More flexibility in federal and state regulations regarding the disbursement of federal funds for education, vocational, and social services (i.e., deregulation).
4. Greater accountability for students' performance at the state level and development of national goals.
5. Local school districts as chiefly responsible for school restructuring (i.e., site-based management, parental choice in schools, magnet schools, more autonomy for teachers).
6. Adult literacy training and on-the-job education.[78]

These six recommendations were stated publicly by President Bush and the governors after the summit meeting. Thus the Carnegie Corporation, through the National Center on Education and the Economy, provided the agenda for the "education president." Thus business leaders associated with the Carnegie Corporation heavily influenced the direction taken by President Bush.

CONCLUSION

The 1989 education summit symbolically announced that new educational leadership was in the hands of politicians—specifically, the president and the governors. Although not included in the summit spotlight, the Carnegie Corporation and business leaders provided influential guidance to the president during the "crisis" in education that linked education and the national economy.

The reader may ask, "What's wrong with the involvement of politicians and business leaders in education? Haven't business partnerships produced some positive results, when professional educators have failed?" In reply I would say that although business leaders and governors professed in the 1980s to be interested in educational reform, major underlying economic factors were at work in this business-political agenda, factors that had their origin in the Reagan years and continued to prevail. Matters of equity were largely ignored in favor of "educational excellence." The crisis in education, I would argue, is that the labor market and education are politically intertwined to create inequity and injustice and to limit widespread public debate of the issues.

Public education has historically been tax-supported and unequal. Despite the infusion of federal funds to poor districts during the depression and the War on Poverty in the 1960s, the data related to the funding of education reveal that inequities among districts persisted in the 1970s and that funding continued to be inadequate to provide high-quality education to *all* students.

The issue of funding equity was raised in the early 1970s, when the difference in expenditures per pupil varied by as much as $1,000.00. Two districts in Cuyahoga County, Ohio (the Cleveland metropolitan area), provide an illustration: Cuyahoga Falls spent $2,067.76 per pupil and had the lowest tax rate in the county, while Olmsted Falls spent $886.34 per pupil and had the highest tax rate, which was four times that of Cuyahoga Falls. Court cases attempted to address this issue. In 1971 the *Serrano v. Priest* decision in California declared that the "funding scheme invidiously discriminates against the poor because it makes the quality of a child's education a function of the wealth of his parents and his community."[79] This was a landmark case among state court decisions. A similar case, *Rodriguez v. San Antonio Independent School District,* was won in a Texas district court, but in 1973 the Supreme Court overturned the lower court decision and ruled that "the consideration and initiation of fundamental reforms with respect to state taxation and education are matters reserved for the legislative processes of the various states.[80] Thus, financing reform is now decided state by state, an approach that would slow the process considerably and makes the political process subject to legislative and business influences.

During the Reagan administration, federal funding to education was cut by one-third, and professional educators were forced to do more with less. Poor districts were unable to provide even minimally adequate education.[81] Inequities among between school districts in the late 1980s are graphically documented by Jonathan Kozol, who describes the vast disparities between some urban "ghetto schools" and lavishly pro-visioned school in neighboring suburbs. In addition to plentiful class-rooms and an extensive curriculum, many suburban schools have well-equipped science labs, music practice rooms, and multiple facilities for physical education. Impoverished urban schools are housed in dilapi-dated, inadequate buildings where classes may be held in converted closets, there are not enough outdated textbooks for the students, and five classes share one gymnasium, making it necessary for the students to stand in line for twenty minutes to shoot one basket. Kozol writes that "children in one set of schools are educated to be the governors; chil-dren in the other set of schools are trained to be the governed."[82] These inequities were not addressed by the governors and the President at the education summit. Instead, an agenda came forward that ignored the harsh social and economic realities plaguing U.S. communities and their schools.

Both the Reagan and Bush administrations looked to the business community to help school districts. Businesses were encouraged to make tax-deductible donations to the schools. Despite some well-documented cases of partnerships between businesses and schools, the overall num-ber of donations and amount of financial support for education has di-minished since the 1970s. According to Labor Secretary Robert Reich, corporate gifts to education increased by 15 percent each year in the 1970s, but the rate of increase slowed in the 1980s. In 1987 the increase was 5.1 percent; in 1988 it was 2.4 percent. Most of these donations were made to higher education, particularly to the alma maters of cor-porate leaders. In 1989 only 1.5 percent of corporate gifts were provided to elementary and secondary schools, a proportion less than the tax abatements received by corporations during the same period.[83]

By the end of the decade, some districts on the verge of bank-ruptcy were turned over to their state departments of education. The most extreme case involved education for the entire state of Kentucky, which was placed under the direction of the governor and the legislature in 1990; in this case, local control of education was completely lost—education became a state-controlled function.

In addition to the vast financial differences among school districts, an inequity exists in the form of taxation that favors big business and the wealthy. Ira Shor states that after 1983, financing schools took the form of regressive taxation and donations. Sales taxes and state lotteries were proposed as the means to finance education; both are "bottom-up" forms of funding in which the middle and lower classes pay a dispropor-tionate amount.[84]

The corporate share of local tax revenues has diminished markedly over a thirty-year period, producing "a sharp decline in the relative weight of taxation in the national economy carried by big business"[85] from 45 percent in 1957 to 15 percent in 1987. This reduction was a consequence of the movement of more than a fifth of American industrial production to foreign countries where wage scales are lower. Tax abatements given to corporations as incentives to move to an area or to remain in place were an additional factor. As one example of the impact of abatements, tax payments were eliminated for the General Motors plant in Tarrytown, New York, where it had been located since 1914. Local revenues were decreased by $2.81 million in 1990, and teachers had to be laid off.[86]

Teachers' salaries are a traditional place to make cuts when budgets are tight. In a sense, these cuts become personal donations to education made by teachers, whose salaries have increased only 4 percent since 1970 when adjusted for inflation.[87] U.S. teachers' salaries were in the bottom one-third in a comparative study with eleven other developed countries.[88]

Unlike the teachers and the poor, the wealthy benefited from the regressive national income tax scales in the 1980s; by 1990, the income tax rate of the wealthiest individuals in the United States was the lowest of any industrialized nation.[89] If the tax codes in 1989 had been as progressive as in 1977, $93 billion would have been collected in federal income tax.[90] This amount would have produced more money to spend on education in order to make one major change that requires funding— reduction of class size. Is it any wonder that the Reagan and Bush administrations have declared that there is no federal money for education?

The last subject for consideration is competition. I offer one final argument against the leadership of education by politicians and business leaders who protest that American students must be able to academically outperform students from other countries. Our students are criticized in the media for not being competitive at the same time that our schools do not receive funding comparable to funding in other industrialized nations. In spending on education, as related to gross national product, the United States ranks between eighth and thirteenth when compared to other industrialized nations.[91] Slashing federal, state, and local education budgets in the 1980s has had international ramifications.

In the 1980s it was in the interest of the wealthy, the U.S. corporations, and political leaders to cut funding to education while making schools, students, and communities the scapegoats for educational and economic problems. The rhetoric of the educational summit meeting in

1989 belies the reality of existing inequities in our educational and social systems.

Notes

1. B. Weinraub, "Bush and Governors Set Goals," *New York Times,* 29 September 1989, 57.

2. "The Statement by the President and Governors," *New York Times,* 1 October 1990, 22.

3. *Education Week* is written primarily for school administrators and has a national and international circulation. It has been published for ten years and is the only educational newspaper of its kind (phone interview with a member of the advertising sales staff, 22 April 1991).

4. David B. Tyack, *The One Best System: A History of Urban Education* (Cambridge: Harvard University Press, 1974), 126–28.

5. Ibid., 126–37.

6. Upton Sinclair, *The Goose-Step: A Study of American Education* (Chicago: Economy Book Shop, 1922), 18–20.

7. Ellen Condliffe Lagemann, *The Politics of Knowledge* (Middletown, Conn.: Wesleyan University Press, 1989).

8. For a history of the Carnegie Foundation for the Advancement of Teaching, see Ellen Condliffe Lagemann, *Private Power for the Public Good* (Middletown, Conn.: Wesleyan University Press, 1983).

9. Ibid., 6.

10. Robert L. Reid, ed., *Battleground: The Autobiography of Margaret A. Haley* (Chicago: University of Illinois Press, 1982), 131.

11. Haley led the CTF in a legal battle against the Chicago city government and some corporations to remedy unfair tax distribution. Reid, *Battleground,* 42–85.

12. Ibid., 132.

13. David B. Tyack, Robert Lowe, and Elisabeth Hansot, *Public Schools in Hard Times: The Great Depression and Recent Years* (Cambridge: Harvard University Press, 1984), 80.

14. Ibid., 105–10.

15. Joel Spring, *The American School: 1642–1990* (New York: Longman, 1990), 321–24.

16. William E. Eaton, *The American Federation of Teachers, 1916–1961* (Carbondale: Southern Illinois University, 1975), 122–53.

17. Maurice R. Berube, *Teacher Politics: The Influence of Unions* (New York: Greenwood Press, 1988), 97–126.

18. Ibid., 78–84.

19. Ira Shor, *Culture Wars: School and Society in the Conservative Restoration* (White Plains, N.Y.: Longman, 1986).

20. See, for example, Joel Spring, *American Education* (New York: Longman, 1989), 209; Thomas Toch, *In the Name of Excellence: The Struggle to Reform the Nation's Schools, Why It's Failing, and What Should Be Done* (New York: Oxford University Press, 1991), 23–29.

21. Berube, *Teacher Politics,* 104–6.

22. Spring, *American Education,* 209–10.

23. National Commission on Excellence in Education, *A Nation at Risk: The Imperative for Educational Reform* (Washington, D.C.: Government Printing Office, 1983), 5.

24. Education Commission for the States, *Action for Excellence: A Comprehensive Plan to Improve Our Nation's Schools* (Denver: Distribution Center, Education Commission of the States, 1983).

25. Toch, *In the Name of Excellence,* 15–16; Spring, *American Education,* 224.

26. Toch, *In the Name of Excellence,* 18–20.

27. Ibid., 21–22.

28. Ibid., 20.

29. Spring, *American Education*, 224.

30. Joel Spring, *Conflict of Interests* (New York: Longman, 1988), 56.

31. See Berube, *Teacher Politics*, 141–46; Toch, *In the Name of Excellence*, 143–51, 155–68.

32. Toch, *In the Name of Excellence*, 18,

33. "Bush Drug Plan: School Policies Required for Aid," *Education Week*, 27 September 1989, 27.

34. Ibid.

35. Martin Linsky, "The Media and Public Deliberation," in *The Power of Public Ideas*, ed. Robert Reich (Cambridge, Mass.: Ballinger, 1988), 218–19.

36. Ibid., 219.

37. Weinraub, "Bush and Governors."

38. "Governors to Analyze Essential Skills for Students," *Education Week*, 6 September 1989, 21.

39. Tyack et al., *Public Schools in Hard Times*, 196–200.

40. Spring, *Conflict of Interests*, 58.

41. Robert B. Reich, *The Work of Nations: Preparing Ourselves for the Twenty-first Century* (New York: Knopf, 1991), 120, 6.

42. Ibid., 110–18, 280–81.

43. Kathryn M. Borman and Joel H. Spring, *Schools in Central Cities: Structure and Process* (New York,: Longman, 1984), 172.

44. Reich, *Work of Nations*, 177.

45. Borman and Spring, *Schools in Central Cities,* 172–82.

46. Reich, *Work of Nations,* 173–80.

47. Ben H. Bagdikian, *The Media Monopoly* (Boston: Beacon Press, 1987), 3–27.

48. Weinraub, "Bush and Governors."

49. Reagan Walker, "Education Summit's 'When' and 'Where' are Settled, but the 'Why' Remains Unsettled," *Education Week,* 6 September 1989, 1.

50. T. Henry, "Seminar Results in Goal-oriented Education Ideas," *University of Cincinnati News,* 29 September 1989, 9.

51. "Bush Wants Education Battle Plan," *Cincinnati Enquirer,* 28 September 1989, 1.

52. Weinraub, "Bush and Governors."

53. Reagan Walker, "Summit Agenda Remains Unsettled," *Education Week,* 6 September 1989, 21.

54. Weinraub, "Bush and Governers."

55. E. B. Fiske, "Paying Attention to the Schools is a National Mission Now," *New York Times,* 1 October 1989, 1.

56. Walker, "Education Summit's."

57. Julie A. Miller and Reagan Walker, "Consensus Builds to Set National Goals," *Education Week,* 20 September 1989, 1.

58. New American Schools Development Corporation, "Designs for a New Generation of American Schools" (Arlington, Va., 1991, Request for Proposal), 7.

59. "A Study in Contrasts—Cavazos' Low Key Style Differs from Bennett's," *Education Week,* 5 April 1989, 5.

60. Julie Miller, "Scrutinizing the Secretary: A Slow Starter or 'On Target'?" *Education Week*, 21 June 1989, 1.

61. Ibid.

62. "Gentleman's 'C' for Bush," *Education Week*, 26 September 1990, 20.

63. Miller, "Scrutinizing the Secretary."

64. Julie Miller, "White House Downplays the Scope of Appointee's Role," *Education Week*, 19 April 1989, 1.

65. "Federal File: Empty Desks," *Education Week*, 2 August 1989, 19.

66. Miller, "Scrutinizing the Secretary."

67. Julie Miller, "Senate Committee Votes $25 Million for Professional Standards Board," *Education Week*, 2 August 1989, 26.

68. Julie Miller, "Bush Floats Plan to Free Schools from Regulation," *Education Week*, 19 April 1989, 1.

69. "Three Year Effort to Create a New Generation of Teacher Assessment Nears Completion," *Education Week*, 23 September 1989, 23.

70. "Bush, Cavazos Convene Seventeen Educators for Meetings," *Education Week*, 27 September 1989, 27; "Participants at White House Pre-Summit Meetings," *Education Week*, 27 September 1989, 18.

71. Reagan Walker, "Accord on Goals Hard to Attain Executives Find," *Education Week*, 31 January 1990, 13.

72. Reagan Walker, "Business Leaders Challenge Bush's School Priorities," *Education Week*, 8 November 1989, 1.

73. "Participants at White House."

74. Lagemann, *Politics of Knowledge*, 147–75.

75. Ellen Condliffe Lagemann, "The Politics of Knowledge: The Carnegie Corporation and the Formulation of Public Policy," *History of Education Quarterly* 27 (1981):207–15.

76. National Center on Education and the Economy, Rochester, N.Y. (Public Relations sheet sent to the author upon request, n.d.).

77. National Center on Education and the Economy, *To Secure Our Future: The Federal Role in Education,* (Rochester, N.Y.: National Center on Education and the Economy, 1989).

78. This summary comes from a comparison of the goals in *To Secure Our Future* and in two postsummit news articles, "Summit Orders New Goals for U.S. Schools," *Cincinnati Enquirer,* 29 September 1989, and Fiske, "Paying Attention to the Schools."

79. Ibid., 289.

80. Ibid.

81. Ibid., 256.

82. Jonathan Kozol, *Savage Inequalities: Children in America's Schools* (New York: Crown, 1991), 176.

83. Reich, *Work of Nations,* 280–81.

84. Shor, *Culture Wars,* 151.

85. Svi Shapiro, *Between Capitalism and Democracy: Educational Policy and the Crisis of the Welfare State* (New York: Bergin & Garvey, 1991), 155.

86. Reich, *Work of Nations,* 181

87. Ibid., 256.

88. "U.S. Spending near Bottom, AFT Charges in New Report," *Education Week,* 17 April 1991, 2.

89. Reich, *Work of Nations,* 246.

90. Ibid., 260.

91. Ibid., 256; "U.S. Spending Near Bottom."

6

IT WAS MORE THAN A THIRTY YEARS' WAR, BUT INSTRUCTION FINALLY WON: THE DEMISE OF EDUCATION IN THE INDUSTRIAL SOCIETY

Erwin V. Johanningmeier

INTRODUCTION

There are four claims on which this chapter rests. The first is that the United States is completing its transition from an industrial to a post-industrial society, a transition that began during World War II. To understand the nature of this transition is to understand that reform of institutions, especially public schools, is counterproductive, for most reform efforts are attempts at restoration. Reformers usually want not to create new institutions but to restore them to a state they believe once obtained. Reforming public schools so they will be like they once were or like we believe they once were is not likely to create schools that will adequately serve children in the twenty-first century. The second claim is that the public school in the United States is a social invention of a new society, a society that had recently created a nation, had invented a new political order, and was preparing to embrace an industrial economy. The public school was designed to serve the political requirements articulated by the founders of the American Republic at the end of the eighteenth century and the requirements of the nineteenth-century industrial nation-state. That nineteenth-century invention, the public school, even as it was modified and rationalized by the progressives in the early twentieth century, may not be an appropriate institution for a postindustrial society. The third claim is that David Hamilton (1989a) was quite correct when he wrote that "schooling is not the same as education" and that it "is a technology designed to domesticate the 'natural processes' of education and bring them within reach of human regulation and control" (279.) The fourth claim is that Frank Smith's (1988) argument that education "backed the wrong horse" when it put its faith in experimental psychology" (111) is perhaps understated but certainly correct. The colonization of public education by psychology contributed greatly to the process whereby education was reduced to schooling, schooling was reduced to instruction, and learning was reduced to specific skills and performances as defined and assessed by psychologists.

SCHOOLS WITHOUT EDUCATION

In "Schools without Education," an article written a generation ago, Carl Bereiter (1972, 391) reported that the traditional school had lost its efficacy. That he could so effectively disassemble the traditional school is more important than his alternative to the traditional school. Indeed, his alternative can be viewed as a celebration of the triumph of instruction, a victory that is here clearly acknowledged but not celebrated. He then argued that "schools should drop their educational function in order to do a better job of child care and training." He wanted schools to "narrow their teaching efforts to a simple concern with getting children to perform adequately in reading, writing, and arithmetic." The distinctions he made among education, care, and training as well as the reasons he gave for insisting upon "schools without education" are powerful, useful, and warrant some review, as does the significance of his ability to make those distinctions so clearly. He clearly and effectively showed that education, training, and care could be separated from each other and insisted that "child care and training should be separated, carried out by different people according to different styles."

Education, according to Bereiter (1972, 391–92), "is *not* development but the *effort to influence* development." While not denying that "intellectual growth" and "personality development" were likely to continue to occur in schools, he maintained that any attempt to direct these processes in any direction could and should be abandoned. Child care, he readily admitted, supports the development of children but "is distinguished from education by its relative neutrality. It consists of providing resources, services, activities, love, and attention for children, but with no attempt to influence the course of development." Training, like education, is directive but only attempts "to provide a certain kind of performance in the children." How a child uses a skill and "how it is integrated into his personality" were not to be considered, for such concerns are "educational."

Bereiter's (1972, 391–94) proposal was based on three claims: (1) the theoretical but practical impossibility of education in schools; (2) the demise of the traditional school; and (3) the exclusive right of parents to educate, a right that, some would argue, became the obligation of mothers. While he did not deny that education was "in principle" possible, he believed in the "impossibility of mass education." He further claimed that his proposal to narrow the scope of schooling was "not immoral," for it was his conviction and argument that "schools do not and cannot successfully educate, that is, influence how children turn out in any important way." The evidence that schools made educative differences was not compelling. The observable and demonstrable correspondence between the values students hold and the values schools teach did not necessarily mean that the school caused the students to hold such values, for it was just as plausible to claim that the correspondence between the two is evidence that "we are merely looking at two sides of the same thing, namely, the prevailing values of society." Similarly, the development of intellectual abilities was not necessarily related to schooling: "As they proceed through school, pupils get better at both mathematical reasoning and mathematical knowledge, but only the latter is related to taking of mathematics courses." As long as the distinction between growth and education is observed, it is seen that the schools take credit (as well as blame) for what would occur even if there were no schools. The education that can be achieved in school is "indoctrination. What does not seem to work in school is anything beyond training, anything that would represent education in a higher sense as the effort to develop a whole person, to draw forth potentialities of the individual and so on."

Bereiter (1972, 396, 398) believed that life in the traditional school was characterized by "peace, enjoyment, and the child's sense that what he [sic] does is important." When Bereiter was writing, however, life in the traditional school, as was soon documented by the Senate Subcommittee to Investigate Juvenile Delinquency's *A Report Card: 'A' in School Violence and Vandalism* (1975), was not what it once was. Life in the traditional school, if not violent and dangerous, was already very much like life in a peacetime army: "Both the child and the peacetime soldier are being readied for future activity, but in both cases the future activity is too remote and unforeseeable to serve as adequate motivation or purpose on a day-to-day basis." The traditional school existed in a society in which many youth, if they so desired, could continue their education in the workplace and begin to support themselves and even contribute to the support of their loved ones or family. After World War II, youth had little choice but to remain in school—at least through high school. As Morris Janowitz (1969, 8–9) so accurately observed, "the transformation and organization of the labor market under advanced industrialization restricted opportunities for youth and assigned a new role to the public schools." Before the Great Depression, "the socialization of youngsters from European immigrant families and of migrants from rural areas was in good measure accomplished through work experiences—part time and full time." After World War II, however, "high school graduation or its equivalent—not only in terms of academic and vocational requirements, but also in terms of social attitude, interpersonal competence, and maturity—[was] defined as a desirable and required goal, even for the lowest income groups."

After World War II, "actual work requirements, changed standards of employment and trade unions, and new legislation about minimum wages" required public schools to "accept responsibility for all youngsters who are not college bound until they develop levels of personal maturity sufficient for them to enter the labor market" (Janowitz 1969, 9). Educators welcomed the consequent expansion of public education, for it seemed a true extension of equality of educational opportunity. The difficulty was that those responsible for administering the schools, especially the high schools, continued to conceptualize and administer them as they always had. They simply did more of what they had been doing for more students. There was no widespread recognition that the schools were serving a new population, a population that was in many instances and in many respects different from those who had traditionally attended high school. Those who had previously dropped out of school to take jobs were encouraged to remain in school, because there was no other place for them. What had once been a population seeking and exercising opportunity became, in large measure, a captive population. That captive population lost its opportunity to be independent (students constitute a dependent class), and it often rebelled against its guardians. The social structure and the social dynamics of public schooling were radically transformed as what was once opportunity became obligation and what was once choice became compulsory. There should be little wonder that attempts at school reform have been so unsatisfactory. Schools, especially high schools, have been serving a new population, a population very different from that for which they were originally designed.

For Bereiter, there was no question that the traditional school lost its efficacy by the end of the 1960s. "Armed attacks on teachers and policemen in the halls" showed that it was neither a safe nor a pleasant place to be. Its "demise" was "clearly underway" and seemed "inevitable." He further observed that

> the perspective of the outer world is penetrating the school. The traditional school cannot survive such an invasion, for if goings on in school come to be judged by the same standards as goings on outside they will be seen as ridiculous and the structure will collapse. You cannot have a room full of ten-year old Paul Goodmans and Edgar Z. Friedenbergs and hope to run a traditional school, especially if the teacher holds the same viewpoint. (Bereiter 1972, 399)

The school, thanks to the efforts of the progressives who took the school out of politics and protected it with an army of professionals, had been isolated from the "outside." Once the protective barriers had been knocked down, there was no way to reverse the effects of its having been placed back in society. It became necessary to conceive of the school as *in* society, but many persist in thinking of the school-*and*-society relationship. Educators may be more successful in the future if they cease explaining their difficulties by relating what the family has failed to do and begin complaining about what society fails to provide.

THE EXPULSION OF PARENTS

Bereiter's (1972, 391) claim that only parents "have a clear-cut right to educate" may or may not have been a tacit claim that mothers needed to assume more responsibility for their children, but it was certainly a rejection of the assumptions on which public education in the United States was founded. It was a position contrary to the professional educators' long-standing belief that the state has the right to educate children to protect the interests of both the state and the child, but especially the state. For example, Samuel Harrison Smith, who shared with Samuel Knox the prize for writing the best essay on a system of education for the new republic, for a contest sponsored by the American Philosophical Society for Promoting Useful Knowledge, in 1795, was among those who believed the state had the right to insist that all children be educated by the public. It was not, however, a new idea. For Aristotle, for example, those systems of education that allowed parents to teach their children whatever and however they saw fit were contrary to the best interests of the state. S. H. Smith (1965, 108–9) argued that the effects of compulsory education were so obviously beneficial that the state could expect " 'a general acquiescence' from the people should it exercise this duty." It was, according to Smith, "the duty of a nation to superintend and even to coerce the education of children." Now it is argued that if the state does not intervene in education even more than it has, the nation itself will be "at risk." "At-risk" children are now important because they place they nation at risk.

Early in the twentieth century, when Ellwood P. Cubberley was promoting the further expansion of public education and reviewing the significance of the educational legislation of the Massachusetts Bay Colony in the seventeenth century, he cited with approval George H. Martin, an early historian of education in Massachusetts, who wrote:

> It is important to note here that the idea underlying all this legislation was neither paternalistic nor socialistic. The child is to be educated, not to advance his personal interests, but because the State will suffer if he is not educated. The State does not provide schools to relieve the parent, nor because it can educate better than the parent can, but because it can thereby better enforce the obligation which it imposes. (Martin quoted in Cubberley 1919, 19)

At the same time Cubberly was writing, Ella Arvilla Merritt (quoted in Cremin 1988, 297–98), a member of the Children's Bureau staff, effectively rejected the notion that "the care of our children was entirely an affair of the home." For her, "it was a great step forward when, after much opposition, the idea that is the duty of the State to furnish schools for its children and to see that they attend those schools, gradually found expression in our public school system and our compulsory education laws." The school was, however, neither solely responsible for, nor completely capable of, tending to children. It was but an instrument of the state. Only the state had the requisite power. According to Lawrence A. Cremin (1988), "her most fundamental point" was this:

> Little by little we have been forced to recognize that neither the home nor the school, unaided, can properly guard the

welfare of the child. We need the strength of the State to protect him [*sic*] from carelessness and selfishness, for the child is weak, and his natural protectors, individually are weak also. (297)

Merritt claimed that "government was better equipped than any other agency" to assume responsibility for determining what constituted good care.

Bereiter's claim that the right of education belonged to the family constituted a rejection of the liberal progressive tradition. It was also understandable, for it is a widely held belief. That such a belief is commonly and widely held may be explained by how professional educators who are products of progressivism have behaved since the end of the nineteenth century and even before then. As Cremin (1988, 295) observed, "though progressives asserted the primacy of familial education, they advanced the pre-eminence of schooling." Parents were quietly, subtly, and effectively excluded from decisions about school processes. A trusting and compliant citizenry relied on the professional educators, the experts, to educate and care for their children. That educators are now trying to bring parents into the school and cooperate with them is a sign that the school is not being reformed but is ready to be transformed. The effective exclusion of parents from school may have run its course. If it has, schooling may be very different in the near future.

The commitment to the proposition that the state has the right to educate created the conditions that eventually allowed instruction, as conceptualized by modern psychology, to rout education from schools. Once it was decided that the modern nation-state required an educated citizenry and that the necessary education should be conducted in schools, conditions (institutional arrangements and beliefs in the efficacy of scientifically based processes for effecting or predicting desired human performance) that would in all likelihood, if not inevitably, lead to the ascendancy of instruction and the demise of education were accepted and set in motion. The public school, eventually framed within what Ernest R. House (1981) has described as the "technological perspective" became the arena in which education and instruction did battle. Instruction, as Bereiter unwittingly demonstrated, won. Neither improved instructional programs nor improved systems for their delivery have made or can make the schools educational institutions. Ironically, better-designed programs and methods for supervising teachers' performances (delivery of prescribed curricula in prescribed ways) have not even improved student performance. That should have been no surprise, for cultural ills, if new and different performance levels are ills, cannot be cured with psychological palliatives.

Bereiter's proposal for schools without education was as much a statement about what had become of education in public schools as it was a proposal. The situation he effectively documented began in the early nineteenth century and gathered considerable momentum after Appomattox. It was virtually realized shortly after the end of World War II.

SELECTING AND INVENTING THE COMMON SCHOOL

Before the American Revolution, *education* and *teaching* had been related almost exclusively to an individual ideal, the growth in the private wisdom and the piety of the unique individual being educated. The commitment to schooling created teaching as an object of concern and inquiry and allowed the eventual professionalization of education. As Robert McClintock (1971, 162) observed, before the professionalization of education, many of those who wrote on education wrote about "study" and "self-culture." Montaigne and Erasmus, for example, preferred "a theory of study to a theory of teaching." Even vocational education was a private and individual affair. The master did not have a class of apprentices. He usually had one, maybe a few; and the master's obligation extended beyond teaching his charge the technical aspects of a trade.

In the United States the common school was seen as a logical extension of the new knowledge and the new politics introduced and popularized by Enlightenment thinkers. From the Enlightenment, Americans learned to believe in the efficacy of human reason and in the possibility of creating a rational, just, and sensible social order. The common school was selected and designed to effect the realization of the new social-political vision. The adoption of the common school was the acceptance and the institutionalization of the program of the Enlightenment thinkers who firmly believed that humankind could improve, and perhaps even perfect itself and society, through education.

As the new American society was establishing itself, the explosive expansion of knowledge, especially during the latter half of the nineteenth century, made universal and uniform participation all the more necessary. Neither the new state nor the new economy could function without an educated, or literate, citizenry. Eventually, some citizens would need specific skills. Maintenance of the new political and economic orders required the rapid and widest possible extension of schooling and ultimately the wholesale recasting of the traditional school curriculum. It required the deliberate teaching of subjects that had not needed to be taught except to those already prepared to undertake them—reading and writing, for example. Both the new political order and the emerging economic order required literacy. The common school—a new, universal institution designed to conduct mass instruction—was the invention selected to satisfy the new requirements. It was to teach people to accept, and how to perform in, the new developing order. It was expected to teach the personal and civic virtues that would incline people not to riot and thereby insure preservation of domestic tranquility.

The success of the American War of Independence and the first suggestions that science could be applied profitably to human endeavors created social, economic, political, and cultural conditions that required that the problem of educating be approached in a new manner. *Education* and *teaching* had to be examined systematically, critically, and institutionally. The word *education* continued to be used, but it increasingly meant *schooling*. As education became schooling, the relationship between student and teacher changed. Discussions about whether education should be an individual process whereby students were privately tutored or a group process conducted in public—in view of all other students—gave way to questions about how to establish and administer the public group process, schooling. As Americans accepted the idea of the common school, they accepted new conceptions of education and teaching. Before they entered the twentieth century, most believed a national system of education had been built.

Education in the form of schooling was selected as the most effective means for creating citizens, for what Benjamin Rush (1965) explicitly described as the need for "republican machines" (10). The newly articulated democratic theory and the new democratic institutions required an education not only for the individual but chiefly for the good of the newly founded society. The new society created by the American Revolution could only be maintained by means of informed and disciplined participation of all its citizens (a class that did not yet include all adults). Society could not depend, as it had for Locke, for example, on the wisdom and virtue of an elite that, if set right, would shape the body politic. The "rubbish heap" was to be raked so those with genius and virtue could be identified, properly schooled, and assigned to the elite. Identification, preparation, and sometimes even the assignment were to be done in state-supported public schools. All those who developed national plans for education during the early years of the republic—for example, those who entered the essay contest sponsored by the American Philosophical Society in 1795—agreed that the school was the appropriate instrumentality for creating citizens (Hansen 1926; Rudolph 1965).

Before the adoption of the common school, the consideration of educational theory and practice was a widespread but largely amateur endeavor. Their origins were not scientific but traditional and metaphysical. The development of educational theory was a speculative undertaking. It was not based on systematic and tested observations. Educational theory and prescriptions for educational practice were often founded on advice from one whose authority in some other field was transferred to his or her pronouncements on education, a topic upon which any learned and accomplished person was supposed to be an expert. Informed opinion ruled. Those who offered advice on education were often more concerned with the character of the teacher, often the tutor, than with his or her other accomplishments. The eloquence and the status of the writer were the criteria by which educational theories were evaluated. Milton, Locke, Kant, and Wollstonecraft are examples of such writers. Late-eighteenth- and early-nineteenth-century developments undermined the rule of the amateurs, especially in the United States. The rise of the nation-state committed to an industrial economy required a new conception of education. Once the common school was accepted as the place and process of education, the utility of traditional educational theory was severely limited: "Whether we like it or not, many former educators considered education to consist of neither teaching nor learning; instead, they found the diverse forms of study to be the driving force in education" (McClintock 1971, 167). The common school required the invention, management, and evaluation of instruction.

Education was no longer a private activity in the new republic. By the 1830s it was clearly becoming a public institution, a universal social, political, and cultural instrumentality. As such, it was conceptualized as a process of general schooling rather than as an essentially tutorial relationship. Notions of individualized instruction gave way to mass instruction. For Horace Mann, for example, mass, or group, instruction was "not merely a practical necessity, but a social desideratum." He believed "that the tutorial relationship could never serve the social ends of education, that only with a heterogeneous group of students could the unifying goals of the common school be achieved" (Cremin 1962, 11). The new educational institution devoted to mass, or group, instruction eventually created new vocations, the *professional* teacher and then the *professional* school administrator and the *professional* supervisor, some of whom supervised instruction and some of whom supervised curricula.

Once the notion of the common school was invented, it was recognized that no merely accidental definition of teaching and schoolkeeping would suffice for the new public schools that were being spread across the land. Social agencies—school board members—had to do more than select and supervise teachers. They had to tend to their preparation; they had to teach them how and what to teach. Preparation of teachers became a social concern, and that social concern became part of higher education's responsibility once college and university presidents decided to demonstrate the social utility of higher education to their patrons and trustees. Universities organized themselves to serve society's institutions and its commercial and industrial needs by preparing personnel to work in the newly emerging bureaucratic enterprises, public and private. First they opened schools of agriculture and engineering to assist the farmers and the railroads. Now there are schools or colleges for business, library science, social work, education, and even physical education. Now it is generally believed that whatever personnel society needs, it can presumably secure properly trained professionals from the appropriate department of the nearby university, personnel who know how to apply scientifically sanctioned treatments to clients. Consequently, students are prepared for specific economic roles and functions in the schools. Program development and curriculum development are driven by the economic and political requirements of the nation, not by any commitment to the tradition of the liberal arts or any conception of what constitutes an educated person. By the end of the progressive era, as Lazerson and Grubb reported (1974, 32), the public accepted that "the primary goal of schooling was to prepare youth for the job market." Subsequently, whenever the nation's economy was not sufficiently robust to employ all those who wanted to work, it was assumed that something was wrong with public education. Economic difficulties were, and continue to be, transformed into the failures of public education.

James G. Carter early recognized the need for a new kind of institution to serve the common schools. He asked for a school specifically devoted to the preparation of teachers. Recognizing that the new kind of school could be described as neither a school of science nor a school of literature, he described it in this way:

> The institution from its peculiar purpose must necessarily be both literary and scientific in its character. And although, with its design constantly in view, we could not reasonably expect it to add, directly, much to the stock of what is now called literature, or to enlarge much the boundaries of what is now called science; yet, from the very nature of the subject to

which it would be devoted, and upon which it would be employed, it must in its progress create a kind of literature of its
own, and open a new science somewhat peculiar to itself—
*the science of communicating knowledge from one mind
to another while at a different state of maturity.* (Carter
1826, 47)

Carter understood that the common school was a new invention,
that it required a new process—teaching, and that attention had to be
paid to the administration of that process. Like Herbart, he understood
that teaching—instruction—was a necessary object of study and inquiry. He not only identified the activity that is now the object to which
professional educators and professional researchers claim to attend but
also clearly showed that it was indeed a new undertaking. Subsequently,
educators allowed their new territory to be colonized by psychologists,
who cast the educators' concerns to fit the interests and requirements of
their own field. For the most part, educators did not resist but welcomed
the invasion.

Teachers are increasingly directed to *train,* to use Bereiter's language, students in the basic skills. The belief that it is possible to find a
process that teachers can be trained to administer, so that teachers and
students will perform according to predetermined standards, without regard to the content or skill that is being taught, persists. Method reigns
supreme, for the medical model has been widely adopted by teacher educators. Consequently, there is virtually no recognition that the choices
teachers must make are often ethical choices. Schools are designed to
shape behavior, not to teach the art of choosing.

Carter believed that something was communicated in the teaching
process. Now many either act as though the process can be easily and
cleanly separated from subject matter (Shulman 1987, 6–7) or claim
that the nature of the process can be ignored if the teacher has mastery
of the subject. The commitment to a universal process prevails. One side
invests in the delivery process (instruction); the other invests in the
goods that are to be delivered (subject matter). Each subscribes to the
same conception; each has succumbed to the notion that education is
simply the transportation of information from one place or person to another, from one who allegedly has it to one who allegedly needs it. It is
a conception, notwithstanding the rhetoric of educators and some psychologists, that tacitly assumes that the student is passive. Students are
seen as passive recipients of instruction. They often respond by being
passively aggressive, and educators respond by looking for new methods.

AFTER APPOMATTOX

Except in the South, the pattern of what was beginning to be viewed as a national system of education had emerged by the time the nation celebrated its centennial. As Americans were preparing to celebrate the centennial of their independence, they were, according to Daniel Calhoun (1969, 295), "becoming confident that they had a genuine 'system' of education." The United States Bureau of Education, under the direction of William Torrey Harris, even sponsored a description of the nation's schools. Harris acknowledged the differences among the states, but "the very sureness with which he described regional or other differences among schools only underscored the sureness of the system he felt." The national system may not have been de jure but it was rapidly becoming de facto. Most states had exercised their authority to establish school systems, and about half the nation's children were attending school. The National Education Association was beginning to assume its modern form and by the 1890s was creating a national agenda through its issuance of reports, such as those issued by its Committee of Ten and Commission on the Reorganization of Secondary Education. Through such reports the NEA framed how the nations's schools were discussed. As its scope, power, and importance increased, public school increasingly mirrored the industrial society of which it was part and parcel. The industrial system strove for standardization and universal standards, and the schools did not lag too far behind as professional educators competed with each other to build what David Tyack (1974) called the "one best system."

Eighteenth-century developments did not reach their full strength until after the Civil War. The nation was then neither fully industrialized nor fully urbanized, but it was well on its way. Bert James Lowenberg (1942, 341) observed, "The end of the Civil War closed an era and ushered in an epoch." The modernization process changed the face of the nation, and Americans required a new *Weltanschauung* to make sense out of and to adjust to what was happening to them and about them. Like their counterparts in Europe, Americans were entering the "high machine age" and doing so with enthusiasm, "for the late nineteenth century, the cradle of modernism, did not feel the uncertainties about the machine age that we do." Then "no statistics on pollution, no prospect of melt-downs or core explosions lay on the horizon" (Hughes 1981, 11).

To celebrate the new age, nation after nation hosted world's fairs, what Robert Hughes called "those festivals of high machine-age capitalism" where they displayed their manufactured goods, and spectators could marvel at new inventions: the telephone, the typewriter, the duplex telegraph, and the Singer sewing machine in 1876 at the Philadelphia Centennial Exposition; Edison's phonograph in 1889 at L'Exposition de Paris; electricity in 1893 at the World Columbian Exposition in what is now Chicago's Jackson Park; and television in 1939 at the New York World's Fair. Then, as now, monuments were built for those celebrations. The precedent began at mid century when, in 1851, Victoria's Prince Albert gave the world Paxton's Crystal Palace—a "cathedral of the machine age" "with its vaults of glittering glass and nearly invisible iron tracery in London's Hyde Park. It was the forerunner of the mirror faced towers that now reflect each other in American cities" (Hughes 1981, 9–10). The greatest of these monuments was, of course, built for the 1889 Paris fair. Significantly, Gustav Eiffel was not an architect but an engineer. Accordingly, he used iron to build the great gothic spire of the high machine age. The Americans built no iron tower, but they did bind their nation together with steel tracks and iron bridges. Rationality, efficiency, and utility were as important, if not more important, than beauty. How to realize a vision was becoming more important than the vision itself. Method was separated from content and purpose and made an object of study. There was widespread belief that an efficacious universal method, the scientific method, could be found and then applied to virtually any undertaking, political, social, economic, industrial, educational. Even management became scientific, and professional school administrators of the progressive era, as Raymond Callahan (1962) documented, tried to become scientific managers. Subsequently, school administrators changed their approaches to school management and administration whenever the commercial sector of society changed its approach to management.

With other nations in the industrial society, the Americans participated in "those festivals of high machine-age capitalism." When they did so, they displayed not only examples of their industrial prowess but also evidence of their cultural development, especially their public schools. They did not neglect to show the marvels of their public school system, the instrumentality for the development of the modern nation-state that was supporting their development. In fact the American educational exhibits were more impressive than the industrial exhibits. The manufactured goods the Americans exhibited in Vienna in 1873 were not especially impressive, but, Merle Curti (1950, 842) reported, "the exhibit of an American school, with its maps, charts, textbooks, and other equipment, helped dispel the prevailing critical European view of American education." The educational exhibits the Americans presented at the 1867 Paris and the 1873 Vienna fairs "prepared Europeans for what was accomplished at Paris in 1878."

The 1878 exhibition of educational accomplishments covered private as well as public education and every level of education. "The international jury awarded the American educational exhibitors twenty-eight more honors than those of any country save France; and although the educational exhibits comprised only one one/hundredth of the American section, they took nearly one sixth of the prizes given American participants." The educational exhibit was so impressive that "both Paris and London bid for the permanent possession of the American educational display." The 1878 exhibition, "with its illustrations of educational buildings, furniture, fittings, appliances, with the 2,500 volumes of educational literature, including reports of city superintendents, state boards of education, regents, and trustees, and the 400 volumes containing specimens of the work of American school and college students, won merited praise in many circles." "American superiority in textbooks the backbone of the American school curriculum was generally admitted" (Curti 1950, 852).

In just half a century the Americans had built an impressive school system, and there was a textbook industry that supported it and that was supported by it. That the textbooks received such recognition at the 1878 fair is significant, for the textbook is the means used to standardize and reduce, if not eliminate, variability from class to class and school to school. The curriculum is the course set out to control students and teachers, and the textbook, especially the graded text or reader, is designed to keep teachers and students on course. The textbook became an instructional material built according to allegedly scientifically determined specifications. Psychologists produced word lists that limit the words authors may use, and must use, in preparing texts. Textbooks are found in schools; and other books, trade books the vocabularies of which are not controlled by psychologists, are found in bookstores. There are few trade books in schools.

The Americans' greatest "festival of high machine-age capitalism" was, of course, the Philadelphia Centennial Exposition (1876). Nearly ten million celebrants viewed the machines then proudly displayed and now enshrined at the Smithsonian in Washington. Americans spent over five years and over $11 million not just to celebrate its centennial but to show that it too was a major competitor in the Western world's quest for industrial supremacy (Cremin 1962, 23). Functional relationships and processes were becoming more powerful in holding people together than were shared beliefs and values. Even the view the Americans had of the space they inhabited was being transformed by the time the centennial was celebrated. The fairs celebrated, sanctioned, and perhaps even legitimatized the transformation of how people worked, where they worked, how and where they lived, and how they viewed their world.

At the Centennial Exposition, Americans were impressed by the work of Della Vos of the Moscow Imperial Technical School. From him they learned about an instructional process that broke down tasks and trades into their specific components or skills. Pedagogy now mirrored the industrial process. Schools became the sites designated for teaching people how to function in the new and transformed spaces. Schools took children from the home and prepared them for the workplace, a function the family, professional educators claimed, was not prepared to fulfill. The home was the place where children were prepared for school, prepared for what was accepted as education. In time educators would account for their failures by giving accounts of what the ever-failing families did not do to prepare their children for school.

NEW SPACES, NEW FUNCTIONS, AND NEW INSTITUTIONS

Once the frontier, what Frederick Jackson Turner (1962, 3) called "the meeting point between savagery and civilization," was closed, the West was vast space to be exploited, settled, and transformed. It became a space to be filled with people and the artifacts of the industrial society, not just a place where soldiers and native Americans engaged and enraged each other. The wilderness was connected to the settled areas by iron bridges, iron rails, copper wire. It was quickly divided into specific spaces for specific purposes. The pattern that began to emerge after Appomattox was clear by 1890. Some of the West had been given to the railroads, and the railroads and the telegraph did bind the land together. Some of the West was reserved for the Indians; some for play; and some was to be wilderness for ever. Burton J. Bledstein (1976, 7) observed, "In the newly founded national parks—Yellowstone in 1872, Sequoia and Yosemite in 1890—spatial boundaries now protected wild nature itself." Nature had become a cultural artifact. Natural became a special, if not manufactured, quality. Curiously, *natural* became a contrivance (Boorstin 1977, 288). Educators and psychologists invented conceptions of the *natural* child, and then *adolescence,* on which they based their instructional programs. Education became a regularized and prescribed process. It became a series of treatments applied to children after their abilities, capacities, and learning styles were properly diagnosed and assessed.

America's mid-Victorians not only tamed the wilderness but organized all the time and space about them. The world of their youth was, depending upon one's perspective, either being transformed into something new or being disassembled. Whether they saw destruction or new possibilities, they saw the demise of what they had known. They responded by giving to virtually everything and everybody a time and a space. They took the simplest, the most fundamental categories—time and space—and applied them relentlessly to create a new and seemingly orderly world. "Mid-Victorians turned their interest toward identifying every category of person who naturally belonged in a specific ground-space: the woman in the residential home, the child in the school, the man in his place of work, the dying person in the hospital, and the body in the funeral parlor; the immigrant in the ghetto, the criminal in the prison, the insane in the asylum, the Indian on the reservation, the Negro in his segregated area, the Irishman in the saloon, the prostitute and the pimp in the red-light district" (Bledstein 1976, 56). Even animals were given special places—zoos. The newly created space for little children—the *Kindergarten*—was another social invention of this era.

Spaces could not be distinguished from each other unless they were marked off by boundaries. Those boundaries not only protected the spaces and the people in them but also regulated and controlled the behavior of those assigned to their allegedly appropriate spaces. The conviction that children and youth belong in school was so great by the middle of the twentieth century that since then enormous energy and effort have been spent trying to retain them all in school. Little attention has been given to asking whether school, as presently constituted, is a good place for all youth. The public school has become the instrument for maintaining age segregation in our society.

To help people adjust to their spaces and learn the behaviors appropriate for those spaces, there developed specialists of all sorts. Nurses helped people in sickness. Social workers helped people learn how to live in the slums. Teachers tended to students in schools. The specialists earned their credentials by completing professional courses controlled by colleges and universities.

The instruments of the modernization process—industrialization, immigration, and urbanization—transformed the social, as well as the physical, landscape. Cities gave people a new kind of independence and more opportunities than ever before, but they also destroyed traditional notions of community as well as the sense of community. Many, especially John Dewey, called upon the schools to do what the community could no longer do. He wanted the school to tend to the process whereby humans become human as well as teach subject matter, combat illiteracy, and realize the social, political, and economic purposes of the nation-state, for he realized, at least tacitly, the significance of age segregation. While Dewey wanted the school to be an educational as well as a political instrumentality, others were tending to improving instruction. Dewey did not prevail, for the newly arrived professional educators turned to psychology to professionalize and legitimize their new places in the university. Ellen Condliffe Lageman (1989, 185) concluded, "One cannot understand the history of education in the United States during the twentieth century unless one realized that Edward L. Thorndike won and John Dewey lost." Dewey wrote about education. Thorndike investigated ways to increase the efficiency of the curriculum and the instructional processes in schools. Consequently and subsequently, little attention was paid to education.

PROFESSIONALIZATION

Universities established specialized departments, institutes, schools, and colleges to train and to certify all the specialists who were to tend to people in their assigned spaces and roles. Progressives threw out tradition and metaphysics and turned to science, bureaucracy, and professionalism to manage the newly created spaces. Even the public school became a collection of specialized units. They were bureaucratically organized, and departmentalization was introduced. Professionals quickly developed ways to study and gather information to use in the rationalization and standardization of the complex system they were creating. By World War I, virtually every institution and every group had been surveyed and measured, not once but many times. Professional educators were especially enthusiastic about surveys. Before World War I, Edward L. Thorndike (1912, 34–35) claimed that "an educational survey of one state would seem to be at least as elaborate a task as a geological survey of a continent." Schooling and the administration of schools became increasingly complex, important, and regulated by two standards: science and democracy. Each standard required the application of public principles in uniform ways. Education was equal for all as long as instruction was uniformly administered. Eventually, researchers and evaluators accepted that it was appropriate and to the advantage of the profession to focus on how well a process was administered or how well a treatment was applied rather than on whether a process or treatment made any significant difference. Now it is possible for a teacher to receive high marks for his or her teaching if his or her teaching behaviors are seen to be those that have been documented to be associated with student learning. It is a system that does not necessarily require an examination of what that teacher's students have or have not learned.

Public school administrative and supervisory positions grew significantly during the progressive era, for public education was being professionalized. Ironically, teaching, not withstanding the rhetoric of the professional educators, as Jurgen Herbst (1989) demonstrated, was not being professionalized. The administration of schooling and the supervision of teachers, a work force that was essentially not very well educated, powerless, and mostly female, were responsibilities that required new professional personnel. For the year 1889, according to the U. S. Commissioner of Education, 484 cities reported an average of only four supervisors per city. Between 1890 and 1920, as Tyack (1974, 56) reported, the growth of supervisory positions in public school systems was phenomenal. It increased from 9 to 144 in Baltimore, 7 to 159 in Boston, 31 to 329 in Detroit, 58 to 155 in St. Louis, 235 to 1,310 in New York, 10 to 159 in Cleveland, and 66 to 268 in Philadelphia. To support this cadre of professionals, city school systems founded bureaus or departments of educational research, and universities did likewise. Before 1918 there were eighteen bureaus or departments of educational research in public school systems and only seven such organizations in teacher-training institutions. By 1925 there were sixty-nine bureaus in the school systems and twenty-nine in teacher-training institutions (Monroe 1928, 58; Liu 1945; Scates 1939). Special spaces had been created for new professionals, educational researchers whose research models, more often than not, came from psychology. They filled their time and space with countless studies designed to support the administration and supervision of the schools and their teachers.

The specialization of administrative and supervisory personnel extended down through the ranks of teachers. As the diversity of students and their needs increased with the growth of the total school populations, the viability of establishing special programs increased: programs for the retarded, the physically handicapped, the delinquent, and the gifted as well as special programs with vocational emphases. States quickly revised and differentiated their certification standards and categories. "In 1900," Tyack (1974, 185) observed, "only two states had specialized credentials; by 1930 almost all states had elaborate certification laws." By 1916, for example, Teachers College (Columbia University) gave its students a choice of work leading to specialized diplomas for fifty-five different positions (Katz 1966, 328). Specialization of teaching required more supervisors and administrators and the further professionalization of education.

Professionals were required to manage public institutions, including public schools, in effective, efficient, and accountable manners. Yet educators were also obliged to attend to the desires of the public who created the public institutions as well as to the standards of their profession or discipline. What the public wanted was sometimes different from how professionals believed schools should be managed. By definition, professionals needed a knowledge base for what they did. They needed something other than tradition to justify their ways of doing what they did. Educational research became not only useful but also politically necessary. In part, it provided a knowledge base for the new social functionary—the public school administrator. It was a source of authority different from the authority that resided in the community. Some even presumed it to be a greater authority, for it was scientific.

Professional educators and educational researchers focused not on education but on instruction. Education always entails the possibility of controversy about fundamental values that cannot be clearly and definitively resolved. In principle, instructional questions seem to have answers. Effectiveness of methods can be assessed—even, within certain confidence intervals, measured. Values cannot. Educational administrators, as Tyack and Hansot (1980, 295) recorded, "tried to turn political issues into administrative ones." The educators', especially the professional administrators', use of science and practices based on science turned out to be a way of exercising power while not assuming responsibility. It also turned out to be a way to limit choice and avoid discussions of purpose. Thomas B. Greenfield (1988) observed:

> A commitment to science in organizational affairs is not simply a commitment to rationality; it is rather, a commitment to a restricted framework of rationality. Such a framework, called science, eases the sense of responsibility for powerful actors in organizational administrative settings. It denies both responsibility and personal choice in the making of everyday decisions and in the making of decisions in a powerful world of organized reality. Such science takes sides in conflicts about the rightness of organizational purpose and about appropriate means for achieving them, but it denies it takes

sides and claims to look dispassionately at such reality. . . . obedience to a truncated concept of rationality has become a cover for the powerful administrator: science and rationality provide the ultimately persuasive and irrefutable excuse for the abdication of personal choice and responsibility. (139)

It is a system that is essentially and thoroughly impersonal.

FULL ENROLLMENT

The goal of professional educators was eventually realized. By the 1930s, it was generally accepted that high school attendance was desirable for all. After World War II, the schools began to experience full enrollment. By 1950, nearly 90 percent of American youth between ages fourteen and seventeen were attending secondary schools, 80 percent more than in 1900. Full enrollment had its price. It required schools to carry out two seemingly contradictory functions: a sorting function and a custodial function. They had to sort and to tend to students who were frequently there because they had no place else to go. When choice became compulsion, the social dynamics of schooling were, as already has been noted, radically transformed. The differences in deportment between those who wanted to attend school and those who did not was quite often quite impressive. As Cremin (1962, 128) observed, "the dreams of democratic idealists may have resided in compulsory-attendance laws, but so did the makings of the blackboard jungle."

As long as school attendance was voluntary, school authorities could easily manage the behavior of students by threatening them with expulsion from school. Compulsory attendance laws and their enforcement eliminated that threat. School officials had to find new ways to manage and to control students. As students openly rebelled in school or resisted by becoming passively aggressive in the classroom, educators invested their efforts in the application of psychologically derived behavior management and behavior modification techniques. They did not confront the situation by examining the curriculum (Ruchin 1977, 238). They looked not so much at content as at the processes of delivering the content and at ways of modifying behavior. Frequently, especially in the early 1970s, they discarded content. Required courses gave way to electives that promised to be relevant. Not surprisingly, indices of student performance subsequently showed declines—the SAT scores fell. Few observed that students tend not to do very well on tests that assess their mastery of material they have not studied.

It was once recognized that compulsory attendance required development of a variety of programs and even different kinds of schools. As early as 1910, some understood that compulsory attendance required school systems to organize different kinds of schools for different kinds of students:

> (a) Those pupils who have become quite incorrigible, and whose parents have lost control of them, must be sent to an institutional school, committed for a term of years. Only thoroughgoing reform is adequate. (b) A day truant school, where hours are long and manual work abundant. This school, while allowing pupils to sleep at home, should aim primarily to keep them off the street and away from the contagion of bad company. Such schools do not exist in America, but are found in English cities. (c) Special classes should be provided for pupils who cannot easily be brought under the ordinary school discipline. These classes may have the same programs as the ordinary classes, but should be under charge of teachers of sufficient maturity, experience, and personal character to cope with this type of child. (d) Possibly a fourth type of class should be for those who by irregular attendance have fallen away from the regular class attainments. ("Attendance" 1911, 294).

Compulsory attendance clearly required more of teachers and of schools than did voluntary attendance. Once compulsory attendance was instituted, teachers had to know more than what they were assigned to teach. They needed to know how to handle their students, how to interest and motivate them, and how to control their behavior. Once compulsory attendance was instituted, schools had to plan not a curriculum but a variety of offerings and a variety of ways to present those curricula in a variety of institutional settings to a great variety of children. According to Cremin (1962),

> Compulsory attendance marked a new era in the history of American education. The crippled, the blind, the deaf, the sick, the slow-witted, and the needy arrived in growing numbers. Thousands of recalcitrants and incorrigibles who in former times might have dropped out of school now become public charges for a minimum period. And as the school-leaving age moved progressively upward, every problem was

aggravated as youngsters, became bigger, stronger, and more resourceful. (127–28)

Compulsory attendance was the beginning of the differentiated curriculum, the beginning of what some describe as course proliferation, or the abandonment of standards. The differentiated curriculum is the device that allows the school to perform both its sorting and its custodial functions. It necessarily entails differentiation of the student body—the separation of some students from others. As early as 1861, John Philbrick of the Boston schools was arguing for the establishment of industrial schools for "a class of children, more or less numerous, which is too low down in the depths of vice, crime, and poverty, to be reached by the benefits of a system of public education" (quoted in Tyack 1974, 69–70). A generation later, California's superintendent urged that compulsory attendance legislation be supported so that the people would be saved "from the rapidly increasing herd of non-producers . . . from the wretches who prey upon society like wild beasts." The "non-producers," or "wild beasts," were not to be placed in schools, for they needed "labor schools, school ships, industrial and technical schools"—schools where they would be taught "how to work" as well as how to read (quoted in Tyack 1974, 60–69.) Before compulsory education, schools did some sorting of students. Some failed and a few were expelled. After compulsory schooling, schools had to do more sorting. Following World War II, schools had to find ways to sort and to retain students in school.

COLONIZATION

After Appomattox, higher education was being reorganized so it could supply the new social-economic order with a cadre of experts to tend to the specialized function in the newly defined spaces. Charles W. Eliot, who had been appointed to the presidency of Harvard in 1869, was making Harvard into a modern university by attending to science and the professional schools. He also worked on shaping the public high schools so they would serve the purposes of his new vision of a university. To guide and to motivate him there was Johns Hopkins, which became an important model for advanced graduate education in the late nineteenth and early twentieth centuries. When the opening exercises were conducted at Johns Hopkins in 1876, a new era in higher education was effectively announced. Denominational exercises and even prayer were conspicuous by their deliberate exclusion, and among the speakers was Darwin's "bulldog," Thomas Huxley.

Darwin was largely accepted in the academy and was being used to establish a new scholarship and new scientific disciplines, disciplines that would presumably serve the new cultural order. Psychology was one of the new disciplines that constituted the seedbed out of which educational research and instructional methods grew. When educators charged with maintaining public education allowed social scientists, especially psychologists, to colonize their own newly developing field (Hamilton 1989b), the possibility of public schools' being educational institutions was virtually eliminated.

The expectation that the imposition of the colonists' conceptions of mind and human learning and their investigative techniques and protocols would be productive and useful was founded on the assumption that education was not an independent enterprise but only a collection of applications from a variety of other disciplines. The colonists could not give effective direction to education. As Foster McMurray (1955) explained:

> What is important to recognize is that the empirical findings of research conducted in or concerning the schools, when problems and procedures are those of the recognized social sciences, do not tell us how to teach nor what to teach. In the same way that application of pure science to the industrial process is not found by simple deduction from basic knowledge, but is rather the product of creative invention, so also the "meaning" of the social sciences for education must be discovered by activities of a higher intellectual order than following suggestions, analogies, or supposed "implications" from foundational sciences. (134)

McMurray was making a point that William James, the founder of American psychology, made a half century earlier. In *Talks to Teachers*, originally delivered as a series of lectures to Massachusetts teachers, James instructed:

> You make a great, a very great mistake if you think that psychology, being the science of the mind's laws is something from which you can deduce definite programs and schemes and methods of instruction for immediate schoolroom use. Psychology is a science, and teaching is an art; and sciences never generate arts directly out of themselves. (James 1962, 3)

James's admonitions were not heeded. Since he offered them, the practice of education and educational research have been closely tied to psychology and psychometrics. Educators continue to pursue the educational implications of psychological theories and speculations, not realizing that the number of possible implications is limited only by the number of people looking for the possible implications or the imaginations of those who are looking for them. The irony is that those who have been trying to build the "one best system" have made procedural commitments that can give them systems but not *a* system.

While James was expressing his doubts about the utility of psychology for education, an entire generation of prospective school administrators, educational leaders, and educational researchers who were to determine how the problems of public education would be conceptualized and how research questions would be framed were preparing for their careers by studying psychology and how it might be applied to the newly and rapidly developing field of education. Psychologists saw the opportunities the new field offered and quickly made their "new science" available to education. Between 1900 and 1920, "three-quarters of those psychologists who cultivated applied concerns did so in the field of educational psychology" (O'Donnell 1985, 277). Colonization was apace with a vengeance.

By 1920, American psychologists had rejected introspection, were more interested in human performance than the nature and quality of human experience, and were keenly interested in becoming useful to society. They generally agreed that human behavior was thoroughly observable and therefore, in principle, predictable and even subject to modification and control. They believed their usefulness to society was their ability to predict and to control how humans would perform in given situations at given tasks.

As Americans embraced the "high machine age" and ever greater numbers of immigrants, it seemed necessary that citizens and workers be taught how to behave at their stations in the new social-economic order. The nation's economic and productive processes required people to appear at specified places at specified times to perform specified tasks. Public schools obliged by emphasizing punctuality and attendance, and parents continue to urge their children not to dawdle, so they won't be late for school. Psychologists provided educators "a model that proposed to raise the pupils' performance to meet pre-established norms" (O'Donnell 1985, 229). They gave education learning theories that addressed what could be observed and measured, and it was soon accepted that that which could not be observed and measured did not exist. As long as there was an abundance of people seeking places, the differences among learning, control, and prediction could be overlooked; and they were.

For too many, there was no question that the application of science, as defined by the psychologists and sometimes the sociologists, to the problems of public education was the way to render the means and the newly defined ends of education—specific performances and skills— more efficient than they had been. Inquiry into child development, learning, how to assess and measure learning and development, and how to predict who would and would not learn were high on the researchers' agenda. Study of Monroe's *Teaching-Learning Theory and Teacher Education, 1890 to 1950* (1952) shows not only how convinced so many were that psychology had to be the basis for the study of education, but also how long that belief endured. Monroe showed that teaching came to be conceived not as a problem to be studied directly, but rather as practices that were deduced from whatever was allegedly known about learning theory. Research in teaching became little more than the attempt to derive pedagogical principles from one of the many learning theories psychology offered, to do what James correctly argued could not be done. Monroe accepted the notion that education was essentially defined by learning theory and that there could be no educational research without measures of learning and measures of one's ability to learn.

During the 1960s, educational researchers seemed prepared to define educational research out of existence. The colonization was virtually complete. Certainly, there was an attempt to minimize the differences between educational research and research in the social and behavioral science disciplines. In the fourth edition of the *Encyclopedia of Educational Research,* Fred M. Kerlinger (1969) defined educational research in a way that emphasized how similar educational research was to that conducted by practitioners of the social-science disciplines. Educational research, he wrote,

> is social scientific research for a simple reason: an overwhelming majority of its variables are psychological, sociological, or social-psychological. Consider some of them: achievement, aptitude, motivation, intelligence, teacher characteristics, reinforcement, level of aspiration, class atmosphere, discipline, social class, race. All of these but the last two are psychological constructs. If the large portion of the variables are psychological, sociological, or social-

psychological, then the conceptual and methodological problems of educational research are very similar to the problems of psychological and sociological research. (1127)

For Kerlinger, educational research that was neither historical nor social-scientific was simply "not as important as" that which was.

Kerlinger's focus was not on the purposes of education or of public schooling but on how problems were conceptualized and how methods were selected and employed. His neglect of purpose was significant. To the extent that he accepted that either scientific or even philosophical (speculative) constructs constitute an adequate reconstruction of processes that in fact occur in the time and space we actually inhabit, it was a mistake and a denial of the purpose of the educator. He effectively denied or overlooked that the purpose of the educator is different from that of the psychologist. McMurray's (1955) observation about the difference between the two is still relevant:

> An educational theorist is interested in distinguishing true belief from false belief, or in distinguishing learning which accords with reality from learning which does not, and this is a kind of interest which a psychologist cannot share. For many psychologists at the present time, the process of learning what is in fact true is no different from the process of learning what is in fact false. And the construction of the standards by which truth is distinguished from its opposite is not the psychologist's business. But it is the business of an educational theorist and very close to the heart of his concern.
>
> Psychologists are interested in how people perform. Educators are interested in determining what is worth learning and how that learning can enlighten and inform the choices people make. (140)

Through the media the ever-present establishment continues to tell us that student performance is still not good enough, and educators strive to bring all up to a *minimum* performance standard. To some, *minimum* performance suggests improved standards or even excellence, but they are wrong. It means "just good enough." Perhaps it is time for professional educators to expel the colonists and recognize that the institution they are trying to improve may not be appropriate for the postindustrial society most of the world has entered. In the nineteenth century, when the public school was invented and established, most people lived in an information-poor society, compared to contemporary conditions. Children secured most of their information from direct experiences in the family, neighborhood, and church. Those experiences were "supplemented by a few windows to the outside world opened up by reading material at home or in school" (Coleman 1971, 116). Levels of vicarious experience were directly related to the children's growth and their reading abilities. Those who learned to read well increased their level of vicarious experience, but for the most part, those levels "were very unevenly distributed throughout the population of children" (117). Now the ratio of direct experience to vicarious experience has been turned upside down, and the ability to read, while it is perhaps more important than ever before, is not the only way children secure information. They have more access to vicarious experiences and less opportunity than ever before for direct experiences; yet the structure of the school is not fundamentally different from what it was at the turn of the century. The arrival of new media and the transformation of the nation's economic structure have changed the cultural context in which schools exist, as well as the people, teachers, and students who spend so much time in schools.

Our culture is different from what it was in the nineteenth century, but the structure and purposes of the public school are not much different. That the school is only one of the many educational institutions in which children and youth participate is only casually acknowledged. Little attention is paid to determining how all the educational institutions fit, or do not fit, together. That educators persist in seeking remedies, remedial solutions, and in seeking resources to establish either remedial or compensatory programs is evidence that many, too many, still view the school and *the* educational institution. It may be time not only to acknowledge the difference between schooling and education but also to consider seriously the nature and importance of the difference. It is time to examine the relationships among the school and the other educational institutions, to ask whether those relationships may need to be reconfigured, and how the school itself may need not to be reformed, restructured, or refurbished, but perhaps invented anew. In doing so, it may be profitable to ask what kinds of choices people want to make about their schooling and about their education, what they value, and what they want to know. If educators could see fit to ask what people wanted to know in place of asking how we can make people perform, school could become interesting and even useful. It might even become educational.

Notes

This chapter is a revision of a paper presented at the annual meeting of the Society for Applied Anthropology, 29 March 1990, University of York, York, England. The revision was supported by the Institute for At-Risk Infants, Children, and Youth and Their Families, University of South Florida.

References

"Attendance." 1911. In *Cyclopedia of Education.* Vol. 1 edited by P. Monroe. New York: Macmillan.

Bereiter, C. 1972. "Schools without Education." *Harvard Educational Review* 42:390–413.

Bledstein, B. 1976. *The Culture of Professionalism: The Middle Class and the Development of Higher Education in America.* New York: Norton.

Boorstin, D. 1977. *The Image: A Guide to Pseudo-Events in America.* New York: Atheneum.

Callahan, R. 1962. *Education and the Cult of Efficiency.* Chicago: University of Chicago Press.

Calhoun, D., ed. 1969. *Educating the Americans: A Documentary History.* Boston: Houghton Mifflin.

Carter, J. 1826. *Essays upon Popular Education Containing a Particular Examination of the Schools of Massachusetts, and an Outline of an Institution for the Education of Teachers.* Boston: Bowles & Darborn.

Coleman, J. 1971. "Education in Modern Society." In *Computers, Communications, and the Public Interest,* edited by M. Greenberger. Baltimore: Johns Hopkins Press.

Cremin, L. 1962. *The Transformation of the School.* New York: Knopf.

Cremin, L. 1988. *American Education: The Metropolitan Experience, 1876–1980.* New York: Harper & Row.

Cubberley, E. 1919. *Public Education in the United States.* Boston: Houghton Mifflin.

Curti, M. 1950. "America at the World Fairs, 1851–93." *American Historical Review* 55:833–856.

Greenfield, T. 1988. "The Decline and Fall of Science in Educational Administration." In *Leaders for America's Schools,* edited by Griffths, D., R. Stout, and P. Forsyth, eds. 1988. Berkeley, Calif.: McCutchan.

Hamilton, D. 1989a. "Beyond the Stable State." *History of Education Quarterly* 29:279–285.

Hamilton, D. 1989b. *Towards a Theory of Schooling.* London: Falmer Press.

Hansen, O. 1926. *Liberalism and American Education in the Eighteenth Century.* New York: Macmillan.

Herbst, J. 1989. *And Sadly Teach: Teacher Education and Professionalization in American Culture.* Madison: University of Wisconsin Press.

House, E. 1981. "Three Perspectives on Innovation: Technological, Political, and Cultural." In *Improving Schools: Using What We Know,* edited by R. Lehming and M. Kane. Beverly Hills, Calif.: Sage.

Hughes, R. 1981. *The Shock of the New.* New York: Knopf.

James, W. 1962. *Talks to Teachers on Psychology.* New York: Dover.

Janowitz, M. 1969. *Institution Building in Urban Education.* Russell Sage Foundation.

Katz, M. 1966. "From Theory to Survey in Graduate Schools of Education." *Journal of Higher Education* 37:325–334.

Kerlinger, F. 1969. "Research in Education." In *Encyclopedia of Educational Research,* edited by L. Ebel. Toronto: Collier-Macmillan.

Lageman, E. 1989. "The Plural Worlds of Educational Research." *History of Education Quarterly* 29:185–214.

Lazerson, M., and W. N. Grubb, eds. 1974. *American Education and Vocationalism.* New York: Teachers College Press.

Liu, B. 1945. *Educational Research in Major American Cities.* New York: Kings Crown Press.

Lowenberg, B. 1942. "Darwinism Comes to America, 1859–1900." *Mississippi Valley Historical Review* 28:339–368.

McClintock, R. 1971. "Toward a Place for Study in a World of Instruction." *Teachers College Record* 73:161–205.

McMurray, F. 1955. "Preface to an Autonomous Discipline of Education." *Educational Theory* 3:129–140.

Monroe, W. 1928. "Ten Years of Educational Research, 1918–27." *University of Illinois Bulletin* (Urbana, College of Education) 25:15–139.

Monroe, W. 1952. *Teaching-Learning Theory and Teacher Education, 1890 to 1960.* Urbana: University of Illinois Press.

O'Donnell, J. 1985. *The Origins of American Psychology: American Psychology, 1870–1920.* New York: New York University Press.

Ruchin, J. 1977. "Does School Crime Need the Attention of Policemen or Educators?" *Teachers College Record* 79:225–243.

Rush, B. 1965. "Thoughts upon the Mode of Education Proper in a Republic." In *Essays on Education in the Early Republic* edited by F. Rudolph. Cambridge: Harvard University Press.

Scates, D. 1939. "Organized Research in Education: National, State, City, and University Bureaus of Educational Research." *Review of Educational Research* 9:576–590.

Senate Subcommittee to Investigate Juvenile Delinquency. 1975. *A Report Card: 'A' in School Violence and Vandalism.* Washington, D.C. U.S. Government Printing Office.

Shulman, L. 1987. "Knowledge and Teaching: Foundations of the New Reform" *Harvard Education Review* 57:1–22.

Smith, F. 1988. *Further Essays into Education.* Portsmouth, N.H.: Heineman.

Smith, S. H. 1965. "Remarks on Education: Illustrating the Close Connection between Virtue and Wisdom." In *Essays on Education in the Early Republic,* edited by F. Rudolph. Cambridge: Harvard University Press.

Thorndike, E. 1912. "Quantitative Investigations in Education: With Special Reference to Co-operation within This Association." *School Review Monograph No. 2: National Society of College Teachers of Education Yearbook.* Chicago: University of Chicago Press.

Turner, F. 1962. *The Frontier in American History.* New York: Holt, Rinehart & Winston.

Tyack, D. 1974. *The One Best System.* Cambridge: Harvard University Press.

Tyack, D., and E. Hansot. 1980. "From Social Movement to Professional Management: An Inquiry into the Changing Character of Leadership in Public Education." *American Journal of Education* 80:291–319.

PART II

RHETORIC VERSUS REFORM AND RESTRUCTURING IN THE DISTRICT AND COMMUNITY

The purpose of the four chapters in Part II is to move the analysis closer to the "realities" of school change. Each of these chapters examines a case (or set of cases) of attempts to bring about structural change.

The lessons learned from current efforts to alter the forms of American education are sobering. The multiple political spheres in each context of school change frequently occupy very different and often colliding orbits. Understanding the agendas brought to the process of school change by community members, parents, elected officials, superintendents, teachers, and students is the minimal first step that must be taken before forging successful strategies for change. Frequently, however, the trajectories taken by events do not allow opportunities for reflection and a "rational" problem-solving atmosphere to develop. Events hurry participants along, as in the Chicago reforms described in two of the following chapters. Thus, structures are changed, erected, and weakened or destroyed by the most well-intentioned persons involved in school change.

The dilemmas and contradictions described in the following three chapters in the end, however, do not signal us to abandon hope. Rather, a central message is that complex political environments require complex and multiple strategies. The chapters in this section of the volume offer concrete examples of the complexities of urban school change.

7

COMMUNITY INVOLVEMENT AND STAFF DEVELOPMENT IN SCHOOL IMPROVEMENT

William T. Pink and Kathryn M. Borman

Improving schools is a difficult task. Two issues are especially problematic in this process. First, those engaged in improving schools must develop consensus on the definition of an effective school and the goals a school should strive to realize. Once goals are determined, a second problem remains—that of developing consensus on both the strategy and the content of a restructuring model to achieve the objectives. Both issues are exacerbated in the case of urban schools situated in complex, hierarchical district contexts and located in communities characterized by both values and ethnic pluralism (Chubb and Moe 1990; Hess 1990; Pink 1990).

In recent years in the United States, the effective-schools literature has been the most accessible place for school reformers to seek help in resolving these and other school-restructuring issues (Brookover 1979; Edmonds 1979; Levine and Lezotte 1989). In this literature, already formulated, reformers have found (1) a powerfully seductive view of a (primarily elementary) school that promotes both equity and social justice by calling for schools to realize student acquisition of the basic curriculum, independent of factors such as race and social class, *and* (2) a set of schoolwide "correlates" associated with student academic and additional outcomes. As schools embrace a school improvement strategy grounded in the mainstream school-effectiveness literature, they take on a series of domains for attention, such as strong leadership and an emphasis on basic skills.

While noting the caution that school improvement is a time-consuming activity and that change may result in measurable gains in student achievement only after several years, the literature, nonetheless, remains sanguine, proclaiming the successes of schools that have adopted and implemented the effective-schools model (Pink 1984; Project SHAL 1982; Teddie, Kirby, and Stringfield 1989). However, it is not simply intensive and extensive investment of time and energy that is required to bring about significant change. Schools seeking to create new structures and outcomes and to change rules, roles, and responsibilities must look beyond the effective-schools rhetoric to mobilize individuals who will be fundamentally involved in creating change, namely, members of the surrounding community and members of the school staff.

In this chapter, we argue that the effective-schools model misses two elements that appear to be critical to the successful conceptualization and implementation of school improvement. They are community involvement and staff development. The effective-schools literature is virtually silent on these two elements, although recent variants, such as Levin's Accelerated Schools, the so-called Comer Schools, and Sizer's Coalition of Essential Schools, give these factors more emphasis (Fullan 1991; Pink 1986). If school improvement activities are successful, fundamental rather than cosmetic changes in existing practices and school organization will occur. School improvement is dependent on two important features. The integration of parents and other community representatives as equal stakeholders with school-based educators in the conceptualization, implementation, and evaluation of school change is the first feature. The second involves construction of a staff development model—one that includes coordinated activities for teachers, administrators, and parents. Such activities should initially empower and subsequently support these key actors in their school improvement tasks.

A major point argued in this chapter is that successful collaboration among individuals who have a long history of confrontational relationships will not happen overnight, and may never occur unless staff development addresses *and* sustains productive interactions. While this statement may seem obvious to those working in the schools, evidence suggests that failure to recognize its importance, *and* to alter school practices that block the collaboration of parents, teachers, administrators, and community representatives, function to inhibit school reform based upon local decision making.

The remainder of this chapter will use case data from two in-depth studies to illustrate the importance of community involvement and staff development to improving schools. While both studies examine cities in the same region, the issues confronting each school district are very different.

COMMUNITY INVOLVEMENT: NORTH RIVERSIDE
FAILS TO MAKE CHANGES

In the United States, boosterism has long characterized a city's desire for an easily recognizable public image. Indeed, in his analysis of American cities, the sociologist Anselm Straus (1961) points to the importance to the citizenry in urban places of a widely understood, easily recognized identity that distinguishes one city from the next. Although we may speak of a broad American midwestern landscape, cities throughout the United States actively cultivate distinct community identities based on economic, sociocultural, and other indicators that allow them to differentiate themselves from other urban centers in this region and throughout the country.

The city of Riverside in southwestern Ohio is actually composed of two distinct sociocultural communities, although the city itself is a political entity governed by a single political structure including a mayor, city council, and city school superintendent. Thus, while citizens in both predominantly white North Riverside and exclusively black West Riverside elect the same mayor and enroll their children in the same school system, they have separate community allegiances and institutions. These include community recreational centers, churches, and informal social groups. Historically, the city's formal political bodies, including both the city council and the school board, have not had elected representation from the black community. Blacks, therefore, have invested their energy in neighborhood-based formal and informal institutions.

Compounding the issue is the fact that although both communities are working-class enclaves, they have had different and distinct racial compositions and have varied in the sizes of their populations. While the white community of North Riverside has a population currently close to eleven thousand, the black citizens of West Riverside number less than forty-eight hundred. Although both communities are largely made up of homeowners, property values in the primarily white North Riverside community are much higher, on the average ($47,000 vs. $23,000). Finally, the two communities, particularly with regard to educational issues, have historically experienced an uneasy alliance under a single political structure. For example, when the North Riverside district was mandated by state law to desegregate its elementary schools in 1957, the closing of Stern School in the West Riverside community fanned hostilities. It was widely understood that Sterne, although a relatively new and well-appointed facility, was targeted for razing to appease the white residents of adjacent North Riverside who had no desire to send their children to a school in the black West Riverside community.[1]

The influential, primarily white citizens of North Riverside see their community as struggling to maintain its integrity as a family-oriented, hard-working, and caring community with relatively low real estate taxes. Its location immediately north of a large midwestern city has limited its growth as a major population and industrial center. Indeed, the city throughout its development has been and continues to be a bedroom community, but one with appealing amenities despite its working-class character. It is a highly conservative community, and its local business association has actively attempted to draw commercial enterprises to the city. Specifically, Don Banks, the city mayor, placed the expansion and improvement of the city's business district as a primary goal when he took office in 1988. His dream has been to transform North Riverside into the "shopping center of the northern hills area." An expanded service-sector base would, of course, translate into additional tax dollars for the community. These dollars have been badly needed by the city to improve sidewalks, streets, and other aspects of the infrastructure, including the city's two elementary schools and combined junior-senior high school.

Insufficient operating funds to manage the school district was only one of several concerns that plagued the new school superintendent, Solomon Williams, when he was selected as the new superintendent in the late spring of 1988. Having suffered a series of financial catastrophes as a result of a number of failed tax levies and the fiscal mismanagement of a recent superintendent, the district was sent reeling in April 1988 when a midmorning fistfight among several students in the North Riverside High School building closed the school for the day and charges surfaced from West Riverside parents of pervasive racial inequities.

Despite repercussions from the racial confrontations during Williams's first year in office, voters in the North Riverside school district, including both North and West Riverside, passed the school district's $8.9 million operating levy, casting 1,754 votes for and 1,239 against (58.6 percent to 41.4 percent). The levy generated $750,000 for operating expenses, offsetting a projected $683,000 deficit that the district anticipated by June of that year (1989). Williams reflected on the favorable outcome of the levy to a reporter from the suburban press in this way: "I think that we had a nucleus of people who were convinced of the need for the levy. It is typical of the North Riverside community that when there is something essential, they respond in kind."

The identity of North Riverside as a community that rallies behind a common cause to support its local institutions is clear in the superintendent's rhetoric. However, given the basic differences between the two enclaves, when a crisis arose, as in the aftermath of the April fistfight at the high school, the two communities responded quite differently. The analysis that follows illustrates how the black community of West Riverside, in particular, created its own agenda for reform and change in the schools.

West Riverside's Strategies

Several strategies contributed to the increased visibility and political strength of the black West Riverside community in the months following the spring 1988 fistfight. They include (1) recognizing and utilizing local, state, and national sources of political pressure to bring to bear on the school system administration, (2) influencing the media, (3) eliciting the participation and subsequently monitoring activities of the university-based evaluators of the district's racial climate, who came on the scene in July 1988, and (4) putting forward a community-supported candidate for political office in the fall of 1989.

Political activities ultimately resulted in pressure on the new superintendent and his school board to address issues of long-standing concern to the West Riverside community, namely, lack of diversity at the administrative staff level, widespread absenteeism and suspension of black students, teacher over- and underreaction to student cultural differences, and lowered expectations for black students' academic performance. These complemented a host of issues at the school level, including fair administration of discipline, equitable assignments, homework, course placement, and parent governance. Also, students in the high school reported tensions in the hallways and cafeteria at school events and sports competitions at other schools.

The black community's efforts to influence district policies arose initially in response to the district's poor handling of the fistfight by attempting to dismiss it as a nonevent. First, members of the West Riverside community, through its local community council, formed the Student Affairs Committee (SAC) and elected an articulate, politically sophisticated chair. Its mission statement asserted that SAC's purpose was to bring about positive changes in the district, specifically in relation to practices, policies, programs, and personnel, in order to benefit all students by creating a "better, more productive educational atmosphere" via a process that was "logical, peaceful, bi-partisan, and harmonious."

Next, a letter written to the state superintendent of instruction requesting intervention was filed in Columbus. The letter charged the district with (1) the psychological oppression and physical abuse of black students, (2) the failure to recruit and hire blacks as administrators or to elect black representatives to the school board, and (3) the fiscal irresponsibility of the former administration, which had lead directly to "a decrease in teacher morale and an increase in teacher apathy toward students, especially black students." The SAC also sent copies of the letter to a number of highly influential politicians, including the two prominent U.S. senators from Ohio, John Glenn and Howard Metzenbaum, in addition to then U.S. secretary of education, William Bennett.

The immediate response of the district to this flurry of political activity in the black community was to propose to SAC leaders that "a cultural assessment" of the district be conducted by a neutral third party. There is little question that the district, in agreeing to carry out an evaluation of its practices, not only was responding to the demands of the highly vocal West Riverside community, but was also bowing to pressure from the state superintendent's office. This office, sensitive to both community concerns and the district's financial perils, provided $5,000 to partially support a year-long evaluation of district practices, requesting that the district provide an equal sum. The superintendent then approached the dean of the college of education at the local university to get a neutral, third-party assessment of district practices. A faculty-graduate student team including the second author was organized to design and implement an evaluation plan. State department of education dollars were used to leverage additional funds from local foundations. When it was completed, the evaluation of the district, in sum, provided both the black community (and particularly its political arm, the Student Affairs Committee) and the district with a number of recommendations based on responses to surveys and interviews conducted with district teachers, administrative staff, students, and parents. The recommended action steps encompassed several areas: multicultural education, race relations, administrative practices, and home-school relations. For example, in the area of multicultural education, the report recommended that the district establish a resource center at each school, housing "culturally inclusive" instructional materials for use by teachers. In addition, the absence of representation for the West Riverside community on the school board was seen as a perennial problem. Election to the board is conducted at-large in the district, a practice that had contributed to the fact that a black member has never served on the board. In this connection we recommended that the school board and administration position black community leaders to receive electoral support from the white community by recognizing their leadership and drawing West Riverside activists into policy deliberations.

Because the West Riverside community remained mobilized around these issues for more than a year following the April fistfight and through the period of study, it was able to campaign for a community representative to the school board in November, four months after the release of the report. The superintendent, who had at one point assured the research team that he would support such a candidate, became indifferent to the black community following the successful passage of the school levy shortly before the report was released in June 1989. Although the candidate put forward by the African-American community had superior credentials, including a doctoral degree in political science, and an impeccable reputation as a highly regarded minister, he was defeated by his white opponent.

The defeat of this outstanding candidate despite his well-organized and effective campaign, in addition to the withdrawal of the Student Affairs Committee's vocal and energetic chair, seemed to cripple the effectiveness of SAC and indeed of the West Riverside community as a whole. Although the superintendent kept discussion of the report alive in the district through regularly scheduled meetings of a task force he had organized for this purpose, the task force appeared to lack focus and concluded its year-long effort without recommending changes in district policies. Without the presence of vocal leadership in the community or continuing pressure from the state superintendent's office, this outcome was not surprising.

It was clear during our follow-up interview nine months after the release of the report that the superintendent considered our presence in the district to be intrusive and unhelpful, delegitimating the district's indifference toward the report's recommended action steps. In fact, the superintendent threatened to attend the national meeting of a major educational research association (AERA) to "defend the district" against what he perceived to be our inaccurate portrayal of North Riverside's "cultural environment."[2]

Given this unhappy ending to the story, are there any guidelines that can be put forward to assist in understanding how grassroots community action can be sustained and mobilized effectively to produce change in school district policies and practices? We think that there are at least three:

1. The vision and direction of vocal and well-respected community leaders is essential. Leadership may be present in one person, or it may be present in an active group, such as the SAC, that sustains and provides momentum for the community's political agenda.
2. In the case of disenfranchised groups, as was true here, other powerful groups or figures, especially those with authority to censure the district, can helpfully serve as monitors of the progress toward change and the redirection of district policies and practices.
3. Whether by coercion or by moral force, the appropriate school-based administrator (the superintendent, as was the case here) must provide the leadership to the district to achieve the goal of quality, integrated education. Clearly, in this case, Superintendent Williams's leadership was superficial and expedient.

   Moreover, the majority of the community's white residents, like the superintendent, simply wanted the problem to go away without their having to do anything about it. In his defense, the superintendent had taken on a district beleaguered by enormous debt and low morale, especially among the teachers of the district. Nonetheless, he missed an opportunity to pursue objectives that, had he worked collegially with community leaders, might have led to the creation of what the community most desired—"a better, more productive educational atmosphere."

We believe these three postulates are transferable to other school district contexts. All three have the force of moral suasion and call upon a district's and community's finest motives.

STAFF DEVELOPMENT: CHICAGO SEEKS
TO REFORM ITS SCHOOLS

The ambitious attempt to reform Chicago's schools is predicated upon the democratic control of schools at the local level. However, without rethinking staff development, designed explicitly to enable the key actors to work productively together *and* make good decisions based on appropriate theory, research, and practitioner reflection, school reform in Chicago is likely to remain mired in a web of ethnic distrust, localized power politics, and uninformed "faddish" practices.

Chicago is one of the major cities in the United States. It has a rich variety of older, ethnically diverse neighborhoods and is surrounded by a number of suburban communities that are largely white-collar and more affluent. It is rich in culture, commerce, industry, and architectural significance. Its central location has made Chicago a major transportation center. Recently, it has changed its image from being the "butcher to the world" and the home of Al Capone to being an exciting tourist and convention attraction.

The rich ethnic diversity of Chicago has made its politics world-renowned—"vote early and often" remains an oft-heard comment at election time. Long dominated by Mayor Richard J. Daley (1955–76), ward politics has helped fashion a thriving city, virtually impervious to economic recession. However, these same ward politics have had two related negative consequences. The involvement of some minorities in city government and its "spoils" system has been limited and has contributed to the creation of a school system that has become significantly less effective at the same time as its students have become progressively more black, Hispanic, and Asian. While the city school system is the third largest in the country (behind New York and Los Angeles), enrolling approximately 450,000 students, there are also approximately 750 private schools enrolling an additional 250,000 students.

In the last ten years, the Chicago Public Schools have had a succession of black superintendents (Ruth Love, Manfred Byrd, and Ted Kimbrough) and have undergone fiscal crises, reorganizations, teacher strikes, reduced enrollments, and declining student achievement. Historically, the school board has been appointed by the mayor, and the large district, with close to six hundred schools, has been managed through twenty-one subdistrict offices. It is only in the last two years that the school board has been selected by the mayor from slates provided by a citizens' committee.

Chicago's Education Reform Act of 1988 mandated major changes in the ways that the city schools do business. Interestingly, neither the current mayor (Richard M. Daley), the current superintendent (Ted Kimbrough), nor the current school board played any significant role in conceptualizing the Reform Act and moving it through the legislative process.

The major push for reforming the Chicago schools has come from the business community, whose primary concern was that too many graduates were unemployable, in addition to several public interest groups, primarily concerned about declining student achievement, and too-frequent teacher strikes. Local neighborhood community dismay about the quality and responsiveness of schools has also been a factor. The Reform Act symbolizes a significant event in the history of Chicago. It is one of the few times when ethnic and ward politics have been put aside to achieve a common goal, namely, school reform.

To address key themes in the reform of Chicago schools, the remainder of this chapter is organized in four sections: (1) a brief background to the recent reform legislation; (2) an examination of the various types of collaboration mandated by the reform legislation; (3) a discussion of how collaborative arrangements are working currently; and (4) a conclusion in which we offer a new conception for staff development. The latter addresses the importance of involving teachers, administrators, parents, and community representatives working together in sustained individual growth activities that target both interpersonal skills and state-of-the-art knowledge about teaching, learning, and school change.

The Chicago Reform Legislation

To better understand the importance of collaboration in the "new" governance of Chicago's schools, a brief summary of the evolution of the reform legislation follows. We will emphasize three major events.[3]

The first milestone was the passage of the Urban School Improvement Act (PA 84-749) in 1985. The state-level action was a response to the financial bankruptcy of the district, which had been ongoing since 1979. The Urban School Improvement Act compelled the development of power from a highly bureaucratic central office and provided parents new powers through school-based local school improvement councils (LSICs) to develop three-year school improvement plans (SIPs). However, this legislation also greatly restricted parental involvement by mandating both achievement goals for schools and a set of operating policies for councils.

Interestingly, the act contained a provision for promoting "staff improvement and stability." The language stated, however, that schools "may" develop a staff development plan—no money was set aside to support such a plan. Subsequent legislation has also ignored staff development.

The act also changed the role of the principal. Principals were charged to (1) form the LSIC, (2) aid in the development of the SIP, and (3) subsequently implement the SIP. Changed roles for both parents and principal are problematic because inner-city parents—primarily young, poor, and undereducated—generally lack the skills to work on committees to develop an SIP, while many principals are ill-prepared to share authority with parents and teachers or to govern their schools free of central-office mandates. In addition, white, middle-class leaders frequently lack the skills to recognize and utilize low-income leadership skills and experiences.

Second, in 1987, Mayor Harold Washington, the first black mayor of Chicago, formed an Education Summit to address a range of issues. The summit was the result of the heated, vocal discontent in the city of parents, teachers, and the business community concerning consistently falling test scores, escalating disciplinary problems, a high dropout rate, and a recent protracted teacher strike. Mayor Washington convened the major stakeholder groups—teachers' union, school administrators, business leaders, and parent and community groups—to enter into a sustained negotiation about the future of public education and jobs in the city.

The mayor had no specific package of reforms in mind. In fact, Washington's style, beyond an infrequent appointment to the school board, had been a "hands-off" approach to education in the city. The expectation was that ideas would emerge from community-based public dialogue, percolating to the top from the wards. The balance of the summit's fifty-four representatives *by the mayor's design* favored nonprofessional, parent and community representatives (44 percent) over professional (19 percent) representatives. The prevailing idea in the mayor's office and in much of the business community was that professional educators had created the mess in the schools and were thus unlikely or unable to clean it up. As the political forces were played out in this highly visible forum—a forum that included several public hearings where parents gave testimony "on the record"—the ideas of influential public interest groups, that is, Designs for Change and the Chicago Panel on Public School Finance (CHIPS), concerning democratic localism and school-based decision making, emerged as the foundational ideas for a reform model. A major outcome of the process followed in Chicago is that parents, rather than school board employees as in New York City's decentralization efforts in the 1970s, became the key decision makers about changes in the schools.

At the mayor's untimely death (November 1987), the power base shifted to Springfield, the state capital. Extensive lobbying followed—by teachers, parents, public interest groups, and business leaders. Those most able to articulate a reform bill, the public interest groups and the business leaders, played the major role in shaping the resultant legislation.

Finally, Senate Bill 1839 was passed in 1988 and contained much of the intent and language of Mayor Washington's earlier Education Summit activity. A slightly amended bill (SB 1840) was subsequently signed into law by Governor Thompson in the fall of 1988. Parents gained significantly in this legislation: (1) Parents, through majority membership on the newly mandated local school council (LSC), have the authority to hire and fire the principal; (2) parents approve the school-based budget, which includes the allocation of Chapter I and other discretionary funds; and (3) parents approve the school improvement plan (SIP).

The local school council at each school (comprising six parents elected by parents, two teachers elected by teachers in the school, the principal, and two community representatives elected by the community) has become the centerpiece of school governance. Significant regulatory and decision-making powers have been devolved from the central office under the rubric of the "central support system." Principals must function within a changed environment. They must consult regularly with the LSC about the SIP, annual expenditures, new hires, and the physical plant. They must also work collaboratively with both teachers and parents on issues concerning discipline, attendance policies, and the instructional program.

The five-year evolutionary process in Chicago is interesting because it illustrates the difficulties for parents of gaining access to the decision-making process in a large urban school system. In this case, however, the scope of the involvement they have won is sweeping, and the potential for changing schools is great. Time alone will indicate their effectiveness in improving schools for their children. The grand experiment is too new to make summative pronouncements, but we can make some preliminary observations.

Predictably, the first year (1989–90) for the schools under the new legislated governance structure was difficult. With relatively little support from the central office, schools struggled (1) to elect members to the LSC, (2) to develop an SIP and an operational budget, and (3) to make a decision, as occurred in 50 percent of the schools in the first year, on releasing or retaining the principal. These were difficult tasks to complete, for urban parents confronted for the first time with such decision-making powers in a public forum.

Parental and community involvement in conceptualizing and implementing school improvement is critical to fundamental change both in the organizational features of the school and in practices concerning teaching and learning (Hess and Easton 1991). However, the prior history of the Chicago Public Schools is replete with examples of governance by centralized top-down policy mandates and educational stagnation. LSCs in their first year varied in their levels of success. Less successful LSCs are those with principals unwilling or unable to share authority and where attendance at and/or participation in council meetings is low. More successful are those LSCs that are functioning well as decision-making teams as they begin to entertain serious questions about curricula and instruction. This bold and innovative governance structure holds much promise for effecting significant school reforms (Easton and Storey 1990).

Types of Collaboration Mandated by the Reform Legislation

The Reform Act changed both the balance of power and the system of decision making in the Chicago schools. The long-established pattern of oppressive central-office control, a system that required strict adherence to standard operating procedures, was abolished in a single legislative act. It was replaced by a system that required the "local school community" to govern itself. While novel for a system with a very long history of dependency on an "imperial" central office, it also created a set of collaborative arrangements that placed many actors, several for the first time, on the same side of the table with respect to school improvement. Several key collaborations were created by the reform legislation:

1. Collaboration among members of the local school council (LSC). In this context six parents, two teachers, two community representatives, and the principal are charged to make policy for their school. Power has shifted from the principal to the council. There is considerable role ambiguity and a range of expertise in the council that may polarize council members or that may heighten the group's inability to act creatively and resourcefully.
2. Collaboration between the LSC and the principal. Now the principal works for a council that has the authority to hire and fire, yet the principal must administer the school. How are power and decision-making negotiated? What role(s) can the principals play with his or her new "employers"?
3. Collaboration between the LSC and the District Superintendent's Office (DS) and the central office, now renamed the Central Service System. The reform legislation has moved decision making from both the central office and the subdistrict offices and placed it at the school level. Yet the LSC must continue to do business with both of these offices, even as all the actors must work to define new roles for themselves. Who decides what is still unclear. Who decides who decides is perhaps even more problematic.

4. Collaboration among the LSC, parents *not* sitting on the LSC, and the greater community the school serves. Moving decision making to the schools gives responsibility and new roles to previously disenfranchised groups. Does the creation of the council focus decision-making power in the hands of fewer or more stakeholders? How are the wider interests of parents given "voice" in the council deliberations?

5. Collaboration between the LSC and PPAC. The Reform Act created the Professional Personnel Advisory Committee (PPAC) to provide teachers a way to influence school improvement at the building level. Teachers can decide how to structure this committee—some schools have elected members, others have operated as a committee of the whole. The problem is that there is no formal mechanism beyond the two teacher representatives on the LSC to represent teacher views. The PPAC is an advisory body. How can the broad range of teacher expertise be given an appropriate voice in the new governance structure? To what degree does community empowerment restrict teachers' empowerment?

6. Collaboration between the LSC and public interest groups interested in providing "training" to assist school reform. Here, as with other factors, new working relationships need to be created as an outcome of the reform legislation. Schools have had little experience designing their *own* staff development needs, while outside agencies frequently have a view of effective schools and reform that they are all too happy to package and bring to the schools. What is the appropriate role of the not-for-profits and the business community in shaping school goals and staff development programs? Where does support stop and advocacy begin?

7. Collaboration among the LSC, PPAC, principal, and local universities. Again, the new governance structure creates the opportunity for different kinds of collaboration among these groups and the resources of the universities. The issue is, who is controlling the school improvement and staff development activities? What models of staff development do university "change agents" bring to school reform activities? What is the impact of unequal access to knowledge about school change and best instructional practices on the shape, scope, and pace of school reform?

This list illustrates the kinds of collaborative arrangements created by the reform legislation that have surfaced during the first two years. All these arrangements require *both* new roles *and* new game rules. Not only does it take time to develop new roles and game rules, but the process is further complicated when actors come to the table with (1) differing cultural beliefs and expectations about schooling, learning, and change, (2) differing levels of sophistication concerning the dynamics of group decision making, and (3) differential knowledge and access to "best practices" concerning schooling, learning, and change. The next section will explore these issues in greater depth.

How Is Collaboration Working in Year 2 of the Reform Act?

To begin to find answers to questions about how well these new collaborative arrangements are working, the first author drew on two sources of data. One source was initial interview data gathered from teachers, administrators, parents, and community representatives collected as part of a citywide survey of stakeholders concerning the future research needs in the Chicago Public Schools. These interviews were conducted by the Consortium on Chicago School Research. In each individual or focus group interview a standard protocol was used. These data are useful because they reveal perceptions of what is and what isn't working from the viewpoints of several stakeholder groups.

The second source of data is interviews with and observations of teachers, administrators, parents, and community representatives actively engaged in a school improvement project involving outside "change agents" in four schools. These four predominantly black, low-income, elementary schools are working with the Center for School Improvement, a consortium of the Chicago Public Schools, National-Louis University, and the University of Chicago. Two of the schools are also members of the School-Parent-Community Project conducted by National-Louis University that is designed to provide assistance in implementing reforms in reading and writing.

In analyzing data concerning collaboration from both the stakeholder survey and the subsequent interviews and observations of actively engaged reformers, several clear patterns emerge. These patterns are informative because they highlight the problematics of expecting collaboration without providing support for preparing and sustaining the actors in this new activity. It reveals, unfortunately, a second example of mandating a top-down change in a school district while ignoring the need to plan for and support, both fiscally and with personnel, the mandated behaviors. To illustrate these problems, themes for each of the first three collaborations are outlined in the three sections that follow.

Collaboration among Members of the Local School Council A number of themes surfaced from interviews and observations concerning the difficulties of initiating and sustaining collaboration among six parents, two teachers, two community representatives, and the principal. These six themes were also apparent in the earlier survey:

1. Individuals on the LSC come with vastly different perceptions of their roles and agendas for reforming schools. Some parents and community representatives come with the agenda to advance themselves politically, others to advocate exclusively for a racial or ethnic segment of the school population. Many come to the LSC with the perception that they will "run the school" and make every decision for the principal. Fair representation of the diversity of the community was also seen as problematic when many groups were unable to elect their own candidate to the LSC. Who talks for them in LSC deliberations? Team building and developing a common vision for the school were also seen as highly problematic.

2. Individuals come to the LSC with different kinds of experiences concerning "procedures for organizing and running a meeting" *and* with divergent views concerning substantive issues germane to school improvement. The way parents and community representatives can play a role equal in status to professionally trained peers, teachers, and the principal is problematic.

3. The chair of the LSC, mandated to be a parent, is frequently elected on the basis of popularity. His or her inability to manage sometimes-hostile audience participation, and to organize and orchestrate the agenda, results in less-productive meetings.

4. LSCs have difficulty prioritizing issues vis-à-vis school improvement. The different agendas (see #1) brought by members of the LSC tend to fragment the LSC around items of self-interest (e.g., hiring and firing of relatives, sequencing of buses at dismissal, firing all white teachers vs. school improvement issues involving pedagogy and instructional materials). Problematic, again, is the limited ability, at least in the short term, to forge a collaborative approach to problem definition and solution.

5. The lack of consistent attendance by LSC members makes gaining a quorum impossible. Decision making is compromised when members of the LSC drop out, but don't resign. Procedures for replacement are not yet widely known.

6. There is a lack of vision concerning both the intent and scope of the LSC—a function of years of dependency on an "imperial" central of-

fice. LSCs have difficulty understanding the differences between policy and implementation.

Parents and community representatives are getting some information about their schools for the first time. Thus, there is much interest in confronting the principal about issues that should not necessarily concern parents while ignoring larger issues of policy that should concern them—since the principal cannot chair the LSC, she or he is at the mercy of the chair in these deliberations. Agenda setting and developing a vision for each school is seen as a cause for concern.

Collaborations between the LSC and the Principal The reform legislation changes the nature of the principalship in the Chicago Public Schools. Principals lose their tenure and seniority in the system and are now hired and fired by the LSC on a four-year term. They have been shifted from being *the* decision maker in the school, working for the central office, to being one member of an eleven-member team (the LSC) responsible for making decisions about how that school will operate. Three themes concerning this collaborative activity emerged across the interview and observational data:

1. The question "Who is in control?" has yet to be resolved in most schools. In many schools it has been difficult for principals to share power with the LSCs and for the LSC to assume power previously unavailable to them. This new governance structure is seen by those closest to it as both complex and fluid. Some principals have been frustrated by what they perceive as slow progress in approving and implementing the SIP and have responded by dominating the LSC by manipulating the agenda items and controlling the time in LSC meetings available for parent participation from the floor. In other cases, principals have become so concerned about job security that they have avoided making controversial (but needed) decisions. The mechanisms for negotiating the operational rules of the LSCs are not yet in place—there are few guidelines in the legislation to resolve such problems.

2. Members of the LSC see access to information as important to their ability to make informed decisions. A common concern voiced by LSC members was principals who withheld information to influence decision making. This demonstrates for LSC members a "lack of trust" on the part of the principal. Information about the budget and the legalities of alternative solutions to policy issues surfaced most frequently.

3. Teachers serving on the LSC sometimes find themselves compromised in "voting their conscience" against the wishes of the principal, when the principal must legally complete their employment evaluation. The role relationships among the various members of the LSC need clarification.

Collaboration among the LSC, the District Superintendent's Office, and the Central Office (Central Service Center) The Educational Reform Act created the LSC while removing decision-making power from the central office and the subdistrict superintendent's office. In doing so, the relationships among these three entities were not clearly spelled out. Four themes emerged from the data concerning what is currently occurring:

1. Role ambiguity currently exists throughout the Chicago Public Schools. The question "Who is responsible for what decisions?" surfaced in every stakeholder group. LSC members report calling the central office and being passed from one telephone station to another—"nobody wishing to be quoted as giving information"—and being told by their subdistrict superintendent to call the central office if they need information. They express considerable frustration when trying to understand "what is going on."
2. The lack of general information and data about their own school available from the central office is seen as a major roadblock to decision making by the LSCs. Questions about budget issues and the legalities of doing things differently (e.g., evaluating the principal and developing ways to spend discretionary funds) are the items most frequently mentioned. There is a strong suspicion voiced by LSC members that this lack of information is intentional, because they perceive that the central office is opposed to the reform legislation and want to see parents fail.
3. The subdistrict superintendents perceive themselves in limbo as a result of the legislation. They feel unconnected to the central office (they are now hired by a district council made up of one representative from each LSC in that subdistrict) and yet "relatively powerless" to help LSCs in significant ways because they have "limited staff and almost no operating budget." Again, role ambiguity and unclear lines of communication act as barriers to successful governance.
4. Local community governance, as mandated by the reform legislation, is viewed by many as signaling the dissolution of the Chicago Public Schools. Unclear to many is how individually governed schools can be a part of a school district—many LSC members, previous disenfran-

chised by the bureaucracy of the Chicago Public Schools, are distrustful of the motives of the central office. The tension is between those who see the individual schools as the *only* focus for educational improvement and those who see a continuing leadership role for centralized services. Presently, there is a lack of clarity concerning which model of governance is currently in place, and no consensus concerning which governance model would be "best" for Chicago's schools.

Putting Collaboration as the Centerpiece of Reform

With respect to the question of how well these new collaborative arrangements are working in the Chicago Public Schools, we must say that it is too soon to offer a definitive answer. Presently, however, there are a number of problems that make the development of productive collaboration problematic. While some schools have created strong and productive decision-making structures, most are struggling to create an organization that supports collaborative decision making.

Interviews and observations with teachers, administrators, parents, and community representatives indicate that visions of improved schools fail to recognize or acknowledge (1) that productive collaboration among all the actors in the new governance system must be the centerpiece of school improvement, and (2) that schools must develop sustained staff development activities and must nurture such productive collaboration. Almost without exception, visions of "good schools" were framed in some variant of the "effective schools" model and thus ignored both collaborative governance and staff development. The following list is typical of components included in visions of good schools:

1. Children and staff are safe.
2. Children are actively involved in learning, and they are happy to be there.
3. The school staff believes their students can succeed.
4. The principal is strong and actively promotes a school vision and sets a positive school climate.
5. The physical plant is safe and conducive to learning.

We suggest that without a shift in focus that mobilizes staff development activities designed to improve the various collaborative arrangements mandated by the reform legislation, school reform in Chicago will continue to be stalled by a combination of ethnic distrust, local politics, and uninformed decision making about school improvement activities.

CONCLUSION

Staff development remains a missing element in school reform (Pink 1986). Where staff development activities do exist, they are often based on a deficit model of teachers' and parents' skills and abilities. Staff development grounded in the dominant positivistic paradigm seeks to *remediate* teachers' perceived technical and instructional weaknesses. However, staff development grounded in an ecological or interpretive paradigm seeks to engage *all* those playing a role in school improvement (e.g., teachers, administrators, parents, and community representatives) in an examination of their taken-for-granted assumptions, beliefs, and values, which, in turn, drive their behaviors and conceptions about school improvement (Pink and Hyde 1992).

Clearly, the paradigm employed governs the discourse about school improvement. Those using a positivistic (process-product) paradigm view school improvement primarily as a process of "tightening-up" teacher behavior in the classroom (see figure 7.1). Thus, emphasis in staff development is placed on eliminating teachers' perceived weaknesses through activities such as "active teaching," "time on task," and "assertive discipline." In this paradigm, issues concerning pedagogy, school organization, and even curriculum content become reduced to "training" teachers and parents to use the "effective" behaviors and techniques in order to produce greater student achievement on standardized tests.

In contrast, those employing an ecological (Shulman 1986) or interpretive (Erickson 1986) paradigm place a very different emphasis on staff development (see Figure 7.2). Here school improvement turns on the taken-for-granted assumptions of all the major actors, not only teachers, concerning learning, together with an understanding of the cultural context of the school. Staff development now focuses on an extended examination of assumptions, beliefs, conceptions, and behaviors that drive *school-level* pedagogical, organizational, and curricular decisions.

We suggest that collaboration must be viewed from an ecological or interpretive paradigm. When this happens, staff development can be focused on an extended examination of the problematics of collaboration and the subsequent development of activities that facilitate productive collaborative arrangements. In short, collaboration itself is made problematic, and staff development systematically interrogates the elements that make it so.

In addition, school reform must be locally based, fixed in the community. Collaboration in this context must lead to (1) development of a shared vision for schools (with *each* school developing its own vision),

Figure 7.1. Staff Development Based on a Process-Product Paradigm

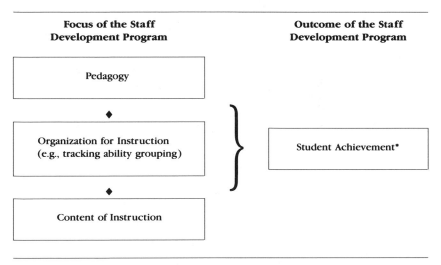

| **Focus of the Staff Development Program** | **Outcome of the Staff Development Program** |

Pedagogy

♦

Organization for Instruction (e.g., tracking ability grouping)

♦

Content of Instruction

Student Achievement*

Source: Pink & Hyde, 1992

*Student achievement is the prime concern of researchers and staff developers who employ a process-product paradigm

and (2) the development of school improvement strategies generated via consensus by an LSC or a similar body. To continue to ignore how best to achieve these two goals, is to keep the journey for school reform in a permanent stall. Staff development, reconceptualized in an ecological or interpretive paradigm and targeted specifically to correct this stall, must synthesize theory, research, and practitioner reflection (Pink and Hyde 1992). When a staff development program is based on theory, research, and practitioner reflective thinking, *and* linked to collaborative work on tasks that teachers, parents, and community representatives perceive to be important, school improvement efforts are likely to be successful in the short term and, perhaps most importantly, sustained over time. The importance of destroying the myth of the one-size-fits-all staff development program cannot be over emphasized (Pink 1990). The culture of individual schools must be fully understood, personnel and fiscal resources must be available, and school improvement must remain a top priority at the district level (Pink 1984, 1992a).

In addition, in order for improvement activities to change urban schools, the problem of schools' failure to educate children at risk must be perceived not only as a technical one but also as a political one (Apple 1987; Pink 1992b; Williams 1989). As has been demonstrated

Figure 7.2. Staff Development Based on an Ecological or Interpretive Paradigm

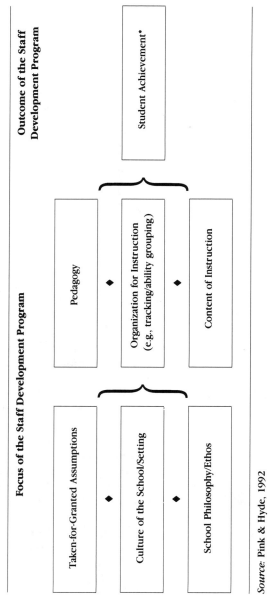

Source: Pink & Hyde, 1992

*While student achievement is frequently not the prime concern of researchers and staff developers who employ an ecological or interpretive paradigm, we use it here to illustrate the major difference with the assumptions indicated in Figure 7.1.

elsewhere, when an effectively organized neighborhood group interacts regularly and over the long term with both the district and the individual school to advise, monitor, and evaluate the implementation of reform activities, outcomes can be impressive. Specifically, such grassroots political engagement can improve the climate of the school, alter ineffective or harmful policies, and attract resources (Williams 1989; Borman et al. 1990).

The major objective of this chapter has been to explore how staff development and community political action can spur school reform in two settings. A second objective has been to suggest strategies for teachers, parents, and neighborhood citizens to begin to work collaboratively in local schools to effect school improvement. In our work, outcomes of these efforts have focused on activities such as decreased absenteeism, lessened teacher over- or underreaction to student cultural differences and subsequent lowered expectations of students, enhanced parent governance structures, and fair administration of discipline, homework, classroom, and course assignments.

A particularly pressing question that we have attempted to address here is, How do specific sites successfully solve the problem of goal displacement? A "you do it for us" mentality by which parents, teachers, or administrators will have *their* issue highlighted can destroy essential cooperative planning, monitoring, and evaluating efforts. A second question concerns the various ways schools can best mobilize school and community resources to collaborate to conceptualize, implement, and evaluate a school improvement plan. A third question focuses on the role and "custom design" of staff development to support the conceptualization, implementation, and evaluation of the school improvement plan. We see this chapter making an important contribution to framing key concerns for the success of school improvement activities at the district *and* school-site levels.

As schools wrestle to reform themselves, it is evident that they must think in bold and innovative ways. As the saying goes (with a minor addition): "If you continue to do what you have always done—and think in ways you have always thought—you will continue to get what you have always gotten."

Notes

1. School board meeting minutes from this period contain a quite candid account of the response of both communities to the desegre-

gation plan that included the closing of Sterne School. These minutes contain lengthy discussion by the members of the all-white board at this time.

2. Because anonymity has been requested by the superintendent, a full citation of the report cannot be provided here. However, a chapter written by researchers Kathryn Borman, Patricia Z. Timm, Zakia El Amin, and Markay Winston, based on the report, appears in *Research Directions for Multicultural Educations,* edited by Carl Grant (New York: Falmer, 1992).

3. The development of the reform effort in Chicago is given comprehensive treatment in Hess's (1990) account of the same period.

References

Apple, M. W. 1987. "Producing Inequality: Ideology and Economy in the National Reports on Education." *Educational Studies* 18(2): 145–220.

Borman, K. M., P. Timm, Z. El-Amin, and M. Winston. 1990. "Using Qualitative Methods to Explore Multicultural Education." In *Research Directions for Multicultural Educations,* edited by Carl Grant. Barcombe Lewes, England: Falmer.

Brookover, W. B., 1979. *School Social Systems and Student Achievement.* New York: Praeger.

Chubb, J. E., and Moe. 1990. *What Price Democracy? Politics, Markets, and America's Schools.* Washington, D.C.: Brookings.

Easton, J. Q., and S. L. Storey. 1990. *Local School Council Meetings during the First Year of Chicago School Reform.* Chicago: Chicago Panel on Public School Policy and Finance.

Erickson, F. 1986. "Qualitative Methods in Research on Teaching." In *Handbook on Research on Teaching,* 3d ed., edited by M. C. Wittrock. New York: MacMillan.

Hess, G. A. 1990. *Chicago School Reform: What It Is and How It Came to Be.* Chicago: Chicago Panel on Public School Policy and Finance.

Hess, G. A., and J. Q. Easton. 1991. "Who's Making What Decisions: Monitoring Authority Shifts in Chicago School Reform." Paper presented at the American Educational Research Association meeting, Chicago, Illinois.

Pink, W. T. 1984. *Effective Schools Pilot Project.* Kansas City, Mo.: Department of Planning, Research, Evaluation and Testing, Kansas City Public Schools.

Pink, W. T. 1986. "Facilitating Change at the School Level: A Missing Factor in School Reform." *The Urban Review* 18(1): 19–30.

Pink, W. T. 1990. "Staff Development for Urban School Improvement: Lessons Learned from Two Case Studies." *School Effectiveness and School Improvement* (1):41–60.

Pink, W. T. (1992a). "The Politics of School Improvement." *Education and Urban Society* 25(1): .

Pink, W. T. (1992b). "A School-within-a-School for At-Risk Youth: Staff Development and Program Success." In *Effective Staff Development for School Change,* edited by W. T. Pink and A. A. Hyde. Norwood, N.J.: Ablex.

Pink, W. T., and A. A. Hyde. 1992. "A School-within-a-School for At-Risk Youth: Staff Development and Program Success." In *Effective Staff Development for School Change,* edited by W. T. Pink and A. A. Hyde. Norwood, N.J.: Ablex.

Shulman, L. S. 1986. "Paradigms and Research Programs in the Study of Teaching." In *Handbook on Research on Teaching,* 3d ed., M. C. Wittrock. New York: MacMillan.

Straus, A. 1961. *Images of American Cities.* New York: Free Press.

Williams, M. R. 1989. *Neighborhood Organizing for Urban School Reform.* New York: Teachers College Press.

8

MONITORING THE IMPLEMENTATION OF RADICAL REFORM: RESTRUCTURING THE CHICAGO PUBLIC SCHOOLS

G. Alfred Hess, Jr. and John Q. Easton

On 2 December 1988 the Illinois State Legislature voted to pass the Chicago School Reform Act (PA 85-1418). The act fundamentally changed the structure of public education by creating Local School Councils consisting of two teachers, six parents, two community representatives, the principal, and in high schools a nonvoting student. Based on the business theory of participatory decision making, the councils are the vehicle through which the goals of Chicago school reform are to be achieved.

Chicago school reform has been called the most radical experiment in the history of public education. Its success or failure will have a major impact on how American children are educated. This chapter depicts the major elements of Chicago's particular type of school reform, from the actual restructuring of the Chicago Public Schools system to the effort to implement radical change through providing freedom and enabling support for local school leaders to break away from the stultifying sameness of bureaucratically controlled school programming. A primary question in the Chicago experiment is whether the reality of school improvement will live up to the rhetoric of change that was utilized to win passage of the mandating legislation.

This chapter describes the conditions that gave rise to the reform movement, the restructuring reforms enacted by the state legislature, and the first year's implementation.

THE CHICAGO PUBLIC SCHOOLS: IN NEED OF REFORM

The Chicago School Reform Act builds upon the unique history of the Chicago Public Schools system (a fuller account of the reform act and the conditions that led up to its enactment is provided in Hess 1991. In 1985, the Chicago schools enrolled some 435,000 students, down from a high of 585,000 in 1968 (Chicago Board of Education 1985). The school system was recovering from a fiscal crisis in 1979–80, when it had failed to meet its payroll and required a state financial bailout. This bailout included subjecting many of its financial decisions to the review and approval of an oversight board, the Chicago School Finance Authority. Under the terms of the bailout, the system was forced to cut more than eight thousand positions from its budget (Hallett and Hess 1982).

The school system was also operating under a desegregation consent decree and had increased minority enrollment in formerly predominantly white schools. However, in a school system that had only about 15 percent white enrollment, that left the vast majority of minority students continuing to attend completely segregated schools and not benefiting significantly from desegregation (Hess and Warden 1987).

The school system had involved parents in advisory roles for a number of years. Local advisory councils had been established at virtually all schools. Chapter I parent advisory councils were maintained at Chicago schools even after they were no longer required by the federal government. Bilingual advisory councils were functioning in most schools serving large numbers of Limited-English-Proficient students (Chicago provided special instruction to students who, collectively, spoke more than eighty different languages). Further, the local school advisory councils or PTAs had been involved in the selection of school principals for nearly fifteen years, interviewing candidates and recommending their three preferences, which were almost always followed in the general superintendent's recommended appointments.

However, the system was not being very successful in educating the children enrolled in its schools. In January 1985, Designs for Change, a Chicago-based educational research and advocacy group, released a study that showed that only one out of three graduating seniors was capable of reading at the national norm, and that at inner-city schools the proportion was much lower (Designs for Change 1985). Two months later, the Chicago Panel on Public School Policy and Finance released a complementary study that showed that 43 percent of entering freshmen dropped out before graduation, with dropout rates in inner-city schools reaching 67 percent (Hess and Lauber 1985). When combined with the

Chicago Panel's earlier study, which showed that the eight thousand positions cut during the financial crisis were disproportionately teachers and other student contact staff (Hallett and Hess 1982), a picture was created of a school system failing its students and more interested in protecting bureaucratic jobs than improving its schools. It was from this base that the school reform movement was launched.

THE INEFFECTIVENESS OF PREVIOUS STATE REFORM EFFORTS

In 1985, Illinois, like other states before it, enacted statewide school reform legislation in response to the report *A Nation at Risk* (National Commission 1983). The 1985 reform act (PA 84-126) was long on accountability and short on serious efforts to improve the state's schools (Nelson, Hess, and Yong 1985). It did not seriously address the shortcomings of the Chicago schools, though the reports of high dropout rates and low graduate reading scores appeared as the bill was being debated. In a special section devoted to Chicago, the act did create Local School Improvement Councils at every school that were encouraged to engage in school improvement planning and given the right to review discretionary spending by the principal.

However, the accountability provisions may have been more important, in the long run, because they helped highlight how poorly Chicago schools were performing. In 1987, the state report card showed that thirty-three of sixty-four Chicago high schools scored in the lowest 1 percent of all high schools in the country on the American College Test (ACT). In fact, Chicago schools dominated that lowest percentile, which included only fifty-four schools nationwide. Only seven Chicago high schools scored higher than the tenth percentile. At the elementary grades, 60 to 70 percent of all students were reading below the national norms on the Iowa Test of Basic Skills.

It is not surprising that state school reform had little effect on Chicago. Chicago is not very different from other large urban school systems. Dropout rates in Boston (Camayd-Freixas 1986), for instance, when calculated in the same way we calculated Chicago rates, are 53 percent, and that does not include the 35 percent of middle school students the Massachusetts Advocacy Center (1988) reports never make it to high school. Using similar statistics, the Dade County Public Schools, which include both the city of Miami and its suburbs, report a 28 percent dropout rate (Stephenson 1985). New York reports a 33 percent rate, though knowledgeable critics point out that that figure would be much higher if New York counted the kids who transferred into night school and then dropped out ("Chancellor Seeks Dropout Program" 1988). Meanwhile, suburban schools graduate upward of 95 percent of their students.

Urban schools are not like suburban schools, a fact recognized by most people. Rural schools are often different from either urban or suburban ones. But state policymakers too-frequently ignore these differences, except to complain about their costs to the state. Urban districts are frequently described as "black holes," and the color reference is usually not unintentional. Rural districts are too small and inefficient. Both cost the state too much and perform too poorly. Suburban districts cost the state little and perform well. Even without much state aid, they spend much more on each pupil than the rest of the state.

If we all know these differences exist, why do states continue to search for the "one best solution"? Why do we try to enact the one set of policies that will fix all of these schools? In fact, the problems faced by urban schools are quite different from those faced by suburban schools, and the solutions must be different as well.

The Council of Great City Schools (1987, 2) reports that a quarter of all youths live in central cities. Students who attend urban schools are predominantly from disadvantaged homes, and these students dominate inner-city schools. In Chicago, more than half of the entering freshmen at Austin High School come from low-income homes, and 82 percent of those freshmen are reading at least two grades below normal. These students are not a few problem kids on the margin of the school population; these disadvantaged kids dominate the school enrollment. Yet from a policy perspective, we treat Austin like any other high school in the state!

In addition, urban school districts are organized differently than other school districts in the state. Outside of Chicago, the average school district in Illinois has 1,385 students in about four schools of 300 to 350 students each. Chicago enrolls 410,000 students in 542 regular-attendance centers and 55 other specialty sites. There are 36 high schools and 10 elementary schools with more students enrolled than in the average Illinois district! In the suburbs, most districts have 10 or fewer administrators. In Chicago, in 1988, there were 4,380 persons who worked in administrative units in the central or subdistrict offices. There were another 38,000 employees working in the system's schools. Unlike most other districts in the state, the Chicago Public Schools like most urban school systems, is a large, rigidly bureaucratized system, far removed from its large and failing schools.

The Chicago School Reform Act attempts a restructuring solution geared to the urban school problem. It is not necessarily an appropriate solution for problems in suburban or rural schools, except in those states using large county districts with their own bureaucracies. There may be aspects of the Chicago restructuring effort that would be appropriate in other settings, but the effort as a whole is aimed at the urban problem. States with large urban centers may find elements of the Chicago experiment that would address their own urban problems.

THE CHICAGO RESTRUCTURING PLAN

The restructuring of the Chicago Public Schools is mandated by PA 85-1418, the Chicago School Reform Act. This act was adopted by the Illinois General Assembly on 2 December 1988 and signed into law by the governor ten days later. There are three major components to the act: a set of goals, a requirement to reallocate the resources of the system toward the school level, and a system of school-based management that is centered upon the establishment of Local School Councils at every school.

The ten goals included in the legislation focus the attention of the system to providing every urban student the opportunity to experience the full breadth of academic opportunities available in suburban schools (art, music, drama, foreign languages, physics and chemistry, journalism, international perspectives). At the same time, the goals stipulate that student achievement and behaviors should increase so that all schools reach national norms in reading, mathematics, higher-level thinking, attendance, and graduation rates.

A major enabling mechanism in the legislation is to reallocate the system's resources so that a larger portion is spent at the school level and is under the discretionary control of local school leaders. The legislation uses two complementary approaches to accomplish this effort: a cap on noninstructional administrative expenses and a targeting of state poverty impaction aid. The legislation requires the Chicago Public Schools to spend no more on noninstructional costs than the average percentage for such expenses in all other school districts in the state. This provision required moving about $40 million of the board's $2.3 billion budget from the central administration to the school level. In addition, Illinois provides additional weighting in the school aid formula to school districts with more than the average number of students from poverty homes. In the 1987–88 school year, Chicago received $238 million in such State Chapter I funds. Although previous legislation required all of these funds to be allocated to schools, the Chicago system had illegally diverted $42 million to the central bureaucracy through the euphemism of charges for "program support." The reform act required that all of these funds be allocated to schools, with an increasing proportion targeted to schools on the basis of enrolled disadvantaged students. Further, these funds eventually become entirely discretionary for purposes beyond the base level of funding provided to every student. The effect of this provision was that the average elementary school received $90,000 in new discretionary funds in the first year of reform implementation (1989–90); that figure will grow to about $450,000 by the fifth year of reform.

But the heart of the Chicago reform experiment is the change in governance. Chicago's school restructuring makes

> the individual local school the essential unit for educational governance and improvement and to establish a process for placing the primary responsibility for school governance and improvement in furtherance of such goals in the hands of parents, community residents, teachers, and the school principal at the school level. (PA 85-1418, Sec. 34-1.01.B)

This change is accomplished through the establishment at each school of a Local School Council composed of six parents, two community representatives, two teachers, and the principal.

Local school councils have three essential functions:

1. The adoption of a *school improvement plan,* based upon a thorough needs assessment and a proposal prepared by the principal in consultation with the school faculty;
2. The adoption of a *local school budget* designed to implement that improvement plan using funds allocated in lump sum fashion by the central Board of Education; and
3. The decision to retain or change *the principal* employed at the school.

The rhetoric of reform in Chicago has been that decisions that affect the education offered to students should be made at the school site, because it is school-level leaders who understand the real needs of their students. Further, the rhetoric claimed that those local leaders would have the interests of their students at heart, rather than being focused upon maintaining the status quo of the bureaucracy and its stable employment opportunities. By changing the accountability of the principal from higher bureaucrats to local parents and community residents, the focus of the staff should be on improving the achievement of students. In a very real sense, the rhetoric was aimed at recreating the notion of the community school, and freeing the school from the layers of bureaucracy that have been the result of the progressive movement's efforts throughout the twentieth century to install rational administration in public governance.

A second dimension of the rhetoric was that reformers already knew what the elements of an effective school were. The Chicago reform movement drew heavily on the body of literature known as the "effective-schools research" (see Purkey and Smith 1983; Edmonds 1979; Brookover and Lezotte 1979; this literature and its impact on the Chicago reform effort is reviewed more extensively in Hess 1991). What the Chicago reformers noted was that there had been little success in efforts to *make schools effective*. The literature had successfully isolated characteristics that marked off effective schools from ineffective ones, but there was little success in converting ineffective schools into effective ones, and even less in converting *a system* of ineffective schools into *a system* of effective ones. For better or worse, the Chicago reform experiment is an effort to create the conditions under which a whole system of effective schools could emerge.

MONITORING OF EFFECTIVENESS OF THE CHICAGO RESTRUCTURING EFFORT

If the key conception of the Chicago School Reform Act is that local people are better positioned to create programs to meet the educational needs of students attending individual schools than are central office bureaucrats setting systemwide mandates, then the key implementation question is, "Do local people seize the opportunity provided by reform to radically alter their schools in an educationally meaningful way?" It is unlikely that there will be significant changes in student achievement if nothing significantly different happens in the classrooms and schools that they attend.

The Chicago Panel on Public School Policy and Finance, the organization the authors lead, has launched a major effort to monitor the implementation of school reform in Chicago and to assess its effectiveness in meeting the goals of the reform legislation. The monitoring effect is designed to run for five years, the period described in the legislation it-self as the focus of reform. The authors recognize that it is wildly opti-mistic to think that student achievement on all the measures included in the goals of the act can reach national norms within five years, but that is what the act demands. The authors intend to continue monitoring the effects of the reform effort far beyond the time period included within the act.

The Chicago Panel has released nearly twenty studies examining different aspects of the programs, practices, and policies of the Chicago Board of Education. Its early studies focused on the board's finances (Hallett and Hess 1982; Hess and Greer 1984) and management prac-tices (Hess and Meara 1983). As the board's fiscal crisis eased in the mid 1980s, the panel's attention turned to the educational achievement of students in the system, particularly to the dropout problem. The panel produced five dropout-related studies during the second half of the 1980s (Hess and Lauber 1985; Hess et al. 1986; Hess and Greer 1987; Hess et al. 1988; and Hess, Lyons, and Corsino 1989). These studies included both large-scale quantitative studies (e.g., a thirty-thousand-student cohort analysis of dropout rates systemwide and at each high school in the system) and in-school qualitative research in four matched pairs of high schools with similar student bodies but differing dropout rates. Thus, the Panel was familiar with the school system, had estab-lished working relationships with its staff, and had the expertise to de-sign and implement a comprehensive monitoring project.

During the spring and summer of 1989, as school reform was mov-ing toward its first year of implementation, staff of the Chicago Panel de-signed a "Plan to Monitor School Reform in Chicago" and submitted proposals to the city's major foundations to support that effect. A related "Research Proposal to Study the Effects of School Reform" was submit-ted to the Spencer Foundation. Both sets of proposals were funded, with initial support for the monitoring project provided by Woods Charitable Fund, the MacArthur Foundation, the Field Foundation of Illinois, and the Chicago Community Trust.

The monitoring plan is composed of eleven subprojects organized under three basic rubrics. Four of the projects focus on school gover-nance issues; three focus on school improvement issues; and four on the outcomes of reform:

    I.   School governance
        A. Local School Council composition
        B. Local School Council operation

C. Principal contracts
    D. Personnel changes
II. School improvement
    E. School improvement plans
    F. Resource allocation
    G. Implementation of school improvement plans
III. Outcomes of school reform
    H. Student achievement
    I. Attendance and graduation
    J. Grade retention
    K. Teacher and parent attitude

Thus, the monitoring effort will focus on assessing what the actual change in governance is, how it operates, and the effects it has on staffing, particularly at the school level. It will examine what improvements are planned at schools, what changes in resource allocation occur, and whether real change follows from the effort to implement those plans. Finally, the project will monitor changes in student achievement and behavior, as measured by test scores, grades, retention rates, attendance rates, and graduation rates. It will also assess changes in the attitudes of teachers and parents as the restructuring effort proceeds.

An interrelated research plan was designed to examine the relationships among the various changes noted during the monitoring effort. A statistical school-effects study will use regression techniques to assess changes in student achievement during reform implementation. Moving beyond simply tracking changes in median reading scores at each grade in each of the system's 542 schools (which we will also do), this approach allows us to aggregate individual student improvement to the school level, accounting for individual characteristics of students. Further analyses will relate changes in achievement to other changes occurring in schools the students attend. The research project includes surveying attitude changes in teachers and principals, which will be examined both as outcomes of the reform effort and as inputs into the change process. The attitudes of staff have been identified as a critical characteristic of effective schools (Edmonds 1979). Funding from the research project allows greater in-depth examination of the change process in local schools, which will focus both on the planning and implementation of improvement efforts and on changes in classroom instruction. The ultimate focus of the monitoring and research plans is upon the effects of school restructuring on classroom instruction. The monitoring and research design we have created can be imaged as a huge funnel with massive data inputs at the systemwide level, and more limited, but ethnographically richer, data from the school governance level, all focused on perceived changes in classrooms where children receive and engage in the instruction process. It is the Panel's hypothesis that reform must affect changes in classroom instruction if it is to be effective in changing student achievement on the multiple measures included in our plan.

The design of our monitoring and research efforts includes both massive quantitative measures and more intense qualitative approaches. At one level we will be doing studies that emulate classical productivity studies, correlating changes in educational inputs with changes in outcomes. At the same time, we will be working intensely with a representative sample of sixteen schools in which we will be attending every Local School Council meeting; observing faculty meetings; interviewing key staff, parents, and area residents; and observing classrooms. Through this combination of methodological approaches we hope to be able to produce an assessment of the implementation and effects of school reform in Chicago that is rich in texture and comprehensive in results.

ESTABLISHING THE QUANTITATIVE BASELINE

During the first year of reform implementation, the monitoring and research staff developed the data base that they will use for the five-year study on school reform. The completed data base focuses on the 1988–89 school year, and contains the following information:

- *Basic information about each school* such as the Board of Education unit number, the old and new district numbers, the community area in which the school is located, school type (magnet, special education, vocational, etc.), whether the school has a local school council;
- *Characteristics of the student body* such as racial composition, number and percent low-income, percent limited English-proficient;
- *Data about the educational setting* like enrollment, number of students from outside of the school's attendance boundaries, attendance rate for the last four years, mobility rate, average class size, percent of elementary students not promoted in each grade and overall, high school students completing a general vocational, or college-bound curriculum, high school students enrolled in various subject areas, high school graduation rate, and 1986 dropout rate;
- *Data about achievement on standardized tests,* including third-, sixth-, and eighth-grade reading and math achievement on the Iowa Test of

Basic Skills and the Illinois Goal Assessment Program test, eleventh-grade achievement on the Test of Achievement and Proficiency, and twelfth-grade achievement on the American College Test.[1]

Annually, the monitoring and research staff will update this data base and calculate year to year changes for all data points.

The data base was created using a variety of sources. One of the largest sources of information was the Illinois State Board of Education, which provided the data compiled for the Illinois School Report Card. The Chicago Board of Education has provided other information from its computer system, and the monitoring and research staff entered some of the data manually from printed board sources.

A number of reports have been generated in establishing the baseline data for the entire monitoring and research project. At the beginning of the first year of reform implementation, the Panel surveyed a sample of teachers from predominantly minority schools. Some 146 teachers (a 31.5 percent response rate) provided insights into the understandings and attitudes teachers brought to the initiation of reform efforts in these schools, where reform was most needed but which skeptics suggested would be the most unlikely to be affected by the Chicago reform experiment. This survey (Easton 1989) showed that about 60 percent of the teachers thought they had a good to excellent grasp of the school reform mandate, which they had received primarily from school administrators and the media. Teachers reported that they had urged parents to run for the Local School Council (LSC), but fewer than a fifth of them intended to run for the teacher spots on the councils. Overall the teachers were somewhat skeptical about the prospects for reform, but thought the largest benefit would be increased parental involvement in schools. However, their largest concern was that greater parent involvement might also mean parent interference in the way they conduct their classrooms and operate the school. Thus, teachers appear to have entered the reform era skeptical, somewhat reluctant to be directly involved, and leery of the potential for confrontation in the new relationship with empowered parents.

The baseline data for student achievement was compiled in a resource book, *Chicago Public Schools DataBook* (Chicago Panel 1990), distributed to every principal and every LSC chairperson. The *DataBook* provided basic student and staff characteristics data about each school and listed relevant student performance data on test scores, attendance, and graduation rates. Since the reform law sets as a goal that at least half the students in each grade in each school will be performing at or above the national norms in reading and math by 1994, the databook was organized to show what percentage were now achieving at that level and what percentage of students would have to improve their performance to reach that goal. This databook became a valuable resource for LSCs as they entered the school improvement planning process. Thus, the process of monitoring has had some direct effect on the process being monitored.

The panel has released several interim reports on the reallocation of resources during the first year of reform implementation (Hess 1990a, 1990b). Despite the doubts of both reformers and critics, the Board of Education did dramatically reduce its expenditures and staffing at the central and district administrative offices, and did make about $40 million available in new program resources at the local school level. Over one thousand positions were cut from the administrative budget, and another five hundred staff were now budgeted to the local schools they had previously served on an itinerant basis (e.g., speech therapists who might have served five different schools, each on a different day of the week). While this budgeting change did not increase the number of personnel working in schools, the budget change indicated a change in supervisory authority and a more direct responsibility to the principal of each school these staff were to serve. At the end of the first year of reform implementation, data were being collected to analyze how the newly available resources were utilized at the local school level.

Two other baseline reports were issued toward the end of the first year of implementation, one assessing the level of grade retention in elementary schools in June 1989 (Easton and Storey 1990b), the other examining attendance rates for the last four years in all schools in the system (Easton and Storey 1990a). Both of these reports played a dual function. The first function was to provide the panel and each LSC with an objective report of the starting point for reform in these two areas in which the law mandated improvement should be made (retention rates were to decline by 10 percent during the reform period, and attendance rates were to improve annually by 1 percent over the previous year; PA 85-1418, Sec. 34-1.02.3 and 34-1.02.2). The second function was to provide LSCs with a review of the literature on improvement efforts in each of these arenas.

The retention study showed a systemwide elementary school retention rate of 4.3 percent, considerably lower than in Boston (9.4 percent) or New York (6.1 percent). Retention rates were highest in the first grade (8.9 percent) and lowest at the sixth grade (3.0 percent). More troubling was the variation in retention rates from school to school. While 81 of 434 elementary schools retained fewer than 2 percent of their first graders, more than a third of the schools retained at least 10 percent. Twenty-three schools retained more than 20 percent of their first graders, with one school retaining more than half. These statistics were particularly troubling given the panel's previous findings that grade retention, even in the earliest grades, is directly associated with later dropping out of high school prior to graduation (Hess and Lauber 1985; Hess, Lyons, and Corsino 1989).

The attendance study also showed a pattern of variation from school to school, but the major variation among elementary schools was restricted to specialty schools, known in Chicago as "EVGCs" (Education and Vocational Guidance Centers) in comparison with regular elementary schools. The median elementary school attendance rate for 1988–89 was 93.0 percent. However, EVGCs regularly had attendance rates in the 65 to 80 percent ranges, while most elementary schools had attendance rates above 90 percent. The picture changed dramatically at the high school level, where the median attendance was only 81.3 percent. In other research (Hess 1986) we have shown that Chicago has operated an educational triage system in which the best-prepared elementary students are guided into magnet and selective-entrance specialty schools or neighborhood high schools in more affluent communities, while the least well prepared are trapped in "holding pen" high schools with high dropout rates. High school attendance rates across the system underscore this tracking of students into a two-tier system. Attendance rates in 1988–89 varied from a low of 65.3 percent to a high of 91.3 percent.

These quantitative studies have provided the baseline from which improvement is to be achieved and measured. The Chicago Panel will continue to monitor and track changes in these various measures during the five years of the educational reform effort. It will compute changes in these various measures on a school-by-school basis. These data will be reported both for their systemwide effects and for each school. In this way, the panel hopes both to keep the wider public abreast of changes experienced by the Chicago schools under the reform effort and to keep individual local schools aware of the progress or lack of progress they have experienced in moving toward the goals articulated in the reform act.

QUALITATIVE ASSESSMENTS OF SCHOOL-LEVEL IMPROVEMENT EFFORTS

As part of our overall monitoring effort, the Chicago Panel has worked closely with a sample of schools willing to be closely observed as they go through the reform process. The initial focus of the monitoring project is on the composition and operation of the Local School Councils (LSCs), the development of school-based management (SBM) and increased local governance, expansion of leadership roles in the schools, and the development of the school improvement plans. During subsequent years of this study, the emphasis will shift from governance to implementation issues, including the implementation of any new instructional practices. During the final years of the project, the emphasis will be on documenting improvements in the schools. This section reports on the first phase of the monitoring project.

Our plan for monitoring school reform in Chicago calls for intensive study of sixteen schools. Using a random sample stratified by race and geographical region, we identified forty-eight schools as possible participants—three sets of sixteen schools meeting the sampling requirements.

Securing Entrance into Observed Schools

We first approached schools by phone and set up appointments to meet with the principal. Two Panel staff members met with the principal (and in many instances, the LSC chairperson) to discuss our study. One staff member subsequently remained in contact with each school, attempting to secure its participation.

Specifically, we explained that in order to conduct this monitoring and research project, we wanted to conduct interviews with the principal, selected teachers, staff, parents, and students; and observe all Local School Council meetings, some faculty meetings, gatherings of the Professional Personnel Advisory Committee (PPAC—the vehicle for faculty input into the school governance process), and other school events.

By March 1990, after discussing this study with eighteen schools, a total of twelve schools had formally agreed to participate. At that time we decided to concentrate our efforts on studying these twelve instead of continuing to spend time on securing the participation of additional schools. (We also attended the LSC meetings at one other elementary school that had not yet been asked to participate. Our sample will be increased to sixteen schools for the second year of implementation of reform.) The twelve schools that agreed to participate included eight of the intended twelve elementary schools and all four projected high schools. Three schools officially voted not to participate, and three others remain undecided. Although the process of securing the participation of schools proved more difficult than anticipated, much was learned from it, especially when the process is considered in light of the literature on school-based management.

Findings from the Entrance Process

The literature on school-based management emphasizes that this form of governance is a process that takes time to implement successfully (David 1989), and cautions that districts adopting this form of governance cannot expect to make major improvements in a short period of time. Consistent with this, we found that the process of requesting schools to cooperate took more time and effort and a higher degree of involvement than we had anticipated. This is in sharp contrast to the ease of entry during our earlier ethnographic study (Hess et al. 1986), when a deputy superintendent's decision and one interview with each principal was all it took to study eight schools. Most schools required two to three months to decide whether or not they wanted to be included in the study, and for many of the LSCs, this was their first major, and sometimes controversial, decision.

We found that parent and community LSC members were more apt to want to participate in our study than were principals and teachers. Even with the support of parents and community members, securing a school's participation was often a long process. Generally, we visited each school four to six times between December 1989 and March 1990. A typical sequence of the process involved in securing a school's participation follows:

- *5 December 1989.* JE and JQ (two Panel staff members) met with the principal of School A to explain our study and request permission to make a presentation to the LSC. The principal was receptive, partly because of a positive reaction to a previous Panel study, and endorsed the idea of a presentation to the council.
- *10 January 1990.* JQ presented our request to the LSC. He explained the study verbally and distributed written material about it and the Panel's other monitoring projects. Although the LSC seemed prepared to vote in favor of participating in the study at this meeting, they decided to table the request until the PPAC had been informed of and voted on the study. They took this action after one of the teacher members of the LSC raised several questions.
- *17 January 1990.* JE and JQ attended a PPAC meeting that included the entire faculty. JE presented the study to a wary group concerned about possible intrusions from outsiders. After the meeting, a teacher leader

discussed the negative reactions and suggested that we attend a second PPAC meeting.

- *2 February 1990.* JQ returned to the PPAC. After the PPAC vented a great deal of frustration with school reform (primarily related to the low representation of teachers on the LSC), it voted to support the Panel's proposal.
- *7 February 1990.* The Local School Council unanimously voted to participate in our study.

Although this represents a typical sequence, we also encountered the extremes. In one school, we met with the principal in the morning and secured council agreement to participate that evening. In another school, we made seven visits and presentations before finally gaining approval.

The above sequence identifies issues that seemed to be of key importance in securing the participation of schools. For example, the principal greeted us favorably and endorsed the idea of us making a formal presentation to the Local School Council. Generally, where the principal was supportive of participating in the study, we secured formal consent from the council. In seven out of the twelve schools that agreed to participate, the principals expressed interest in our work and were willing to be included. In one school, the principal stated that she felt comfortable with our presentation, that she preferred to present our information to the council herself, and that she was confident that she could persuade the LSC to participate. Similarly, the principal in another school readily agreed to have the school participate in our study, stating, "The LSC is meeting tonight. I'll explain the study and they [LSC members] will approve it." The Local School Council unanimously voted to participate.

By contrast, the schools where principals did not express an interest were less likely to participate. In one school where the LSC and its chair seemed receptive to participating in the study but the principal was hesitant, the council voted against participation. The LSC chair explained, "I think the school should participate in the study, but the principal does not want to because she has a policy that does not allow classroom observations." Continuing, the chair stated, "I don't agree with the principal's closed classroom policy, but she has a lot of other good programs at the school." In only one school did we find a council that voted to participate even though the principal was reluctant about the study.

The significance of the leadership of principals reflects the experience of those who have studied other systems utilizing school-based management (Lindquest and Mauriel 1989; Malen and Ogawa 1988). The importance of the professionals (principals and teachers) in school decision making was underlined in both studies.

Several other interesting findings related to school reform emerged during our attempts to secure participation. Teachers played little role in shaping the reform legislation or in the initial planning for implementation. As reported in the attitude survey above (Easton 1989), they were skeptical of reform in general and concerned about intrusions by parents. However, the depth of their feelings was more fully revealed in the process of securing permission to observe these schools. For example, in one school that voted against participating, teachers were vehemently against participating in our project. This became apparent during one of our formal presentations at that school when a teacher began to complain that teachers had been "shut out" of the school reform process. This teacher asked the presenter what the Panel would do if the teachers were opposed to the study but the council voted to participate. When the staff member stated that the Panel would go ahead with the study, the teacher became angry and stated that this was proof that no one respected teachers.

Similarly, teachers in another school expressed their dissatisfaction with school reform. At this school, we made a formal presentation to an unenthusiastic faculty during a PPAC meeting. At the invitation of a teacher representative on the LSC, we made a second presentation to the school's PPAC. During this presentation, the members of the PPAC vented their frustrations over school reform. They explained their sense of powerlessness because of their opinion that teachers are underrepresented on the Local School Council. Furthermore, they did not like the council's being composed of parents and community representatives who, in their view, were least equipped to make crucial decisions. Ironically, after venting these frustrations, PPAC members voted overwhelmingly to support our study. Interestingly, the Local School Council in this school was initially supportive of our study, but would not vote to participate until after the PPAC had been informed of and voted on the study. After the PPAC voted to support the study, the LSC voted unanimously to participate. This indicates that in this school, the opinion of the "professionals"—the PPAC—carried weight, and that the parent and community representatives on the council respected the opinion of the faculty, though the faculty members did not seem to appreciate this fact.

Another issue emerged in a school that voted to participate in the study even though the faculty did not seem eager. In an initial LSC vote, four members favored participating, four abstaining from voting, and one member voted against participating. The one vote against was cast by a teacher member of the LSC who stated that he had to vote according to the wishes of his constituents, the majority of whom were against participating for all the familiar reasons. This illustrates an issue that recurs in all governing bodies—whether elected representatives are obliged to vote as their constituents would want or to vote their own conscience. This matter has not been resolved for many Local School Councils.

We found that some principals felt reform had actually reduced parental participation. One principal noted that a number of active parents in her school also held part-time jobs at the school. These parents were ineligible to serve on the LSC, due to their employee status. She also felt that the extensive time demanded for service would hinder parental involvement. The Panel has not yet been able to assess actual changes in parent involvement at the school level.

We also learned that Local School Councils had been required to make many decisions in a short period of time; at times members on the council lost track of the decisions they had made. For example, in one school a researcher attended a meeting expecting the council to make a decision about participating in our project, but our study was not an agenda item and was not discussed during the meeting. After the meeting, the staff member asked the LSC secretary whether the council had decided to participate; she responded that a special meeting would have to be called to make that decision. The staffer then asked the principal about the decision. The principal responded that the school had already voted to be a part of our study and that a letter stating this had just been mailed to the Panel. The secretary then apologized and said she just did not remember the decision having been made. Similarly, the Local School Council chairperson added: "There are so many things going on, I forgot too."

The process of securing the participation of schools in our observational study has been useful in identifying issues that we must take into account as we conduct our research. We will examine the role and influence of key council members: principals, chairpersons, and teachers. We will examine the development of the roles of the other parent and community members on the council. We must give further attention to the feelings of powerlessness and underrepresentation on the part of teachers. We want to assess whether some councils are able to make decisions in a more efficient manner than others and try to identify why this is the case. Finally, we want to account for the possible nonrepresentativeness of the schools we are working with, in that principal willingness was a key condition of our entry into these schools.

How Local School Councils Worked during Year One

It is important to note that our observations began in the second half of the school year and therefore do not represent what the councils accomplished for the first year. By the time we began systematic observation, LSCs had elected officers, and most had developed committee structures. We were not present to observe this important business.

Collecting data After a council had approved our request to study the implementation of school reform in its school, we attended every meeting we could and recorded attendance of members, attendance of guests (children and adults), availability of agenda and minutes, and who chaired the meeting. We took notes throughout the meeting, organizing these notes around "topics" that the councils considered. (A topic is a discrete item or subject that is reported or discussed at a meeting. Often a topic is equivalent to an agenda item. At other times an agenda item covers many topics.) For each topic considered at a meeting, the observer recorded what LSC member led the topic discussion, which members participated in the topic discussion, whether special problems occurred during the discussion, and whether the topic came to a vote.

Observing LSC meetings We analyzed the content of seventy-four LSC meetings at twelve schools between late January and mid August, 1990. During this period, these LSCs conducted a total of ninety meetings; we missed a total of sixteen meetings. Some meetings were missed because of schedule conflicts between special meetings and regular meetings at other schools.

Length of Meetings and Attendance In the twelve schools, the average meeting length was 127 minutes, slightly more than two hours. Of course there was great variability from meeting to meeting and from school to school. The school with the shortest meetings averaged 89 minutes (an hour and a half); the school with the longest meetings averaged 162 minutes (about two and three-quarters hours). Of the seventy-four meetings we observed, the shortest was 15 minutes long and the longest was 220 minutes (three hours and forty minutes).

Usually 8 of 11 LSC members attended the elementary school meetings (an average of 7.7, or 70 percent attendance). In the eight elementary schools, the lowest average number of members present at meetings was 6.8, and the highest was 9.3. In the four high schools in this sample, 9 of 12 members attended meetings (an average of 9.1, or 75.8

Table 8.1. Attendance Rates for LSC Members

	Average Rate	Highest Rate	Lowest Rate
Principal	97.3%	100.0%	83.3%
Chair (Parent)	87.8%	100.0%	66.7%
Other Parents	61.7%	82.5%	37.5%
Teachers	87.7%	100.0%	68.8%
Community	67.1%	100.0%	16.7%
Students	52.2%	80.0%	28.6%

percent). High school LSCs have an additional nonvoting student member. The high school attendance ranged from a low average of 7.2 members to a high of 10.1. With the student member removed from the calculation, the high school average attendance as 8.7 members (an attendance rate of 79.1 percent). In this sample, attendance was higher in the high schools than in the elementary schools.

The average adult "audience" size ranged from about two at one elementary school to nearly thirty-four at one high school. Overall, about six adults attended the average elementary school LSC meeting while attendance at high school council meetings averaged eighteen. A few children were also present at council meetings.

Table 8.1 shows the average overall attendance rates by "role" in the council. Of the seventy-four meetings, the principal attended 97.3 percent, the chairperson attended 87.8 percent, the other parents attended 61.7 percent, the teachers attended 87.7 percent, the community members attended 67.1 percent, and the student members in the four high school LSCs attended 52.2 percent of the meetings. Thus, collectively, the principals attended all but two of the seventy-four LSC meetings, and the chairpersons missed only nine, or less than one per school.

These attendance rates differed from persons to person within role, as well as from school to school. Some of the school-to-school variation is shown in table 8.1. Whereas the principals and chairpersons had high attendance in all of the twelve schools, other parent and community members had more variable attendance. Attendance for other parents ranged from a high of 82.5 percent at one school to a low of 37.5 percent at another. (This average rate does not indicate whether one or more parents have very high attendance and others very low attendance or whether all parents have equal attendance.)

Teachers' average attendance rates ranged from 100 percent in one school to 68.8 percent in another. There is a much greater range in

Table 8.2. Distribution of LSC Member Attendance Rates

	Principals	Chair	Other Parents	Community	Teachers	Students
Above 75%	100.0%	83.3%	32.3%	50.0%	88.0%	25.0%
50%–74.9%		16.7%	37.1%	25.0%	8.0%	25.0%
25%–49.9%			21.0%	4.2%	4.0%	50.0%
Under 25%			9.7%	20.8%	0.0%	0.0%

the average attendance of community members—from 100 percent in one school to 16.7 percent in another. The students in the four high schools attended about half of the meetings. The student with the highest attendance attended four out of five meetings (80.0 percent), and the student with the lowest participation attended only two out of seven (28.6 percent).

The average attendance rates do not answer an important question about differences from one person to another. Do a few members miss many meetings, or do most members miss about the same number? In order to summarize these comparisons, we classified all members by their attendance rates, counting those who attended 75 percent or more of the meetings, those who attended more than 50 percent but less than 75 percent, those who attended more than 25 percent but less than half, and those who attended fewer than 25 percent of their meetings.

All of the principals attended more than 75 percent of the meetings, as did 83.3 percent (ten of twelve) of the chairpersons. As we have already seen, the principals and chairpersons had very high attendance. Most of the teachers (88.0 percent) also attended 75 percent or more of the council meetings. Only one teacher (4.0 percent) attended fewer than half of the meetings.

The attendance of other parents (nonchairpersons) is highly variable. Table 8.1 shows the range in average parent attendance rates from school to school. Table 8.2 shows that only about one-third of the parents had high attendance, one-third attended between 50 percent and 75 percent of the meetings, and that slightly less than one-third of the parents attended fewer than 50 percent of the meetings. Almost 10 percent of the nonchair parents attended fewer than a quarter of all LSC meetings.

Community members attended more meetings than "other parents" (the five nonchair parents), but they had roughly the same attendance rate as all parents combined (including the chairs). Half of the community members attended 75 percent or more of the meetings. However, a larger proportion of community members (five of twenty-four) than parent members had very low attendance (less than 25 percent), indicating a higher rate of nonattending community members.

Thus, about 14 of the 132 LSC members attended a quarter or fewer of all LSC meetings. On the average, this would mean each LSC had one member (either a parent or community resident) who attended infrequently, but in fact, five of the schools had no infrequent attendees. However, at four schools, multiple members (four, three, two, and two, respectively) attended infrequently. Some schools had some vacant positions, due to resignations, for part of the year.

Topic Categories Observers recorded the content of meetings in discrete "topics." We defined a topic to be subject or content matter brought before the council. Topics often corresponded to agenda items but at other times were narrower. For example, "principal's report" was a common agenda item. We recorded topics in relation to the content of the report, like "test scores," "summer school schedule," or "new assistant principal." We recorded all of the business of the council meetings with the exception of approving minutes from the previous meeting. We entered each topic into our database and then assigned them to categories. We developed seven broad areas, each of which is subdivided into categories. The research team developed these categories out of the data by making continual reference to observational notes. We made very effort to avoid imposing arbitrary categories upon the data.

We recorded a total of 466 topics in the seventy-four meetings. With the expected variability from school to school and meeting to meeting, on the average, each LSC considered about six topics per meeting. These topics are "unweighted" for time or importance and are simply classifications of the matters that the councils considered in their meetings. A further analysis will examine the topics in greater depth by considering how many members participated in discussing each topic and whether the topic came to a vote. The participation and voting information will suggest the relative importance the councils attached to various issues. This analysis is not yet available.

Figure 8.1 shows the distribution of the 466 topics by broad groups of categories. The most prevalent topics related to school programs (28.6 percent); an almost equal number of topics dealt with LSC procedures (27.6 percent). School safety, buildings, and security was the next most prevalent set of topics (13.3 percent), followed by budget (10.9 percent), personnel (10.7 percent), parent and community involvement (4.3 percent), and other (4.5 percent).

Figure 8.1 Distribution of Topics in LSC Meeting

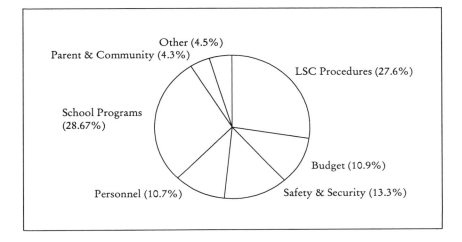

School Program Nearly half of the discussions on school program focused on matters of curriculum and instruction, including program content (reading programs, summer school, gifted, creative writing) and testing and test scores. A quarter of the program topics involved direct participation in creating the school improvement plan, reports from council members on the progress of the plan, or presentation of the plan to the school community. Reports to LSCs indicate subcommittees were also working on the improvement plans, but we have no direct evidence of the extent of this effort, which appears to have varied significantly from school to school. Another quarter of the LSC discussions focused on school administrative issues such as calendars and events; this topic was frequently a part of the principal's report. One school spent a number of sessions discussing overcrowding.

LSC Procedures and Training The second most frequent set of LSC topics dealt with the business of running the council itself. Three-quarters of these discussions (or one-fifth of all topics considered by the LSCs) focused on council procedures: election of officers, establishing committees, developing bylaws, absence of members, filling vacancies. Absence of members was an important issue for several councils; two formally requested that one or more nonperforming members resign. On thirty-eight occasions, LSCs discussed training specifically designed for LSCs. They discussed or heard reports on several different types of training, including lump-sum budgeting, boardsmanship, principal evaluation and selection, strategic planning, and school improvement planning.

Safety, Security, and Buildings The third most frequent area of discussion involved student discipline and safety and problems related to school facilities. Gang issues featured prominently in these discussions, with dress codes as a potential tactic to reduce gang identification in school. Other topics included parent safety patrols, in-school suspension centers, and crime prevention programs featuring police officers. About a quarter of the safety and facilities discussions focused on building rehabilitation, particularly in one school where major repairs were needed.

Budget The next most frequent set of topics related to the financing of the school. About two-thirds of these topics related to the formal budget of the school, including expenditure plans for discretionary spending, staffing, and special programs. A third of these discussions revolved around fund-raising, including developing proposals for foundation support.

Personnel Almost as frequently, LSCs discussed staffing issues. With seven of the twelve schools involved in the principal selection process this year (systemwide, half were to choose principals in the first year of reform implementation, half in the second year), more than half of the personnel items focused on evaluating, selecting, and contracting with their choice of principal for the next four years. It should be noted that in this report we are only discussing topics on LSC agendas; the principal selection process was frequently conducted primarily by an appointed committee, with only the procedures or the final decision discussed in the LSC meeting. LSCs discussed other staff positions twenty-two times.

Parents and Other Issues On twenty occasions, these LSCs discussed issues related to parent or community involvement in these schools, either through parent clubs, volunteer opportunities, or fund-raising. There were ten other items discussed that did not fit any of the foregoing categories.

Summary

Through the presentation of these data from our observation of Local School Councils during the first year of reform implementation, we have tried to show the high level of activity of LSCs in launching school reform. All of the observed schools elected full slates of LSC members. Most had some experience with a nonperforming member. Naturally, in the initial year, procedural issues played a major role. But it was encouraging to find that the most frequently discussed topics related to the educational programs of the schools. Safety, the budget, and personnel items were less frequently discussed. Of some surprise, greater parent involvement was only infrequently discussed.

YEAR-END ANALYSIS

After only one year of reform implementation, it is much too early to offer an assessment of the probable successes or failures of the Chicago restructuring experiment. It is important to note, however, that all of the basic elements of the school reform plan, as embodied in the mandating legislation, are now in place, with the single exception of an approved set of Systemwide Goals and Strategies for Reform. The school board's efforts to develop a systemwide plan have been pathetic, and were regularly rejected by the overseeing School Finance Authority during the preceding planning period and the first year of implementation. Thus, the reform effort goes forward without a formal systemwide plan guiding the board's effort. But thanks to careful guidance in the legislation itself, the essential elements of the reform structure were in place as the first year ended.

Entirely unanswered is the question as to whether local school leaders will be able to take advantage of the new opportunities put before them to radically alter the current patterns of classroom instruction and student learning opportunities. Local school leaders have learned to operate the new structures created by the reform act. They have begun to discuss issues related to the educational programs of their schools. The step that is still to be taken is to make decisions that will change the way in which Chicago's 410,000 public school children experience these 542 schools. The Chicago Panel will continue to monitor the implementation of school reform and report on progress in taking that next step as it happens.

The authors would like to acknowledge the participation and contribution of other staff members of the Chicago Panel in preparing the research and monitoring reports on which this chapter is based, specifically Cheryl Johnson, Jesse Qualls, Sandra Storey, Darryl Ford, and Hilary Addington. G. Alfred Hess, Jr. is the Panel's executive director; John Q. Easton is its Director of Monitoring and Reseaerch.

Notes

The authors would like to acknowledge the participation and contribution of other staff members of the Chicago Panel in preparing the research and monitoring reports on which this chapter is based, specifically Cheryl Johnson, Jesse Qualls, Sandra Storey, Darryl Ford, and Hilary Addington. G. Alfred Hess, Jr. is The Panel's executive director; John Q. Easton is its Director of Monitoring and Research.

1. The Chicago Panel recognizes the limitations of standardized tests and sees the use of such test scores as providing only part of the evidence on school improvement. However, improvement on these test scores is an explicit goal of the reform act. Further, this assessment has been complicated by the board's decision to use a series of versions of the Iowa Test of Basic Skills during the five-year reform period. These tests have not been equated to each other. To overcome this problem, with the cooperation of the board's Department of Research, Evaluation, and Planning, the Panel has conducted the first of a series of equating studies to relate the annually reported outcomes on these various tests.

References

Brookover, W. B., and L. W. Lezotte. 1979. *Changes in School Characteristics Coincident with Changes in Student* East Lansing: Michigan State University.

Camayd-Freixas, Y. 1986. *A Working Document on the Dropout Problem in Boston Public Schools*

"Chancellor Seeks Dropout Program in New York's Elementary Schools." *New York Times,* 24 September, 1988.

Chicago Board of Education. 1985. *Racial/Ethnic Survey—Students.* Chicago: Chicago Board of Education.

Chicago Panel. 1990. *Chicago Public Schools DataBook, School Year 1988–89.* Chicago: Chicago Panel on Public School Policy and Finance.

Council of Great City Schools. 1987. *Challenges to urban Education: Results in the Making.* Washington, D.C.: Council of Great City Schools.

David, J. 1989. "Highlights of Research on School Based Management." *Educational Leadership,* 46(8):50.

Designs for Change. 1985. *The Bottom Line: Chicago's Failing Schools and How to Save Them.* Chicago: Designs for Change.

Easton, J. Q., and S. Storey. 1990a. *Attendance in Chicago Public Schools.* Chicago: Chicago Panel on Public School Policy and Finance.

Easton, J. Q., and S. Storey. 1990b. *June 1989 Grade Retention in Chicago Public Elementary Schools.* Chicago: Chicago Panel on Public School Policy and Finance.

Edmonds, R. 1979. "Effective Schools for the Urban Poor." *Educational Leadership* 37:15–18.

Hallett, A. C., and G. A. Hess, Jr. 1982. *Budget Cuts at the Board of Education.* Chicago: Chicago Panel on Public School Finances.

Hess, G. A., Jr. 1986. "Educational Triage in an Urban School Setting." *Metropolitan EDUCATION* No. 2, Fall, 39–52.

Hess, G. A., Jr. 1990a. "Changing Illegal Use of State Compensatory Aid." Unpublished paper delivered to the American Educational Research Association, Boston.

Hess, G. A., Jr. 1990b. Testimony before the Chicago Board of Education. 16 July.

Hess, G. A., Jr. 1991. *School Restructuring: Chicago Style.* Newbury Park, Calif.: Corwin Press.

Hess, G. A., Jr., D. O. Green, A. E. Stapleton, and O. Reyes. 1988. *Invisibly Pregnant: Teenage Mothers and the Chicago Public Schools.* Chicago: Chicago Panel on Public School Policy and Finance.

Hess, G. A., Jr., and J. L. Greer. *Revenue Short Falls at the Chicago Board of Education: 1970–1984.* Chicago: Chicago Panel on Public School Finances.

Hess, G. A., Jr., and J. L. Greer. 1987. *Bending the Twig: The Elementary Years and Dropout Rates in the Chicago Public Schools.* Chicago: Chicago Panel on Public School Policy and Finance.

Hess, G. A., Jr., and D. Lauber. 1985. *Dropouts from the Chicago Public Schools.* Chicago: Chicago Panel on Public School Policy and Finance.

Hess, G. A., Jr., A. Lyons, and L. Corsino. 1989. *Against the Odds: Early Prediction of Dropouts.* Chicago: Chicago Panel on Public School Policy and Finance.

Hess, G. A., Jr., and H. Meara. 1984. *Teacher Transfers and Classroom Disruption.* Chicago: Chicago Panel on Public School Finances.

Hess, G. A., Jr., and C. A. Warden. 1987. *Who Benefits from Desegregation?* Chicago: Chicago Panel on Public School Policy and Finance.

Hess, G. A., Jr., E. Wells, C. Prindle, B. Kaplan, and P. Liffman. 1986. *"Where's Room 185?" How Schools Can Reduce Their Dropout Problem.* Chicago: Chicago Panel on Public School Policy and Finance.

Lindquest, K. M., and J. J. Mauriel. 1989. "School-based Management—Doomed to Failure?" *Education and Urban Society* 21(4): 403–16.

Malen, B., and R. T. Ogawa. 1988. "Professional-Patron Influence on Site Based Governance Councils: A Confounding Case Study." *Educational Evaluation and Policy Analysis* 10(4): 251–70.

Massachusetts Advocacy Center. 1988. *The Way Out: Student Way Exclusion Practices in Middle Schools.* Boston: Massachusetts Advocacy Center.

National Commission on Excellence in Education. 1983. *A Nation at Risk: The Imperative for Educational Reform.* Washington, D.C.: GPO.

Nelson, F. H., G. A. Hess, Jr., and R. Yong. 1985. *Implementing Educational Reform in Illinois.* Chicago: Chicago Panel on Public School Finances.

Purkey, S. C., and M. S. Smith. 1983. Effective Schools: A Review. *Elementary School Journal* 81(1): 426–452.

Stephenson, R. S. 1985. *A Study of the Longitudinal Dropout Rate: 1980 Eighth-Grade Cohort Followed from June 1980 through February 1985.* Miami: Dade Country Public Schools.

9

EDUCATIONAL REFORM AND THE URBAN SCHOOL SUPERINTENDENT: A DILEMMA

Louis Castenell, Cornell Brooks, and Patricia Z. Timm

As we approach the twenty-first century, concerned citizens know that we are not preparing all children to lead productive and informed lives. The ultimate consequence to our nation is catastrophic. In 1989, 31.5 million Americans, or 12.8 percent of the population, lived in poverty. According to a 1986 longitudinal study of high school students (National Center for Education Statistics 1986), the dropout rate hovers around 25 percent and affects most minorities disproportionately (Native Americans, 42.0 percent; Hispanics, 39.9 percent; African Americans, 24.7 percent; whites, 14.3 percent; Asians/Pacific Islanders, 9.6 percent). By the year 2000, one-third of our nation's children will be members of ethnic minorities; by 2050, one-half will be non-Anglos.

As agents of change, superintendents are expected to create curriculum programs to enrich and inform all students, to produce workers better prepared for the labor market, and to instill the values and virtues articulated in the common school movement. How superintendents satisfy these educational demands is the focus of this study.

Today's urban superintendents are confronted with greater problems and fewer resources than ever before. Compounding the difficulty is the unchanging power distribution in education, whereby elites continue to direct and/or manipulate educational outcomes predicated on their values and political views (see, for example, Susan Martin's chapter, this volume). A review of the literature confirms our hypothesis that school boards and their agents, superintendents, are generally consciously or unconsciously controlling educational opportunities for children along race, gender, and socioeconomic lines as a consequence of what we term "indirect institutional discrimination" (Button and Provenzo 1983; Katz 1975; Kincheloe and Pinar 1991; Shor 1986; Staples 1987).

Indirect institutional discrimination refers to practices that have a negative and differential impact on minorities and women, even though the organizationally prescribed or community-prescribed norms or regulations guiding those practices were established, and are carried out, with no prejudice or no intent to harm (Feagin and Feagin 1978). This point helps us to understand the apparent contradiction in decisions made by superintendents, regardless of their race or gender, that promote the status quo, when in fact they intended to do otherwise. We believe this is the result of role confusion between boards of education and superintendents.

Nearly every day we read or hear of a superintendent who resigns or is terminated primarily because of unresolved issues between the board of education and himself or herself. An inherent problem is that the board that conflicts with the superintendent seldom consists of the same individuals who were serving at the time of the original appointment. Boards of education create policies but not necessarily practices; therefore the superintendent is frequently the "whipping boy" for prevailing concerns articulated by influential groups that control members of the boards. Because of the lack of a clear-cut belief system regarding the limits that a board of education must observe, the result is role confusion, which causes perpetual problems for the school superintendent. This situation leads to differences in expectations, which in turn lead to conflict.

Perhaps more germane to this chapter, the board and the superintendent are seldom aware of the historical background of their respective roles, and accept their roles uncritically. Specifically we refer to instances of indirect discrimination: the conscious attempts to discriminate by boards of education and superintendents in regard to improper testing and placement of students; using curricula that are substantially unchanged from the past and thereby not challenging the status quo; stressing basic skills at the expense of critical thinking; and marginalizing meaningful parental involvement.

HISTORICAL BACKGROUND

The superintendency always has been a contentious position. Originally it was born of conflict (Knezevich 1975). Largely because expanding school districts made it impossible for lay boards to regulate daily school activities effectively, this task was given to city superintendents as early as 1837 in Louisville and Buffalo (Blumberg and Blumberg 1985). These early superintendents were charged with supervising and hiring teachers, buying supplies, and developing a uniform curriculum for all children (Cuban 1985). Spring (1986) adds that these individuals were given directives to protect the power and values of middle-class and native-born groups.

With the advent of the progressive education movement, the concept of the superintendent as instructional leader gave way to a managerial approach (Cuban 1984). It became popular to conceptualize management of schools as an extension of the industrialized model common in factories. This reform effort attempted to centralize all school activities and to apply principles of scientific efficiency, as envisioned by social engineers such as W. W. Charters (1875–1952) and Franklin Bobbitt (1875–1956). These individuals argued for a standardized curriculum and more precise testing of students' performance to promote the virtues of industrialization and the prevailing social, political, and economic hierarchy of that time. These endeavors were regarded as neutralizing schools politically, though Apple (1985) cogently concluded that the values vested in these concepts were far from neutral and instead legitimated the structural bases of inequality.

Since the 1960s, the static position of the superintendency has come under heavy fire from various boards of education, community groups, business communities, and local and federal government. A case in point is the events that led to the resignation of Joan Raymond, superintendent of the Houston Independent School District. According to Walters (1991), when five new members were elected to the board in 1990 a conflict arose over restructuring, which culminated in a 6-to-3 vote expressing dissatisfaction with the superintendent in a public job evaluation. The issue over restructuring was sparked, in large part, by dissatisfaction among many Hispanic families with the quality of schooling. A complaint was filed with the United States Department of Education's office for Civil Rights. As Walters (1991) pointed out, some members of the board concluded they could not give the situation more time, a position maintained by Superintendent Raymond. Superintendent

Raymond subsequently negotiated a contract buyout and agreed to resign at the end of the school year.

Recent reforms have called for superintendents to reclaim their leadership role in assuming responsibility for developing relevant and diverse curricula to meet the needs of all children. Yet, paradoxically, many superintendents are permitted to complete advanced degrees with little or no coursework in curriculum development (Marks 1981).

In a recent survey, 1,957 superintendents agreed that "climate building" and developing curriculum were among the two most important performance areas (Glass and Sclafani 1988). The authors of the survey questioned whether superintendents actually were committed to these goals or whether these were a rankings response to the rhetoric of the current reform movement.

A closer examination is warranted in view of the leadership role that superintendents are expected to play in educational reform. Therefore the purpose of this chapter is to inquire into the meaning of curriculum development and climate building as articulated by superintendents, primarily in large urban school districts. In an attempt to understand the contradiction between superintendents' interest in these two areas and their apparent lack of suitable training, we analyzed data from a national sample.

In analyzing the data, we hypothesized that all superintendents, regardless of their race or gender, would support liberal concepts for progressive education but would promote practices (e.g., focusing on basic skills, standardized testing, and managing teachers' time) that contradicted their aims. In this vein, Bullough (1988) concluded that schools are helping to establish and justify a three-tier occupational structure (the elite, skilled professionals, and unskilled workers) while trying to maintain a commitment to social equality.

METHOD

Subjects

In the spring of 1989, we sent surveys to superintendents in the Council of the Great City School Districts and in other large urban districts. Because not all large urban school districts belong to the council, we supplemented the list by using urban school districts that receive Chapter I funds. We requested that the survey be completed by the superintendent.[1]

Procedure

The study consisted of two major stages: instrument development and questionnaire distribution. We constructed a self-report questionnaire that contained items representing current issues in the management of school districts today. The questionnaire included specific items about the superintendent and about characteristics of the school district. The superintendents were asked for basic information about their ethnicity, gender, years as superintendent, and other characteristics. The questions about the district included the percentage of students receiving free or reduced-price lunches, the ethnic makeup of the student population, and other items. Educational items included questions about ethnic history, concerns for the future, and levels of funding.

This instrument, with a cover letter and a stamped self-addressed envelope, was mailed to each superintendent in the sample. The cover letter described in general terms the purpose of the study and stressed that the validity of the study depended on obtaining a high return rate. The letter also stated that all surveys would be kept confidential, and that all data analysis would be limited to aggregated regional information and would not be reported by individual school districts. As an added incentive, the letter stated that the researchers would send a copy of the final analysis to the participants.

It is often difficult to obtain high return rates for mailed surveys (Altschuld and Lower 1984). Thus, to maximize the return rate, we sent a follow-up survey to the subjects who did not respond to the initial mailing. This step resulted in a slight increase in the overall number of surveys returned.

RESULTS

We analyzed the completed surveys using frequency counts of the responses and various cross-tabulations. We abandoned the effort to examine regional trends, because of insufficient responses from some parts of the country. Results of this survey were compared to those of similar surveys of communities, teachers, and students. The demographic characteristics of the responding superintendents are presented in table 9.2. Table 9.3 presents the demographic characteristics of the responding superintendents' school districts.

The data confirmed descriptive information about superintendents, particularly in urban school districts: They are mainly male and

Table 9.1. Demographic Characteristics of Superintendents

Age:	Range: 41–60	Mean 51.2
Race:	Black	7 (33.3%)
	Hispanic	1 (4.8)
	White	12 (57.1%)
	No response	1 (4.8%)
Sex:	Male	20
	No response	1 (4.8%)
Highest level of education:		
Doctorate		18 (85.7%)
Master's Degree Plus 30 credits		1 (4.8%)
Master's degree		1 (4.8%)
No response		1 (4.8%)
Number of years as superintendent:		
Range: 1–12 years		Mean: 3.65
First minority superintendent?		
Yes		5 (23.8%)
No		4 (19.0%)
No response		12 (57.1%)

white, possess a doctorate, and have fewer than five years of experience. The majority of the children in the districts are poor and belong to minority groups. The superintendents most often attribute the unacceptably high dropout rate to lack of interest (see the Appendix). This form of resistance challenges the concept of "climate building," if one assumes that school is for all children. With regard to curriculum, the superintendents reported that the most serious concerns relate to teacher effectiveness, basic skills, parental involvement, and improvement in standardized test scores. These findings are consistent with Shor's (1986) argument that programs featuring basic skills, standardized testing, and teacher efficiency create anti-intellectualism, which leads to low performance from teachers and students.

DISCUSSION

These findings support the thesis that superintendents are interested in reform but have not engaged their systems in meaningful change. Cuban

Table 9.2. Demographic Characteristics of Responding Superintendents' Districts

Percentage of ethnic groups served:

	Range	Mean
Black	2.6–91.4	37.0
White	3.6–90.0	44.0
Hispanic	0.2–48.1	12.5
Asian	0.4–24.3	5.1
Other	0.0–5.8	1.2

Percentage of ethnic groups receiving free or reduced-price lunch:

	Range	Mean
Black	22.7–62.0	34.3
White	10.0–37.0	18.4
Hispanic	33.4–71.7	48.1
Asian	16.1–54.9	30.9
Other	1.0–54.6	34.7

Percentage of students in the district receiving free or reduced-price lunch:

0–25%	1 (4.8%)
25–50%	11 (52.4%)
50–75%	7 (33.3%)
75–100%	1 (4.8%)

Dropout rate for the district:

Range:	1.2%–16%	Mean: 8.5%

Dropout rate for each of the following ethnic groups:

	Range	Mean
Black	1.7–22.0	5.1
White	1.2–37.0	6.7
Hispanic	4.1–61.8	8.7
Asian	1.2–11.1	2.5
Other	3.0–13.9	3.8

(1985) offers the theory that superintendents are subject to conflicting demands from individuals and groups, to whom they must pay varying degrees of attention. Because of the superintendents' history and academic training, the managerial needs quickly supersede the leadership role in many instances. Superintendents are directed to address new public goals and objectives; as a result, many are defining these tasks in terms that are conveniently manageable. Thus the directive to foster curriculum development becomes a nontransformative matter of improving basic skills, teachers effectiveness, test scores, and parental involvement. Concomitantly, schools become places that are intellectually sterile; hence the high dropout rate.

Are superintendents responding to the rhetoric of educational reform in meaningful ways? The answer appears to be negative. In view of their background, the power of the school board, and the neoconservative policies of the federal government, superintendents are left to fend for themselves, thereby abdicating their transformative opportunities. For instance, in 1991, top CEOs in a large midwestern city decided to address the decline in school achievement of its largest public school district. A subsequent task force selected by this group made recommendations to reorganize the administrative structure of the school district. The lead officers of this corporate organization chortled, "The rest will take care of itself, because we own the [school] board and superintendent." Eventually, all recommendations were approved by the school board and endorsed by the media.

For many students, lost opportunities frequently result in high dropout rates. Ironically, high dropout rates are one of the major concerns of superintendents. English (1991) cogently observed that students who cannot tolerate school environments drop out or are forced out. These youngsters are disproportionately females, poor, and students of color (Borman, Mueninghoff, and Piazza 1988). If one primary purpose of schooling is to prepare people for the world of work, superintendents need to do a better job of insuring that school practices and policies are formulated to assist youths in making the transition from school to work (Borman 1991). Schools concerned with basic skills, performance on standardized tests, and teacher efficiency in achieving those goals will only steer us toward new forms of oppression and not educational reform as posited by superintendents. Thus Greenman's insightful argument, in an earlier chapter of this volume, that we must close the gap between the rhetoric of educational reform and the social reality, is noteworthy. Alas, for too many superintendents their reality is restructuring schools consistent with conservative national goals and narrow state interests, thereby negating the possibility of developing a critical awareness that must undergird meaningful educational reform.

APPENDIX. ADDITIONAL ITEMS COVERED IN SURVEY

Most common reason for dropping out:	N	(%)
Lack of interest	7	(33.3%)
Other	3	(14.4%)
Low academic ability	2	(9.5%)
Need for money	1	(4.8%)
Peer group pressure	0	(0.0%)

Curriculum concerns ranked from highest to lowest:

1. Teacher effectiveness
2. Improved basic skills
3. More parental involvement
4. Improved standardized test scores
5. More or improved business-school relationships
6. Improved classroom discipline
7. More ethnic studies

Notes

1. The following is a list of responding school districts: Baltimore, Buffalo, Cleveland, Dade County (Fla.), Dallas Independent, District of Columbia, Flint (Mich.), Iberia Parish (La.), Jefferson County (Ky.), Kansas City (Kans.), Long Beach Unified (Calif.), Lowell (Mass.), Milwaukee, Montgomery County (Md.), New York City, Oklahoma City, Portland (Oreg.), Pueblo (Colo.), Saint Paul Public Schools, Spokane, Tulsa.

References

Altschuld, J. W., and M. A. Lower. 1984. "Improving Mailed Questionnaires: Analysis of a 96 Percent Return Rate." *New Directions for Program Evaluation* 21:5–18.

Apple, M. 1985. *Education and Power.* Boston: APA Paperbacks.

Blumberg, A., and P. Blumberg. 1985. *The School Superintendent.* New York: Teachers College Press.

Borman, K. 1991. *The First "Real" Job.* Albany: State University of New York Press.

Borman, K., E. Mueninghoff, and S. Piazza. 1988. "Bowing to No One." In *Class, Race, and Gender in American Education,* edited by L. Weis. Albany: State University of New York Press.

Bullough, R. 1988. *The Forgotten Dream of American Public Education.* Ames: Iowa State University.

Button, H., and E. Provenzo. 1983. *History of Education and Culture in America.* New Jersey: Prentice-Hall.

Cuban, L. 1984. "Transforming the Frog into a Prince: Effective Schools, Research, Policy, and Practice at the District Level." *Harvard Educational Review* 54:129–51.

Cuban, L. 1985. "Conflict and Leadership in the Superintendency." *Phi Delta Kappan* 67:28–31.

English, F. 1991. "Visual Traces in Schools and the Reproduction of Social Inequities." In *Contemporary Issues in U.S. Education*, edited by K. Borman, P. Swami, and L. Wagstaff. N.J.: Ablex.

Feagin, J., and C. Feagin. 1986. *Discrimination American Style.* Malabar, India: Krieger Press.

Glass, T., and S. Sclafani. 1988. "Superintendents Rate Their Jobs." *Executive Educator* 10:19–20.

Katz, M. 1975. *Class, Bureaucracy, and Schools: The Illusion of Educational Change in America.* New York: Macmillan.

Kincheloe, J., and W. Pinar. 1981. *Curriculum as Social Psychoanalysis.* Albany: State University of New York Press.

Knezevich, S. 1975. *Administration of Public Education.* New York: Longmans.

Marks, W. 1981. "The Superintendent as Social Architect." *Theory into Practice* 20:255–59.

National Center for Education Statistics. 1986. Washington, D.C., U.S. Dept. of Educ.

Shor, I. 1986. *Culture Wars.* Boston: Routledge & Kegan Paul.

Spring, J. 1986. *The American School 1642–1985.* New York: Longmans.

Staples, R. 1987. *The Urban Plantation.* Oakland: Black Scholar.

Walters, L. 1991. "Big City Schools: Turmoil at the Top." *Christian Science Monitor,* 83(139): 10–11.

10

IMPROVING PARENT INVOLVEMENT AS SCHOOL REFORM: RHETORIC OR REALITY?

Marianne N. Bloch and B. Robert Tabachnick

While legislation and rhetoric support the notion that parent[1] participation in school decision making is possible and that "parent involvement" in education is "good," the reality of school practice is often quite different from the rhetoric. Adding to the potential for confusion are the varied meanings for the term *parent involvement,* and its variations in practice in different localities and by groups of people with power and without power.

In this chapter, we try to illustrate the rhetoric and reality of the current wave of reform in parent involvement by questioning the terms as they are used, and by illustrating the variety of ways in which researchers as well as parents and school personnel have used the terms and engaged in parent involvement practices. In addition, this chapter documents the rhetoric and reality of parent involvement in three elementary schools in one school district in Wisconsin that we call Lakeland. "Parent involvement" has been articulated as a priority in the state, in this district, and for the particular schools that were studied. The discussion section of this chapter focuses on parent involvement in the broader context of educational reform. The notions of reform as symbolic ritual, rhetoric versus the reality of change, and the possibility of transformation of the social realities of parent involvement in schooling will be examined.

The phrase *parent involvement in education* includes notions of caring for children as well as specific programs directed at parents' ways of caring for and educating their children. Parent involvement encompasses parents' participation in school events, volunteer efforts in classrooms and schools, and meetings with teachers. The term *parent involvement* also includes current efforts to decentralize urban school systems by creating "parent councils" (e.g., in the Chicago Public Schools) or efforts to give parents educational vouchers or "choice" about which schools their children attend. Parent involvement in education within a community includes local school board participation and influence on financing, school policy-making, and the structuring of schools in the community; voting for the election of school board members is also often considered part of parent involvement in education within a community.

THEORY VERSUS PRACTICE

In theory, parents and communities have a variety of ways of influencing school policy, including their participation in election of local school board officials, and, in many states, superintendents of public instruction, who set state-level policy. Parents also have ways to influence and support local school practice through school level Parent-Teacher Organizations or Associations (PTOs or PTAs), which have been in existence in most of the nation's schools since the early twentieth century (Schlossman 1976). In practice, voter turnout is very low for school board and state school superintendent elections; participation in PTAs/PTOs is also low, and principals and teachers complain chronically about how few parents attend and work for PTA/PTO-type school organizations. Both school boards and PTA/PTO organizations have memberships that do not fully represent the families that send children to school. Those who are rarely found on school boards or at PTA/PTO meetings are, typically, from low-income or minority families. There is a cost to participating in these ways, an "opportunity cost foregone" (activities that participation prevents someone from doing instead, possibly including work for pay) as well as an immediate cost—of campaigning for an elected office, of finding child care in order to be able to attend a meeting, and so on.

In theory, there are various other formal and informal mechanisms that schools typically use to involve parents in schools and in the education of their children. These usually include conferences at least once a year, open houses for families to visit classrooms and schools, other family events at school, providing homework that parents may be involved in, and the opportunity to participate in volunteer activities in children's classrooms (see Lareau 1989 for a more extensive description of these types of informal parent involvement activities). These are the activities with high parent participation rates, activities that are likely to create home-school linkages in typical American public schools. In practice, only very brief times are available during any of these activities when a teacher and a parent can meet together and discuss a child's work, an educational issue, a school policy. During an open house or a similar activity, a teacher is host to many visitors and cannot linger to develop an idea or a conversation in depth. After an orientation (usually brief) for a parent volunteer, a teacher is immersed in teaching a class full of children, meeting teaching demands that allow little time for discussing questions of school policy or curriculum. Parent conferences are often scheduled so tightly that there is rarely time, in the twenty minutes typically allotted, to do more than tell a parent about his or her child's work, possibly to try to interpret it to the parent, rarely to discuss it (i.e., for each participant to share interpretations, conclusions, and meanings with the other[s]). In practice, parents and teachers hold different beliefs about the value of homework and how parents should interact with children when homework is given. Some research shows that homework disadvantages children whose parents cannot help them (e.g., Richardson et al. 1989), while others stress interactive homework as an extremely effective ingredient of parent involvement programs (Epstein 1986).

In theory, parents and teachers complement each other's education of children, and their interactions or communication can represent a collaborative effort to help children. In practice, the social structure of parent-teacher interaction is frequently one of unequals interacting and often seems competitive rather than collaborative. While in some sense inequality is "natural"—parents and teachers have different knowledge, training, roles, and obligations—in other ways inequality or competition that does not serve children well is not natural, but a social construction that can be altered to serve children better.

While parent-teacher communication ideally aims at helping parents and teachers with children, teacher-parent interactions in public schools are most frequently aimed at helping the *teacher* meet professional responsibilities more effectively or to make it easier for the *teacher* to teach so that each child is successful in doing schoolwork and has positive social relationships with other children and with teachers. This purpose, better teaching, is something teachers and parents both want, but it does not address other parent interests or help parents achieve nonschool purposes. It is also something everyone expects teachers to know more about, to be more skilled and expert in, than nonteachers or parents would be; indeed, it is exactly in the area of the teacher's professional expertise and an area in which great struggles have been made to achieve recognition and status for teachers. Unfortunately, inequality is engendered by the notion that teachers are experts and parents are not. The social relations of "unequals" also at times encourage self-protective and competitive behavior rather than a cooperative search for mutual interests and solutions to shared problems. Teachers sometimes perceive power given to parents as a loss of power to them, rather than as an addition or complement to their classroom program. Thus, in practice, parent and teacher communication is fraught with hidden meanings, perceptions, and concerns that are independent of that which is best for children.

VARYING DEFINITIONS OF PARENT INVOLVEMENT

As suggested above, the term *parent involvement* in children's education is a catchword that is relatively ill-defined but universally acclaimed to be of importance[2] by professional educators and by many groups of parents.[3] In addition, parent involvement with schooling can take place along several different dimensions. Along a *social dimension,* parents may interact with their children in such a way as to demonstrate that they care about the child's schooling and, more generally, about the child's education. Parents may express values that support schooling as an institution, teachers as professionals, children's activities that exhibit intellectual curiosity or use academic talents and skills (e.g., dramatic play, artwork, reading library books). If the social response to a school or teacher is negatively critical, this response itself takes place within a context of caring about the purposes and effects of schooling and teaching as important social institutions that have consequences for a family's and a child's well-being. Along a *technical-participatory dimension,* parents may engage in a variety of activities outside of school: teaching a child the alphabet, reading to children in the evening, asking a child to add up a restaurant bill, discussing a TV show, helping a child with homework, or monitoring whether or not a homework assignment has been completed. Parents may come into the school to volunteer as aides, to chaperon trips, to attend parent conferences or school events. Along this technical-participatory dimension, parents use technical skills to participate in activities with their children at home or in school that further school purposes for academic achievement, either directly or indirectly. Finally, along a *political dimension,* parents may serve on school district or local school policy-making boards or committees, campaign or vote for candidates for school-related positions, lobby through various political or religious groups in an attempt to influence school policy or activities. Any single effort or action by parents over time may be along one or two or all of these dimensions at once.

In a recent volume, Lareau (1989) reviews research that suggests that the term *parent involvement* usually includes *preparing* children for school (e.g., teaching children the alphabet or teaching them how to act in a classroom) *before* school entry, *attendance at a variety of school functions that include parents* (e.g., PTO meetings, parent night, conferences), and *fulfilling requests teachers make of parents* (e.g., sending in food for snacks or field-trip permission slips, volunteering in the classroom when requested, helping children to complete homework). In another report, Epstein (1987) adds to Lareau's summary the role parents can play in management or advisory capacities in a school or community; she also adds fulfillment of parental obligations, which can include simply care and love for children as well as the more traditional list of ways parents can be involved in schooling.

Cultural, institutional, and individual beliefs and practices influence which definitions of parent involvement are valued and practiced within different contexts. Cultural, ethnic, gender, and class relationships affect the meanings and the ways in which people think of "involvement" and understand how they might participate in parent involvement opportunities. In practice, then, the definitions, meanings, and perceptions of power and opportunity affect school and home participation in what is most frequently simply referred to as "parent involvement in schooling."

THE IMPORTANCE OF DIFFERENT PARENT INVOLVEMENT STRATEGIES

Epstein suggests that more research is needed to speak to which aspects of parent involvement are most important to parents or effective for children. Others (e.g., Henderson 1987) review research that suggests that effective parent involvement programs must include a comprehensive set of strategies, including most of the types of parent involvement described above. Comer (1980, 1988) highlights the importance of parent preparation of children for the "school role," especially for children of color, where the "school culture" and "home culture" may be discontinuous or even "culturally incompatible" (Tharp 1989; Vogt, Jordan, and Tharp 1987). Comer's work (e.g., Comer 1980) also stresses the importance of parent involvement in decision making and advisory roles in schools, especially where parent power has historically been low or nonexistent; other researchers and practitioners using the concept "parent involvement" may not even include parent political power in discussions. Few assess which practices parents believe in or feel are most effective (Epstein 1986).

In summaries of research on parent involvement, the importance of a "comprehensive" approach to improving parent involvement in children's education is cited as "critical to highly effective parent involvement programs" (Henderson 1987). Studies suggest that "highly effective parent involvement programs" help to improve children's achievement in school reading and on other standardized test scores, and that increased parent involvement with children enhances children's self-concept and social development in school. Parent involvement in programs such as Head Start has also been associated with increases in parent knowledge about child development and school skills, parent perceptions about school, and, in some programs, parents' own attitudes and skills (e.g., self-concept or vocational skills; Powell 1988). In situations where communities have been involved in significant decision making in schools or communities, parent "involvement" can affect power and status relationships in a community—or society—at a more substantial level.

THE CONCEPT OF PARENT INVOLVEMENT AS REFORM

In theory, *if* a school were to include parents and community members in all of the feasible aspects of parent involvement, reform at individual, familial, school, and broader community levels might occur. For example, in the case of parent management or community control as reform in the Chicago Public Schools system, school reformers hope for change in the structure of school system organization and governance as well as the possibility of schools becoming different and better, with different teaching methods and significantly higher student achievement (Ayers 1989; Hess 1991).

Despite perennial hopes for reform, Cuban (1989) points out that reforms go in historical cycles and that reform through parent involvement, of each type, including the notion of community control, is no exception to this. Indeed, the notion of parent involvement as "reform" has reoccurred over the nineteenth and twentieth centuries in various forms, styles, locations, and effects (Cuban 1989; Powell 1989). Despite recurring efforts to reform schooling through parent involvement efforts of various kinds, these reforms, such as the community control reforms of the late 1960s in New York City, rarely have resulted in long-term or substantial structural or even pedagogical change (Cuban 1989; Popkewitz 1988).

In general, the majority of reform efforts are nontransformative in their end result, and far too frequently seem to be more on the rhetorical, and ritualistic or symbolic, side of a change equation than on the other side where classroom actions might occur (Popkewitz 1988). Indeed, the purpose of reform seems to be to change some components of a system, but to keep the basic social structure and relationships the same.

In the next section, we briefly describe the context and methods of our study, followed by vignettes and discussion that illustrate the complexity of parent involvement in practice within these three fairly typical school situations.

PARENT INVOLVEMENT IN THREE ELEMENTARY SCHOOLS

The study we will describe was situated in the state of Wisconsin in a moderate-size, largely middle-class and Euro-American, city of approximately 250,000 people. The school district gives significant local autonomy and control to elementary and secondary schools, but provides priorities for change.

The city can be divided into four primary areas: North, South, West, and East. The three elementary schools we have been studying fall into the North and East quadrants of the city.

While the school district gives schools a surprising amount of decision-making autonomy, the district has mandated several recent changes as a result of an increase in the number of low-income children of color in schools. Through a policy of siting low-cost subsidized housing projects throughout its area, the city has distributed children of low-income families, often children of color, to about one-third of its schools. Even so, in 1983, a suit by parents led to a city plan to "pair" two schools that had high percentages (approximately 80 percent) of children of color from low-income homes, with two other schools that had more than 90 percent of enrollment from Euro-American families.

All children in grades K–2 from the two school attendance areas attend one school in a "pair," while all children in grades 3–5 in the two school attendance areas attend the other school in the pair. Half of the children in each school are bused from their neighborhoods to and from the school. The school district has also mandated additional efforts, districtwide, to increase the "involvement" of parents of color in schools. Two of the schools described in this paper have been part of the voluntary "pairing" integration plan; the other school has a high percentage of people of color enrolled for the city (approximately 28 percent). The three schools have multicultural populations that include Euro-American, African-American, Asian-American, and Latino-American children.

The Schools

School 1: Oakhill School. Oakhill School is a K–5 grade school of about 425 children. It is in a well-to-do neighborhood in the city's North area. More than 70 percent of the children are Euro-American, but only 66 percent are from middle- to upper-middle-class family backgrounds, while 33 percent receive free or reduced-price breakfasts and hot lunches. Northville low-income housing complex is in the Oakhill School neighborhood. Northville families are Latino (mainly Mexican-American and other Latino-American country origins), Southeast Asian (primarily Hmong refugees from Laos, Cambodia, and Thailand), African-American, and low-income Euro-American. We chose to work with Oakhill School kindergarten teachers because of the Latino families in this particular school and because the school appeared to be initiating a variety of reforms in the area of parent involvement for families of color. The school has a male principal and primarily Euro-American female staff. One of the two ESL/parent liaison staff members spoke Spanish. A Latino parent was employed as an aide in the school. The two kindergarten teachers in our project were Euro-American females.

School 2: Greendale School. Greendale School is a K–2 grade school in the same North area of town as Oakhill School. In 1983, the voluntary integration plan resulted in the school district "linking" Greendale School (then a K–5 school in a largely middle-class Euro-American neighborhood) with Fillmore Elementary, an East-area school that had approximately 80 percent children of color attending the school and had the largest percentage of African-American children in the city. Many parents from both school neighborhoods were very upset by the decision to link these two schools, although reasons varied. Busing was unattractive to most parents, as was the loss of a neighborhood school opportunity for half the children. Many parents, especially in the affluent neighborhood, were active and vocal in opposing the plan. A greater number were willing to give it a try, convinced by predictions that no children or school programs would be hurt academically and also by their support of integrated schools. The school district also added to the resources available in each school (e.g., full-day kindergartens, extra staff, a computer lab, and other resources).

Children from several low-cost housing projects go to Greendale from the East-region Fillmore School neighborhood. One of these, Moonhill housing project, has received negative attention from the media over the past four or five years largely because of a public perception of crime and drug-related issues in the complex.[4]

The majority of the families living in the Moonhill project are both low-income and African-American, although some low-income Euro-American, Asian-American, and Latino-American families also live in the complex. Most of the African-American families are recent immigrants to the city from nearby larger urban areas.

Many of the African-American parents say they've moved to make a better life for their children and because they've heard the schools are good. Despite this, suspicion and distance still characterize the relations between families from Moonhill and school staff members. The physical distance between Greendale School and the Fillmore neighborhood, the largely Euro-American background of the school staff, and Fillmore neighborhood parents' perceptions that the school staff has more frequent problems with Fillmore neighborhood children than with Greendale School neighborhood children contribute to the climate of distance.

Close to the time when we began our project with this school, a new principal was hired for Greendale School in order to try to reduce distance in parent-teacher relations and to improve instruction for children. The principal is female and Euro-American in background; she had been a teacher and principal for approximately twenty years before being assigned to Greendale School. The two kindergarten and two first-grade teachers we worked with at Greendale School were Euro-American in background and female, as were the majority of other staff members in the school. There were two African-American female teachers and one native American teacher in the school, as well as an African-American parent liaison staff member and a Hmong interpreter.

School 3: Lakelawn. Lakelawn was a K–2 grade school situated in the East area of the city. As a result of the voluntary integration plan, Lakelawn neighborhood children were paired with another school, which we call "Washington School," in the North area of the city for third through fifth grades. Thus, unlike the Greendale-Fillmore pairing, children who live in the Lakelawn neighborhood, which is a mixed middle- and lower-income neighborhood, stay in their neighborhood school for kindergarten through second grade, and are bused to Washington School for third through fifth grades. Children from the Washington School neighborhood, a middle- and upper-middle-income neighborhood with many professionals, were bused for their early grades (K–2) to Lakelawn and stayed in their neighborhood school for third through fifth grades. As with the Greendale-Fillmore pairing, many parents were fearful toward the pairing as it was initiated; Washington neighborhood parents did not want their young children bused away from the neighborhood school and feared that the generally high reputation of the school in terms of academic preparation would go down with "pairing."

A very experienced Euro-American male principal in the city who had been principal of Washington School moved to become the principal at Lakelawn School. The principal's already established good reputation reduced some Washington School parents' concerns. Our project worked with three of the six kindergarten teachers at Lakelawn and four of the eight first-grade teachers; one kindergarten teacher with whom we worked was an African-American female, while all the other teachers at the school were Euro-American, including one male first-grade teacher who participated in the study. There were no Asian-American classroom teachers, although several ESL teachers or parent liaison staff members were of Hmong or Southeast Asian (Thai) origin.

While Lakelawn is in a relatively mixed income neighborhood, many of the Hmong children we followed at this school live in a low-income housing complex, Runnymeade, situated in part of the Lakelawn neighborhood. The majority of the city's Hmong population go to Lakelawn, where, in 1989–90 when our study began, children of color represented 38 percent of the total school population. Approximately half of the minority ethnic population at Lakelawn are African-American and nearly half are Asian-American. The majority of the Asian-American children attending the school are children of Hmong refugees.

Our report in this chapter relates to the issues of rhetoric and the reality of parent involvement as we have seen it from varying viewpoints during the past two years in Greendale, Fillmore, and Oakhill schools.

Methods

We have studied the three schools described above through participant observation strategies for two years (September 1989–June 1991). We have followed children from the beginning of kindergarten through the end of first grade. We have spent time with the children and their families at home in children's communities, as well as with their kindergarten and first-grade teachers at all three of the schools. In the first two months of kindergarten, with the seven kindergarten teachers who agreed to participate in our study (three at Lakelawn, and two at each of the other two schools), we selected a small sample of children from African-American families ($n = 6$, all of whom are at Greendale School), Asian-American families ($n = 8$, all of whom were Hmong and at Lakelawn School), and Latino-American families ($n = 6$, all of whom are at Oakhill School). Each teacher was interviewed regarding parent-teacher communication with the targeted children in their classroom (our sample children) and concerning general practices with parents of all the children in their classrooms. During the kindergarten year, and somewhat less so during the first-grade year, specific information about parent-teacher relationships with each child's parents was ascertained during interviews in order to determine whether parent-teacher involvement and communication were similar for sample children and their families compared to all children in a teacher's classroom. Sample children were also observed in their homes over the two-year period, and sample children's parents were interviewed periodically over the two years, with a particular focus on parent-teacher involvement and their perceptions and understanding of school-based communications, including report cards, conferences, and newsletters. Parents were also interviewed at home about their interactions with the school and with their children's teacher, and about their perceptions of children's reactions and progress in school. School principals and a variety of other staff members (e.g., the parent liaison staff member, social workers, other teachers involved with parent involvement efforts and our collaborative efforts) have also been interviewed informally and formally.

Project staff consisted of two Euro-American principal investigators. In addition, research staff, over the several years of the project, included two African-American research assistants who worked primarily with the teachers and families of African-American children, four research assistants with specific or general experience with Asian-American or Hmong families who worked with teachers and families of the Hmong children, and a Peruvian bilingual research assistant who worked with teachers and the families of Latino-American families.

The first two years of our research project can be characterized as a period of low-key participant observation, where we observed, interviewed, participated, and intervened in modest, unobtrusive ways.

In the next few pages, we describe vignettes from the first and second years of our study (the kindergarten and first-grade years for children) of participant observation and low-key intervention, to show some of the issues we have encountered in our examination of schools' current parent involvement efforts. We also illustrate reactions to some initial intervention efforts we instigated in collaboration with school staff members in one school and with a selected group of parents. The vignettes have been selected because they illustrate common types of parent involvement efforts in the schools with which we've worked, and because they illustrate some of the issues we saw that relate to whether real or rhetorical efforts to involve parents were being made in the schools.

It is important to note that the vignettes have been selected out of many possible examples because they illustrate certain general points we want to make in this paper. While they represent certain common occurrences, they do not represent the beliefs, statements, or actions of every teacher we have interviewed or observed, nor can they be construed to represent the general actions or philosophy of any of the three schools or communities with which we worked. Nonetheless, we do believe the events portrayed in the vignettes illustrate important and general issues that permeate the environment of reform related to parent involvement in the schools we've studied, and, with some likelihood, elsewhere.

Vignettes Focusing on Parent Involvement

One Teacher. One of the kindergarten teachers, who we call here Teacher X, elected to participate in our study because she was interested and willing to work to improve home-school relationships between African-American parents and Greendale School. She chose to move to Greendale School after the pairing plan began. She reported some prior experience working with children from low-income and diverse ethnic backgrounds in her previous school assignment in the Lakeland School district and perceived that teaching at Greendale, a newly integrated school, would be a new challenge for her. When we invited teachers (during the summer after our first year in the school) to attend a summer teacher-parent workshop, she was also one who chose to attend. Based upon observations of her classroom practice, she is an effective classroom teacher with children. She stays late into the afternoon preparing for school the next day. Her parent involvement practices include the regular once-a-year conferences the school requires, and other contacts initiated by parents (for instance, during their participation in school events such as the once-a-year open house or Thanksgiving Day celebration).

She does not have a regular parent volunteer program in her classroom , although some parents participate in field trips, and at least three Euro-American mothers from the Greendale School neighborhood help in the room on a regular basis.[5] About one of these parents, she says:

> I do have a parent who comes in, who works on the computer with the children, and she just very quietly comes in and quietly takes a child and they go in that area. Not at all disruptive. That just flows, very, very nicely. But not all parents will do that.

Concern about the disruptive nature of parents in the classroom is shared by many teachers and is a common problem in trying to involve parents within classroom programs.

However, this teacher had additional concerns affecting her ideas about which parents could help without disruption and which couldn't. The following report from her interviews with us provides background to other concerns she had regarding another parent who wanted to participate in the classroom. The interview is about an African-American parent whose child was in a pilot public program for four-year-old "at-risk" children the prior year at the same school, and who was encouraged to get involved in her son's kindergarten classroom by the "four-year-old" program teacher. The kindergarten teacher says the following to the interviewer's question:

> (Interviewer) "But in terms of other history of contacts with the parents . . . ?" (Teacher X) "Ok, with mother, lots. She's been in twice to come and stay. She ended up having his birthday party in the classroom. She will send me notes if there is something that she needs to know or if there is something she wants me to know. I think she feels very comfortable getting in touch with the school. I do not encourage parents to drop in and she spent a lot of time in the "four year" program and was . . . you know . . . and I don't encourage that sort of thing. So I think that may be a little difficult for her. I'm sorry about that, but I just don't function that way. . . . I guess, I feel that if parents would like to come to

school, I'd like to know before hand, and if they want to come and just observe, that is fine. I would like to know that. If they are to come and involve themselves with children, I'd like to work out with them what they are going to do and how they are going to do it. Sometimes there are parents who will come in and sort of disrupt the whole day. And involve themselves a lot with the children rather inappropriately. The affects my program in the classroom.... The last time I talked with her, somehow or another, we were talking about Halloween and we were talking about what we were going to take to the Halloween feast as a class. I told her that we had baked pumpkin, baked pumpkin cookies. And she said, 'Well, oh, I'll come in and help you.'

Well, I didn't call her and ... I have a hard time with this whole issue. Because when I plan it, such as a cooking activity like that, there are some very specific goals and a certain kind of language used and certain kinds of concepts emphasized, etc. And I also like to encourage, or I also do encourage certain kinds of interaction among, with the kids among themselves with me, etc. And I get somewhat concerned when what I see is inappropriate behavior with parents ... I'm not so sure the children, I think it's more an activity maybe more to, not entertain, but to please the parents than it is a learning activity for the children.

This particular interview segment is used as an example to illustrate some of the perceptions that work against parents of color as volunteers in classrooms. The teacher has no direct knowledge of how this parent would act as a volunteer. The teacher anticipates that the parent might use nonstandard forms of English at times, that the children might make inappropriate demands or behave poorly and that the parent would go along with these, not knowing that the teacher would object. This might create an awkward situation in which the teacher might feel forced to contradict the parent or else correct her in front of the children. Again, none of these expectations is grounded in experience with this parent as a volunteer, but rather in generalized expectations for a group of adults with whom the teacher has had little personal social contact.

It is important to note that many of our teachers were much more active and positive in their encouragement of parents of color as volunteers in their classrooms than the teacher described above. The other kindergarten teacher at Greendale School, for example, encouraged *all* parents to volunteer if they were able to do so, but had few African-American or Asian-American parents who did choose to volunteer. One of the other schools, Oakhill School, had received specific grants to support volunteer programs to encourage parents of color to volunteer in the classroom. Through the grants, small numbers of low-income parents from diverse ethnic backgrounds were employed as paid aides and participated in a monthly parent-child workshop. The goal of this volunteer program was, in the words of the principal, to help make parents feel comfortable in the school in the beginning of their children's public school career, hoping that "once parents are in the school, they'll keep coming." This goal will be discussed in the next section.

It's Not So Simple. It's not so simple to say we're going to increase parent involvement in the school. The principal of Greendale School wants to encourage Fillmore neighborhood parents to feel that Greendale School is *their* school; above all else, she wants the parents to feel comfortable in the school and to come into the school (Interview with M. B., 21 March 1990). While the parent liaison questions whether "just getting parents into the school" is an adequate goal for parent involvement,[6] the principal would be happy to start at this point. As mentioned above, this same goal, "starting by getting parents to feel comfortable with the school," was also mentioned by the principal at Oakhill School as the basis for their special grants to encourage kindergarten parents to volunteer in that school.

Given Greendale teacher X's response to one of the few African-American parents who tried to volunteer in a kindergarten classroom, the Greendale School principal's goal was not easy to achieve in that particular classroom; indeed, only a few Euro-American parents did volunteer to help in that class during the particular year we were working with Teacher X. Of greater importance, perhaps, is the need to define whether parent comfort in the school is a critical first goal for public school parent involvement programs, and/or whether broader visions of parent-school relationships and the school's role toward families, as suggested by the parent liaison, is important. According to one informant, the Oakhill School program, which supports low-income parents' volunteering in the classroom and attendance at parent-child workshops, and supports one or two paid regular aides, has increased parent self-concept, some parents' willingness to seek additional work, and parents' positive communication with the school. Our data also suggest, however, that some Latino parents at Oakhill, even after such efforts and activities, do not feel "comfortable" with teachers and the school; there is still some feeling of psychological distance and suspicion. In both the kindergarten and the first-grade years of our study, parents have reported that they know little about the children's progress in school or how the school curriculum (e.g., the reading program) works in general or for their children.

At Lakelawn, where the principal, ESL teachers, and the one Hmong interpreter have had numerous meetings with Hmong parents outside the school, Runnymeade housing complex parents have rarely come to the school; here the language differences, sizes of families, and needs for child care, as well as a lack of understanding about the school, influence parents' low attendance at in-school functions and within the classroom. At Lakelawn, where the principal has also tried hard to help parents feel comfortable at the school, as well as to understand what their children are doing in school, parent comfort is slowly being achieved through frequent meetings and explanations given to parents with the intervention of ESL staff and one Hmong interpreter. This level of comfort has been achieved after great effort by some staff and is still at a questionable level. Hmong parents are still suspicious, and do not understand why the school wants them to be involved, or how, given low English language skills, they realistically can be. While certain ESL-related staff have made important efforts to communicate and involve Hmong parents, many teachers still have little knowledge about Hmong customs or how these parents might be involved successfully in the school. Because the ESL staff do much of the direct work and communication with parents, teachers and parents rely on them and have little direct communication with each other—and, perhaps, too little knowledge of each other to work together in the ways the involvement programs intend.

Can Comfort and Communication Be Achieved by Simply Bringing People Together to Get to Know One Another? The principal at Lakelawn School believes that a long-term commitment of knowledgeable personnel to work on parent comfort and knowledge of the classroom and school will eventually help the children. However, the majority of the effort is done through specialized staff and does not involve classroom teachers, who see Hmong parents relatively rarely at conferences in their classrooms.

At Greendale School, we initiated a workshop to bring parents and classroom teachers together to develop joint goals for enhanced parent involvement and to try to define, collaboratively, goals for parent involvement. This vignette shows dilemmas that were faced when these two groups of people, who rarely interacted with each other, came together.

When we began our project with Greendale School, we recognized that there were fear, distrust, suspicion, and, for a few, stereotyped expectations influencing some of the school staff members' perceptions. This wasn't unique to Greendale School; stereotypical information about certain minority groups exists throughout the school district (and nation). Most Euro-American teachers in the district have had little real experience with members of any minority ethnic or linguistic groups; few live near minority ethnic group families, and few have social contacts outside of school with members of minority ethnic groups (see Ladson-Billings 1990 for similar comments about school staff nationally). Few teachers are bilingual in Spanish, and virtually no regular classroom teachers speak any Hmong or other Asian languages.

When the project with Greendale and Fillmore schools began, it was clear that only a few members of the school staff in either building had been in Moonhill complex or had met African-American community leaders from the Fillmore School neighborhood; these were the principal of Fillmore, a few of the teachers, including the African-American teachers in the schools, the African-American parent liaison staff member, and the social support staff (e.g., the social workers). This was true four years *after* the initiation of the integration effort in the schools, and four years after the beginning of reform efforts toward increasing minority parent involvement in the schools.

We thought bringing the community members and school staff together might help to initiate discussion; certainly, we hoped it wouldn't hurt. When we broached the subject to the principal of Greendale School, for whom we were coordinating a three-day summer workshop, she said, "Perhaps it's too soon for the staff . . . the staff needs to have a chance to talk together first to think about parent involvement." After some discussion, we agreed to the idea that the first day of the workshop would be with teachers and other school staff alone, and that community members (African-American, Hmong, and Latino) from the South area, as well as minority ethnic group parent representatives from Greendale School, would get together with school staff for days two and three.

When the workshops did occur, they were moderately successful. During the morning of day two, community leaders identified problems with parent-school relationships that school staff felt they had identified themselves during the first day of the workshop, when they were alone.

School staff members felt pleased that there was so much agreement. By the beginning of afternoon of day two, there was joviality among the members of the group; we could break down the barriers. However, by the middle of the second afternoon, things became more tense. Several community members suggested that there was some racial prejudice involved in school relations with the East community and Moonhill complex. One leader of the African-American community stated (with emphasis), "Don't think we don't know who is working for our children in your school, and who isn't! These things are known." Several teachers became defensive, and several members of the workshop, including the African-American teacher from Greendale, tried to smooth things over. When one Euro-American teacher claimed the workshops were turning into a "teacher bashing" meeting, one of the African-American teachers stated that she disagreed and that the meetings were productive. Several Euro-American teachers supported her. The conversation calmed down and became less hostile and defensive. Some issues were raised and discussed (see the next section). By the end of the third day of the workshop, some specific strategies were identified to begin reforms; an extra fourth workshop day was planned before the beginning of school, at the group's suggestion, to refine these ideas. The ideas were not bold (see the section "The Question of Conferences" below), but they represented some movement. We all felt good. Teacher and community participants' evaluations of the workshops were extremely positive and confirmed this perception. The question was, and remains, were these ideas symbolic? Were we working together and communicating, or were we simply engaging in rhetoric, or participating in a symbolic reform activity that would eventuate in little change, as so many reforms have done in the past (Cuban 1989; Popkewitz 1988). This issue will be discussed more fully in the final section of this chapter.

The Question of Homework. At the summer workshops, one or two African-American, Hmong, and Latino parents from Greendale School spoke about their own and other parents' concerns. Interestingly, while there were some differences, all of the parents mentioned *homework* as an issue.

> "If minority children are doing so poorly at school, why aren't teachers sending homework?"

> "Parents want to help children, but don't always know how."

"Teachers send home notes that suggest parents play with their children, or go to the library with them, or read to them at night. But this isn't real homework."

"Parents don't have time to sit down with their children after school and read to them or go to the library . . . but children can work on their own if they have homework."

"Children waste time outside, or watch television inside; if they're doing so badly at school, teachers should send homework with them to keep them busy after school."

Teachers and other staff members responded to parents' comments in several ways. Several teachers suggested, "Children work hard all day; young children shouldn't have homework." Others suggested that "developmentally appropriate homework for K–2 graders involved enjoyable reading with parents, sharing an interest in books by going to the library, even talking with children while cooking." In general, the teachers were opposed to homework that would be similar to classroom assignments or completion of workbook pages on letters or numbers.

In this exchange, a commonly expressed parent concern was communicated by parents in a context in which they could be respected, their opinions were asked, and they were, we thought, empowered to speak. However, teachers, who had different beliefs, assumptions, and training than parents, found no middle ground with parents. Teachers, with teacher education and national standards to support their notion of developmentally appropriate curriculum for young children, stood their ground with respect to the way "homework" might be given (not at all, or as "fun activities for parents and children to do *together*"). They spoke from their own knowledge base and perspectives, without accommodating the valid points parents were trying, hesitantly, to bring to them. They did not dig into the meaning of parents' requests or concerns or open negotiations about meanings for homework and homework activities that both teachers and parents could support. There was little real communication.

At this juncture, we ("the university staff") could have helped, but did not. We thought we understood the issues, and we sensed the lack of communication. There was an intensity of emotional commitment to each statement of position that may have made us reluctant to intervene at this time. We understood that teachers were drawing on their professional expertise to protect children from what they saw as ill-conceived practices that would make academic work seem unattractive to children while not actually enhancing the children's in-school academic achievement. We understood that parents were asking for help; they were expressing their deep concern for children and their desire to help them achieve in school. They were also saying: We are busy, we cannot do too much ourselves, and we don't know how exactly to help. Give us, and our children, structured assignments to help them, and we'll make sure they do them.

While the teachers were saying "homework isn't good for young children who have been working hard all day," teachers were also negating parents' perspectives that minority-culture children need extra help to succeed in school, and that the parents do not have enough knowledge about school-required activities to generate these on their own. Thus, while the teachers would doubtless have said the same thing to anxious middle-class, better-educated parents, those parents are likely to *know* better what to do with their children to prepare them for school. The low-income, less-well-educated minority parents at the workshop were saying, "We do not know how. Help us." This reflects Lareau's (1989) conclusion that middle-class families have "cultural capital" that enables them to work with and for their children in ways that lower-socioeconomic-class parents cannot; the homework issue raised in this workshop on day two exemplified the differences in cultural capital that different parents bring to parent involvement in schooling. The teachers, following experts' advice for all children and families, and possibly undervaluing the fact that dominant-culture parents do give "homework" to children after school, thought it best not to accede to low-income, minority parents' requests for help to do something the parents thought would benefit their children. The parents in the workshop did not recognize that the teachers were recommending "homework" activities that were often similar to activities that more affluent parents provided for their children and that helped contribute to the children's school success.

The Question of Conferences. At Greendale School, in years past, the once-per-year conference with teachers had taken place at Greendale School during the course of one afternoon and evening (the evening was added on to make it possible for daytime-employed parents to attend a conference) and one full schoolday. Attendance by parents from the Fillmore neighborhood, particularly African-American parents, had been low. During the summer workshop with Greendale School parents and teachers, it was decided to try to aim for 100 percent attendance at this one conference and to hold conferences in the East area of town (at Fillmore School, at a church, and at a local neighborhood community center) to reduce psychological and physical distance for parents from the Fillmore School neighborhood. Parents thought it would be a symbolic act of importance to have teachers come to their neighborhood. Surprisingly, no one suggested that there be more than one conference; the goal of 100 percent conference attendance and moving Greendale School staff to the East side of town for some conferences was considered a big step. Indeed, it represented substantial symbolic and real change, given the distance that existed before the workshop.

One morning of the day-and-a-half conference period took place in the three East-area community locations. Conferences went well, and parents who attended them responded very positively. Teachers felt "safe" in numbers at the three community locations, and also responded very well.

When conference statistics were tallied, 75 percent of the Greendale School parents had attended, an increase from previous years. In a school newspaper that went to all Greendale parents, the principal referred to this as a good turnout, which it had indeed been, and thanked everyone for their help. Nearly 100 percent of the majority-culture, and Greendale neighborhood, parents had attended. However, only 50 to 60 percent of the minority parents had been to a conference, the only one scheduled for the year; this was an increase from previous years' minority attendance, but it fell short of the 100 percent conference attendance goal.

Does True Communication Occur in Conferences Anyway? In Oakhill and Lakelawn schools, where parent involvement programs were somewhat more intensive, principals had "mandated" 100 percent conference attendance for all parents during the same November conferencing period, and 95 percent attendance had been achieved in these schools by December. Teachers were pushed and prodded, and were encouraged by being given additional time to complete conferences. Parent involvement and conferencing, especially with minority parents, had been a high priority for several years. Indeed, based on a school district grant for "minority achievement" to Lakelawn and Oakhill schools during the 1989–90 academic year, kindergarten teachers had been paid to hold an orientation meeting, before school started, for all parents, with a special effort toward parents of color. They had also held "ready-set-go conferences" in late September, where parents, teachers, and children met to identify common goals they hoped to work on together over the first part of the year.[7] By the November conference, the kindergarten teachers we were working with at Lakelawn and Oakhill schools had nearly 100 percent attendance and meetings with all of their parents on at least three separate occasions. Another conference or two were scheduled for the spring. In one school, Oakhill, one of the kindergarten teachers was also paid to do home visits with each of the low-income parents of kindergarten-age children in the school. A Minority Parent Aide program, where parents were paid a stipend to help in the kindergarten classrooms, and an afterschool monthly workshop for parents on kindergarten activities were also being conducted, using funds from an outside grant to the school. A primary goal at Oakhill was to get parents "comfortable" with the school, since, "once they feel comfortable with the school, they'll come back."

During interviews with African-American, Hmong, and Latino parents whose children attended all three schools in our sample, we asked how the conferences had gone. What were parents' reactions? Did they understand, feel comfortable? What kind of information did they still feel they needed?

With almost no exception, the parents from all three schools felt very uncomfortable at conferences. According to one Latino parent from Oakhill School, they attended conferences "because otherwise the teachers would think we don't care"—but, the parent continued, "I felt terrible at the conference. I hardly said anything. . . . I went in by myself and there was the kindergarten teacher, an ESL teacher and a Chapter 1 teacher. The Spanish-speaking (but Anglo) parent liaison staff member was also there. There I was alone with four of them . . . how do you think I felt?"

All of the parents, regardless of the schools their children attended, responded that conferences provided little information that they understood. They believed teachers were neither telling the whole truth about their children, nor providing much useful information that they could use to help their children at home. All of the parents wanted additional information about what they could do to help their children; all wanted additional time to talk to teachers, interestingly enough, but they wanted that time to be more honest, open, and "concrete," to identify what their children were doing poorly so that they could help correct these "deficiencies." It is a curious contradiction that parents in all three schools said that one of their primary purposes for coming to the conference was to discover if their child's teacher was a nice person who liked their child and wanted to help their child do well; at the same time they were suspicious of the positive language used by teachers and the limited, sometimes elliptical references to academic inabilities. For their part, the teachers tried to be very careful to report academic lacks in a context of a more positive overall picture of a child's presence and performance. Especially for kindergarten children, the wide range of "normal" development curves for children led them to see almost all children as developing appropriately (unless there was angry, acting-out behavior or a pattern of inattention and movement around the classroom that disobeyed teacher instructions). Any negative comments were usually well insulated by many positive comments, both before and following, and became difficult for parents to recognize or evaluate, particularly for parents who were not facile or comfortable in using English.[8]

Was communication occurring, even at the schools that were making extra efforts to involve parents? According to parents, not very much, not enough. Teachers suggest they intend to give parents accurate information about their children's school behavior, but the school conference activities were not accomplishing this goal.

Rhetoric or Reality?

The rhetoric of parent involvement is similar across all three schools—for example, all teachers want parents to feel comfortable in the school, and all talk positively about the need for greater parent involvement in, and understanding of, the school, school programs, and classroom practices as they affect children. The schools with which we worked are also different from one another (e.g., some have more meetings with parents than the others, some employ community residents as parent liaisons, while others employ parents to assist in teachers' classrooms). Within the same school, some teachers are more active in parent involvement efforts, while other teachers have highly structured parent involvement programs that severely limit or restrict the ways in which parents may enter the classroom. According to research reported by Epstein (1986), there are significant differences in teachers' practices and in beliefs about the importance of parent involvement. Teachers who believe that parent involvement practices are important appear to engage a greater number of, and a greater diversity of, parents in activities with schools and with children in and out of schools; teachers who feel that parent involvement practices are less important are less likely to involve parents in such activities. Thus, while all teachers may express verbal support of parent involvement, there are multiple definitions of parent involvement, beliefs about the importance of parent involvement, and practices that seem to accompany these beliefs. The definitions that are used by individuals, or by individual schools, seem to represent different "realities" about parent involvement. What may be more likely is that contradictory impulses, aims, and meanings create a complex multilayered reality.

As the phrase *parent involvement in schooling* suggests, the focus is on children's school achievement and school behavior. In addition to the children themselves, teachers, who spend eight to ten hours a day working or preparing to work with children, are the major players.

For some teachers, the words about parent involvement layer over attitudes toward parents as outsiders. The effort to orient parents and find tasks for parents to do in the classroom makes parent volunteers seem like more trouble than help. Time constraints often make orientations to classroom assistance rushed or nonexistent, and the negative apprehensions of both parents and teachers may be confirmed by the experience. The language of parent-teacher conferences, as of messages from school to home, usually flows in one direction only and contains terms that are often not well understood or that may be misinterpreted by nonprofessionals. Time pressures may limit the opportunity to check for understanding during a conference or the effort to compose a newsletter home that parents with limited English proficiency might be more likely to understand or have their children tell them about. Time constraints become an ally in maintaining distance, keeping parents well outside the action of the classroom.

Another group of teachers center their efforts to get parents involved in schooling in their deeply felt attitude that parents are their partners in the effort to have children succeed in school. Even though parents may be a minor presence in the classroom, these teachers recognize the potentially powerful contribution that parents can make to children's school success. So, they search for ways to bring parents into their classrooms more often, to use parent expertise and skills in the curriculum, to have parents appear to their children as honored and important participants in their children's schooling. But time pressures are not an invention of those who might want to keep parents at a distance. There is little time for teachers to meet often or at length with parents, little time to confirm whether communication has taken place or missed the mark, whether teacher or parents have sent messages that the other does not interpret appropriately.

There are real and important differences in belief, priority, definition, and practice within the realm of "parent involvement" that nest themselves within the context of expectations, encouragements, ideologies, and the economics of the time demands and different priorities teachers experience within their work and a school or school district.

What is confusing is that some of these differences result in similar words of support for parent involvement in schooling and even in similar practices (e.g., rushed, closely scheduled parent conferences, inadvertent use of specialized professional terms). The differences are discernible in the "close encounters" of parents and teachers, where nuances of meaning are found in the tone and language used when teachers and parents meet and talk or work together. These nuances of meaning may encourage and welcome parent participation; they indicate teacher confidence in parental support and cooperation toward achieving a common purpose, a child's school success. Alternatively, these subtle messages may discourage participation, send suggestions of lack of trust by teachers and parents of one another's interest or capability to help a child succeed in school, while the participants retreat behind a firm belief in their own good intentions.

Parents are not passive players in the process; parents also differ from one another in their definitions of how, who, and toward what ends one should "be involved" with schools and schooling. Parents have defensive stances and different roles to play as they assess the necessity or value of attending a conference or volunteering in their children's classroom. Some (e.g., the Hmong families with whom we worked) perceive the roles of parents and teachers as distinct, with little overlap, while other parents believe there should be more shared visions, communication, or collaboration between teachers and parents over the education of their children. Parents are made aware that they should be doing something, helping somehow, but they are not always sure how to help or what to do. They don't want teachers to think that they don't care about their children, so they attend conferences where they may feel uncomfortable and outnumbered in a contest whose rules or purpose is not clear to them. The notes sent home may be difficult to understand if parents' English is limited or if the notes contain specialized professional terms that are common place for teachers but new to parents. Requests to participate in out-of-school activities with their children (e.g., to take them to the zoo or to cook and measure ingredients together) seem not to make sense in terms of parents' understanding of the academic knowledge and skills that they expect children to acquire; possibly these requests don't make sense to them in terms of their usual practices for family activities such as cooking.

The distinctions between parents and teachers have been described by many others (e.g., Epstein 1986; Lareau 1989; Lightfoot 1978), but our data support the fact that there are cultural as well as individual differences in the ways in which these roles are viewed and affect parent-teacher relationships. Parents also face a multilayered reality in their perceptions of "parent involvement." That reality is nested within the cultural context of the families, individual expectations, and possibilities, and within the history of the experiences families have had and continue to have with schools and teachers as agents of a cultural institution.

Teachers are well intentioned and genuinely attempt to act out what they believe. Feedback as to the effectiveness of what they try would help to make current efforts succeed and or be modified to achieve goals. In addition, different actors (administrators, teachers, and family members) need to clarify what parent involvement might mean, and they should facilitate setting of and sharing goals and priorities that could be based upon shared beliefs about the value and intent of parent involvement efforts. With greater clarity, support for shared goals and strategies might be identified and provided. For example, if, to help parents help children, teachers were clear that they wanted parents to know how children were behaving or doing in school, then there would be more feedback to find out when communication failed, and other ways devised to help parents understand what children are doing in school. But it is more complex; the differential power relationships between some parents and teachers influence how much a teacher might tell an influential parent—or a perception that parents would punish a child for poor academic behavior, rather than help the child, might influence a teacher to hide a true picture of performance. The lack of relationships between teachers and parents, and the lack of good knowledge and respect for each other's knowledge, behavior, and intentions to help children, constrains their ability to engage in more complete communication.

Reform or Transformation?

In our study, school activities aimed at increasing parent involvement in schooling represented reform efforts but did not seem to transform relationships, the structure of status and power relationships, or, to a great extent, the actions and communication teachers or parents had with each other or with children. While improvement of parent involvement was a state, district, and school priority, while lip service was paid to parent involvement, and where, in numerous cases, real efforts were made to improve communication by the schools, little substantial improvement in relations, communication, or power occurred.

Why? What is meant by the term *transformative relationships,* versus *reform?* If transformation is desirable or necessary, what are the constraints to such change?

In the context of this chapter, we suggest that transformations of social relations between parents and teachers, schools and communities, need to be changed to facilitate trust, a valuing of competencies each other brings to the relationship and to their parenting/teaching work with children, and concepts that collaborative work can facilitate each other's work rather than detract from it. We suggest that parents and teachers could develop ideas together, and would work collaboratively toward school change, respecting and using the types of knowledge and skills that each brings to the relationship, and using the differences in roles and relationships with children as additional strong points brought to the collaborative effort. For example, parents have long-term interests for their children, whereas, as schools are most often structured, teachers have shorter-term commitments to individual children. The longer-term knowledge and commitments of parents provides great strength as parents look at a school and curriculum and instruction over, for example, the five or six years of elementary school. Parents have knowledge of their rich history and the strengths of their own culture and language that can be used in school to provide continuity for children between home and school. Rather than shutting parents out of the process of school-based education, the relationships of power need to reflect an honoring of parents' as well as teachers' expertise and power as they collaborate in the education of children. While this solution or strategy may seem to reflect "old reforms" (e.g., community control, site-based management solutions, multicultural education where parent ideas are brought into the curriculum), the type of collaboration and respect for families that we think is important incorporates shared power and ideas through collaboration (not competition), and respect for parents' ideas, skills, and ability to motivate and work with children, and their motivation to help children be educated within schools. In some fundamental way, the relations between parents and teachers would change so each could learn from and help each other. Power to parents would not be subtraction from the power that school personnel have, but a complement.

Barriers to Communication and Collaboration: Barriers to Transformative Change

History and the Struggle to Become Professional. Teachers have been struggling for a hundred years in the United States to discover their expertise and have it acknowledged as something valued. Should we expect teachers to deny their expertise in order to strengthen home-school relations? Clearly that is not reasonable, and teachers resist. We can, however, work toward a situation in which people who have been en-culturated to different knowledges, beliefs, priorities, and affiliations learn to recognize one another's point of view, to value it, and to find ways to use these viewpoints constructively for each other's and for children's benefit.

It is reasonable to expect administrators and teachers to take the lead in these efforts. When they do not, as in the case of Chicago, and perhaps in some of our schools, parents have the right to push. Collaborative discussion, training, and support for change would need to occur for parents as well as teachers and their administrators, when and where necessary.

Teacher Time. Involving parents in transformative ways requires time. Teaching is in general a gendered occupation. The majority of the staff we described in schools studied were women, with teaching as their occupation but not their only employment. Time required to go to communities, to meet with parents and children at homes, or even to prepare for appropriate use of parents as volunteers added to teachers' already heavy professional and personal burdens. Parent involvement, while appearing to be worthwhile in principle, required additional burdens. Teachers, faced with many options as to how to use their time as professionals, often chose efforts that seemed to have a direct link with children (e.g., a new lesson or activity for the next day; reviewing multicultural literature to add to their readings in the classroom). Parent involvement, or lack of activities or emphasis toward greater transformative involvement of parents, was highly related to the time demands already placed upon teachers and teacher resistance to increased demands.

Prejudice and Stereotypes. At the bottom of many issues lie stereotypical thinking and prejudice. Teachers must be pushed in preservice and inservice education to work in communities and with parents and children from *all* backgrounds. Leadership and resources to overcome the poor job we've done educating children and future teachers have to be targeted; within current schools, principals, teacher leaders, and empowered parents must step forward and push teachers and parents to work together to develop stronger relationships and, when possible, share power in an effort to collaboratively help children.

Power and Structural Change. It's so easy to keep the little power one has and to not share this. But schools need to work *in collaboration* with parents. Is it so terrifying to include minority parents' opinions in decision making? Some schools, such as Lakelawn and Oakhill, want parents to help with the school, and all school principals want parents to feel "comfortable" with the school. Parents of color also want to feel comfortable with the schools, but more importantly and less "symbolically" want to be able to help their children succeed. It is an error to think parents don't care about their children. But it is true that many parents with minority ethnic and linguistic backgrounds perceive, with school culture and expectations as they are, that they do not know how to help children and do not have the power or relationships built within schools to push for important change or to learn ways to help.

Why? Schools often maintain power, status, and expertise because they are fearful of sharing the little they have with others, especially those they do not know and sometimes fear.

Why? Schools represent the power and culture of the dominant culture—often without realizing it. Change prompted by a real structural transformation in relationships and valued behavior and knowledge would endanger current practices and beliefs in schools that dominant culture values still hold to be true and that serve some children better than others.

Thus, while there are some that want the reality of change, the majority have many reasons for maintaining the status quo—or working toward symbolic change, simplistic reform, or nontransformative change.

The rhetoric and the reality of parent involvement, despite the good intentions of actors and participants in such programs, appear to us to be symbolic reform. The concept of parent involvement, as currently used in the schools we've examined, is an "educational quick fix" that is constrained by economic, ideological, and social relationships of power as well as perceptions of unequal expertise. The concept of parent involvement is good, but it is constrained by the lack of clarity in meanings, goals, and visions of accomplishments for children. Despite this apparently negative assessment, the potential for change is good, given the good will and hopes of many members of school staffs and families with whom we've worked.

Notes

Inquiries about this paper should be addressed to the authors at the Department of Curriculum and Instruction, University of Wisconsin-Madison, Madison, Wisconsin 53706. The writing of this paper, and the research that is reported, was supported primarily by a grant from the Spencer Foundation, as well as grants from the School of Education, University of Wisconsin-Madison and the University of Wisconsin-Madison Plan. The authors want to thank members of the school staff with whom they worked, families who participated in the project, and Jay Hammond Cradle, Carolyn Dean, Miryam Espinosa-Dulanto, Joann Koltyk, and Seehwa Cho, who were research assistants with the project. All names used in the text are pseudonyms to protect the confidentiality of participants.

1. Although we use the term *parent,* our referent is to adults responsible for children out of school, regardless of relationship; uncles, aunts, grandparents, legal guardians, and informal guardians who are family friends would be examples of people included through the use of either *parent* or *family.*

2. Here again the word *important* could be highlighted as rhetoric. Parent involvement's being important is like saying that apple pie and motherhood are important. No teacher or administrator would say that parent involvement is unimportant; the meanings attached to the phrase, however, can be and are very different from one another, depending upon individuals and the social context. Lareau (1989) suggests that all teachers cared about parent involvement; while this may be true at some level, the general picture we get from our research is of a wide variety of interests and practices. Some of these practices encourage and invite participation and having both teachers and parents learn more about one another through informal social interaction as well as through collaborative work in the interest of children's improving school academic or social behavior. Some of the practices discourage parent involvement and/or suggest that parent involvement competes unsuccessfully with other priorities school principals and teachers have. In the latter case, pronouncements that parent involvement is "important" appear to be more rhetorical than a representation of reality.

3. Although rarely noted in the literature on parent involvement, there are clear cultural and class differences in parents' definitions of and beliefs about parent involvement practices (e.g., Lareau 1989; Delgado-Gaitan 1990). In our own study, for example, Hmong parents believed parent involvement was important at home, but that parents should not interfere with "school business".

4. Collections of newspaper clippings over the three years of the study show significant negative attention to this complex in a city that

has other areas where crime and drug-related problems are also occurring, and were less media attention is directed. In 1990–91, media attention began to include more community protest about the negative portrayal of this housing complex and some positive images; earlier, almost all media coverage fanned community opinion that people (including children in this complex) were "different."

5. This volunteer pattern was quite common across a number of kindergarten and first-grade teachers across all three schools with which we worked.

6. The parent liaison's concern was that if parents are to give up the protection of distancing themselves from the school, there need to be school programs and activities that insure that the parents participate in ways that create positive feelings about themselves as well as about the school. He felt it was important for the school to help parents meet their own goals, to improve parent literacy and job opportunities, and to act in general ways to serve wider community needs.

7. Greendale School was given a Minority Achievement grant and held Ready-Set-Go conferences beginning the next year (1990–91).

8. Report cards seemed to represent the same problem.

References

Adams, R. S. 1978. *Educational Planning: Towards a Qualitative Perspective.* Paris: HEP.

Comer, J. *School Power.* 1980. New York: Free Press.

Cuban, L. 1990. "Reforming Again, Again, and Again." *Educational Researcher* 19:3–13.

Delgado-Gaitan, C. 1990. *Literacy for Empowerment.* Bristol, Pa.: Falmer Press.

Delgado-Gaitan, C., and H. Trueba. 1990. *Crossing Cultural Borders.* New York: Falmer Press.

Epstein, J. L. 1986. "Parents' Reactions to Teacher Practices of Parent Involvement." *Elementary School Journal* 86:277–94.

Freire, P. 1970. *Cultural Action for Freedom.* Cambridge: Center for the Study of Development and Social Change.

Freire, P. 1973. *Education for Critical Consciousness.* New York: Seabury Press.

Henderson, A. T. 1988. "Parents are a School's Best Friends." *Phi Delta Kappan* 149:149–53.

Hess, G. A. 1991. *School Restructuring, Chicago Style.* Newbury, Calif.: Corwin Press.

Huberman, A. M. 1973. *Understanding Change in Education: An Introduction.*

Lareau, A. 1989. *Home Advantage.* Basingstoke, England: Falmer Press.

Lightfoot, S. L. 1978. *Worlds Apart.* Cambridge: Harvard University Press.

Papagiannis, G., S. Kless, and R. Bickel. 1982. "Toward a Political Economy of Educational Innovation." *Review of Educational Research* 52:248.

Popkewitz, T. S. 1988. "Educational Reform as the Organization of Ritual: Stability as Change." *Educational Theory* 38:77–93.

Popkewitz, T. S. 1991. *A Political Sociology of Educational Reform: Power/Knowledge in Teaching, Teacher Education, and Research.* New York: Teachers College Press.

Powell, D. 1988. *Parent Education as Early Childhood Intervention: Emerging Directions in Theory, Research, and Practice.* Norwood, N.J.: Ablex.

Powell, D. 1989. *Families and Early Childhood Programs.* Research Monographs of the National Association for the Education of Young Children, no. 3. Washington, D.C.: National Association for the Education of Young Children.

Richardson, V., Casanova, N., Placier, P., and Guilfoyle, K. 1989. *School Children at Risk.* Basingstoke, England: Falmer Press.

Sack, R. 1981. "A Typology of Educational Reforms." *Prospects* 11:39–53.

Schlossman, S. 1976. "Before Home Start: Notes toward a History of Parent Education in America, 1897–1929." *Harvard Educational Review* 46:436–67.

Tharp, R. 1989. "Psychocultural Variables and Constants: Effects on Teaching and Learning in Schools." *American Psychologist* 18:349–59.

Vogt, L., C. Jordan, and R. Tharp. 1987. "Explaining School Failure, Producing School Success: Two Cases." *Anthropology and Education Quarterly* 18:276–86.

PART III

RHETORIC VERSUS REFORM AND RESTRUCTURING IN THE SCHOOL AND CLASSROOM

Whatever else is involved in the enterprise of educational change, we usually identify the bottom line with regard to outcome as to what impact it has on the students. Obviously, this eventually has an impact on the community, which in turn may shape what is allowable. Decisions may technically be made elsewhere, but schools and classrooms are the loci of action.

Reform of the 1980s removed whatever involvement in the change process teachers and other professional educators may have had. The restructuring rhetoric proposes to bring change back to this fundamental level through participatory site-based management. The lived reality sometimes aligns with this goal, but more often does not. Discrepancies between what we say and what we do arise on innumerable levels—often evolving from discontinuity of expressed philosophy and existing structural realities, through conception of policies and programs, to implementation of policies and programs at various levels of the educational enterprise.

Parts I and II of this volume provided a forum for discussion of some of these discrepancies through critical analysis on both theoretical and practical levels. The contributions in Part III focus on identification of discrepancy at the practical, grass roots level of education, and on aligning rhetoric and reality.

Fortunately, examples exist of successful teaming and collaboration, as well as models of social bonding and empathetic interaction that foster understanding and communication and yield hope for transformation of the way we "do school." The purpose of Part III of this volume is to provide a sample through specific case studies, of the problems resulting from attempts to recapture the past and the promise of forays into inventing the future.

11

CAN MULTICULTURAL EDUCATION FOSTER TRANSCULTURAL IDENTITIES?

Dorothy Angell

INTRODUCTION

The title of this chapter is a species of shorthand. I use the term *multicultural education* to stand inclusively for all the efforts currently being made in response to the changing cultural complexity of the classroom, and I use *transcultural identities* to connote what Erik Erikson (1964, 206) called "more inclusive identities." Thus, while I ground this chapter in the realities of the culturally diverse U.S. classroom, I want to shift attention from the usual focus on helping students from other cultures to "adjust," or even on teaching U.S. students about other cultures, and instead ask whether and how all of us—teachers and students—may learn to stretch our identities to meet or include the culturally defined "other": not simply to "help" the Punjabi child, or even to learn about Punjabi culture, but to put ourselves in the shoes of that child and enlarge ourselves in the process.

I wrote the first version of this essay in the winter of 1989–90, as a paper for presentation at an anthropological conference in England in the spring.[1] That winter was a heady one—perhaps especially so for a social anthropologist who has long been interested in Erik Erikson's (1964, 242) concept of "a more inclusive human identity." The Washington, D.C., newspapers were full of new proposals for international education, the TV screen was alight with astonishing images of cultural change, the Congress warmly hosted Havel's moving speech about creating "the family of mankind [*sic*]." A heady time indeed. But a dismaying one, too: The same media simultaneously told us that students in the United States are geographically illiterate, incurious about what has happened in Eastern Europe, and poorly prepared to work in the international and intercultural world at their doorstep. It has become axiomatic that we need to expand our students' knowledge about the rest of the world. Of course I agree. But I will also maintain in this chapter that something more than knowledge "about" others is needed. Let me tell you what I think it is, and why I think so, through the experience of my own students.

I have been teaching an anthropology of education course that is now being required for certification of new elementary teachers in order to prepare them for the culturally diverse classroom. In working with these prospective teachers over several years, I have identified two problems, shared by all but a few students, that hamper their classwork and may decrease their effectiveness in culturally diverse classrooms. My students, primarily junior and senior education majors, have great difficulty with the concept that personal identity is culturally mediated. Their received notion of culture prepares them to accept the idea that their students will have different holidays, heroes, and histories—the cultural "heritage" model. But grasping the reality that particular social arrangements, and particular symbolic communications, actually produce distinctive sorts of persons—particular ways of enacting personhood—and (this is the hardest part to grasp!) that this is true of themselves, too—this is a tough one. And it is precisely this "aha" experience—what Louis Dumont (1980, 5) called the "*sociological apperception*" (author's emphasis)—that I believe teachers (and of course all of us) must internalize if they are to see their students' lives as in any way linked to their own. And my students' second problem is closely related to the first: They have difficulty putting themselves in their culturally different students' places—imagining what it would be like to be a new immigrant in a big U.S. city, for example, or to try to follow classroom directions in a strange language. In short, their capacity for empathy is underdeveloped.

Unhappily, the experience these student teachers have in their senior year practice teaching, in culturally diverse classrooms throughout the Washington, D.C., metropolitan area, does not, apparently, ameliorate these deficits of understanding and empathy and in some cases seems to exacerbate them. Probing this observation of mine with my students highlighted some of the disjunctions between the rhetoric about these classrooms and the lived reality of the classrooms. On the one hand, the student teachers hear me and (at least some of) their in-school practicum teachers affirm the integrity of each culture and the virtues of cultural diversity; on the other hand they can scarcely think of an example of something new and valuable they have learned from the culturally "different" students. Unfortunately helping to concretize this contradiction between rhetoric and reality is a dominant teacher education model (informed by its own rhetoric) of "problem solving" as being at the heart of what teachers do. In the lived reality of current multicultural classrooms, the major "problem" student teachers see is the presence of culturally and linguistically "different" students. It is only a short step to seeing the differences themselves as the problem, and their elimination, circumventing, or softening as the solution. The ease with which this step is taken shows up readily in student teachers' exams and papers and in classroom discourse.

Is there then a bridge between the rhetoric about valued cultural diversity and the reality of "troublesome" cultural differences? Can we translate the rhetoric into a reconstituted classroom reality? What might that reality look like? The task I set myself in this essay is to outline a feasible, concrete project for developing wider identities and enhancing empathy in the classroom. I seek to ground this project by exploring two pieces of work: an exposition of a semiotic model of identity, and a group of empirical studies on empathy. I take this effort to be an example of an "intentional subject" working to construct an "intentional world" by seizing some of the meanings and resources of her sociocultural environment—to borrow Schweder's (1990, 1) clarifying language.[2] I shall return to the notion of intentionality in a brief closing comment on the rhetoric-versus-reality issue that grounds this volume.

IDENTITY AS DIALOGUE WITH THE "OTHER"

The semiotic model of identity is crucial. It will be clear that I refer to the identity not of groups but of the person—an individual who is both a social actor and a reflexive self. In common with Milton Singer and others who have followed in the footsteps of G. H. Mead and C. S. Peirce, I take the identity of this individual to be simultaneously personal *and* social—and both of these through dialogue. We have to mend the Cartesian split in order to grasp this nondualism. The essential point is this: I am continuously in dialogue—an external dialogue with all those whom I meet in shared social space, and an internal dialogue with my new self that is just coming into being. If I understand this, I can come to apprehend that the "locus, identity and continuity" of myself is not in my individual organism but in what Singer (1984, 56–57), following Peirce, calls an "outreaching identity"—which connects my feelings, thoughts, and actions to those of others.[3] For Singer, then, the interesting question about identity is not the supposed conflict between personal and socio-cultural identity, since the identity of any of us is simultaneously both. Rather, it is the empirical problem of "discovering the bonds of feeling that hold people together or tear them apart, and what their interrelations and conditions are" (Singer 1984, 71–72). I take empathy to be a critical aspect of the "glue" that holds us together, and I turn to it now.

EMPATHY AS FEELING FOR THE "OTHER"

There is substantial consensus among a group of new studies in psychology and education (Eisenberg and Strayer 1987) that differentiate empathy from sympathy, from personal distress, and from projection—with each of which it has often been confused. Unlike sympathy, which draws heightened attention to one's own feelings, empathy directs attention to the other: Its response must be consonant with the other's reality, not with one's own. Unlike personal distress, which may lead to aversive action, empathy is associated with action on behalf of the other. And unlike projection, in which I place my own feelings in the other, the capacity for empathy permits me to insert, so to speak, the other's feelings into myself (Eisenberg and Strayer 1987, 6–8). All three of these discriminations underline the essential point: Empathy requires a clear ability to differentiate myself from the other, to take the other's experience imaginatively into myself, and to be ready to act for her or his welfare.

Most of us probably find it easy enough to conceptualize what empathy does for the species or the group. It is clearly associated with survival value in evolution, by promoting group behavior. Indeed, it makes group life possible, and without it we would live only by constant reference to rules (Staub 1987, 109). But what of individuals? Apart from making them more caring to their children and more proactive in groups, what does it do for the "self"? Don't "I" lose something for myself if I'm busy feeling for you? Extraordinarily interesting new research reported by Barnett (1987) indicates that empathy is positively associated with imagination, emotional competence and stability, communications skills, and cohesion between the cognitive, affective, and interpersonal aspects of behavior (148). But further, and perhaps coun-terintuitively, empathy appears to be precisely the source of the self-concept and indeed of self-expansion, according to the interpersonal theory of Harry Stack Sullivan (Staub 1987, 110). Without the capacity to feel for the other, we do not fully know or develop ourselves. It is not just that we become better selves through empathy, then, but that we become selves at all.

If we're sold on empathy, how do we generate it? And how might it be enhanced in the culturally diverse classroom? What identifiable fac-tors work against it? And how, if at all, could these factors be minimized? It seems clear that empathy cannot be produced through a reasoning process. Merely explaining about another's affective state does not pro-duce empathy in children. True empathy must be produced through experience that is itself emotional (Barnett 1987, 154). Rational expla-nation—teaching "about" the other—may produce "social perspective taking" (Bryant 1987, 245), an instrumental skill that enables us to ne-gotiate more successfully with others. But empathy is an "expressive competence" (Bryant 1987, 245)—the ability to experience a variety of feelings even though we may gain no material advantage thereby. The "gain" from empathy is the intrinsic enjoyment of expressivity and the experience of emotional connectedness to others. While contemporary U.S. culture clearly has put a premium on the instrumental side of the ledger, clinicians daily observe (and we all observe, and pay) the costs of the despair that results when people, of any age, fail to experience emo-tional connectedness to others.

Not surprisingly, this emotionally charged experience of connect-edness is apparently best produced through concrete sharing and help-ing and through an intimate friendship during childhood (Barnett 1987, 156–58). While the groundwork for empathy is ideally laid in childhood, Duggan reports that in a project designed to produce empathy in disad-vantaged adolescents the experience of helping younger children (many of them with equal or worse handicaps) was indeed effective in enhanc-ing the adolescents' empathy. Duggan (1978, 8) suggests that adoles-cence, with its heightened "cognitive maturity and growing awareness of others' feelings," may in fact be the optimum time to foster this vital quality and that it will be increasingly difficult to accomplish thereafter.

What this seems to mean is that if we want more of the gains that empathy brings us, we need to encourage expressivity and intimate friendship, sharing and helping, in young people—and accomplish this before the end of adolescence. Minimally, we need to diminish the two factors that apparently inhibit empathy: interpersonal competitiveness and the perceived lack of commonality between persons (Barnett 1987, 154–55). Since the culturally diverse classroom is a par excellence location of both competitiveness and exaggerated attention to apparent differences, the challenge defines itself.

ENHANCING EMPATHY AND ENLARGING IDENTITIES IN THE CLASSROOM

Competitiveness in the classroom has been heavily researched. The work of Robert Slavin and his colleagues at Johns Hopkins has documented the effects of cooperative learning in redirecting competition and raising test scores of all students—including racial and ethnic minorities and (contrary to the fears of their parents) the already high-achievers. I shall not discuss cooperative learning (also known as "team learning") here, but the "model" I now outline assumes its incorporation, in some form, into any classroom that aims to increase cooperation, let alone empathy.

I thus confine myself to the similarity issue, about which we apparently know less than we need. Those scholars who have researched empathy agree that children respond more empathically to persons whom they perceive as similar to themselves. While it appears that "similar" can be defined more abstractly—and thus perhaps more broadly—with increasing age, and that much depends upon how "large and inclusive" are the categories of commonality that are taught to children (Barnett 1987, 154–55), we still need to know more about this decisively important area.

I suggest that if our goal is both to celebrate each child's distinctive identity and to make it possible for that identity to become more inclusive, more empathic, and more open to commonalities with others, we won't achieve it primarily by telling students *about* other cultures (on the usual model of multiethnic education) or by telling them how similar we all are as human beings (on the usual model of global education). We will best achieve the goal by enabling students to enact their distinctive identities—both personal and cultural—*and* see their connections to others through that process. The scheme I propose for enhancing communicative identity and empathy in the classroom is extrapolated from this principle. It has three major components, corresponding to the three "bundles of habits" (Singer 1984, 159) that constitute identity: thinking and feeling, acting, and symbolizing. Each of these components explicitly connects the "I" to the "you," and each is adapted for use at different classroom levels and in teacher education. The first component, corresponding to thinking and feeling, is telling and hearing stories—especially stories about the self, the life story. The second (acting) is expressive and creative activity (such as dance, music, poetry, painting). And the third (symbolizing) is the use in the school's public space of powerful visual symbols that combine the local and the global (for example, a world map large enough to take changing overlay displays about particular countries and cultures). And of course it would include a photo of the beautiful "blue marble" upon which we all reside: the image of the Earth as seen from space, to which Margaret Mead found children responding empathically as a symbol of pan-human unity and hope for the future. I confine myself here to the use of life stories and what they might contribute to expanded identity and enhanced empathy.

LIFE STORIES

I have been exploring the use of life stories with my students' major advisor and have had an enthusiastic response to the stories' potential for eliciting the personal consciousness of vocation and direction that this education department's faculty want their prospective teachers to achieve. My aim is complementary, but different, and builds upon the concept of identity as dialogue. I have asked my students to write the story of their lives, in diary form, the narrative to be kept private if they wish. They will next be asked to analyze their own stories for several features: the important persons in their lives, family traditions, help they have received, ideas and interests they share with friends, and their own feelings about all of this. Through a series of exercises shared with their classmates, they will discover the social and cultural origins of what they think of as "inside" them, and the evidences of their own person in those they are close to. In short, they will discover that they are who they are through others, and that those others have their identity, in part, through them.[4]

Then I will ask them to read and hear similar stories by their age mates from different cultures. I want them to see that, while the contents of the stories may be distinctive to those social settings and cultural meanings, the process by which the narrators become both social and private selves is a universal one. Also universal (or at least very widely shared) are their feelings about what happens to them in that process. It is this process and these feelings that they can share with the culturally diverse youngsters they will teach. My students' own cultural "givenness" is no less particular, no less the intimate foundation of their identity, than that of their culturally "other" classmates and future students. From even brief experimentation with this technique, I believe it can help produce the "aha" experience that alone can bind new teachers intuitively to their students and without which they will always be more or less alien. It wonderfully cuts through the impasse of "We do it our way because it makes sense; they do it their way because it's part of their culture" in which most college juniors (and, for that matter, most adults) otherwise get mired. And it simultaneously supports their own distinctive cultural and personal identities (a support much needed by new teachers) and opens them to greater curiosity about and appreciation for that self-building process in others. Once young teachers have had and enjoyed this experience for themselves, they should have no real difficulty adapting it in classroom activities for whatever age group they may teach.

For culturally "different" elementary schoolchildren, there is nothing more energizing, more confirming of identity, than to be able to tell their stories and have them heard. At this age, children's stories, from whatever culture, are more convergent than not, thus very naturally calling attention to similarities and building a base for empathy. But the differences will also emerge. This is the point where teaching *about* the other culture makes sense—to help children understand and appreciate their differences. Teachers' knowledge base about their students' countries and cultures must be adequate to the task, of course, so that the following horror story—a true one—is not replicated.

A sixth-grade Bangladeshi girl in a U.S. public school needed to bring something to class for show-and-tell. She asked her mother if she could bring some "gold"—some of her mother's gold jewelry and hair ornaments, all handmade in Bangladesh. "So that the kids will know there are good things, beautiful things, in Bangladesh—not just poverty," she said. The mother agreed, and the girl went to school dressed in a silk saree and the gold jewelry. But it was a disaster: The classmates teased her, insisting such finery couldn't be from Bangladesh. And the teacher, as ignorant as the American students, couldn't support the girl's story. The youngster went home in tears, and her mother was still visibly upset when she recounted the story months later.

In a classroom working to enhance students' identities and to nurture "informed empathy" (Bennett 1986), this kind of assault would not be possible. In such a classroom, the particular person can emerge— with a distinctive identity, culturally mediated. And classmates can enlarge their own identities both by hearing and intuiting all the commonalities and by discovering the true (not feared; not imagined; not reified) and interesting differences. The current lived reality of the culturally diverse classroom is overwhelmingly often enacted in terms of heightened cultural differences and the problems they create. It is up to the collective school community—teachers, administrators, parents, neighbors—to encourage the present reality and future potential of inclusiveness and identification among authentically diverse students.

THE TIES THAT BIND

I was led by a convergence between my long-term interest in Erikson's "more inclusive identities" and an on-the-ground problem in my recent teaching to try to deepen my understanding of identity and of empathy, especially as they may be affected by practice in the culturally diverse classroom. Whether we consider a dialogical model of identity that directs our attention to what passes between persons—what binds them together—and thus discover the apparent paradox of a self-identity that is fully social, or whether we review recent research on empathy that suggests that it is by openness to the feelings and needs of others that we become ourselves, we arrive at a relational understanding of human persons that is strikingly at variance with the standard U.S. "individualism" and the standard definition of maturity as independent, even isolated, functioning. Anthropologists have discovered such relational persons in many of the cultures they study: Dorothy Lee found them among the Tikopia; T. N. Madan (and others, including myself [Rutherford 1985]) have identified them among South Asians. Culturally diverse classrooms in the United States usually include such persons—but they typically come from Central America or indeed from South Asia. Many North American teachers and students need to learn, or relearn, this model of human functioning, because, on the strength of the evidence, persons who participate widely and empathically in the lives of others are healthier, more resilient, more imaginative, and more attractive to others than those who do not. That is, they have precisely the qualities and personal skills that our rapidly changing and internationalizing world demands.

The culturally diverse classroom would appear to be a splendid place to start teaching about and nurturing such identities, but we have to get past more tolerance for reified "others." As R. K. Arora (1986, 59–60) puts it, in a stunning essay on multicultural education in England, respect and tolerance are negative virtues. We need to teach children how to foster the dialogue with others, and the empathic connections with them, through which they can apprehend the spirit of other cultures, encounter the reality of their culturally different classmates, and thus together be in a position to forge the new networks and invent the new cultures their collective future will require.

As a social anthropologist long interested in multicultural institutions, I close by suggesting that members of my discipline have a particular responsibility in the conflicted multicultural arena of contemporary schools. We need to remind ourselves and our colleagues in neighboring disciplines how the human community evolved: not primarily through individualistic competition but through collaborative group life and shared symbols. We need to identify examples of inclusive and empathic identities in the world's cultural groups and discern which social arrangements, childrearing practices, and educational strategies foster them. And, in the spirit of this publication, we need to do still more to help translate what we know across the national, cultural, and disciplinary borders that still too often separate scholars with convergent interests.

In this same spirit, I would suggest that we need not set aside the rhetoric about school restructuring or judge reform to have failed when it doesn't match our rhetoric. Rather we can take the rhetoric, in its sense of discourse, as an important indication of the "intentional worlds" we wish to construct in schools. We can then, as I have attempted to do in this essay, identify in some detail both the practices that would likely characterize those worlds and what we know right now about how to generate those practices. It is these "materialized intentional worlds" (Schweder 1990, 22), our own creations, that will reciprocally shape and be shaped by the intending adults of the future—our own students and children. Seen this way, the intentional exhortation to an enhancement of empathy and inclusivity is not "mere rhetoric"; it's bedrock praxis.

Notes

1. An earlier version was read at the annual meeting of the Society for Applied Anthropology, University of York, England, on 28 March 1990. I am grateful to those who attended the session and discussed the paper with me, and especially to Nancy Greenman and E. V. Johanningmeier for encouragement and useful suggestions.

2. Intentional subjects and intentional worlds are central to the new "cultural psychology" as outlined by Schweder (1990) and exem-

plified in the volume he has coedited (Stigler, Schweder, and Herdt 1990). I was not able to study this important work until too late in the present effort to permit even suggesting a synthesis, but I want to acknowledge its very stimulating and clarifying effect. Centering as it does on the concrete social contexts of "intentionality" in which human subjects and their worlds are coconstituted across cultures (Schweder 1990, 13, 22), this volume should be of enormous value to the collective discourse and action on educational, and especially classroom, restructuring.

3. Although, once again, there is not sufficient scope here to undertake its explication, I see a substantial convergence between the concept of persons as constituted through this dialogical and outreaching identity and the concept of persons as "intersections of an array of relational units" that Kenneth Gergen (1990, 585) suggests as more fruitful than our conventional notion of single individuals. The "prototype" of a relational unit, for Gergen, is the mother-child unit.

4. This project was interrupted by a serious illness—thus the evident division between what has been done and what I intend to do. My expectations for its outcome are based on a prototype project undertaken in another classroom setting with young adults and on comparable undertakings by colleagues.

References

Arora, R. K. 1986. "Towards a Multicultural Curriculum—Primary." In *Multicultural Education: Towards Good Practice* (47–61), edited by R. K. Arora and C. G. Duncan. London: Routledge & Kegan Paul.

Arora, R. K., and C. G. Duncan, eds. 1986. *Multicultural Education: Towards Good Practice.* London: Routledge & Kegan Paul.

Barnett, M. A. 1987. "Empathy and Related Responses in Children." In *Empathy and Its Development,* edited by N. Eisenberg and J. Strayer, 146–62. Cambridge: Cambridge University Press.

Bennett, C. I. 1986. *Comprehensive Multicultural Education: Theory and Practice.* Boston: Allyn & Bacon.

Bryant, B. K. 1987. "Mental Health, Temperament, Family, and Friends: Perspectives on Children's Empathy and Social Perspective Taking." In *Empathy and Its Development,* edited by N. Eisenberg and J. Strayer, 361–73. Cambridge: Cambridge University Press.

Crandall, J. E. 1981. *Theory and Measurement of Social Interest: Empirical Tests of Alfred Adler's Concept.* New York: Columbia University Press.

Dumont, L. 1980. *Homo hierarchicus: The Caste System and Its Implications.* Chicago: University of Chicago Press.

Duggan, H. A. 1978. *A Second Chance: Empathy in Adolescent Development.* Lexington, Mass.: D.C. Heath.

Eisenberg N., and J. Strayer. 1987. "Critical Issues in one study of empathy." In *Empathy and its Development* (3–13), edited by N. Eisenberg and J. Strayer. Cambridge: Cambridge University Press.

Eisenberg, N., and J. Strayer, eds. 1987. *Empathy and Its Development.* Cambridge: Cambridge University Press.

Erikson, E. H. 1964. *Insight and Responsibility: Lectures on the Ethical Implications of Psychoanalytic Insight.* New York: Norton.

Gergen, K. J. 1990. "Social Understanding and the Inscription of Self." In *Cultural Psychology: Essays on Comparative Human Development,* edited by J. A. Stigler, R. A. Schweder, and G. Herdt, 569–606. Cambridge University Press.

Lee, D. 1959. *Freedom and Culture.* Englewood Cliffs, N.J.: Prentice-Hall.

Lee, D. 1976. *Valuing the Self: What We Can Learn from other Cultures.* Englewood Cliffs, N.J.: Prentice-Hall.

Madan, T. N. 1982. "The Ideology of the Householder among the Kashmiri Pandits." In *Concepts of Person: Kinship, Caste, and Marriage in India,* edited by A. Ostor and L. Fruzzetti, 99–117. Cambridge: Harvard University Press.

Rutherford, D. A. 1985. *Bengalis in America: Relationship, Affect, Person and Self.* Ann Arbor, Mich.: University Microfilms.

Schweder, R. A. 1990. "Cultural Psychology—What Is It? In *Cultural Psychology: Essays on Comparative Human Development,* edited by J. A. Stigler, R. A. Schweder, and G. Herdt, 1–43. Cambridge: Cambridge University Press.

Singer, M. 1984. *Man's Glassy Essence: Explorationsin Semiotic Anthropology.* Bloomington Indiana University Press.

Slavin, R. E. 1981. *Synthesis of Research on Cooperative Learning.* Alexandria, Va.: Association for Supervision and Curriculum Development.

Staub, E. 1987. "Commentary on Part I." In *Empathy and Its Development,* edited by N. Eisenberg and J. Strayer, 103–15). Cambridge: Cambridge University Press.

Stigler, J. A., R. A. Schweder, and G. Herdt, eds. 1990. *Cultural Psychology: Essays on Comparative Human Development.* Cambridge: Cambridge University Press.

Wolf, E. 1988. *Treating the Self: Elements of Clinical Self Psychology.* New York: Guilford Press.

USING THE FUTURE TO CREATE COMMUNITY AND CURRICULAR CHANGE

Julie Binko

In reforming curriculum in the United States, it is important to consider the current state of theoretical design for curricular systems. Presently the dominant sociocultural ideologies that are used to transmit and maintain the culture are Western European and middle-class. These ideals and leadership styles are used to legitimize cultural, political, and economic avenues of bourgeois culture (Anyon 1988, 176). Preordained middle-class, sociocultural ideals are also employed as sounding boards for expectations in curriculum. Performance measures gauge the success or fulfillment of social agendas that bind, rationalize, and narrow the boundaries of acceptable performance and production within the educational system (Huebner 1974, 48). The consequence of these curricular concepts is the creation of a "museum of virtue" or the preservation of an idealized culture that is outdated and antiquated (Wax, Diamond, and Gearing 1971).

To maintain outdated ideals in society, curricular agendas "explain" (flatten out) and "re-present" (introduce or exhibit) the sociocultural ideals through the educational system (McDonald 1988, 101).

"Ex-plaining" initiates organization of social life and development of one-dimensional institutions. These institutions, such as schools, neutralize social contradictions and absorb all opposition. As a result, society loses its means for revitalization or for synthetic and creative adaptations of future ideals and culture (Marcuse 1966).

"Re-presenting" ideology can be complex. In order to simplify complexity and variety, current curriculum unpacks rules, concepts, and ideas, making them conform to the middle-class norm. This pedagogy "disallows" possible contradictory or unintended meanings for the student (Apple 1976). Both of these one-dimensional concepts assume rationality and acceptance of a technological value system. The rationality implies a right/wrong, good/evil dualism. Performance in the present educational system is based on the ability to reproduce the fixed ideal rather than to create or adapt culture into appropriate forms to meet future situations.

Time-referenced learning is probably one of the most effective tools for teaching people to transcend present reality. If we are sincere about curricular change, time-oriented learning must be incorporated into the educational system. Learning how to recognize time orientation is the first step in this process. Next, learning to create new meanings of time helps students to transcend their being and to discover that their past, present, and future realities are not fixed.

Changing curricular meaning is the first step to acknowledge the temporality of people's frame of thinking. Human beings are cognizant of past, present, and future (Freire 1970), but patterning, fixation, and conditioning prohibit them from creating and forming new ideologies and cultures. People's ability to address the future allows them to transcend the boundaries and rationalities constructed in culture (Huebner 1975, 241).

In the context of learning, knowledge should take on certain characteristics. "Past" is the knowledge of memory and tradition. "Present" is the knowledge of interpretation of self to others as it is expressed in interpersonal relations, roles, career, and recreation. People view their future through present situations and knowledge. Combining "past" and "present" types of knowledge will help people transcend present temporality. Their new views of the future will evolve from new time contexts until individuals and their community "arrive at a mutual understanding in the conduct of public affairs [and] caring collectivity in which individuals share memories and intentions" (Huebner 1974, 37).

These three dimensions of time will direct the evolution of meaning for a reformed, procreative, proformative curriculum. Creating, developing, and nourishing a "three-dimensional human" will be the direction of recommendation for curriculum. The three-dimensional human will be capable of dialectical, dynamic exchanges. These exchanges will occur on three levels: on the intrapersonal, on the interpersonal, and between the natural world and social groups, such as communities.

In summary, the present educational system in the United States uses middle-class norms that are becoming outdated as the basis of performance measures. People need to learn how to create new cultures and ideals so they can adapt to changing situations.

ETHNOGRAPHY AND CRITICISM: A POSSIBLE CHANGE TOOL

The purpose of this study was to design several possible futures for Cambridge, Minnesota. We used ethnographic techniques to describe Cambridge's present reality, and we used ethnographic futures research (Textor 1980) to help the citizens describe desirable futures for their community. Comparison between the two methods yielded sociocultural paradoxes related to moving from the present to the future. The study of Cambridge uses paradoxes in such areas as youths' participation and aspirations, family services, small-town image, and ruralness. I prescribed curricular reform based on a normative future for Cambridge as the vehicle used to move designed change, resolution of paradoxes, and to provide direction for the community toward 2010.

If curriculum is defined as the spiral and dialectical process of knowledge and experience mediated by the learner and the teacher within an adapting and changing sociocultural community, curriculum can reflect meaningful and significant change (Bruner 1966; Dewey 1916; Freire 1970). Change and transformation through education have been successful in the past, in both developing and industrialized countries (Textor 1981). Therefore I consider in this chapter how the reformation of the K–12 curriculum can be used to direct a community.

The method for interpreting data from our study of Cambridge is to juxtapose the paradoxes of ethnographic data with the parameters of a three-dimensional human. The juxtaposition of present and future scenarios with levels of human interaction discloses an array of suggestions on how to resolve these paradoxes.

The recommendations are normatively prescriptive. If we assume a desirable future collated from the data from our research study, "if-then" situations that need to be resolved are created. Moving beyond the present situation can provide catalysts for change.

The process of interpretation follows the tenets of critical praxis in curriculum theory. These tenets emphasize a critical view of the phenomenon and the theory being considered, in this case the future and the three-dimensional human. Phenomenology in curriculum theory critiques curriculum within a specific framework to create meaning. Here the meaning is the resolution of a paradox between present and future. Gail McCutcheon (1981) believes that individually critical praxes and phenomenological interpretations fall short in recommendations or practical implementation for clarifying the future. Therefore in this chapter I use the interplay of the two approaches to produce an understanding that provides "foresight, [and] intervention/control and provides vision in resolution and recommendation" (McCutcheon 1981).

JUXTAPOSITIONS AND RECOMMENDATIONS

Juxtaposition 1

A community of memory and tradition seems to be a vivid image for the people of Cambridge. Change has occurred, however, even in the historical development of this community. Cambridge has evolved from a lumbering village of Swedish immigrants to a bustling retail and government center including a variety of ethnic groups. Citizens are concerned that local leadership is "fragmented, conservative, and afraid of change."

Recommendation 1

Change should be understood as a constant state and should become a goal of the curriculum. Change should be emphasized through the study of community, state, and national history and traditions. Historical comparison should include studying the evolution of cultural diversity in Cambridge and beyond. Nonconformity and variety should be stressed in the positive sense.

For example, the founders of Cambridge established the community under the same premise as our nation was established under by its founders: They fled to the United States to escape various forms of oppression stemming from nonconformity, such as economic deprivation or religious persecution. Nonconformity and acceptance of variety, as mentioned above, helped Cambridge evolve to its present state.

Change in "traditional" roles and patterns must be recognized for the future. For example, demographics show a shift in family makeup to now include single-parent families, blended families, and elderly citizens. Also, shifting economic forces need to be reconciled now as throughout history. Even as early as the 1870s, Cambridge continued as Cambridge citizens described, to develop through shaky times. The acceptance of the aforementioned factors will be the first step in transforming Cambridge's future.

Juxtaposition 2

Spirituality, both theological and social, is valued in Cambridge. Many citizens commented on "the high moral standards of the community." The "I"-centeredness and the lack of social agenda for youths, however, seem to be the basis for a division between young and old. Young people feel that their paying jobs contribute in important ways to the community. Adults claim that work reduces the "time to do volunteer work." The preoccupation with material wealth among all people of all ages seems to be in conflict with the social theology of assisting or participating in the community. Youths feel that they are contributing to Cambridge by what was described as "spending money on things such as clothes, cars, recreation, and other consumer goods." Adults feel that they are "too caught up" in work. The future holds a vision of informed, concerned interpersonal relations and community caring.

Recommendation 2

Spirituality and self-knowledge for personal enrichment, goal setting, and transcending material accumulation should be an aim of the curriculum. The definition of spirituality should be broadened to include knowledge of one's self and one's potential as well as of the common good. Enrichment courses in philosophy, poetry, literature, and art could focus on the expression of self. Career and avocational guidance could provide outlets for exploring and creating the whole person. Concern for commonality could be encouraged through civic and social participation in community activities sponsored by the school as part of coursework. This would be the first step in encouraging self-initiated participation in interpersonal and community affairs.

Juxtaposition 3

The family is an important referent in Cambridge. This social structure furnishes perceived closeness, security, emotion, and affection. In addition, specific definitions and expectations exist for the family social unit.

For the future there is a vision of extended and nuclear families, but the present reality shows divorced, single-parent, and blended families.

Recommendation 3

Living skills should be an essential goal of the educational curriculum. Teaching about these skills should include the changing demographic makeup of family life and the associated possibilities. Attempts should be made to enlighten and incorporate all supportive living arrangements, granting them legitimacy. The first step to addressing these issues is to educate and inform the citizens of Cambridge.

Support for single parenthood and blended families should be built into these skills. Such support could address stress management, budgeting, and household maintenance. Because teen pregnancy is increasing in Cambridge, the importance and responsibility of parenthood also should be emphasized, including child psychology, discipline, and what it means to be a responsible parent.

A high infant death rate, an increase in the elderly population, and a lack of social support services are reasons to include physical, mental, and emotional health issues in the curriculum. There is a need for preventive and medical advice on topics such as nutrition, disease control, personal health, and hygiene. Increases in drug and alcohol abuse show a need for attending to mental and emotional health. Programs could include peer support and substance abuse education and support.

Juxtaposition 4

Currently the younger segment of the population is isolated. In the vision for the future, "all kinds and types of people" will be involved in the community. Isolation of individuals, both intergenerational and intragenerational, must be alleviated to encourage this vision. Intergenerational conflicts include the degree of involvement with family and extended family members. "Many youths do not go to their parents for help," stated one student. "[Only if] you get a real big problem, then [I] go to them," said another. Other issues between the generations are community participation and appropriateness of recreational and job choices. Our data also showed that youths have little direct contact with younger siblings or with other children. Citizens desire exposure to other lifestyles, ages, cultures, and values to encourage the perspective of equality and social justice.

Recommendation 4

Social or community service activities should become a part of the curriculum. These should be directed at specific populations such as the indigent, the elderly, infants, and children. They could include self- and peer counseling, adopting a grandparent, tutoring and mentorships, social justice campaigns, or community-oriented services such as beautification, recreation, or other socially altruistic activities.

Juxtaposition 5

Social interaction within peer groups, both formal and informal, is very important for youths, but many adults view social interactions such as "hanging around" as a nuisance and trouble. Formal activities are approved by the community, but our data show that these are poorly attended and rank low in importance in youths' lives. Formal activities are directed and initiated by adults: Their role is to command respect and cooperation from participants. Youths feel that often nobody listens to their input and opinions. Formal extracurricular activities must become youth directed and youth guided.

Recommendation 5

Youths should have their own time and space to explore adult roles and relationships to others. Planned activities should be initiated by young participants; adult sponsors should play equal, cooperative roles. Options and responsibility of choice should be present in this learning environment. This change will allow participation by youths on their own terms and will encourage future participation in adult roles and within the community.

Juxtaposition 6

Competition seems to be implicit in Cambridge, as exhibited in the striving for material accumulation, the emphasis on school performance, and the role of competitive sports. On the other hand, the community wants caring and cooperative relationships in the future.

Recommendation 6

Self-directed cooperative experiences should be included throughout the educational process. Collective efforts should be expanded to extracurricular activities, including sports. The emphasis in these activities should shift from competition, winning, and "putting Cambridge on the map" to teamwork and cooperation. The annual spring drama presentation, for example, seems to be a collective and appreciated effort. Our research showed that youths are uncomfortable with individual recognition in sports, but feel that recognition of team effort is appropriate.

Cooperative, creative problem solving and group accountability should be used in the classroom. This approach would encourage the combination of peer-group interaction and common interest in the completion of a product. The initiation of this type of extracurricular and educational activity would catalyze young people's ability to carry this new tradition into their adult and communal roles.

Juxtaposition 7

Presently newcomers, youths, and other residents are not involved in the decision-making process. The citizens believe that a clear division exists between the "haves" and the "have-nots," and that "cliques and exclusiveness" are present. Many people say that the community leaders currently do not make enough effort to encourage participation. The vision of the future calls for cooperative participation and full representation in decision making. Various ages and social and economic statuses will be represented. Decision makers in this vision are described as "those who might have a vested interest, such as people with children, property owners, business persons, commuters, and the everyday working-class stiff." Strong formal leaders also will initiate caring cooperative efforts.

Recommendation 7

To help the community to move in this direction, representational, participatory government should be encouraged in the educational environment. Cooperative, participatory governing and leadership styles must be established within schools to train youths for these roles. The student governing board might be encouraged to run its affairs in town meeting fashion. Educational planning and policy should incorporate input and consideration rather than nonparticipatory planning from the people involved. For example, the school administration's nonattendance and grade penalization policy were chosen without community input. Our study found that students and other citizens were very unhappy with this policy because their opinions were not even solicited beforehand. Educational experiences must be training grounds for future leadership that is cooperative, representative, and participatory.

Juxtaposition 8

Growth is viewed ambiguously in Cambridge: Although it might "bring better jobs," it also will support a larger population. Cambridge would be in danger of losing its small-town image, which citizens described frequently as "friendly," "nice," "homey," or "peaceful." People in Cambridge describe their town with pride: They "have a stake in it and an identification with the community that people in the suburbs lack." Increased population means more crime, drugs, and other social problems for residents. At the present there are few social services for youths, families, and the elderly. Additional growth would put stress on an already inadequate system, further lowering the quality of life for some individuals.

Recommendation 8

One approach to growth is to include the goals of planned growth and maintenance of social and other quality-of-life standards. Planned growth allows communities to anticipate future economic and social needs. Such anticipation will permit citizens to prepare for growth and control growth in accordance with their desired future. So that this process can be understood, the concept of planned growth and social planning must be incorporated into curricular goals. The educational system can provide activities for appreciation of "small-townness." For example, our data indicated a need for transport of the elderly. An increase in the elderly population is projected in the demographic data, so this service would be useful. The school system could promote community-service fund drives for transportation or carpooling for the elderly.

Citizens also believe that historic architecture and sites enhance "small-townness." Cambridge contains several examples of turn-of-the-century houses. The historical society already has preserved a one-room schoolhouse. Another activity would be participation in historical preservation. Planning and construction of parks and playground equipment will preserve the rural quaintness that citizens fear would be lost through population growth.

Finally, social services for youth support are currently lacking. Educational activities that could be initiated to enhance the quality of life must include youth fellowship and counseling or health and chemical abuse awareness and prevention. As one citizen suggested, "a youth health service clinic with pregnancy, drug, alcohol, and marriage counseling as well as a community help line could be a viable support organization."

Juxtaposition 9

The overall direction or image that Cambridge wants to portray for the future seems to be undecided. Data show that community members believe the future is dictated by economic demands and interests.

Recommendation 9

If this is so, several options or directions are available. Health and medical opportunities are plentiful in Cambridge, which has the largest hospital in the region and contains a regional mental health center. Even if the regional health center were closed, health-related care still would be in demand. Because the surrounding areas show a high infant death rate and a large increase in the elderly population, preventive and medical support is needed.

Government and related enterprises seem to be another option for economic development. County services currently are housed in Cambridge and could be expanded to incorporate more information and administrative services.

Encouraging Cambridge to become a regional retail center is another option for planned growth. Currently retail is the largest business in the area, but the citizens still request more variety. With an expanding population of commuters and professionals, demand possibly might be supported by consumers' dollars.

Curriculum and courses need to be directed to the future community image and must be relevant to future career aspirations. Each of these economic paths demands specific education and training for people in the community. So that young people's aspirations for gainful employment can be met as they enter the adult world, jobs with relevant information and training must be incorporated into the curriculum. Whatever direction Cambridge chooses for its economic future, that choice should dictate the course of the curriculum. Cambridge must decide upon the developmental focus.

Juxtaposition 10

Currently the rural and natural environment surrounding Cambridge commands respect and appreciation. There are many tree-lined streets, small parks, lakes, and wildlife habitats, as well as a canoeing river. Even in such a small community, however, environmental woes are beginning to appear. Untreated waste is dumped in the nearby Rum River. Traffic congestion and pollution plague the main thoroughfare. The agricultural base is evolving from family farms to specialty agricultural crops, livestock, and hobby farms. The surveyed citizens wish overwhelmingly to keep Cambridge's rural quality.

Recommendation 10

Environmental, agricultural, and rural components are needed to maintain the rural quality of life in Cambridge. Environmental components should continue to be incorporated into the curriculum and should expand from mere appreciation to management, maintenance, and conservation. The people also wish to preserve an agricultural lifestyle. Different types of farms might encourage truck farming, specialty crops, and livestock, as well as traditional agriculture livestock. Agricultural coursework and activities should be enhanced to include management, irrigation, proper and safe fertilization, and possibilities in specialty farming, farm crops, and livestock. These steps would help to preserve the environment in the future Cambridge.

CONCLUSION

This chapter attempts to contribute to reform in K–12 curriculum from a normative futures perspective. Normative futures research, combined with critique, can be beneficial in transcending present definitions and reality in the educational process. This tactic must be adopted so that current curriculum and community can be moved beyond the present into the future.

A common choice of a future can be the first step toward directing actual change in the community. Incorporating diversity and creativity in choosing a vision can result in multiple views of the future. Experimentation, risk taking, and reflection must be used so that alternative futures can be "tried on for size." After critical reflection, a common future can be chosen more wisely. Goals and new parameters then must be defined, prescribing the best-fit situations for a community's transition to the future.

The educational process can be most useful in implementing planned change for future vision. This process has been used to aid developing countries and should be considered for developing futures. The use of data-based, community-level paradoxes between the perceived, observed present and the desired future is one way to attempt creation of catalysts for change. The three-dimensional human can evolve by transcending the present time and sociocultural interaction to create new curricular meanings. Other evolutionary methods for promoting proformative, procreative, dialectical, and dynamic community and curricular futures should also be explored.

Notes

The research that is reported was initially collected for a report, "Cambridge today and tomorrow: Designing an optimistic future for 2010." Support was granted, for the initial report, through the Center for Urban and Regional Affairs, College of Education, Department of Educational Policy and Administration at the University of Minnesota and the City of Cambridge, Minnesota. The views expressed in this chapter do not reflect those of the funders.

References

Anyon, Jean. 1988. "Schools as Agencies of Social Legitimation." In *Contemporary Curriculum Discourses,* edited by William Pinar, 175–200. Scottsdale, AZ: Gorsuch Scarisbrick.

Apple, Michael. 1976. *Cultural and Economic Reproduction in Education: Essays on Class, Ideology, and the State.* London: Routledge & Kegan Paul.

Bruner, J. S. 1966. *Towards a Theory of Instruction.* Cambridge: Belknap Press.

Dewey, John. 1916. *Democracy and Education.* New York: Macmillan.

Freire, Paulo. 1970. *Pedagogy of the Oppressed.* New York: Continuum.

Huebner, Dwayne. 1974. "Toward a Remaking of Curricular Language." In *Heightened Consciousness, Cultural Revolution, and Curriculum Theory,* edited by William Pinar, 3–53. Berkeley: McCutchan.

————. 1975. "Curriculum as Concern for Man's Temporality." In *Curriculum Theorizing,* edited by William Pinar, 237–49. Berkeley: McCutchan.

Marcuse, Herbert. 1966. *One-Dimensional Man.* Boston: Allyn & Bacon.

McCutcheon, Gail. 1981. "On the Interpretation of Classroom Observations." *Educational Researcher* 10:5–10.

McDonald, James B. 1988. "Curriculum, Consciousness, and Social Change." In *Contemporary Curriculum Discourses,* edited by William Pinar, 156–74. Scottsdale, AZ: Gorsuch Scarisbrick.

Textor, Robert B. 1980. *A Handbook on Ethnographic Futures Research.* 2d ed. Stanford: Stanford University Press.

————. 1981. "Development Education and Futures Research." *Journal of Cultural and Educational Futures* 2 (2–3): 34–41.

Wax, Murray, Stanley Diamond, and Fred Gearing. 1971. *Anthropological Perspectives on Education.* New York: Basic Books.

PERSONALIZING THE SOCIAL ORGANIZATION OF MIDDLE-LEVEL SCHOOLS: DOES INTERDISCIPLINARY TEAMING MAKE A DIFFERENCE?

Joanne M. Arhar

MIDDLE SCHOOL ORGANIZATION AND ADOLESCENT SENSE OF BELONGING

Since the early 1970s, there has been a drive to increase academic rigor in our schools. Federal and state legislators, the business community, and the media have joined forces to reshape America's schools to fulfill a vision of academic excellence. The results have been a narrowing of the elementary school curriculum to concentrate on cognitive achievement and an increase in academic requirements for high school graduation. Even while the school's purpose has narrowed, the social, psychological, physical, and economic needs of our nation's children command attention. As teachers struggle to cover an increasing amount of required academic content, dimensions of school curricula designed to meet the expanding needs of students have diminished.

At the center of this struggle to meet competing demands of higher academic achievement and the social, psychological, physical, and economic needs of an increasingly diverse student population is reform of the middle school. Educators and policy leaders now recognize the importance of restructuring middle schools to be more responsive to the needs of young adolescents in order to help them succeed and stay in school. This reform movement is unique because of its persistent belief in the importance of building a school program around students' academic needs as well as other needs, such as enhanced self-esteem and the capacity to work cooperatively. A growing body of literature discusses the characteristics of early adolescence and the theory and design of middle schools as educational organizations suited to adolescents' developmental needs. Many middle school reformers, aware of this body of literature, have developed and organized innovations that balance the needs of academic content, the individual adolescent, and society; this orientation has been associated with "middle-level philosophy." Yet they often are caught between the elementary school drive toward mastery of simple, measurable, academic goals and higher standards of academic achievement prized by the high school. Regardless of the defensive position in which middle school educators find themselves, advocates of middle-level philosophy maintain their belief that unless we pay attention to the multiple dimensions of learning, many middle school students simply will not be able to learn academic material.

The basic concern in middle school philosophy is the creation of a school social environment that fosters personal relationships between teachers and their colleagues, between teachers and students, and between students and their peers. Middle school reformers believe that within personal relationships, students and teachers will develop a sense of belonging and identity with the schools. They regard this sense of belonging not only as an intermediate step toward academic achievement, but as an outcome worthy in and of itself. This belief is bolstered by research that supports small school size as a structural feature that strengthens personal relationships, a feature especially important for holding at-risk students in school (Byrk and Thum 1989).

Interdisciplinary teaming is the key to middle-level restructuring and the link between what we know about young adolescents and a school organization that meets their needs effectively. Middle-level experts advocate interdisciplinary teaming because it addresses the unique concerns of young adolescent students (Alexander and George 1981; Carnegie Task Force 1989; Epstein and Mac Iver 1990; George and Oldaker 1985; Johnston and Markle 1986; Merenbloom 1986).

INTERDISCIPLINARY TEAMING AND THE ORGANIZATION OF WORK IN THE MIDDLE SCHOOL

Interdisciplinary teaming has a variety of meanings; we here focus on the social organization of students and teachers into teams rather than on either an integrated curriculum approach or team teaching strategies. Interdisciplinary teaming as defined here is the organization of two or more teachers from different disciplines who teach the same group of students and share the responsibility for the curriculum, instruction, and evaluation of those students (Alexander and George 1981). Team teaching strategies and the development of an integrated curriculum unique to the middle school are viewed by many educators as a natural outgrowth of reorganizing the work environment of teachers and students.

Theoretically, teaming meets the adolescent's need to belong to a meaningful group. It is a way to break down the isolation and anonymity that adolescents frequently feel in large, impersonal schools. It thus enables them to develop academically and personally. Middle-level reformers argue that teams have the potential to create conditions conducive to the formation of close, stable relationships between teachers and peers. In such environments, relationships are founded on intimate and personal knowledge rather than on prescribed roles. Motivation and academic engagement are based on social contracts rather than on authoritarian rules. A personalized environment is important to many educators and policy makers because "it is thought to be a powerful means of promoting students' commitment to school and their engagement in learning" (McLaughlin et al. 1990).

Learning theory tells us that learners must use prior knowledge as the scaffolding on which to build new knowledge. Thus personal knowledge about students' current understandings is critical if teachers are to help students move toward new knowledge. In the case of at-risk students, this information is particularly important, because such students' school experiences frequently differ in radical ways from home and other social experiences. Personal knowledge enables teachers to help students make links between existing knowledge and new understandings. If it is not used to label or stereotype, such knowledge can benefit students who might otherwise be unable to adjust to the academic and social demands of school.

In most organizations, primary organizational tasks rather than individual preferences determine institutional structures, routines, and roles. For this reason, McLaughlin et al. (1990) state that "personalization is more a matter of organizational design than of individual teachers' values and practices" (235). From their study of schools with personalized school environments, McLaughlin and her colleagues found that when personalization is the leading priority of the school, "the rewards, the supports, the routines, the expectations, the moral and intellectual authority that govern day-to-day interactions ... inside and outside the classroom are consistent with the ethos of personalization" (235). Thus, middle school reformers believe that in the long run it is more effective to restructure schools around teams as a way to enhance relationships than to leave this task to individuals within a structure that promotes isolation.

Equally important, teaming has the potential to create a more professional work environment for teachers. By providing them with the opportunity for joint work through a common planning time and a shared group of students, teaming offers teachers opportunities for reflective practice, ongoing professional development, enhanced decision-making rights, control, and autonomy. These are factors associated both with collaborative work environments and with increased efficacy, professional satisfaction and productivity (Lieberman 1990; Rosenholtz 1989). Thus if teaming is part of a positive work environment, it will enable teachers to develop attitudes and practices more responsive to the developmental needs of young adolescents than is traditional organization of teachers into academic departments. Teachers in departments more typically are held accountable for their students' academic achievement than for any affective-social outcomes.

Two recent national surveys of middle-level practices show that interdisciplinary teaming is on the rise. Alexander and McEwin (1989) report that interdisciplinary team organization of the four core subjects has increased in popularity over the past twenty years at every grade level from fifth to eighth. In a survey of practices and trends in middle grades, Epstein and Mac Iver (1990) report that an overall increase of 10 percent or more in the use of such teams is anticipated over the next three years. Yet little systematic research on the outcomes of teaming for students has been conducted.

My study of the influence of teaming on students' social bonding was framed to address the concerns of practitioners and policymakers about the efficacy of teaming in light of its increased cost: financial, because of the need for additional planning time and teacher development for collegial work; professional, because of the commitment and energy needed to reorganize the work environment. I also undertook this research as a contribution to the study of the social organization of the school and its impact on students' social and academic development. Finally, I wished to address in both empirical and theoretical terms what middle-level writers have been saying at a philosophical level—that middle-level schools need to be responsive to the young adolescent's need for belonging. Accordingly I tested the rhetoric associated with the virtues of teaming by asking the question, "Does the structure of inter-disciplinary teaming, in fact, produce stronger student social bonds to peers, to teachers, and to school than does the traditional organization of middle school teachers into academic departments?"

ADOLESCENTS AND THE SOCIAL ORGANIZATION OF SCHOOLS

Adolescents are particularly vulnerable to feelings of disengagement and alienation as they try to meet their needs for both independence and so-cial integration in a world that provides little stability as turf on which they can develop their identity. The basic human need for caring rela-tionships with adults and for the security of belonging to a constructive peer group is threatened frequently during this critical stage of devel-opment. Some students handle the early years of adolescence more suc-cessfully than others. For those who cannot cope with all of the changes and demands they encounter, "the engagement . . . in learning dimin-ishes, and their rate of alienation, substance abuse, absenteeism, and dropping out of school begins to rise" (Carnegie Task Force 1989, 9).

LeCompte and Dworkin (1991) aptly describe the contexts, both inside and outside of school, that lead many students and their teachers to conclude that disengagement is the only path they can take:

> Like other institutions, schools are not purposefully con-structed to facilitate alienation and incompetence; they have evolved to be that way in response to changes in the social, economic, political, vocational, and cultural life of modern society. In fact, they reflect the structure of modern soci-ety. However, modern society and its institutions . . . have changed faster than the capacity of their participants to cope. The result is strain—among the demands of society, its op-portunity structure, the structure of schooling, and possible human responses. When the strain becomes too great, alien-ation . . . results. In schools, the symptoms of this strain are the burning out and quitting of teachers and the turning out and dropping out of students (10–11).

Alienation, as defined by Farnworth and Lieber (1989) and developed by LeCompte and Dworkin (1991) in *Giving Up on School: Student Dropouts and Teacher Burnouts* is the gap between expectations and experiences. An individual's sense of alienation is thus a function of an individual's perception of the discrepancy between personal goals and the likelihood that such goals will be met. According to LeCompt and Dworkin, expectations are culturally defined and measured. Expectations for satisfying work, financial independence, and academic achievement have changed in the past few decades because of political, economic, vocational, social, and cultural upheavals. For example, because of the lessening of the value of educational credentials, students can no longer expect that hard work in school will ensure success. From the perspective of students seeking ways to accomplish their goals, "school is as irrelevant as current events and the political system over which they believe they have no control" (LeCompte and Dworkin 1991).

The structural and social organization of many schools contributes to adolescents' alienation. Although schools are not purposely organized to alienate and fragment student experiences, common organizational practices may have just that effect. A host of such practices contribute to student disengagement: Large school size; tracking of students; differential treatment of students based on race, class, and gender; increasing specialization of staff into departments; diversification and irrelevance of curriculum; fragmentation of time through scheduling; teachers' transient relationships with large numbers of students in departmentalized structures; an emphasis on individual achievement at the expense of cooperative group work; impersonal rules and regulations; lack of students' involvement in decision making; and institutional control of educational goals and means (Calabrese and Seldin 1987; Carnegie Task Force 1989; LeCompte and Dworkin 1991; McPartland 1987; Newmann 1981; Wehlage et al. 1989). And if students do not interpret school structure and organization as alienating, the gap between expectations and experiences is communicated to them by reference groups that include families, the media, and public figures, as well as teachers, peers, administrators, and counselors.

Adolescents, who need a sense of belonging to a larger social group, for a variety of reasons, often do not get their need for belonging met through traditional channels such as family or community. These same students are also often alienated by school organization and structure. According to Wehlage et al. (1989), schools impose impediments to membership in a community. The four common impediments to school membership are adjustment to new demands experienced in the transitions between elementary, middle, and high school; difficulty in academic matters; incongruence in the personal and social match between the student and the school; and isolation from meaningful interaction with adults and peers. Wehlage and his colleagues argue that these impediments are particularly potent in their effect on at-risk youths. As the number of youths at risk of school failure increases, schools and families must both examine the ways they place adolescents at risk. Educators and families must view the process of disengagement as an interaction between personal and institutional factors.

On the one hand, the literature on adolescent alienation describes the isolation, apathy, incongruence, and lack of academic engagement experienced by many academically unsuccessful young adolescents. On the other, successful middle-level schools offer new ways of organizing school routines to enhance student success and promote a sense of membership, identity, self-esteem, and engagement. Reorganizing middle-level schools into interdisciplinary teams has been proposed as a way of reducing students' alienation and increasing their sense of membership. When interdisciplinary teaming is implemented as it is designed, students are much more likely to be known by name and to feel that at least one adult cares for them. When teachers' expectations and rules are consistent, students find it easier to figure out how to interact with their teachers. Common planning time allows teachers to share information about individual students who may need extra help or who have difficulties in adjustment. In this situation, teachers are more likely to integrate curriculum and adapt it for individual needs. Teaming also provides students with a small focus group that may help them to identify more strongly with the school, its policies, and its practices, because "school" becomes more personal and more relevant. Finally, teams provide the opportunity to promote interdependence among students, thus fostering peer friendships. These peer interactions may occur across racial and economic lines. Nevertheless, the question remains: Does interdisciplinary teaming really make a difference in students' sense of belonging to a school and to meaningful groups of adults and peers?

A THEORY OF SCHOOL MEMBERSHIP

Why is it important that students feel "bonded" to their peers, their teachers, and their schools? Young adolescents have a strong need to belong, to be accepted by others, and to be actively involved with friends, family, and classmates, as well as the school and larger community.

Bonding to peers is critical to the development of adolescent identity. Through interaction with peers, adolescents learn to distinguish themselves from those around them while developing a sense of social responsibility that goes beyond their own individual need for self-esteem.

Although adolescents want the acceptance of their peers, they also want approval and support from adults. When students feel that they are cared for by adults, they are more inclined to want to participate in school activities and to conform to standards for achievement and behavior established by the school. This sense of reciprocity between students and teachers may lead students to identify with the school and to value its goals and welfare.

Bonding to school implies involvement in both academic and nonacademic pursuits. Exclusionary practices may tell students that they are not welcome. Encouraging the involvement of students in activities that promote school values and lead students to believe that their involvement is important to the school and to their success in school. Involvement thus has the potential to encourage students to exert the effort to graduate.

One of the key assumptions underlying social bonding theory is that belonging to a school community is inherently good. It implies that educational credentials help students to achieve long-term social, political, and economic gains as well as academic benefits (Hirschi 1969). However, a school culture and climate may actually harm individuals. Rejecting a school that harms social and personal development may be the healthiest thing a student can do. As schools seek to enhance a sense of community, the values of that community require careful consideration.

Social bonding is a measure of attachment, commitment, involvement, and belief in the values of the institution. Attachment is concern with the opinions of others. Commitment is a rational decision to behave in acceptable ways. Involvement is the expenditure of time and energy in institutionally encouraged behaviors. Belief is the view that the principles encouraged by the institution are valid. According to social bonding theory, bonds to institutions may operate to control behavior. When these bonds are weakened, the individual is "free" to engage in behavior that is not sanctioned by the institution.

Using Hirschi's work as a foundation, Wehlage et al. (1989) developed a theory of school membership that explains school failure as a function of lack of belonging. They believe that membership depends upon social bonding—the extent to which an individual forms meaningful and satisfying links with a social group and the extent to which the group encourages the formation of those bonds. The theory hypothesizes school membership as the foundation of educational engagement. Engagement and membership are viewed as intermediate goals that school must promote as a way of helping students to attain the outcomes of achievement and personal and social development. Thus, a lack of bonding to peers, to teachers, and to school increases the likelihood that students will not accomplish the purposes of school. By not helping students to bond to school, the institution in effect may negatively influence student success. Following this logic, dropping out of school is the end result of a disengagement process, heightened in the middle school years by attendance problems, exclusionary disciplinary practices, nonpromotion, and lack of social bonding (Finn 1989; Natriello, McDill, and Pallas 1990; Wehlage et al. 1989; Wheelock and Dorman 1988).

The concept of school membership includes a greater degree of reciprocity between students and school than does traditional social control theory. In a reciprocal relationship, schools and students have a mutual obligation to establish a social contract rather than adhere to impersonal rules and regulations. They have a mutual obligation to set and reach realistic, not overly idealistic, goals.

Extending the theory of school membership to teachers offers a way of understanding how interdisciplinary teaming has the potential to create a professional working environment that ultimately may enhance students' social bonding. Teachers engaged in collaborative work as members of interdisciplinary teams have the opportunity during common planning time to help each other grow professionally by sharing instructional practices, curriculum ideas, and information about students. Although not all teachers enjoy the benefits of joint work, because of the difficulties associated with collaboration and the inherent threats to autonomy, the potential of teaming for changing long-standing attitudes and practices of isolated work has led some observers to consider it solely in terms of its impact on teachers. Underlying this view that joint work will produce positive outcomes for teachers and students is the belief that the problems faced each day by teachers cannot be successfully solved alone. The belief that educators can make professional decisions alone about such complex, uncertain work is challenged further by economic and social conditions that threaten the safety and well-being of educationally disadvantaged adolescents. Addressing these concerns requires wisdom, experience, and effort from multiple sources.

AN EMPIRICAL RATIONALE FOR TEAMING

Because of its popularity, educators believe strongly that interdisciplinary teaming benefits students. A handful of studies have attempted to give empirical support to that belief. Although the overall results of studies have been inconclusive (Arhar, Johnston, and Markle 1989), one study is particularly relevant because it compared teacher-student relations in schools that assigned sixth-grade teachers to self-contained classrooms with relations in schools that assigned sixth-grade teachers to traditional academic departments. McPartland (1987) found that although departmentalization is associated with weaker teacher-student relationships than self-contained classrooms, it strengthens instructional quality in more-specialized subjects such as science and social studies. He concludes that intermediate practices such as teaming potentially offer high-quality instruction from subject-matter experts in combination with methods for addressing the students' individual needs. Other studies have linked interdisciplinary teaming to students' psychosocial outcomes. Studies of school climate consistently associate small school size, "school-within-a-school" organization, and programs that increase student-teacher interaction and flexible scheduling of time with positive outcomes that may affect achievement indirectly. In addition, several middle school studies have shown a positive relationship between teaming and many other outcomes, such as positive interracial relationships (Metz 1986; Damico 1981); positive attitudes of students toward teachers, interest in subject matter, sense of personal freedom, and sense of self-reliance (Gamsky 1970); students' perceptions of the school environment as more supportive (Sinclair 1980); improvement in school discipline, students' personal development, and self-esteem, as well as more-productive peer relationships and reduced conflict (Ashton and Webb 1986; Doda 1986; George 1987; George and Oldaker 1985); and a sense of caring between teachers and students (Lipsitz 1984).

In a national survey of principals of schools containing grade seven, Mac Iver and Epstein (1990) found a comparatively deeper commitment to teaming in schools in which principals predicted a higher dropout rate than would be predicted otherwise based on background and demographic variables. The results supported their hypothesis that schools with high dropout rates may adopt teaming and other practices responsive to the needs of young adolescents in an effort to rescue potential dropouts. Thus, the growing literature on the psychosocial outcomes of teaming provides empirical support for assumptions under which many practitioners are operating currently.

THE EFFECTS OF TEAMING ON SOCIAL BONDING OF
SEVENTH-GRADE STUDENTS

My study of middle school organization attempted to answer empirically the question "Do students in middle level schools with interdisciplinary teaming develop stronger social bonds to their peers, their school, and their teachers than students in traditional nonteamed schools?" Because teaming is not distributed randomly, I used a matched-pairs design. I compared approximately twenty-five hundred seventh-grade students in teamed middle-level schools to twenty-five hundred seventh-grade students in nonteamed middle-level schools on the three measures of social bonding: (1) bonding to peers, (2) bonding to school, and (3) bonding to teachers. I matched eleven teamed with eleven nonteamed schools on a number of criteria, including school size, percentage of minority students enrolled, percentage of students receiving free and/or reduced-price lunches (used as a measure of SES), geographical region, and urban/suburban location. The first three criteria are considered to be related to social bonding. All of the criteria help to establish similarity between the teamed and nonteamed schools.

Teamed schools were selected on the basis on nominations from a panel of middle-level experts for the quality of their interdisciplinary team programs. I determined the level of implementation through phone interviews with principals of the teamed schools, a questionnaire administered to principals, and a questionnaire for seventh-grade team teachers.

Nonteamed schools then were nominated by the principals of the teamed schools. The principal of each teamed school nominated a nonteamed school in his or her region; these schools were similar to their own schools on all of the criteria listed above. I validated the matching through phone interviews with each nonteamed school principal and through a questionnaire administered to principals. The principals agreed that the matches were adequate. I also used phone interviews with principals in teamed and nonteamed schools to gather additional information about the operation of departments or teams and about principals' perceptions of students' bonding in their own schools and of the factors that influence bonding.

I administered a twenty-five-item Likert-type social-bonding scale (Wehlage 1989) to seventh-grade students in both teamed and nonteamed schools. This scale served as a dependent measure of students' bonding to peers, to teachers, and to school. Construct validity and internal reliability were established by Wehlage (1989).

I selected the schools for their representativeness, level of team implementation, and adequacy of matches. The eleven pairs represented four main geographical areas of the United States: East, West, South, and Midwest. Six of the pairs were located in urban areas and five in suburban areas. The proportion of minority students enrolled in these schools ranged from 64 percent to 3 percent. SES ranged from 55 percent to 1 percent. School size ranged from 1,160 students to 230 students.

To determine whether teaming in fact was implemented at a level that experts agree constitutes adequate commitment to this arrangement, I collected data from teachers and principals about common planning time, individual planning time, and presence of team leadership. Commitment to reorganization is critically important if any meaningful and long-lasting change is to be made. A change in organizational structure from strict departmentalization to interdisciplinary teaming may not be sufficient to give students a greater sense of belonging. Teachers and principals also must be committed to teaming as an organizational arrangement. The administration's provision of resources to teachers to accomplish the purposes of teaming and the teachers' use of those resources reflect school norms and commitments to a child-centered approach to schooling. In other words, without common team planning time, teachers have no opportunity to collaborate for the improvement of curricula, instruction, and evaluation of students. Nor will they have the time to deal collectively with the unique needs of individual students. When teachers are given that opportunity, teachers' use of that time reflects their commitment to carrying out the intentions of teaming. In theory, teachers on teams will cross disciplinary lines to help students understand how mathematics, science, English, social studies, and other subjects are integrated in real life. Ideally, these teachers on teams not only coordinate content, but also jointly address problems and needs of individual students, meet with parents, revise schedules for classes that need more time, group and regroup students to match lessons to abilities, and plan assemblies, trips, and other special events. According to Epstein and Mac Iver (1990), the greater the amount of common planning time scheduled for teachers (in addition to individual planning time), the greater the amount of time teachers will devote to the above activities above and beyond preparing for their individual subjects. Without officially scheduled common planning time, team members would be forced to meet before or after school to carry out their responsibilities. Thus a school's commitment to teaming entails the allocation of planning time as well a provision for team leadership, so that time will be directed toward work by the team. Such resources, however, are becoming extremely difficult for schools facing budget crises. For many schools, time for collaborative work is viewed by the community as an unaffordable luxury.

Teachers' commitment to teaming is in theory based on personal beliefs that teaming is worthwhile. These beliefs may be reflected in the kinds of activities undertaken by teachers during common planning, class time, and out-of-class time. If teaming is to meet the academic and psychosocial needs of young adolescents, many levels of the school must be involved in implementation.

In selecting the teamed schools for my study, I wanted to ensure that both the school and the teachers were committed to interdisciplinary teaming and that teaming was in fact practiced. Thus I selected teamed schools according to the level of commitment demonstrated by their school and teachers on the criteria just described above. All of the teamed schools regularly scheduled at least three hours of common planning time and three hours of individual planning time per week. Nine of the eleven teams had leaders. Teachers reported that 63.2 percent of the common planning time focused on needs of individual students. Of that proportion, 45.91 percent was spent in diagnosing students and 17.29 percent in conferences with parents. The remainder of the planning time was divided among other team-related rather than individual planning activities: coordinating content (11.77 percent), revising schedules (6.62 percent), regrouping students (4.62 percent), and planning events (13.89 percent).

Teachers also largely agreed that the time they spent on diagnosing individual students in particular was adequate; this finding indicated satisfaction with the personal emphasis of their planning time. They expressed less agreement that the time spent on the other activities was adequate; perhaps this was a sign of difficulty in using the full potential of the team planning time for curriculum development and in employing class time for anything other than grouping students into traditional academic time slots.

Finally, because a sense of commitment influences the implementation of an innovation, I asked teachers to rate their own commitment as well as their school's commitment to teaming. In seven of the eleven teamed schools, all of the one hundred teachers who participated stated that both they and their school had a strong commitment to teaming. In the other four teamed schools, a handful of teachers felt that their commitment and the commitment of the school could be greater.

The final determination about the selection of the matched schools was agreement between principals that the matches were adequate for their geographical location. To substantiate the principals' perceptions, I found a significant correlation between teamed and nonteamed schools within each pair on size of school, percentage of minority-group students enrolled, and SES. When one school was compared to its match, it was more similar to its match than to all of the other schools on those factors thought to be related to social bonding.

WHAT THE SOCIAL BONDING SCORES REVEALED

I analyzed the effects of interdisciplinary teaming on the social bonding of middle-level students on several levels: individual students, matched pairs of schools as a set, and individual schools within matched pairs. I also calculated effect sizes and summed them overall to determine the impact of teaming on students' social bonding scores. The purpose and the results of each analysis are discussed below.

Using a multivariate analysis of variance and follow-up analysis of variance on each measure of social bonding to determine the effect of school organization on three measures of social bonding, I found that teaming has a significant effect on students' bonding to peers, to teachers, and to school at the $p < .05$ level of probability. The social bonding means for teamed and for nonteamed schools are presented in Table 13.1.

As Table 13.1 shows, seventh-grade students in the study overall have positive feelings about their peers, their teachers, and their schools. When asked to respond to twenty-five items related to social bonding on a Likert scale ranging from 1 (strongly disagree) to 4 (strongly agree), students showed that they felt a stronger bonding to their peers (2.97) than to their school (2.87) and teachers (2.75). This finding is not surprising, since young adolescents form their identity through identification with their peers. As parents lose touch with their children at this age, peer groups and special teachers become more important in self-definition.

Next, I conducted a MANOVA for matched pairs to determine the influence of school organization overall on teamed and nonteamed schools in each pair. This analysis was made to determine whether teamed schools in pairs differed overall from nonteamed schools in pairs. Results show that teaming has a positive effect at the $p < .05$ level of probability on students' bonding to teachers and to school, but not to peers. Although mean bonding scores were higher on bonding to peers than on bonding to teachers and school, the team structure does not ap-

Table 13.1. School Means and Standard Deviations on Three Measures of Social Bonding: To Peers, to Schools, to Teachers

School A = Team B = Non-team	Sample Size	Peer Bond Mean	Peer Bond SD	School Bond Mean	School Bond SD	Teach Bond Mean	Teach Bond SD
1A	180	2.78	.50	2.76	.54	2.83	.62
1B	139	2.91	.62	2.88	.61	2.70	.67
2A	307	2.94	.47	2.75	.47	2.60	.53
2B	341	2.96	.46	2.84	.50	.2.62	.61
3A	330	3.05	.43	2.93	.53	.294	.58
3B	203	2.87	.56	2.92	.55	2.84	.60
4A	82[a]	3.17	.31	3.17	.51	3.05	.52
4B	239	2.94	.56	2.99	.50	2.82	.58
5A	281	2.99	.49	2.96	.50	2.78	.57
5B	246	3.06	.47	2.93	.52	2.78	.58
6A	336	3.02	.47	2.79	.48	2.67	.55
6B	197	3.03	.40	2.87	.50	2.80	.51
7A	309	3.10	.39	2.93	.50	2.89	.52
7B	163	2.93	.46	2.72	.57	2.67	.59
8A	186	3.00	.47	2.88	.53	2.69	.62
8B	185	2.96	.47	2.80	.57	2.66	.65
9A	96	3.06	.56	3.13	.52	3.06	.60
9B	58	3.12	.50	2.71	.46	2.64	.57
10A	161	2.92	.56	2.98	.55	2.90	.63
10B	256	2.92	.42	2.83	.51	2.66	.59
11A	223	2.90	.48	2.87	.53	2.82	.57
11B	247	2.76	.53	2.64	.59	2.52	.65
Grand Mean		2.97		2.88		2.77	

[a]There was only one team in grade 7.

preciably influence peer interactions. It may be that students view themselves as connected more closely to the larger school environment than to their teams, or that peer influence holds stronger power over adolescent networks than do other sources of influence. It also may mean that the teachers' emphasis on individual students in their common planning time is translated into stronger personal relationships with students but not into instructional strategies that foster stronger peer interactions. It is almost certain that other factors outside of the teachers' control are at work.

In order to determine the differential effect of teaming on individual teamed schools within pairs, I performed a MANOVA on each of the separate matched pairs on the three measures of social bonding. This type of analysis is possible because in a matched-pairs design the nonteamed school is likened to a control group, and the teamed school is likened to a treatment group; teaming serves as the intervention. Thus the bonding scores of the teamed schools are treated as posttest scores. The results then can be used to determine whether teaming has different effects on different schools. Table 13.2 presents the analytical findings on each of the matched pairs.

According to the results, teaming produces different effects in different schools. In eight of the eleven pairs, school organization produced a significant difference in at least one of the bonding scores. In four of the eleven pairs, students scored higher in teamed schools than in nonteamed schools on bonding to peers; one pair favored the nonteamed school; six pairs showed no significant difference. In five of the eleven pairs, students scored higher in teamed schools than nonteamed schools on bonding to school; one pair favored the nonteamed school, and five pairs showed no significant difference between the teamed and the nonteamed school.

Potential reasons for the differences will be discussed in the section on social context, but a few will be mentioned here. In some schools, team spirit may compete with school spirit for students' attention. In others, students' social bonding may be encouraged by positive features of the climate, which principals attribute to the support of community, district, and parents as well as to numerous opportunities for students to participate in school-related activities. In other instances, social bonding is influenced by organizational features other than teaming, such as advisory programs and teachers' collaboration at the grade and department levels.

To determine the practical significance of the effect of teaming on students' social bonding, I summed the effect sizes for each of the sub-

Table 13.2. School-by-School Analysis: Overall MANOVA and Separate ANOVAs for Each Pair

School Pairs A = Team B = Nonteam	MANOVA	Peer Bond	School Bond	Teacher Bond
1A 1B	•	−	0	0
2A 2B	0	0	0	0
3A 3B	•	+	0	+
4A 4B	•	+	+	+
5A 5B	0	0	0	0
6A 6B	•	0	−	−
7A 7B	•	+	+	+
8A 8B	0	0	0	0
9A 9B	•	0	+	+
10A 10B	•	0	+	+
11A 11B	•	+	+	+
Overall Differences Favors Teamed (+)		4	5	6
Overall Difference Favors Nonteamed (− +)		1	1	1
Pairs That Showed No Significance (0)	3	6	5	4
Pairs That Showed Significance (*)	8			

Note: * = significant at $p < .05$; 0 = no significant difference; − = significant difference favors the nonteamed school in the pair; + significant difference favors the teamed school in the pair.

scales to produce an average effect size. Estimated effect sizes, weighted to take into account the difference in school size between matched pairs, show that the effect of teaming is greatest on students' bonding to teachers (.159), and somewhat less for bonding to school (.102) and to students (.085). The most potent effect of teaming may be its influence on the creation of positive student-teacher relationships.

Table 13.3 presents a summary of specific questions underlying each analysis and displays the results of each analysis. This table summarizes all of the analyses discussed previously and shows that interdisciplinary teaming makes a difference in student sense of social bonding to teachers and to school and (to a lesser extent) in student bonding to peers. Thus, it has the potential to affect school membership. For schools interested in shaping social bonds, these findings are important.

THE SOCIAL CONTEXT OF TEAMING

Caution is necessary in interpreting these results. A matched-pairs design cannot control for all of the features that affect students' bonding. In addition, teaming does not operate in isolation from other important school programs, practices, and norms. The impact of teaming is affected by individual teachers, whose preferences range from a more personal to a more academic approach to teaching. These preferences are likely to play a major role in the quality and the quantity of interactions inside and outside of the classroom.

An analysis of data collected from interviews with principals and surveys of teachers and principals helps to explain the social organizational variables that form the context in which teamed teachers and students interact. An examination of data from principals yields further evidence in support of the positive effect of teaming on students' bonding scores, even in the three cases where the nonteamed schools produced higher bonding scores than their teamed counterparts. As stated earlier, SES was a stronger predictor of students' social bonding than was school organization. Demographic information about students' socioeconomic status helps to explain low peer bonding scores in some teamed schools. The effects on bonding to peers may be lessened in schools containing a high percentage of low-SES students. This finding may help to explain the lower bonding scores in the teamed school in pair 1. Fifty percent of the students in this school received free and or reduced-price lunches, as opposed to 25 percent of the students in the nonteamed

Question	Unit of Analysis	Statistical Analysis	Peer Bonding	School Bonding	Teacher Bonding
Does teaming have a gross effect on students?	Student	MANOVA $*p = .000$	$+$ $*p = .000$	$+$ $*p = .002$	$+$ $*p = .000$
Do teamed schools, in pairs, differ over-all from nonteamed schools, in pairs?	Matched schools as a set	MANOVA matched pairs $*p = .000$	Difference in means $= +.04$ NS $p = .120$	Difference in means $= +.09$ $+$ $*p = .048$	Difference in means $= +.13$ $+$ $*p = .009$
Does teaming have different effects on different schools?	Individual matched pairs	MANOVA $8*$ 3 NS	$4(+)$ $1(-)$ 6 NS	$5(+)$ $1(-)$ 5 NS	$6(+)$ $1(-)$ 4 NS
How large an impact does teaming have in practical terms?	School	Weighted avg. effect size	.085 (Percentile increase $= 4\%$)	.102 (Percentile increase $= 4\%$)	.159 (Percentile increase $= 6\%$)

Note: $*$ = significant at $p < .05$; NS = not significant; $-$ = significant difference favors the nonteamed school in the pair; $+$ = significant difference favors the teamed school in the pair.

Table 13.3. The Effects of Interdisciplinary Teaming on Social Bonding of Middle-Level Students: Summary of Analyses

school. In this vein, Lightfoot (1978) suggests that dependency and trust in low-SES families tends to be familial. That is, because of close ties within the extended family, children of low-SES families tend to trust and depend on their families for support; in contrast, they show a lack of trust and dependence toward the larger social group. Thus it is not difficult to understand why low-SES students, who already may perceive school as incongruous with their personal lives, would find it difficult to bond with peers from varying social and cultural backgrounds.

In the case of pair 6, several factors help to explain why school and teacher bonding scores were significantly higher in the nonteamed school. First, grade span may be a consideration. The nonteamed school consisted of grades six through eight; thus the seventh-grade students had a one-year headstart in getting to know their peers over the teamed grade seven and eight school. The principal of the teamed school said that although he perceived students' commitment to be strong, he felt that being together for only two years was an impediment to cohesiveness. To compound the problem, the two high schools that draw from this middle school compete athletically; thus they divide the middle school students, who begin to anticipate attending one of the two high schools as early as the seventh grade. Therefore teaming has a differential effect in individual schools. The degree of social bonding may be influenced by the manner in which teaming is implemented and by other school-related factors. Principals stated that other organizational and normative factors, such as advisory programs, parents' involvement, community support, athletic programs, co-curricular activities, teachers' commitment to a middle school as opposed to a secondary school orientation, and grade span also play a role in students' identification with school. Eight of the eleven teamed schools had student advisory programs, which may have had an impact on bonding. Principals agreed, however, that advisory programs were an outgrowth of teams. Rather than having a separate set of goals, advisory programs complemented the purposes of teams to create a more personal and caring environment for students through small support groups.

CAN INTERDISCIPLINARY TEAMING HOLD POTENTIAL DROPOUTS IN SCHOOL?

The answer to keeping potential dropouts in school does not rest solely with the school. A review of the literature on early school leaving (Hendrick et al. 1989) suggests that various dropout intervention strategies are needed. Society must recognize and reward effort and achievement. Parents also must encourage their children to achieve and support them in their efforts. The school, however, plays a major role in creating a climate conducive to learning by creating incentives and removing barriers to learning. Differences in students' academic preparation and in types of school programs and structures also account for differences in school retention rates.

In accordance with the scope of this study, research suggests the existence of a linear relationship between social bonding and dropping out of school (Finn 1989; Wehlage et al. 1989). Dropouts report having fewer social networks in school than nondropouts (Finn and Achilles 1990). Research also suggests that school organization influences retention of students in school (Byrk and Thum 1989; LeCompte and Dworkin 1991; Newmann 1981). If a linear relationship in fact can be established between social bonding and dropping out of school, social bonding as an outcome of the educational process becomes critically important to all educators.

One way to determine the impact of a program (in this case, interdisciplinary teaming) on particular outcomes (in this case, social bonding) is to examine effect sizes. Although the effect sizes in my study are small, they have implications for larger populations. The impact of the effect size found in this study can be understood by examining a z-table to determine the percentage of the population that is affected incrementally by changes in the effect size. To illustrate, students will show, on the average, a net gain of six percentile points when a program has an effect size of .159, and a net gain of four percentile points when a program has an effect size of .102 or .085. Thus a school that scored at the 50th percentile on bonding to teachers in a nonteamed school would score at the 56th percentile on bonding to teachers if teaming were instituted. Likewise, a nonteamed school that scored at the 50th percentile on bonding to school and bonding to peers would score in the 54th percentile with teaming.

Thus an effect size of .159 could reduce the dropout rate by approximately 6 percent. If we consider that the dropout rate in this country averages about 25 percent, and that a considerable number of youths decide during their middle-level years to leave school before graduation, interdisciplinary teaming, a low-cost intervention, may have the potential for making a dramatic change in the number of students who drop out of high school.

WHERE DO WE GO FROM HERE?

One of the assumptions underlying this study is that membership in the schools I studied is generally worthwhile for the well-being of students. Observational studies that examine the organizational structure *and* the messages given to students by peers, teachers, school, and family would yield valuable qualitative information about the nature of student experiences in school.

We need to know what kinds of messages the school, teachers, peers, and counselors give to students. Negative messages may heighten alienation. Does the hidden curriculum, evident in practices such as rigid tracking and mindless remedial classes, construct a set of circumstances that limit access to school experiences that are instrumental to helping students achieve career goals? Do teachers send messages of blame to students for academic failure? Do teachers and counselors convey messages to students that college or particular career goals are unavailable to them? Is the system so overworked that counselors and teachers do not have the time to spell out for students precisely what they have to do in order to attain their goals? Or are teachers and counselors differential in their treatment of students from different economic and social backgrounds? Do organizational and curricular practices deprive poor students, young women, and minorities of experiences that impart social skills and value orientations necessary for success in desirable occupations? In such cases, student bonding would indeed be undesirable.

We need further study of clusters of social organizational variables that influence social bonding. It is difficult to isolate one particular feature from another in its effect, so studies of whole-school efforts to decrease alienation and increase bonding are needed. In this vein, how do multi-age grouping and teacher advisory groups interact with interdisciplinary teaming to bridge the gap between expectations and experiences?

In addition, research on the influence of demographic background variables may clarify the interaction between family variables, students' characteristics, and organizational features of middle-level schools. More specifically, what is the profile of a highly bonded student? What is the profile of the school in which students are highly bonded? How can teachers and students interact on teams in ways that will help adolescents overcome the adjustment difficulties of at-risk students?

How does variation in the organization and implementation of teams affect students' outcomes? Do factors such as multi-age grouping, preparation and certification of teachers, ability grouping, and school grade span influence the extent to which students bond?

Finally, further research on teachers' and students' collaborative behaviors in teamed and nonteamed schools may enable researchers to link specific behaviors and conditions to the bonding of students. Such research may prove beneficial to practitioners concerned with restructuring the work environment of students and teachers to promote bonding of at-risk students.

The issue of engagement, as operationalized in the measures of social bonding used in this study, inevitably arises in the study of student experiences in school. It would seem to be that building a research base in this area would yield useful information for policymakers, practitioners, and families about their roles in creating community.

References

Alexander, W. M., and P. S. George. 1981. *The Exemplary Middle School.* Chicago: Holt, Rinehart & Winston.

Alexander W. M., and C. K. McEwin. 1989. *Schools in the Middle: Status and Progress.* Columbus, Ohio: National Middle School Association.

Arhar, J. M. 1991. "Interdisciplinary Teaming and the Social Bonding of Middle Level Students." In *Perennial issues in middle level education,* edited by J. L. Irvin, 139–61. Boston: Allyn & Bacon.

Ashton, P. T., and R. B. Webb. 1986. *Making a Difference: Teachers' Sense of Efficacy and Student Achievement.* New York: Longman.

Byrk, A. A., and Y. M. Thum. 1989. *The Effects of High School Organization on Dropping Out: An Exploratory Investigation.* New Brunswick, N.J.: Center for Policy Research in Education.

Calabrese, R. L., and C. A. Seldin. 1987. "A Contextual Analysis of Alienation among School Constituencies." *Urban Education* 22(2):1–7.

Carnegie Task Force on the Education of Young Adolescents. 1989. *Turning Points: Preparing American Youth for the Twenty-first Century.* Washington, D.C.: Carnegie Council of Adolescent Development.

Damico, S. 1982. "The Impact of School Organization on Interracial Contact among Students." *Journal of Educational Equity and Leadership* 2:238–52.

Doda, N. M. 1984. "Teacher Perspectives and Practices in Two Organizationally Different Middle Schools." Ph.D. diss., University of Florida, Gainesville.

Epstein, J. L., and D. G. Mac Iver. 1990. *Education in the Middle Grades: Overview of National Practices and Trends.* Columbus, Ohio: National Middle School Association.

Finn, J. D. 1989. "Withdrawing from School." *Review of Educational Research* 59(2): 117–42.

Finn, J. D., and C. M. Achilles. 1990. "Answers and Questions about Class Size: A Statewide Experiment." *American Educational Research Journal* 27:557–77.

Gamsky, N. 1970. "Team Teaching, Student, Achievement, and Attitudes." *Journal of Experimental Education* 39:42–45.

George, P. 1987. *Long-term Teacher-Student Relationships: A Middle School Case Study.* Columbus, Ohio: National Middle School Association.

George, P., and L. Oldaker. 1985. *Evidence for the Middle School.* Columbus, Ohio: National Middle School Association.

Hendrick, I. G., D. L. MacMillan, R. G. Balow, and D. L. Hough. 1989. *Early School Leaving in America: A Review of the Literature.* Riverside, Calif.: University of California Educational Research Cooperative.

Hirschi, T. 1969. *Causes of Delinquency.* Los Angeles: University of California Press.

Johnston, J. H., and G. C. Markle. 1986. *What Research Says to the Middle Level Practitioner.* Columbus, Ohio: National Middle School Association.

LeCompte, M. D., and A. G. Dworkin. 1991. *Giving Up On School:*

Student Dropouts and Teacher Burnouts. Newbury Park, Calif.: Corwin Press.

Lieberman, A., ed. 1990. *Schools as Collaborative Cultures: Creating the Future Now.* New York: Falmer.

Lightfoot, S. L. 1978. *Worlds Apart: Relationships between Families and Schools.* New York: Basic Books.

Lipsitz, J. 1984. *Successful Schools for Young Adolescents.* New Brunswick, N.J.: Transaction.

McLaughlin, M., J. Talbert, J. Kahne, and J. Powell. 1990. "Constructing a Personalized School Environment." *Phi Delta Kappan* 72(3): 230–35.

McPartland, J. M. 1987. *Balancing High Quality Subject Matter Instruction with Positive Teacher-Student Relations in the Middle Grades.* Baltimore: Johns Hopkins University Center for Research on Elementary and Middle Schools.

Merenbloom, E. Y. 1986. *The Team Process in the Middle School: A Handbook for Teachers.* 2d. ed. Columbus, Ohio: National Middle School Association.

Metz, M. H. 1986. *Different by Design: The Context and Character of Three Magnet Schools.* New York: Routledge & Kegan Paul.

Natriello, G., E. L. McDill, and A. M. Pallas. 1990. *Schooling Disadvantaged Children: Racing against Catastrophe.* New York: Teachers College Press.

Newmann, F. M. 1981. "Reducing Student Alienation in High Schools: Implications of Theory." *Harvard Educational Review* 51(4): 546–64.

Rosenholtz, S. 1989. *Teachers' Workplace: A Study of Social Organizations.* New York: Longman.

Sinclair, R. 1980. "The Effect of Middle School Staff Organizational Patterns on Student Perceptions of Teacher Performances, Student Perceptions of School Environment, and Student Academic Achievement." Ph.D. diss., Miami University, Oxford, Ohio.

Wehlage, G. G. 1989. *Wisconsin Youth Survey.* Madison: Center for School Restructuring, University of Wisconsin.

Wehlage, G. G., R. A. Rutter, G. A. Smith, N. Lesko, and R. R. Fernandez. 1989. *Reducing the Risk: Schools as Communities of Support.* New York: Falmer.

Wheelock, A., and G. Dorman. 1988. *Before It's Too Late: Dropout Prevention in the Middle Grades.* Boston: Massachusetts Advocacy Center.

14

BELIEFS, MYTHS, AND REALITIES:
A CASE STUDY OF A
SCHOOL IN TRANSITION

W. Wade Burley and Arthur S. Shapiro

INTRODUCTION

School culture and school change have become increasingly important focal points of both discussion and research during the past twenty years (Rowan 1990; Moll and Diaz 1987; Sarason 1971). In these two decades a more definitive view of what constitutes healthy or unhealthy organizations and productive or nonproductive school cultures has developed (Goodstein 1978; Hollander and Offermann 1990; Offermann and Gowing 1990; Schein 1990; Schmuck and Runkel 1985). Sarason (1971) and Rowan (1990) have highlighted the difficulties and alternatives involved in changing and improving schools. Efforts directed toward intervention and restructuring within specific contexts and schools are often less predictable and may pose a greater variety of questions and potential challenges in the implementation of change (Ashton and Webb 1986; Schmuck and Runkel 1985; Spindler and Spindler 1987; Vogt, Jordan, and Tharp 1987). Each setting may present its special set of conditions, processes, and outcomes, as well as provide implications for the future and for comparable situations.

The case study in this chapter focuses on a specific change process that spanned more than three years in a school that became progressively more burdened with problems in its functioning and in its work with students and parents. This chapter reports on that process and on the patterns of "traditions," perceptions, roles, interpersonal relations, events, and changes that occurred. Some of the processes and events considered in this case study, as well as some of the resulting changes, not only seem to reflect extensions of knowledge about school organizational conditions and change, but also to provide alternative processes for implementing more effective school renewal and improvement.

In the first part we cite the general conditions and initiating circumstances that led to our involvement as consultants with the school. We examine briefly some conditions that appear to be the basis for in-service assistance related to school improvement. Next, we analyze the faculty's cultural beliefs, their myths, and realities through the prism of an organizational diagnostic process and construct that emerged, and note the extensive changes resulting from the three-and-a-half-year process. Finally, we consider current conditions and implications for educational restructuring in the social dynamics involved.

BACKGROUND

This study deals with the processes, events, conditions, relationships, and consequent changes in a single school (grade six to grade eight middle school in a medium-sized school district in the southeastern United States). We served as out-of-district consultants who assisted in addressing that school's needs and in developing a school-based change process. The goal of the process was to improve the school's functioning and its work with its program, the staff and faculty, the students, and the parents and community that it serves.

By the 1987–88 school year the central office of the district was concerned about some practices and conditions that had developed in this school over a fifteen-year period. The nature and extent of these conditions were reflected in incidents brought to the attention of the school board, in the results of a school-based assessment of in-service needs, and in attitude surveys administered yearly to students by the central office. Apparently the school had become bureaucratic, meeting neither its students' nor its teachers' needs. It had become relatively rigid in its structure and operation (Wilson et al. 1969). Strong needs for school-based in-service assistance were identified in the following areas: school improvement, management of student conduct, dropout prevention, crisis intervention, and teacher effectiveness; these areas were reflected in a needs assessment conducted by the county Teacher Education Center. Sarason (1971) notes that the culture of a school may deter change; certainly that condition may have been operative here. Stronger negative attitudes were reflected in the results of the student attitude survey administered at that school than those from other middle schools districtwide. The county Teacher Education Center had designated as one of its goals school-based in-service programs for dealing with special needs during 1988–89. One of us was serving as a university representative on the Teacher Education Center Council when the director asked about obtaining assistance from the university. The other was identified as having an appropriate administrative background, diversified experience at various levels, and a history of working effectively with schools.

Beginnings

In early 1988 we held an initial meeting with a county-level administrator and a supervisor who formerly had worked full-time in the school as a teacher. At this meeting we discussed and analyzed several phenomena. As a result, the administrator and the supervisor concluded that the problems were serious enough to merit action. These difficulties included an increase in discipline problems, a key faculty member's transferring to another school, increasing social distance between faculty and students as well as between faculty and parents, falling morale, increasing teachers' criticisms of the students, and apparently dysfunctional guidance counselors and, perhaps, administrators. The cultural practices of the faculty and the administration appeared to be reactive as well as laissez-faire.

After the district-level meeting, we arranged a lunch meeting with the school principal. At the meeting he said that although the school had some problems, they were not significant. He agreed, however, to form a group of key faculty and staff members to begin inquiring into the problems[1] and identifying major needs for a possible school-based in-service program. Specific survey information given to us by the principal early in 1988 showed that more than half the staff and faculty had been at the school for twelve years or more; the result was a great deal of inbreeding. Other information provided by faculty members and staff revealed needs for in-service and staff development in various areas.

We received a list of the staff and faculty members whom the principal described as "possibly key team people"; this group included content-area teachers, a physical education teacher, an alternative education teacher, a guidance counselor, and one of the deans of students. Over a two- or three-month period we met with this group every two or three weeks. With their support and that of the principal, we made several visits to the school, staying from early morning, before many staff and faculty members arrived, until the end of the school day.

The Consultants' Backgrounds

Our backgrounds contributed to our initial involvement with that school and may have served as an influence for positive change. Consultants may function in a variety of roles and at various levels of intervention, such as acceptant, catalytic, confrontational, and prescriptive (Goodstein 1978). Because of our backgrounds, the intervention work in this case may have been largely a combination of the acceptant and the catalytic types. The credibility and ease of our entry into the school seems to have been increased by the ten-plus years of close involvement with the county by one of us as a representative on the Teacher Education Center Council and by work in other collaborative functions and staff development activities. Another factor was the wide range of district-level experience on the part of the other consultant, which included teaching, school-level administration, and prior district-level responsibilities with other school systems. Our being viewed either as strangers or as naives by members of the organization could have interfered with the process of working within a new or specific school culture (Schmuck and Runkel 1985).

Progressively, our role as consultants seemed to become more like that of members of the school's culture and organization. For example, at some initial meetings with school representatives and later with the total faculty, the administration did not appear to give special consideration to making after-school and before-school meetings especially enjoyable or "sociable." After we provided fruit or doughnuts, however, faculty and staff members began to do so on their own initiative.

These actions reflect possible modeling of group maintenance functions (Cartwright and Zander 1962), a role that was taken on increasingly by members of the school faculty and staff at later work sessions. We may have helped to model and influence some of the important roles and functions significant for leadership and for effective group and organizational functioning. Apparently, a group must satisfy its socioemotional or group-maintenance needs, as well as perform its tasks and achieve its goals, in order to maximize effectiveness (Bales and Slater 1955; Cartwright and Zander 1962; Shartle 1956). Frequently, one of us focused on achieving tasks and goals while the other focused on socioemotional conditions and group members' feelings.

The Analytic Process and Strategies: An Emerging Construct

As the discussions with the school group began to unfold, it became clear that a structure or construct was emerging. (See table 14.1.) Rather than discussing the school's and the people's problems, we structured interaction to focus on *issues and concerns*. Once these began to emerge, we and the staff drew *conclusions and implications* from the issues and concerns, and ultimately discovered *potential lines of action or initiatives*. Then we synthesized the *themes* underlying the process. Finally, we stated the actual *outcomes*.

This analytic process was developed to elicit the beliefs, attitudes, and symbols held by the faculty, administration, and students. Because individuals and groups operate according to their key beliefs and assumptions, any effective change process must expose these beliefs and assumptions in a setting where they can be examined thoughtfully. In short, a professional frame of reference must be developed in which rational, thoughtful discussion of purposes, practices, and behavior occurs. It is particularly important to focus both on underlying beliefs and assumptions and on their impact on the practices and behaviors of staff and students. Then the gaps between stated and implicit purposes, practices, and behavior must be identified. Once this process occurs and is discussed thoughtfully, changes can take place.

The construct that emerged in this process supported this analysis. The faculty's *concerns* were solicited openly in a representative body; their thoughts and ideas were written on two-by-three-foot newsprint so that everything was public. These notes then were reproduced and distributed to the entire faculty. Analysis by the group of these concerns led to discussions of underlying *issues* in the committee. Next, the people present drew their own *conclusions* and then *implications* from the concerns and issues, again writing on newsprint. *Potential lines of action* were elicited. Finally, underlying *themes* were analyzed and written publicly on newsprint (Barnard 1951); minutes of these meetings were distributed to all faculty.

In reviewing the first and second columns in Table 14.1, first with the committee and then with the total faculty, one consultant noted to everyone that all of the indicators were negative. Thus the first step in Lewin's three-phase model of social change (unfreeze, move to a new level of behavior, refreeze) took place (Lewin 1952).

Table 14.1. Analysis of Dynamics of Change

Issues/Questions	Summary/Conclusions	Potential Lines of Action/Initiatives
Socioeconomic changes in → community From single home to duplexes From parents to single parent Reduced intramural participation Reduced parents' participation	Changing students' → values, attitudes Value of education Not doing homework Impact on teachers Reduced standards	Major intramural program → Major recognition program Major involvement of parents Volunteers in school Fund-raisers Administration, faculty involved In-service programs to understand students
Impact on teachers → Feelings of high stress High frustration Morale collapsing "Family" feeling collapsing Considering leaving school	Social organization → holding school together, but fraying Key teacher social systems upset, publicly considering leaving	Develop grade-level → administrative teams Develop teacher teams
Hopelessness →	Need sense of hope →	Develop plan with purpose → Form three committees to reorganize Planning Guidance Classroom management support team
Passive, laissez-faire → administration not functioning One of two deans not functioning Guidance dysfunctional Administrative clock-watching spreading to teachers, students	Administration, → deans, guidance dysfunctional Not cooperating Not proactive Limited work ethic affecting teachers, students Teachers angry at students for this	Proactive leadership to → form and support Planning and guidance committees
Junior high school → departmental organization dysfunctional	Formal organization → blocks effective action Isolates teachers Teachers with same students do not see each other Teachers disorganized	Formal organization must → change to facilitate cooperation Form teacher teams, work in small, decentralized units with same students Form grade-level administrative teams
Departmental organization →	Little accountability	Grade-level teams for → administrators, teachers
Norms (attitudes, practices, → behavior)	Culture dysfunctional → Norms must change	Establish new norms with → above changes

Rationale for Actions	Underlying Themes	Major Outcomes
Develop sense of belonging for all→ Sense that teachers care, that parents care Sense of pride Teach parenting skills Faculty, administration understand, accept students Involve community	Changing community changes → students' attitudes Decreasing respect for teachers, education Teachers increasingly alienated from parents, students, each other, administration, guidance, central office	Major intramural programs Major recognition program for all Major parent involvement program, with staff development In-service program on nature of students
Decentralize → Work/cooperate in small units Makes all visible/accountable Personalizes Increases ownership, morale Increases sense of belonging	Teachers' control over → professional life decreased Feel powerless School sliding downhill	Grade-level administrative teams in place Teacher teams in operation
Teachers involved in → reorganization Increases ownership Empowerment Support groups	Loss of morale, hope, → positive attitude toward work, purpose	Long-range plan developed Reorganization support team functioning Sense of hope Strong teacher ownership of plan and support of reorganization support team
Develop support by all reference → groups (administration, deans, guidance, faculty, students, community, central office)	Passive, laissez-faire administration functioning poorly No accountability	Administration strongly supports plan, reorganization support team, process Accountability clear, visible
Decentralizing facilitates → Personalizing Empowerment Greater responsibility Accountability—all visible Cooperation Interdependent operation	Relationship between form → and function Organization dysfunctional— prohibits teachers with same students from working together Centralized/decentralized Central office indifferent	Formal organization changed from a junior high school to a middle school Grade-level administrative teams Teacher teams with block of students Implementing teacher-as-advisor program
All organizational components → become visible—thus, accountable	Administrators, deans → guidance not accountable	Accountability clear, visible
Decentralization increases → students', teachers' cooperation, responsibility	Norms need to support → changes, work ethic, cooperation, responsible professional behavior, self-esteem, recognition for all, repersonalizing to a family	Cultural norms, beliefs, practices, changed

Lewin's second step was initiated by joint consultants' and faculty members' development of *potential lines of action or initiatives.* The following discussion summarizes the key components of this process as well as the actions taken.

THE SURVEY

After we had begun to dig out key *issues, concerns,* norms, and beliefs, we drew up a survey form with the help of the school group, to which all faculty members responded near the end of the 1987–88 school year. (See appendix A.) Once the construct or framework developed, the principal scheduled a total faculty meeting at which the construct and its results were reported, as were the results of the survey.

Prior to the meeting with the total faculty and the reporting of the survey results, we sent a letter to all members of the staff and faculty. (See appendix B.) This was to communicate to each one directly and individually the perceptions of the consultants and study group and to provide appropriate feedback and personal support concerning possible future directions and effort.

Survey findings revealed faculty members' perceptions of the degree of need for improvement and their degree of satisfaction with key conditions previously identified as areas of concern in the discussions and the reports drawn from the faculty. Faculty members also were requested to list in order their five leading concerns as the basis for developing an in-service plan for the school.

The faculty and staff identified the following four issues as top priorities:

1. The present operational role of guidance and counseling staff
2. Unified, consistent procedures for handling student discipline by the faculty
3. Student attitude toward education
4. Total staff morale (faculty, administration, and others)

After we shared these results with the faculty, we facilitated their planning and decisions at a workshop held before the opening of school. As a result, the committee structure was reorganized into a planning committee, a guidance committee, and a classroom management support team (Van Meter 1979–80). The support team was to give voluntary help, at the principal's recommendation, to teachers experiencing difficulty in managing their classrooms.

RESULTS

The planning and the guidance committees, which sometimes met jointly, recommended that the principal and the faculty establish voluntary teams on the sixth-grade level as a start toward reorganizing the instructional model, and reorganize the school into a grade-level structure with a team consisting of a dean/administrator, a counselor, and a clerk/secretary serving each grade. In addition, major programs with the community and students were considered necessary, and steps were taken in those directions. These included major parent involvement programs such as school volunteers and fund-raisers. Student recognition and intramural programs were designed and implemented.

The recommendations for reorganization then were taken up the administrative ladder to the superintendent of schools; all administrators supported them enthusiastically. (See appendix C.) The Teachers' Association also was consulted, and supported the action. The stage was set for implementing change.

Expectations, Norms, and Realities

New expectations and new norms were developed. Teachers, administrators, deans, and counselors began to attend regularly night meetings of the parent organization of the school, whereas previous attendance by all of these groups had been erratic. A number of the staff and faculty members changed from their previous use of the meeting time for personal recreation to attending and to working on projects and programs with parents. As a consequence, the first fund-raiser produced a gift of $14,000 to the school, which surprised and delighted everyone involved. Other cooperative programs began to surface; as a result, all groups cooperated more and felt less social distance from one another.

Roles and Teams

As the formal organization of the school changed, new roles began to emerge for former deans who had become grade-level dean/administrators, each of whom was teamed with a counselor and a clerk/secretary. The assistant principal became the head of one of the grade levels. These dean/administrators needed in-service training to oversee all teachers and to implement a state-mandated teacher performance observation system, which they used in supervising and coaching both new and experienced teachers.

As the sixth-grade team began to jell, faculty perceptions of its success developed to the point where an additional team was scheduled for the grade for 1990–91 (only two teams could be formed), and one each was scheduled for the seventh and eighth grades.

To facilitate these and other major changes, the guidance and the planning committees were united and retitled the "reorganization support team," a significant title, for 1989–90 and subsequent years. The classroom management support team of high-prestige teachers and deans was retained as a support both for teachers and for the principal. With the increase in personalization, support for decentralization increased considerably; the key social systems of the school were intensely supportive and served on the reorganization support team. Regular meetings have been held with virtually 100 percent attendance. One member even refused coaching duties to retain membership on the team, sacrificing additional pay.

Beliefs, Symbols, and Realities

A number of changes have taken place regarding beliefs, symbols, and realities (Mead 1934). In many schools, as here, teachers traditionally work alone and struggle to perform their allotted functions. This paradigm has shifted considerably to the point where nine out of ten teachers in the sixth grade now work in teams. In-service training has been provided for teams to enable deans/grade-level administrators to supervise teachers and to help counselors and clerk/secretaries to function better. The clerk/secretaries have received in-service training to assist them in their work, because computerization has affected every school in the district. They also serve on the reorganization support team and meet regularly as a group to deal with issues and improve their functioning.

Attitudes toward students also have changed. A major and highly successful in-service program focused on understanding preadolescent personality and learning styles. Now less anger is expressed, fewer students are sent to offices for disciplinary infractions, and closer relationships have developed between the school and the community. As teams jell, they tend to become more effective in handling "problems" with student behavior. Because students and teachers spend several hours together each day, they get to know each other; a "family" atmosphere begins to grow; people develop a greater sense of belonging and start to care for each other. Behaviorally, this is expressed as "taking care of our own." Thus, "discipline" becomes decentralized to the team levels, and social controls become more informal and thus more effective with the small (100 to 130) block of students and four or five teachers. Several changes were revealed in the survey of faculty members' perceptions, completed at the end of the 1989–90 school year and replicating the survey administered in 1988. (See figure 14.1 and appendix D).

We learned a great deal from the self-report information obtained from the faculty at the end of the first year of contact with us as consultants and again two years later, after a reorganized structure had been in place for one year. Figure 14.1 shows a positive change in the faculty's perceptions concerning areas needing improvement; *all* eighteen areas reflect improvement, moving toward "satisfactory" or "very satisfactory." Item 11, the "present operational level of guidance and counseling staff," was regarded in 1988 as the faculty's leading priority, "needing much improvement" or "some improvement." By 1990, perception of this area showed dramatic improvement, and it was rated as mostly "satisfactory" by the faculty. Appendix D reflects changes in priority of areas that the faculty felt were most important for future work. A number of areas that might be considered as goal or task functions collectively seemed to become more important, as did "total staff...morale," a group maintenance function (Cartwright and Zander 1962). We also examined the differences among various subgroups within the school (grade-level groups and those whose responsibilities cut across grade levels) to learn what was taking place internally and possibly to obtain diagnostic information for refinement and improvement of the grade-level groups. (See figure 14.2).

Feedback provided to us by persons working in educational anthropology encouraged us to look at the total context, in which the culture, norms, and expectations of members of the school culture could be considered. We obtained information from an annual survey of a sample of the students concerning their attitudes about various aspects of the school. We used this information as a basis of comparison with other junior high or middle schools to provide a picture of students' perceptions for each of the three years in which we had been consultants. During that time, the school change process was being conducted. (See figure 14.3). Most of the changes appear to be more positive student attitudes toward most areas, in the second and third years, especially regarding some general norms and expectations. At the end of the 1989–90 school year, in

Figure 14.1. Perceptions of Total Staff, 1988 and 1990

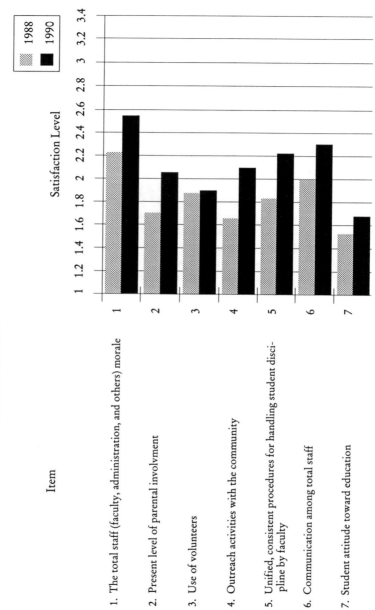

Item

1. The total staff (faculty, administration, and others) morale

2. Present level of parental involvment

3. Use of volunteers

4. Outreach activities with the community

5. Unified, consistent procedures for handling student discipline by faculty

6. Communication among total staff

7. Student attitude toward education

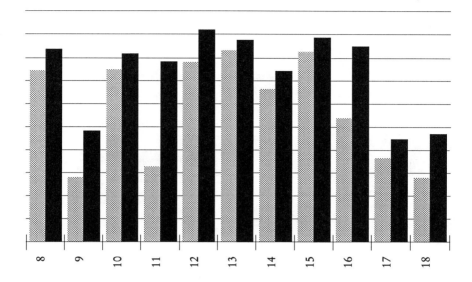

8. Communication between administration and faculty

9. Student completion of required class work

10. Family feeling among total staff

11. Present operational role of guidance and counseling staff

12. Present operational role of grade-level administrators

13. Present operational role of building administrator

14. Impact of extracurricular activities on students

15. Teacher satisfaction with classroom management

16. Student participation in intramural programs

17. Student respect for teachers

18. Student perception of the value of classroom learning experiences

Figure 14.2. 1990 Perceptions of Total Staff by Grade Level

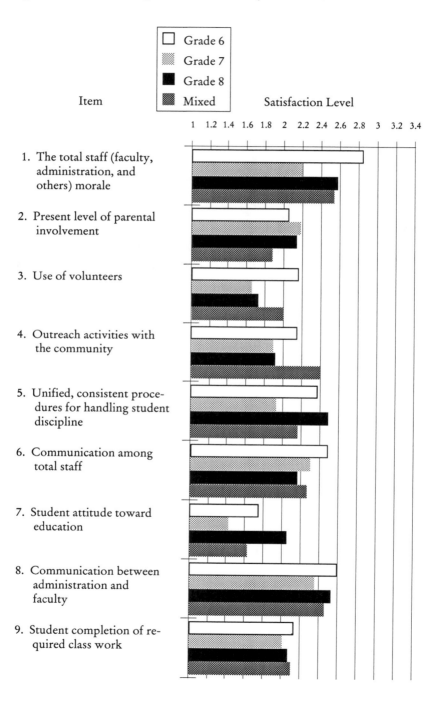

10. Family feeling among staff

11. Present operational role of guidance and counseling staff

12. Present operational role of grade-level administrators

13. Present operational role of building administrator

14. Impact of extracurricular activities on students

15. Teacher satisfaction with classroom management

16. Student participation in intramural programs

17. Student respect for teachers

18. Student perception of the value of classroom learning experiences

item 2, for example, almost 90 percent of the students said they would not quit school today even if they could do so without getting into trouble. In item 19, about 75 percent said that regardless of what their grades might be, they felt they were "learning a lot" this year in all or most of their subjects. Students' high levels of satisfaction in a number of areas likely reflects specific organizational changes.

An improved work ethic among teachers also seemed to develop. At 3:30 the teachers' parking lot is not empty, as it was formerly. As noted above, closer relationships have developed between teachers working on teams and between teachers and students. In addition, accountability and the presence of an extra counselor to serve on one of the grade-level teams have led to considerable improvement in the counseling function. This area was the top-ranked concern in 1988, but in 1990 virtually disappeared into a tie for fifteenth place among eighteen issues.

Various changes and events seem to reflect an interest in meeting the needs for recognition and for working together. Because of awareness of the need to recognize all people in the school, from administrators to students, students' achievement now is recognized consistently. Color photos of students are posted on the windows of the school offices in honor of various achievements, a practice that now has continued more than two and one-half years. The extracurricular program also has been strengthened to meet students' needs. Recently it was decided that each grade level will have two teaching teams for the 1991–92 school year; this decision was virtually unanimous.

CONCLUSIONS AND IMPLICATIONS

A new construct has been developed, which appears useful in diagnosing and analyzing organizations and their dynamics. The process involves searching for the key *issues and concerns* perceived by people in the organization, and then publicly drawing *conclusions and implications* from these perceptions; next, looking for underlying *themes;* and finally, developing *potential lines of action* to deal with the *issues and concerns, themes,* and problems. (See table 14.1.)

In the case of this junior high school, this deliberately designed, highly public process led to a series of major changes in which the school began to be transformed into a middle school. These changes included the following:

Figure 14.3. Student Perceptions, by Year, 1988–1990

Item

Percentage of Students

1. How proud are you of your school: ("Very proud," "Fairly proud")

2. Would you quit school today if you could without getting in trouble? ("No")

3. How many of your teachers seem to care if you learn the subject they teach? ("All," "Most")

4. How often do your teachers clearly explain <u>what</u> to do on assignments? ("always," "Usually")

5. How many of your teachers are willing to give students individual help outside of class time? ("All" "Most")

6. By which method do you usually learn best? ("Discussion group")

7. When a student does not learn, who do you think is at fault? ("Student himself")

8. Are the students allowed to take textbooks home? ("Most of the time," "Sometimes")

9. Do you find the media Specialist in the Media Center helpful? ("Most of the time")

10. Are the books in the Media Center helpful? ("Most of the time," "Sometimes")

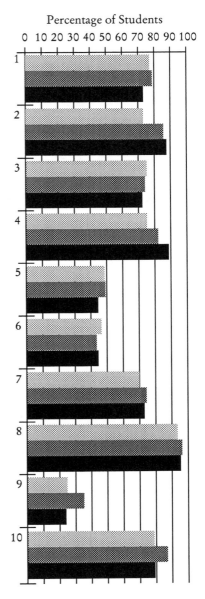

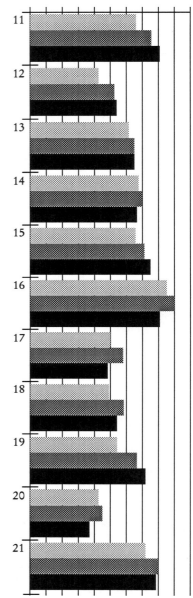

11. Do you know your school counselors ("Yes")

12. How easy is it to get to see your school counselor? ("Very easy")

13. If you met with your school counselors, were they ("Very helpful," "Helpful")

14. If you have a problem or suggestion for the principal, howlong would you have to wait to talk with the principal? ("I could talk . . . immediately," ". . . within a day")

15. If you have a problem or suggestion for the assistant principal, how long would you have to wait to talk with the assistant principal? (". . . immediately," "within a day")

16. If you have a problem or suggestion for the dean, how long would you have to wait to talk with the dean? (". . . immediately, " ". . . within a day")

17. In general, are you satisfied or dissatisfied with the way you are treated by the administration? ("Very satisfied," "Satisfied")

18. In general, how well satisfied are you with the variety of the subjects that your school offers? ("Very satisfied," "Satisfied")

19. Regardless of what your grades may be, in how many of your school subjects would you say you are "learning a lot" this year? ("In all my subjects," "In most of my subjects")

20. How would you rate "school spirit" at your school? ("Excellent ," "Good")

21. In general, how proud or ashamed of your school are you? ("Very proud," "proud"*)

- Reorganizing the school from a dysfunctional junior high school organization, which blocked effective communication, to a middle school model
- Coordinating and cooperating among staff members to support a grade-level administrative reorganization, which facilitated those and other processes
- Revising the instructional model from teachers working alone to working in teams
- Solving the problems of the dysfunctional guidance organization
- Increasing community involvement
- Improving communication among community, parents, teachers, and students
- Major recognition and activity programs for students
- Increasing teachers' control over their professional lives
- Increased morale and sense of hope
- Assisting administration to become more proactive and more effective.

In addition, students' and teachers' attitudes indicated significant changes. To effect the administrative changes, the central office became involved and supportive.

Norms, beliefs, and symbols were altered. To accomplish such massive changes, the entire staff—faculty, administration, deans, and counselors—had to cooperate to establish goals (Barnard 1951; Bennis, Benne, and Chin 1962). The work ethic improved, and both professional behavior and the personalized "family" nature of the school strengthened. Faculty members attempted to improve self-esteem in everyone—administrators, staff, and students. A strong sense of responsibility always had existed; this now was directed toward the goals discussed above and toward accomplishing these goals successfully. One of these aims was to produce success for everyone. In this strong, caring atmosphere, faculty turnover is low, and faculty members' support of each other, of administrators, and of students is high. Support for the plan is equally great.

A major vehicle for this change was the use of external, objective consultants over a long period of time. These consultants made a commitment to the school and the process; we were continuously in contact with the school and spent extensive amounts of time there. This is in contrast to the degree and type of involvement typical of many other school intervention projects by those initially outside of the system and may be more similar to some school change processes in anthropology (Cochran-Smith and Larkin 1987; Moll and Diaz 1987; Schmuck and Runkel 1985).

EPILOGUE

A report of more recent events and outcomes and a few reflective comments related to the transitional events of this school change process seem appropriate to conclude this chapter. These may help provide a useful perspective and some implications from one school's restructuring.

First, the school has continued to change and "improve." Results and reports from 1991 and during the 1991–92 school year reflect continued improvements in *all* areas of concern identified at the end of the 1989–90 findings from the total staff and faculty—especially in the area of "total staff . . . morale" identified as the first priority at the end of 1990 (appendix D). Also, a firsthand report from one of the district's administrators, who initiated concerns related to the school, noted that it is one of the most improved schools in the county. Even though the staff and faculty there are almost the same as four years ago, the school is a different place. It was also reported that many of the potential leaders for the county seem to be coming from that school. At the annual faculty party celebrating the end of the 1990–91 school year, at least seventeen teachers and administrators emphatically stated that this was the best year they had ever had professionally.

The comments that follow were made by staff and faculty members at various grade levels on the survey given at the end of the school year in 1991:

> The office is working beautifully and people seem to know what their roles are and generally are comfortable with them. Because of more effective inservice, there is less negativism and more willingness to try new ideas. Most of us feel we are having a positive effect on our students. Teaming is working well so far.

> There has been a positive attitude at [the] top. . . . accountability . . . visibility of all staff [members] have changed.

> I think the front office alignment has worked out beautifully. Grade level adms. [administrators], counselors, and staff has worked well.

> We have been exposed to new ideas and ways of doing things. Staff has had more opportunities to interact in a vari-

ety of settings and in some cases "forced" to work together. I think this has been beneficial in sharing needs, concerns, and frustrations among staff members rather than in just departments. We have all been looking for an easy "fix" for other problems; but, we are learning that with assistance and input of other experts, we have the answers to the future of our kids if we will patiently and cooperatively put it all together. We are not there yet; but, we have made some huge strides.[2]

These provide some indication of the changed picture of the beliefs and realities and the collective ownership that have evolved in that school. The process and progress in this school seem to have encouraged a relatively nonthreatening opportunity and subsequent internal support for looking at the "why" of school dysfunction and for commitment to efforts toward school success (Vogt, Jordan, and Tharp 1987).

In summary, this case study has focused on the processes and resultant changes that can occur when a faculty's underlying myths, beliefs, and realities operating in a specific school are clarified and analyzed. By developing a high degree of consensus about these myths, beliefs, and realities, this data becomes part of the basis for improvement. The developing ownership, mutual commitment, and continuing growth of those involved provide the ingredients for a thoughtful, major, continuous change process. With this school—as there would be with any school—there are new concerns, and continuing needs for improvement, changing cultural factors, and unresolved issues. Even though there are now in that school higher satisfactions, more congruent "beliefs" and "realities," and improving relationships and outcomes, things are certainly not perfect. The events related to the evolving of educational restructuring and specific school change are really never-ending stories.

Notes

This chapter is in part an expanded adaptation of a paper presented 29 March 1990 at the annual meeting of the Society for Applied Anthropology in York, England.

1. This was the principal's terminology. The organizational diagnostic construct we developed focused on people's perceived "issues and concerns" rather than "problems."

2. These are quotes taken directly from an expanded form of the survey (see appendix D) that was given at the end of the 1990–91 school year. The responses were to Item E: How have things changed at *[the school]* over the past three years?

References

Ashton, Patricia T., and Rodman B. Webb. 1986. *Making a Difference: Teachers' Sense of Efficacy and Student Achievement.* White Plains, N.Y.: Longman.

Bales, Robert, and P. Slater. 1955. "Role Differentiation in Small Decision-Making Groups." In *Family, Socialization, and Interaction Process,* edited by Talcott, Parsons, Robert Bales, et al. Glencoe, Ill.: Free Press.

Barnard, Chester. 1951. *The Functions of the Executive.* Cambridge: Harvard University Press.

Bennis, Warren G., Kenneth D. Benne, and Robert Chin, eds. 1962. *The Planning of Change.* New York: Holt, Rinehart & Winston.

Ben-Peretz, Miriam, and Rob Halkes. 1987. "How Teachers Know Their Classrooms: A Cross-Sectional Study of Teachers' Understanding of Classroom Situations." *Anthropology and Education Quarterly* 18:17–32.

Cartwright, Dorwin, and Alvin Zander. 1962. *Group Dynamics.* 2d ed. Evanston, Ill.: Row, Peterson.

Cochran-Smith, Marilyn, and James M. Larkin. 1987. "Anthropology and Education: What's the 'and' Mean?" *Anthropology and Education Quarterly* 18:38–42.

Fabun, Don. 1967. *The Dynamics of Change.* Englewood Cliffs, N.J.: Prentice-Hall.

Goodstein, Lenard D. 1978. *Consulting with Human Service Systems.* Reading, Mass.: Addison-Wesley.

Hollander, Edwin P., and Lynn R. Offermann. 1990. "Power and Leadership in Organizations: Relationships in Transition." *American Psychologist* 45:179–89.

Lewin, Kurt. 1952. "Group Decision and Social Change." In *Readings in Social Psychology*, rev. ed., edited by G. E. Swanson, T. N. Newcomb, and E. L. Hartley, 459–73. New York: Holt, Rinehart, & Winston.

Mead, George Herbert. 1934. *Mind, Self, and Society.* Chicago: University of Chicago Press.

Moll, Luis C., and Stephen Diaz. 1987. "Change as the Goal of Educational Research." *Anthropology and Education Quarterly* 18:300–311.

Offermann, Lynn R., and Marilyn K. Gowing. 1990. "Organizations of the Future: Changes and Challenges." *American Psychologist* 45:95–108.

Rowan, Brian. 1990. "Commitment and Control: Alternative Strategies for the Organizational Design of Schools." In *Review of Research in Education*, edited by Courtney Cazden. Washington, D.C.: American Educational Research Association.

Sarason, Segman B. 1971. *The Culture of the School and the Problem of Change.* Boston: Allyn & Bacon.

Schein, Edgar H. 1990. "Organizational Culture." *American Psychologist* 45:109–19.

Schmuck, Richard A., and Philip J. Runkel. 1985. *The Handbook of Organization Development in Schools.* 3d ed. Palo Alto, Calif.: Mayfield.

Shartle, C. L. 1956. *Executive Performance and Leadership.* Englewood Cliffs, N.J.: Prentice-Hall.

Spindler, George, and Louise Spindler. 1987. "Cultural Dialogue and Schooling. In Schoenhausen and Roseville: A Comparative Analysis." *Anthropology and Education Quarterly* 18:3–16.

Van Meter, Eddy J. 1979–80. "Planned Change in Education." *Administrator's Notebook* 28:322–35.

Vogt, Lynn A., Cathie Jordan, and Roland G. Tharp. 1987. "Explaining School Failure, Producing School Success: Two Cases." *Anthropology and Education Quarterly* 18:276–86.

Weick, Karl E. 1976. "Educational Organizations as Loosely Coupled Systems." *Administrative Science Quarterly* 21:1–19.

Wilson, L. Craig, T. Madison Byars, Arthur S. Shapiro, and Shirley H. Schell. 1969. *Sociology of Supervision.* Boston: Allyn & Bacon.

APPENDIX A. SURVEY ADMINISTERED TO TOTAL STAFF IN SPRING 1988

_____ SCHOOL INSERVICE SURVEY

Everyone's input is needed to clarify issues, conditions, and concerns and then to prioritize them so that we can develop directions that might be taken in a planned school-based inservice program for _____ .

The following survey tries to focus on your present perceptions of and feelings about conditions and concerns and then asks you to prioritize the most important to you.

A. What is your present perception regarding the following at _____ ?

(To the right of each condition below check the line that best relates to your present perception or feelings about it.)

Column headings (diagonal): very satisfactory / satisfactory / needs some improvement / needs much improvement

1. The total staff (faculty, administration, and others) morale.
2. Present level of parental involvement
3. Use of volunteers
4. Outreach activities with the community
5. Unified, consistent procedures for handling student discipline by faculty
6. Communication among total staff
7. Student attitude toward education
8. Communication between administration and faculty
9. Student completion of required class work
10. Family feeling among total staff
11. Present operational role of guidance and counseling staff
12. Present operational role of deans
13. Present operational role of administrators

14. Impact of extracurricular activities on students   —   —   —   —
15. Teacher satisfaction with classroom management   —   —   —   —
16. Student participation in intramural programs   —   —   —   —
17. Student respect for teachers   —   —   —   —
18. Student perception of the value of classroom learn-
    ing experiences   —   —   —   —

Others:

19. Please specify. _____   —   —   —   —

20. Please specify. _____   —   —   —   —

B. Add any comments or explanations you feel necessary to clarify any of the above.

C. What are your ideas for improving conditions in this school? (use back of sheet if necessary).

D. Prioritize the top five concerns you personally think are the most important to work on first. (#1 would be the most important; #2, the second in importance; #5, the fifth in importance.)

1.
2.
3.
4.
5.

APPENDIX B. LETTER SENT TO EACH MEMBER OF THE TOTAL STAFF

May 27, 1988

Dear Colleague:

We appreciate your attendance and interest shown at the preliminary meetings that were held with the three groups of teachers during recent weeks. We also very much appreciate (the principal's) openness and acceptance of an unrestricted approach to review people's concerns in order to improve the school and its programs for students and total staff—teachers and others. Such wide-open acceptance is unusual and speaks highly of a desire to meet the challenges which schools in our area face.

As you may recall, many of the concerns expressed are faced by all schools with changing populations and were drawn mainly from the planning committee. We are impressed with the strengths and assets _____ has developed and provides, including a strong degree of staff professionalism, a concern for effective teaching and learning, and a commitment to the school and its students and personnel. There seems to be a strong hope that the school can meet its challenges through the possibility and support of a school-based inservice program which is being developed with considerable input from the total staff.

During the times we have been at _____for visits and meetings, those with whom we had contact (staff members, students, and even a few parents we saw) have expressed many positive and supportive statements about _____and those who are a part of its programs. These, along with the comments above, are claims that many schools could not make these days.

We are looking forward to meeting with you at a faculty meeting before the end of the school year. This will give us an opportunity to clarify and develop directions for a school-based inservice program for _____beginning this summer and continuing into the 1988–89 school year.

Sincerely,

Wade Burley   Arthur Shapiro

WWB/AS/sgb

APPENDIX C. RECOMMENDATION FOR REORGANIZATION

PROPOSAL FOR_____

BACKGROUND

The faculty and administration of _____School embarked upon a school improvement process earlier in the preceding academic year. In this process two consultants from the University of South Florida assisted. The process entailed forming a Planning Committee representing every department as well as a dean and a guidance counselor. The Planning Committee structured its inquiry to focus on concerns, issues, and possible lines of action, with minutes of every meeting being distributed to all faculty members and administration. A total faculty inservice meeting discussed concerns and issues. At this time the consultants and the Planning Committee presented some of their tentative findings and conclusions to the entire staff, the faculty and administration.

Concerns/Issues/Rationale

Faculty discussion led to several concerns and issues emerging.

1. The guidance function was seriously misfiring, with much criticism and concern occurring from faculty and even the guidance department itself. Many viewed the department as disorganized.
2. Similarly, the administrative function seemed to be reactive more than proactive.
3. The deanship was a focus of concern as well. Accountability was a goal also for administration and guidance.
4. The student base had significantly changed from upper middle class to many people from duplexes, single parent families generally from lower socioeconomic levels causing changes in student attitudes toward education, doing home work and the like.
5. Student and parent participation and involvement with the school had dropped significantly, and even faculty participation was not as high as desired.
6. Faculty morale and concern were too low and too high, respectively.

Lines of Action/Initiatives

The following lines of action developed in the processes of deliberation

1. A Guidance Committee was formed to wrestle with the problems discussed in that area, and met regularly with the consultants.
2. A proposal was developed to re-organize the front office as follows:
   a. Develop teams consisting of the dean, guidance counselor and clerk to be in charge of each grade level.
   b. This would entail redefining the jobs of all three to focus on their respective grade level.
   c. Each team will follow its grade level as that group of students matriculates through the school.
   d. Inservice training would be required to facilitate team development, and is strongly supported by _____.

Some questions raised regarding how these teams will operate:

1. Q. Will one person in each of these teams have to be in charge?
   A. It looks like that is the approach we have to take.
2. Q. How will teams be selected?
   A. The principal will ask for their input; final decision to be his.
3. Q. How will the person in charge be selected?
   A. The principal will decide after consultation.
4. Q. What would be the role of the assistant principal?
   A. It would have to be shifted into one of the teams; however, _____ is needed for the district's growing data analysis capacity and the district is reviewing its resources for an appropriate placement.
5. Q. Does this require a new counselor?
   A. Yes. The district has indicated its approval of adding this new position.
6. Q. What other questions do we need to consider to implement this restructuring?

APPENDIX D. SURVEY ADMINISTERED TO FACULTY IN 1988 AND 1990, WITH RESULTS

This is the original Survey form that was used in the Spring of 1988. Please respond to it in terms of your current perceptions of *present* conditions related to _____ .

_____SCHOOL INSERVICE SURVEY

Everyone's input is needed to clarify issues, conditions, and concerns and then to prioritize them so that we can develop directions that might be taken in a planned school-based inservice program for _____ .

The following survey tries to focus on your present perceptions of and feelings about conditions and concerns and then asks you to prioritize the most important to you.

A. What is your present perception regarding the following at _____ ?
(To the right of each condition below check the box that best relates to you present perception or feelings about it.)

PRIORITY
Rankings

For items most important to work on first:

1988	1990		satisfactory	very satisfactory	needs some improvement	needs much improvement
4th	1st	1. The total staff (faculty, administration, and others) morale	—	—	—	—
5th	4th	2. Present level of parental involvement	—	—	—	—
		3. Use of volunteers	—	—	—	—
		4. Outreach activities with the community	—	—	—	—
2nd	5th	5. Unified, consistent procedures for handling student discipline by faculty	—	—	—	—
	6.5	6. Communication among total staff	—	—	—	—
3rd	3rd	7. Student attitude toward education	—	—	—	—
		8. Communication between administration and faculty	—	—	—	—
	8th	9. Student completion of required class work	—	—	—	—
	(14th)	10. Family feeling among total staff	—	—	—	—
1st	(15th)	11. Present operational role of guidance and counseling staff	—	—	—	—
	(17.5)	12. Present operational role of deans	—	—	—	—
		13. Present operational role of administrators	—	—	—	—
	(17.5)	14. Impact of extra curricular activities on students	—	—	—	—
		15. Teacher satisfaction with classroom management	—	—	—	—
	(16th)	16. Student participation in intramural programs	—	—	—	—
6th	2nd	17. Student respect for teachers	—	—	—	—
	6.5	18. Student perception of the value of classroom learning experiences	—	—	—	—
		Others:				
	9th	19. Please specify class size	—	—	—	—
		20. Please specify. _____	—	—	—	—

B. Add any comments or explanations you feel necessary to clarify any of the above.

C. What are your ideas for improving conditions in this school? (use back of sheet if necessary).

D. Prioritize the top five concerns you personally think are the most important to work on first. (#1 would be the most important; #2, the second in importance, #5, the first in importance.)

   1.
   2.
   3.
   4.
   5.

15

INTERACTIONS AMONG SCHOOL AND COLLEGE TEACHERS: TOWARD RECOGNIZING AND REMAKING OLD PATTERNS

Chester H. Laine, Lucille M. Schultz, and M. Lynne Smith

INTRODUCTION

Recognizing that it is valuable for high school and college language arts/ English teachers to work together to solve mutual problems and coordinate instructional efforts is not a new phenomenon in this country. The concern that this chapter addresses is that in spite of this recognition and, indeed, a long history of collaborative efforts, the scholarly community has given limited attention to understanding this work. Reports of collaborations are primarily descriptive and anecdotal (Fortune 1986), and for the most part self-congratulatory. In this chapter, we look analytically and critically at interactions between school and college English teachers, then personally and anecdotally at our own experience as collaborators. We begin by summarizing the history of school/college collaboration, then describe the specific collaborative effort in which we all participated. Following the description of our collaborative project, we describe our three individual points of view on our years of collaboration, and attempt to relate our points of view to the larger framework of school/college collaboration. Next, we briefly examine

some of the cultural constraints that affect collaboration, and then consider ways that collaborating teachers can remake the history they have
inherited. While we write in part from our research in this area, we also
write from our own experience with collaboration; for six years, we
were part of a collaborative project between a large urban school system
and a comprehensive research university. As necessary context for what
follows, we begin with a summary of research on the long and troubled
history of collaboration between school and college English teachers.

A NOTE ON THE HISTORY OF SCHOOL/COLLEGE COLLABORATION

A search of more than three hundred essays, editorials, council letters,
presidential addresses, workshop reports, and roundtable notes (from
the *English Journal, College English, College Composition and Communication, Education,* the *Educational Review,* and the *School Review*) reveals that joint projects have a long history (Schultz, et al.,
1988). In 1913, the University of Chicago held a conference with local
schools to discuss school and college work in English. In a paper delivered to the National Council of Teachers of English (NCTE) in 1921,
George R. Coffman outlined ten suggestions for ensuring student preparation for Freshman English, concluding with the pronouncement that
"the only hope for the intellectual life of the higher educational institutions of the country is in intelligent and comprehensive co-operation between the secondary schools and the colleges" (Coffman 1922, 139). It
is also true, however, that these projects have often been fraught with
problems. As early as 1894, Paul Hanus of Harvard University wrote that
"anything like real cooperation between colleges and secondary schools
does not exist" (Hanus 1894, 259). In June, 1918, George Miller of the
University of Idaho spoke of the "evils" of "poor coordination and correlation" ("News and Notes" 1918, 401). And as recently as 1976, Donald McQuade spoke of the "lack of articulation, if not the open hostility,
among teachers of English," their "professional skirmishing," and their
"internal bickering, trading insults which reinforce the prejudices embedded in the hierarchical structure of our system of learning" (Mc-
Quade 1976, 8).

The review of joint projects revealed three patterns that have frequently jeopardized school/college collaborations. The first pattern is
that school and college teachers have often ended up blaming each other
for what has gone wrong in students' preparation for college and, in par-

ticular, for Freshman English. In the worst scenario, high school teachers have accused the colleges of intellectual snobbery and paternalism, of being pontifical, condescending, and arrogant. One panel, for example, during the 1956 conference of the National Council of Teachers of English, was billed as a "frank and friendly panel at which high school and college teachers will tell each other what is wrong with each other" (Archer 1956, 48). A more extended sample of a similar heated exchange occurred in the *English Journal* in the spring of 1958. A college writing teacher wrote to the principal of a local high school saying the school should not teach students how to write a research paper because "the more a student has learned about the research paper in high school, the more difficulty I have teaching him valid research techniques, since I must have him unlearn all that he has learned as well as teach him what he must know" (Boggs 1958, 86). Three months later, in the May issue, a high school teacher responded, "My own experience as a high school instructor of English indicates that you suffer from the myopic viewpoint shared by many—but fortunately not all—college instructors: that high school teachers and principals are hopelessly unrealistic dolts who don't know a scholarly hawk from a pedagogical handsaw" (Jumper 1958, 289).

A second pattern that turns up in reading the historical accounts is that college teachers have often held the balance of power in these relationships. When secondary school English teachers organized to form the NCTE in 1911, they were protesting the domination of their curricula by uniform college-entrance requirements. They saw no reason for teaching all of their students a college-preparatory curriculum when many of those students were bound for something other than college; further, they saw no reason why college teachers should determine what they were required to teach, one high school teacher complaining that "of the sixteen men who prescribe the college-entrance requirements in English, only one is a high school man" ("News and Notes" 1912, 124). Essays of the period speak of the teachers of New York "waging warfare"; of the "shackles," the "ball and chain" the teachers wore; of the "storm and stress" of the controversy. It is also noteworthy that on the panels at some of our earliest national conferences, most of the speakers about school/college interaction were from the colleges, and most of them were men (Tovatt and Jewett 1959, 541).

A third pattern—perhaps the most subtle but also the most powerful—that has jeopardized school/college relationships, is what Donald McQuade (1976), borrowing a phrase from Whitehead (1950), calls the "fallacy of simple location." According to McQuade, this fallacy assumes that the higher you are on the ladder of education, the more important you are. It thus encourages teachers to believe that no matter how poor their work is at their level on the educational ladder, it is necessarily better than the work of the best teacher at the level below them. College English teachers, McQuade laments, thus dare to tell high school English teachers how to teach their classes, without having been there, lecture to teachers in workshops that rarely involve mutual learning and teaching, and continue to ask, "What are *they* doing in the schools?" That the fallacy also affects secondary teachers is evident from their blaming the elementary teachers for sending them underprepared students (8–9). Thus, as it has been lived out in the educational system and to some extent in cooperative projects, this fallacy has meant that "because I am higher up, my work is more important than yours" and also that "I can project onto you the task of getting students ready for my more important work."

What the journal coverage of interactions between school and college English teachers reflects, therefore, is that although they have a long-standing interest in partnerships and their work often focuses on writing instruction, hidden or barely hidden assumptions about the work and/or character of the other party create a dynamic in which one group, usually the college teachers, tries to meet its own needs by imposing—often unthinkingly—an agenda on the other group.

PLACING OUR COLLABORATIVE PROJECT

Purpose

The explicit purpose of our collaborative project, as outlined to the funding agency, was to experiment with, and refine, writing assessment and instruction methods in the high school English classrooms of an urban school system, in an effort to reduce the number of students needing remedial writing instruction when they entered college. However, there were actually many emerging goals. These included:

- the desire to implement mandated curriculum and assessment requirements;
- the goal of improving writing instruction;
- the desire to learn more about writing assessment; and
- the hope of generating research and publications.

One of the most interesting challenges throughout the years of the project was to make our work cross-disciplinary rather than simply multidisciplinary. This type of collaborative work was new for most of us. We did not have to deal with such diverse groups of people in the course of our regular professional responsibilities.

Persons

Two of the university people came from a liberal arts English and comparative literature department. One came from a college of education. Two came from a two-year open-access college. Their backgrounds varied: Some came from traditions of rhetoric and composition, others from linguistics or American and English literature. Still others had training in educational administration and cognitive psychology. Our career paths were very different. Three of the college teachers were men, two were women. The expectations we held for ourselves and that others held for us were unique.

Two of the public school personnel who served on the administrative team for our collaborative project were teacher/administrators; they directed the districtwide staff development writing program. The other was the supervisor of secondary English. All three were women; one was African-American. Over the course of five years we worked with approximately forty experienced high school English teachers. Most were women from the majority, "mainstream" culture. Some were African-American women. Two were men.

Sites

Nine high schools in a large, midwestern, urban public school system were selected for their unique economic and ethnic diversity. The nine schools drew from affluent, middle-class, and very poor neighborhoods and from African-American, urban Appalachian, and non-Appalachian white populations. Five of the nine schools included magnet programs: an admission-by-testing academic high school, a school for the creative and performing arts, an academy of physical education, an international baccalaureate program, and a computer-centered curriculum. Three included extensive vocational education programs. Four were largely comprehensive high schools, with no magnet programs but varied kinds of special educations programs—for blind, deaf, and other differently abled students.

Subjects

At any given time in the course of the collaborative project, we were examining the writing of approximately two thousand students: 17 percent were urban Appalachian, 60 percent were African American, and 23 percent were non-Appalachian white.

Data Collection

During the course of the project, we addressed over thirty thousand pieces of writing generated by high school juniors and seniors. All were produced under impromptu testing conditions and were assessed using established primary trait and holistic methods. Some of the writing was later subjected to many linguistic and rhetorical analyses.

PLACING THIS CHAPTER'S AUTHORS

We continue this chapter by describing how each of us was positioned in this collaboration, because that positioning, the way we were individually contextualized in the project, influenced the ways in which we participated in the work and influenced our perceptions of the "success" of the collaboration.

Point of View: Director, Freshman English Program, Department of English, College of Arts and Sciences

When I, Lucy Schultz, began work on the collaborative project, I was a newly hired assistant professor in a department of English in a college of arts and sciences. My field is composition studies, and I was hired as the associate director of a Freshman English program that served twenty-five hundred students every quarter. From the beginning of my time in the department, I knew that of the three criteria by which I would be judged for promotion, publication was preeminent. When, therefore, I signed onto a collaborative project with the schools, I was excited about the work of the project and by the collegiality it offered, but I also knew that I could not invest the kind of time the project required (we often met two hours a week or every other week, and often worked weekends on the project) and not come away with some published research from it. My agenda, therefore, was to be sure that we were documenting our work in such a way that we would be able to report it in professional journals, for I knew that as much as my department celebrated my participating in the project, our reward system is so constructed that such "service" would have very small bearing on my promotion.

One result of my situatedness is that midway through our project, our team of school and college teachers faced a near standoff when, in order to do a research study, the college teachers wanted to keep a set of student papers at the same time that the school team members insisted that every paper be returned to the students. As we struggled with how to make the decision of whether to keep or return the papers, we realized what should have been obvious but wasn't: that each group was simply being faithful to the beliefs and values of their own cultural scenes, to the contexts in which they spend their professional lives. From the teachers in the schools, the college teachers learned that it is hard to find a more serious sin than to pump up a class about an important writing task and then not return the papers; from those of us in the colleges, the teachers in the schools learned that it is crucial to our careers that any project we take on have a research component. By bringing our conflicting agendas to the surface, we not only came to understand some of the underlying assumptions of each other's cultural scene, we also found the *tertium quid.* The college teachers, persuaded that it was important for the students to have their papers back, agreed to return the originals to the students. The high school teachers, persuaded how important it was for the college teachers to be able to conduct a study based on these papers, volunteered to help with the photocopying of the papers. While photocopying the papers sounds like a simple enough solution, I would add that we were talking about two thousand student essays generated for each of several writing tests over the course of the collaboration; most of the students' papers were two pages long and included two additional pages of prewriting. Not surprisingly, none of us had the kind of secretarial assistance or long-term daytime access to a photocopying machine that a project of this magnitude would require. So what "photocopying the papers" meant was that our team of high school and college teachers spend one entire Sunday and several evenings, shoulder to shoulder at a copy machine, as we photocopied eight thousand pieces of paper, one by one, and re-sorted the originals to return to students. Perhaps from that experience, more than from any other aspect of our work together, I learned what it means to honor someone else's agenda at the same time that I wanted mine honored, and I learned what collaboration means.

Since the outset of the project, I have coauthored five essays that have come from this work (and I have been promoted), so, in fact, I found a way—with the help and understanding of my collaborators—to realize my needs in the projects.

Point of View: Associate Professor, Department of Curriculum and Instruction, College of Education

When I, Chet Laine, began work on the collaborative project, I was entering my fourth year as an assistant professor in a college of education. Even before we began our work, I was linked to many of the individuals in the project. However, as the project unfolded, many new connections were formed. My primary role—preparing apprentices to assume positions as English teachers—brought me in contact with colleagues in the Department of English and in public school classrooms. Over half of the course work required of my students is completed outside of my college, most of it in the Department of English. All of my students spend at least six hundred hours in public school classrooms. Several of the project teachers served as master teachers for the interns I placed in their secondary English classrooms. Other teachers, returning graduate students, attended my evening classes. These same public school teachers and administrators frequently asked me to participate in staff development programs or to serve on accreditation teams. Program development, student admission and retention, student placement, and state and national accreditation reviews provided natural links between myself and the other individuals working on the project. Prior to the project, however, important differences often prevented these links from being very productive. Philosophical differences, contrasting notions about content and pedagogy, faulty assumptions about the quality of teaching in the public schools or about the skills and abilities of education majors, and differences in research traditions were often at the root of these unproductive relationships.

When the project began, common stereotypes framed my sense of these various cultures: for example, the notion that programs in education—like those in nursing, developmental education, or business administration—are of lower status than programs in the humanities, liberal arts, or sciences. It wasn't until much later in the project that I realized that we are all operating on the margins. My colleagues from the two-year, open-access college, for example, are seen as peripheral by most of the university. Their heavier teaching and advising loads prevent them from devoting large blocks of time to research and publication. Indeed, even many of the officials who provided us with funding hoped that our project, and others like it, would reduce or eliminate the need for "remedial" writing instruction at colleges and universities across the state. The urban teachers on our project, also on the margins, are frequently portrayed as the villains when the local newspapers carry stories about student test results. The low-level public school administrators—respected by the teachers—have no real power and very little influence within the central administration of the school district. Even within the Department of English, faculty members in Composition Studies, and particularly in Freshman English, are on the margins, usually of lower status than faculty members in literature. None of the members of this team—the public school teachers and administrators, the faculty from the two-year college, the faculty members from education, or the faculty members from Freshman English—are invested with much prestige, power, or influence.

I became increasingly aware of the differences among these diverse cultures. In 1980, I was hired by the university to teach and supervise prospective teachers. Contact with public school teachers and students is a critical part of what I do. Indeed, one of the minimum requirements specified in the position announcement to which I responded was at least three years' experience as a public school teacher. "Working in the trenches" meant very little to my college promotion and tenure committee; however, my grasp of the constraints that teachers face is crucial to my credibility within my department and in the schools. Although I taught in public schools for a decade, in 1984, when the collaborative project began, I had been out of the classroom for eight years. I was keenly aware of the changing nature of classrooms and worried that I was losing touch with contemporary classrooms, student writing, the politics of assessment, and the culture of urban schools. Throughout the next several years, the project brought me much closer to the public school teachers, their beliefs, their constraints, and the rhythms of their lives.

What I could not anticipate in 1984 were the new insights that would emerge during the course of our collaboration. All of the members of the project, regardless of their situations, were committed to teachers, writing, and young writers. Each brought a particular strength to the project: planning staff development programs; securing a photocopy machine on a Sunday morning; writing a succinct progress report; locating examples of effective assessment techniques; making sense of fanfold computer sheets; writing useful prompts for student writing tasks; managing a budget; insuring that people got paid; supporting a wavering rater at a test-scoring session; writing a diplomatic letter to a school superintendent; picking up doughnuts for a scoring session; writing a grant proposal; identifying bias in a writing prompt; listening to someone who didn't understand; securing a little additional funding from a provost or a superintendent; unlocking a room at 6:30 in the morning; transforming a research finding into an effective classroom strategy; cleaning up the mess when a scoring session was over; or any of scores of other talents and contributions.

The project marked the beginning of many long professional relationships. For some of us, this contact became a stimulus for years of collaborative research, writing, presentations, and publications. For others, new projects were created. For at least two of us, the collaboration contributed to promotion and tenure. For a third, the collaboration contributed to a decision to complete a doctoral program and begin a college teaching career.

Point of View: Writing Program Director, Urban School System

When I, Lynne Smith, began work on the collaborative project, I was a low-level teacher/administrator in a city school system, the director of the Writing Program, an in-service training program for secondary English teachers. Prior to the collaborative effort, several hundred secondary English teachers had completed the thirty-hour in-service training workshop designed to introduce them to teaching writing as a process. I was excited by the teachers' enthusiasm for what they had learned during the workshops, and thrilled by their attempts to apply the ideas of Graves, Atwell, Elbow, and others, in their work with students.

My pride in the teachers' enthusiasm, knowledge, and accomplishments was short-lived however, because it quickly became clear that thirty hours of in-service work was only a beginning. The workshops were just the edge of what could be accomplished if ways could be found to support the teachers' interests in learning more and communicating with one another about efforts within their classrooms, across grade levels, and among schools. For the first few years of the Writing Program my focus was on doing a good job in each thirty-hour workshop, helping the twenty to thirty teachers who participated in each workshop become communities of writers. It was exciting work, but that focus on bringing more and more teachers into the dialogue on what worked and what didn't in the teaching of writing meant that I was not offering much support and assistance to those who had understood and internalized the methods and ideas of the workshop and were more than ready to go on, to learn more, to do more. As with other kinds of education, a little knowledge led to a thirst for more. Specifically, the more teachers learned about the ways writing could be taught, the more dissatisfaction and frustration they felt with the ways writing was being tested in the school district.

Thus, I saw the collaborative project as an opportunity to have expert help in solving my problem within the school district, that is, help in making changes in the ways writing was tested in the school district, so that the testing more accurately reflected the ways writing was being taught. With each passing year, increasing numbers of teachers, armed with their new knowledge of the writing process, were dissatisfied with the school system's districtwide minimum competency tests in writing. An instrument that tested students' editing skills and asked them multiple-choice questions about writing did not accurately reflect the students' ability to write and revise their own writing.

During the first few meetings of those involved in the collaboration, as I got to know Lucy Schultz, representing the university's Freshman English program, Chet Laine, representing the university's Department of Curriculum and Instruction, and others from their respective colleges and the two-year college of the university, the varying agendas, or—as I perceived them then—the hopes and needs of the participants and the constraints of their respective positions, became increasingly apparent to all of us. In retrospect, I can see our playing out of the three historical patterns Lucy described earlier in this chapter. From my point of view (as I attempted to assuage my own guilt, for example, not knowing enough about writing, myself, to meet the increasingly sophisticated needs of the English teachers), my goal was to get help, through this collaboration, in changing the way writing was tested in the school district. That help, I thought, would be in the forms of expertise and affirmation from persons who knew a great deal more than I did about composition and collaboration. As I tacked back and forth between meetings of the collaborators and meetings of English teachers, I realized that the high school teachers feared the college professors—a classic example of the historical patterns. The teachers expressed fears that (1) the professors would blame them for poor student writing and would communicate to school and district administrators that poor writing by students could be traced to poor teaching of writing; (2) the professors were more powerful than teachers and would control whatever new testing methods resulted from the collaboration; and, contrary to the first two suspicions, as it may seem, there was enough self-recrimination among English teachers for poor student writing for them to fear that (3) maybe it was true that the higher the grade you taught, the smarter and more important you were; therefore, maybe it's better to have the college professors design new writing tests, because they're smarter. Spoken and unspoken, these patterns seemed to be a part of the undergirding of the first few teacher meetings hosted by the collaboration team.

For example, at the first meeting of the high school English teachers hosted by the project and held to brainstorm ways a collaborative effort could be conducted, there was an extended discussion of the possibility of a primary-trait writing test, a type of test new to the school district but already in use in other districts. In such a test, it was explained, students would have an English-class period to prewrite (brainstorm, make lists, etc.) and compose a first draft of an essay in response to a written prompt, and another class period the following day to rewrite their essay. One high school teacher made clear his suspicions that a new test meant simply a new kind of teacher accountability, a testing system in which student writing scores would be reported by teachers and teachers would be penalized, somehow, for low student scores.

In looking back at the early activities of our collaborative project, I think we began the collaboration as strangers in some ways, suspicious about one another's motives, fearful that our personal and institutional agendas would be overpowered by the agendas of others. The first step in changing those fears and suspicions seems to have been the gradual building of working relationships that were egalitarian rather than hierarchical. That is, contrary to the high school teachers' prior experiences and their initial expectations of the collaborative project, the college professors who led the initial group work sessions—for creating writing prompts for students, the test-scoring sessions, the summer graduate-credit course, and other aspects of the collaboration—made it clear that the high school teachers were valued and respected. Small, seemingly insignificant actions and interactions helped build trust and counter suspicions. Name tags for teachers and for professors used first names and did not use titles. Professors were sensitive to the parking problems teachers faced when meetings were held at the university. A male college professor made and replenished the coffee for the whole group during the summer graduate-course sessions. A female college professor shared with high school teachers some of her Freshman English students' papers and her dilemmas in responding to their writing; Lucy openly discussed with the high school teachers her fears related to gaining tenure, and Chet enthusiastically praised the work of individual high school teachers to an audience of their peers. I more openly discussed my need for the project to be a continuation of the efforts of the school system's in-service training in writing, an answer to the "What do we do next?" questions of teachers, a way to move beyond my personal grasp of the writing process and ways of teaching and testing writing.

Trust in the professors was increased through collaborative team decisions that clearly respected both students and teachers in the high schools. For example, though the funding agency was interested in improving the writing skills of college-bound students, the collaborative effort involved every eleventh- and twelfth-grade student in the school system—college prep, vocational, special education, and so on. The professors understood the high school teachers' view that such inclusion was important, for teacher morale, and in recognition of the fact that many urban students, for a variety of reasons, do not go to college immediately after high school graduation, but do attend college several years later, after work and/or military experience.

The topic of our collaboration—writing—contributed to the building of personal relationships and increasing trust between and among the collaborators. That is, to share one's writing is a way of sharing oneself, and since much of our time together was spent discussing individual pieces of writing and giving our personal responses to the writing (and, indirectly, the writers), the respect shown for writing and therefore for writers helped us to respect one another, and to argue or agree with each other's perceptions and ideas rather than our respective titles and positions. I believe that such trust is an essential forerunner of change, and that personal changes in perceptions of the ways we saw one another and the ways we saw ourselves preceded and then accompanied changes in the ways we worked together and changes we were able to make in the ways writing was taught and tested in the school district.

CULTURAL CONSTRAINTS ON COLLABORATION

Pitman (1987) describes a culture as a patterned way of life that constrains the choices of its members and constitutes their subjectivities. Spradley (1990) explains that in order for researchers to recognize the tacit principles of another way of life, they must become students. Especially in the early months of our collaborative project, we were students of one another's cultures, learning about the kinds of constraints with which we each worked. Though all the persons participating in our collaborative project lived in the same city, and in some cases on the same street, the respective positions and institutions of our work lives made us members of different cultures. In effect, we were strangers in deceptively familiar lands.

The collaborators from the public school system knew little or nothing about the requirements, rewards, or constraints of the work lives of the university professors. For example, the fact that there was a pecking order among the colleges of the university (as discussed by Chet earlier in this chapter) was not a part of the high school teachers' understanding of the professors' work lives. The fact that the high school English teachers worked with 110–160 students in a single school day was a revelation to some of the professors. Differences in how our jobs were defined, in our work calendars, in our access to resources within institutions, and in the institutional ideologies regarding our positions (i.e., the belief systems about who we were and what we did) all were potential barriers to our understanding one another. Therefore, they were all potential barriers to a collaborative project that any one of us would define as "successful" or "important."

In retrospect, our efforts to understand one another's cultural systems throughout the years of the collaboration were personally very rewarding. Like inexperienced anthropologists studying cultures very different from their own, we had the opportunity to learn about work cultures very different from our experiences. Also like anthropologists, learning more about one another's cultures meant, ultimately, that we learned about ourselves, through our own and one another's eyes. It could be argued that some of us even "went native," in the sense that we not only grasped one another's personal and professional agendas for the collaborative project, but incorporated them into our own agendas.

REMAKING THE HISTORY WE'VE INHERITED

Where does this leave us? We are struck by two caveats for those contemplating similar collaborations. One is the danger inherent in the introduction of *innovations* within complex settings. A second is the care we must take as researchers collaborating with teachers, other researchers, and administrators.

Innovations and Barely Hidden Agendas

Michael Fullan, in *The Meaning of Educational Change* (1982), described the fragile nature of any collaborative effort that hopes to bring about change.

When we try to look at change directly from the point of view of each and every individual affected by it, and aggregate those individual views, the task of educational change becomes a bit unsettling. When we are dealing with reactions and perceptions of diverse people in diverse settings, faulty communication is guaranteed. People are a nuisance, but the theory of meaning says that individual concerns come with the territory; addressing those concerns *is* educational change (Fullan 1982, 295).

This seems to be particularly true of school/college collaborations, efforts that include participants from different cultural settings, the cultures of schools and of universities.

As in all such ventures, there are a number of divergent but overlapping intentions. We are all invested in promoting our own particular agendas. Some of us are primarily driven by research interests; others look for opportunities to collaborate. Others seek to understand another culture better. Some seek accountability. Others want teachers to feel ownership for a program that they will eventually have to accept. Some look for a chance to learn firsthand what "they" have up their sleeves, what is, in fact, going to be coming down in the schools. And, finally, some look for an opportunity to affect what that might be.

As teachers and researchers, we are compelled to help each other. Mary Savage (1988), in *Anthropology and Education Quarterly,* argues that many of us are members of marginalized groups. Members of urban social service agencies, community members, university faculty, and urban teachers are still examples of marginalized groups. In many ways, all lead a kind of marginal existence. Although they lack any obvious signs of power, they can form coalitions and become crucial agents for change.

These efforts could encourage what Mary Savage calls "neighborliness," people from one culture working, at least partially, for the sake of people in another culture. This "neighborliness" could also include individuals from less marginalized populations. However, "neighborliness" is not easy. In our collaboration, personal agendas had to accommodate and serve the interests of the children and communities served by the urban schools. For university faculty, the priority sometimes had to be research and publication—that was a constraint of their institution that they lived with—but they could and did recognize and work for the priorities of others in the collaborative effort as well. For school administrators, the priorities were accountability, public recognition, or the demands of particular parents, but there was a recognition that the priorities of the other collaborators and their respective institutions had a place in the collaboration. For teachers, the priority was professional advancement, additional skills, or recognition, but the priorities of others in the collaborative effort had to be recognized and respected. The key seemed to be recognizing that, some of the time, each person involved must be *working for the sake of the people in the other culture(s)*.

References

Archer, J. W. 1956. "Counciletter, the St. Louis Convention: Friday Program." *English Journal* 45:48–49.

Boggs, W. A. 1958. "Dear Principal." *English Journal* 47:86–87.

Coffman, G. R. 1922. "Correlation between High-School and College English." *English Journal* 11:129–39.

Fortune, R., ed. 1986. *School-College Collaborative Programs in English.* New York: Modern Language Association.

Fullan, M. 1982. *The Meaning of Educational Change.* New York: Teachers College Press.

Hanus, P. 1894. "University Inspection of Secondary Schools and the Schools' Examination Board of Harvard University." *The School Review* 2:257–67.

Jumper, W. C. 1958. "Dear Instructor of College Composition." *English Journal* 47:289–91.

McQuade, D. 1976. "Who Do You Think You're Talking To?" Trading Ideas for Insults in the English Profession." *English Journal* 65:8–10.

Miller, J. B. 1976. *Toward a New Psychology of Women.* Boston: Beacon.

"News and Notes: The New York Meeting." 1912. *English Journal* 1:124–25.

"News and Notes: Inland Empire Council of Teachers of English." 1918. *English Journal* 4:399–402.

Pitman, M. A. 1987. "Women and Leadership in American Higher Education: Marginality and Ritual in Organizational Culture." (University of Cincinnati, Department of Educational Foundations, Cincinnati, OH).

Savage, M. 1988. "Can Ethnographic Narrative Be a Neighborly Act?" *Anthropology and Education Quarterly* 19:3–19.

Schultz, L. M., C. H. Laine and M. C. Savage. 1988. "Interaction among School and College Writing Teachers: Toward Recognizing and Remaking Old Patterns." *College Composition and Communication* 39:139–53.

Spradley, J. P. 1990. "Ethnography and culture." In *Conformity and Conflict: Readings in Cultural Anthropology,* 7th ed., edited by J. P. Spradley and D. W. McCurdy, 21–29. Glenview, Ill.: Scott, Foresman.

Tovatt, A. and A. Jewett. 1959. This World of English. *English Journal* 48:540–41.

Whitehead, A. N. 1950. *Science and the Modern World.* New York: Macmillan.

Contributors

Dorothy Angell is an independent scholar and consultant whose practice is based in Washington, DC. Her work is in social anthropology with a concentration on culture in complex societies. Her primary interest is the process of migration and displacement and its consequences for personal and group identity, family maintenance, and community empowerment. Most of her research has centered on the South Asian diaspora and in particular the experience of Bengalis (from both Bangladesh and India) as immigrants in the United States.

Michael W. Apple is John Bascom Professor of Curriculum and Instruction and Educational Policy at the University of Wisconsin, Madison. A former elementary and secondary school teacher and past president of a teachers' union, he has worked with governments, dissident groups, unions, and educators to democratize educational research, policy, and practice. Among his many books are *Ideology and Curriculum* (1979, 2nd ed. 1990), *Education and Power* (1985), *Teachers and Texts* (1988), *The Politics of the Textbook* (1991), and *Official Knowledge* (1993).

Joanne M. Arhar is an Associate Professor of Educational Leadership at Kent State University (Ohio). She has taught secondary English and integrated studies and served as an administrator at both the high school and middle level school. Joanne also worked as a staff development specialist for the American Association of School Administrators. She has written numerous chapters and articles on the social organization of middle level schools and recently published *Leading Into the 21st Century* with Fenwick English and Larry Frase.

Julie Binko recently finished her Ph.D. at the University of Minnesota. Her thesis, *Dialogic Critical Approaches Towards Educational Reform,* explores the use of the future to change schools. Additionally, she has developed a methodology, Dialogic Critical Ethnography, to help educators understand and use qualitative research information to change schools. Dr. Binko is active in many professional organizations such as the World Future Society, International Society for System Science, and American Educational Research Association.

MARIANNE N. BLOCH is a Professor in the Department of Curriculum and Instruction at the University of Wisconsin-Madison. Her research has focused on historical and cross-cultural investigations of early education and child care. Along with B. Robert Tabachnick, she has most recently been involved in a four study of home-school-university collaborations and communications that impact upon the success of young culturally and linguistically diverse children within school.

KATHRYN M. BORMAN is Professor of Education and Anthropology at the University of South Florida where she also serves as Associate Director of Research in the David B. Anchin Center. During the 1992–1993 academic year she and several faculty colleagues at the University of Cincinnati carried out a series of evaluation projects for Cincinnati Public Schools. Her recent book, *The First 'Real' Job* (1991) examines the experiences of young men and women following high school in manufacturing, clerical, and in-person service jobs. Her ongoing research examines school district restructuring, the influences on, and career decision making among adolescents, the latter with colleagues of the University of Chicago.

MARIE BRENNAN is a Professor in the School of Administrative and Curriculum Studies at Deakin University where she is interested in the effect of the growth of management as the major focus of mass organization in education. Her related research interests lie in the construction of identity and fields of practice arising from new information technologies, pedagogies, and school/teacher/principal work. She draws on wide ranging work experience as a teacher of humanities in secondary technical schools; a researcher concerned with literacy and educational disadvantage, action research, school improvement, and the state; a manager of state education system projects; a policy analyst, and most recently, a teacher of distance education in policy, educational administration, and gender in education.

CORNELL BROOKS is a Professor of Education at the University of New Orleans. His specialty is research and design in education. He is a former director of research and evaluation for the Orleans Parish School District.

W. WADE BURLEY is a Professor in the Department of Psychological and Social Foundations of Education at the University of South Florida in Tampa. He has been a high school teacher, guidance counselor, director of a counseling center, director of teacher education, and a college and university professor. His research and writings include numerous publications in journals and books. He has also worked with teachers from eight Caribbean Island countries involved developing and delivering training as a member of an international cadre.

LOUIS CASTENELL is a Professor of Education, with a joint appointment in Educational Foundations and School Psychology and Counseling, and Dean of the College of Education at the University of Cincinnati. His research interests include race, class, and gender equity in schooling. He is presently working on a text, to be published by Abler which will examine how women and minority leaders influence schools of education.

JOHN Q. EASTON is the director of monitoring and research for the Chicago Panel on Public School Policy and Finance. The Chicago Panel is conducting the major independent effort to assess the effectiveness of that city's school restructuring effort, "Monitoring and Research School Reform in Chicago."

NANCY P. GREENMAN is Assistant Professor of Social Foundations in the Department of Psychological and Social Foundations of Education at the University of South Florida. She holds a courtesy appointment in Anthropology. No stranger to educational change, as a teacher in the Pojoaque Valley (New Mexico) Schools and the Santa Fe Public Schools over a nineteen year period beginning in 1970, she advocated for and facilitated change. She continues to do so through her teaching, research, service, and consulting. Her research focus includes educational change and restructuring, issues in cultural diversity and multicultural education, and oral life history of culturally diverse women.

G. ALFRED HESS, JR. is the executive director of the Chicago Panel on Public School Policy and Finance. The Chicago Panel is conducting a five-year project, "Monitoring and Researching School Reform in Chicago," with support from the Spencer Foundation, the MacArthur Foundation, the Chicago Community Trust, the Woods Charitable Fund, the Field Foundation of Illinois, and the Fry Foundation. An educational anthropologist, Hess is co-chair of the Committee on Ethnographic Educational Evaluation of the Council on Anthropology and Education. He is the author of a participant observation study of the school reform movement in Chicago, *School Restructuring, Chicago Style* (1991).

STAFFORD HOOD is Assistant Professor of Psychology at Arizona State University. He received his bachelor's and master's degrees from the University of Wisconsin at Whitewater and earned his Ph.D. from the University of Illinois at Champaign-Urbana. His broad research interests are post-secondary education, educational policy analysis, program evaluation of inner city schools, and bias in testing. He has written book chapters and journal articles on these topics. His work has been published in *Teachers College Record* and the *Journal of Negro Education.*

ERWIN V. JOHANNINGMEIER received his Ph.D. in History and Philosophy of Education from the University of South Florida, and teaches History of Education at the University of South Florida. He has served as president of the Southeast Philosophy of Education Society, is a member of the Executive Committee of the International Standing Conference for the History of Education, and has lectured in Bulgaria and Poland. He is co-author of *Teachers for the Prairie* (1972), author of *Americans and Their Schools* (1987), and is currently working on a history of educational research.

CHET LAINE is Associate Professor in the Literacy Program at the University of Cincinnati. His scholarly interests include English teacher preparation, writing assessment, and school-college collaboration.

SUSAN MARTIN is Assistant Professor in Educational Foundations at Indiana State University. Prior to earning her doctorate at the University of Cincinnati, she was a teacher and ad administrator in Ohio, Thailand, and New Hampshire. Currently she is the editor of *Philosophic Studies in Education* and secretary of the American Educational Studies Association.

WILLIAM T. PINK is a Professor of Foundations and Research, National College of Education, National-Louis University. He has written a number of pieces in various journals and is the co-author of *Schooling in Social Context: Qualitative Studies* (with George Noblit) and *Effective Staff Development for School Change* (with Arthur Hyde). He is the editor of the *Urban Review* and of a volume for Hampton titled *Understanding Education and Policy.*

THOMAS S. POPKEWITZ is a Professor of Curriculum and Instruction at the University of Wisconsin, Madison. His work centers on a political sociology of educational reform, educational sciences, and professionalization. He recently completed a study of reform in the United States (*A Political Sociology of Educational Reform,* 1991) and an eight country study of teacher education (*Changing Patterns of Power,* 1993). His current work includes investigations of power/knowledge relations in teacher education and an international study of the social relations in which discourses of professionalization occur.

BARBARA SCHNEIDER is Senior Social Scientist at NORC and the University of Chicago. She received her Ph.D. from Northwestern University. Her interests are in the area of educational socialization. She currently is co-principal investigator on a national study of adolescent career formation.

LUCILLE M. SCHULTZ is Associate Professor in the Department of English at the University of Cincinnati. She has written on the history and dynamics of school-college collaboration, on writing assessment, and on literacy acquisition. She is currently studying early nineteenth century figures in composition, especially John Frost and other authors of little known textbooks.

ARTHUR SHAPIRO is Professor of Education at the University of South Florida. He served as a group worker, a teacher, senior high school principal, director of secondary education, assistant superintendent, and superintendent of schools, all in nationally visible districts, before moving to the professorship. His writings have covered topics in the theory and practice of supervision, curriculum development, and decision-making in organizations. He is also a stereo photographer with a life-long interest in people and cultures and serves as an organizational consultant.

LYNNE SMITH is Assistant Professor in the Department of Education Studies at Antioch College. The qualitative research interests that inform her teaching include urban family literacy, women's work lives, collaboration, home schooling, and marginality.

B. ROBERT TABACHNICK is a Professor in the Department of Curriculum and Instruction and Associate Dean for Teacher Education at the University of Wisconsin-Madison. His research has focused on teacher education and social studies. His recent work includes home-school-university collaborations that have focused on the education of ethnically and linguistically diverse children.

Patricia Ziegel Timm is the founder of Cincinnatians Active to Support Education, a community-based advocacy organization. She has been an activist in the social movements of the last three decades, working for civil rights of women and minorities. She is an appointee of the U.S. District Court to monitor the desegregation of Cincinnati Public Schools. Pat has worked in community organizations in Cincinnati and Chicago. Her areas of interest include social policy, cultural studies, and urban education. She is currently completing her doctoral thesis, "The Legitimacy of Early School Leaving: An Analysis Across Three Generations of Urban Appalachian Women."

Index